Electronic
Media Law
and Regulation

Electronic Media Law and Regulation

Kenneth C. Creech

Butler University

Focal Press

Boston   London

Focal Press is an imprint of Butterworth–Heinemann.

Recognizing the importance of preserving what has been written, it is the policy of Butterworth–Heinemann to have the books it publishes printed on acid-free paper, and we exert our best efforts to that end.

Library of Congress Cataloging-in-Publication Data

Creech, Kenneth.
    Electronic media law and regulation / Kenneth Creech.
       p.   cm.
    Includes bibliographical references and index.
    ISBN 0-240-80130-X (acid free pb.)
    1. Television—Law and legislation—United States. 2. Radio—Law and legislation—
United States. 3. Mass media—Law and legislation—United States. I. Title.
KF2805.C74   1993
343.7309′9—dc20
[347.30399]   92-21670
                                              CIP

British Library Cataloguing-in-Publication Data.

A catalogue record for this book is available from the British Library.

Butterworth–Heinemann
80 Montvale Avenue
Stoneham, MA 02180

10 9 8 7 6 5 4 3 2 1

Printed in the United States of America

□ □ □
□ □ □
□ □ □

Contents

Cases

This list includes all cases cited in this book. Page numbers follow each entry.

Abrams v. United States, 250 U.S. 616 (1919), 18, 28, 34–35
Action for Children's Television, 58 R.R.2d 61 (1985), 127
Action for Children's Television v. FCC, 756 F.2d 899 (DC Cir., 1985), 135
Action for Children's Television v. FCC, 821 F.2d 741 (DC Cir., 1987), 135
Action for Children's Television v. FCC, (CA DC, 1991) 18 Med.L.Rptr. 2153, 149
Action Repair v. ABC, (CA 7, 1985) 12 Med.L.Rptr. 1809, 207
Adrian Weiss, 58 F.C.C.2d 342, 36 R.R.2d 292 (1976), 116
American Communications Association v. Douds, 339 U.S. 382 (1950), 36
Anderson v. Fisher Broadcasting Companies, (OR Ct.App., 1985) 11 Med.L.Rptr. 1839, 241
Anderson v. Liberty Lobby, (U.S. Sup.Ct.,1986) 12 Med.L.Rptr. 2297, 227
Anderson v. WROC-TV, 441 N.Y.S.2d 220, (Sup.Ct., 1981), 246
Andren v. Knight-Ridder, (DC E.Mich, 1984) 10 Med.L.Rptr. 2109, 244
Ashbacker Radio Corp. v. FCC, 326 U.S. 327, 66 S.Ct. 148, 90 L.Ed. 108 (1945), 97
Associated Press v. Bell, (NY Ct.App., 1987) 14 Med.L.Rptr. 1156, 285–86
Baia v. Jackson Newspapers (Conn. Sup.Ct., 1985) 12 Med.L.Rptr. 1780, 206–7
Baltimore Orioles v. Major League Baseball Players, (CA 7, 1986) 13 Med.L.Rptr. 1625, 190, 241
Banzhaf v. Federal Communications Commission, 405 F.2d 1082, 14 R.R.2d 2061, (D.C.Cir.1968) 1 Med.L.Rptr. 2037, cert. denied 396 U.S. 842 (1969), 66, 150–151
Barber v. Time Inc., 348 Mo. 1199, 159 S.W.2d 291 (1942), 208
Barry v. Time (DC N.Cal., 1984) 10 Med.L.Rptr. 1809, 208
Beacon Journal v. Lansdowne, (OH Ct.Comm.Pleas, 1984) 11 Med.L.Rptr. 1096, 211
L.L. Bean Inc. v. Drake Publishers Inc., (CA 1, 1987) 13 Med.L.Rptr. 2009, 198
Bigelow v. Virginia, 421 U.S. 809 (1975), 147
Bindrim v. Mitchell, 92 Cal.App.2d 61, 155 Cal.Rptr. 29 (1979), 205–6

Preface

The electronic media are nearing a major evolutionary leap. How we listen to radio and watch television will have changed dramatically by the year 2000. Just as cable television and VCRs in the 1980s changed the role of broadcast television, so will high-definition television and digital audio broadcasting alter the landscape further. Convergence—the coming together of various media—will blur the lines of demarcation between broadcasting, cable, satellite, and fiber optic telephone line delivery of entertainment and information services.

Although new electronic media continue to develop rapidly in the laboratory, the legal and regulatory framework of our society works to moderate change. New technologies, while technically possible, present questions of social policy that may make some of them neither politically nor economically feasible. We have only recently begun to establish legal precedent in media law. The first cases in which the Supreme Court ruled on First Amendment issues occurred in the early 1900s.

The study of the law and regulation of the electronic media remains an important component in the college curriculum. In spite of the deregulation of the '80s, the Communications Act of 1934 remains largely intact. The complex relationships between broadcasting, cable, and other media subject to Federal Communications Commission (FCC) jurisdiction are dynamic, and the relationships these media have with society are reflected in the decisions of the courts, in the legislation passed by Congress, and by the presidents we elect.

This book focuses on the laws and regulations that affect broadcasting and cable communications. It is designed for students and professionals who wish to understand the major issues and regulations facing the electronic media. This book proceeds from the premise that students should engage original text of major court cases and FCC decisions to better understand electronic media regulations. Because this is an introductory text, only the most important portions of these cases have been selected. By reading these cases, the reader can more easily understand the essence and importance of each case to the specific subject under study.

It is difficult to keep abreast of current laws and regulations affecting the electronic media. No one book can accomplish that feat. Readers interested in up-to-the-minute changes should consult periodicals. However, this book does provide a foundation for understanding how and why the electronic media are regulated as they are.

Acknowledgments

I wish to thank the following organizations and individuals for their contributions to this book: the students at Butler University and the University of Southern Indiana who assisted in refining the material presented in this book; the teachers and professionals in the industry who carefully reviewed this text for accuracy; the Annenberg Washington Program in Communications Policy Studies for providing access to the opinions of scholars, policymakers, regulators, and legislators; Phil Sutherland at Focal Press for believing in the project and for his guidance during the editing process. Finally, I thank my family for their encouragement, patience, support, and understanding during the writing of this book.

1 □ □ □
□ □ □
□ □ □

Introduction to the Legal System

America is a nation governed by laws, not by individuals. Since the earliest days of the founding of the United States, Americans have attempted to justify actions by applying laws, rather than relying on the authority of a single ruler. For example, the Declaration of Independence is a beautifully crafted, philosophical and legal statement that justifies the separation of the 13 colonies from England. Nearly 200 years later, the same reliance on law forced the resignation of a president of the United States.

The court cases that result from disputes over interpretations of American laws could easily be used as the basis for writing an accurate history of the United States. Court cases reflect the tensions present in American society at a given time. For example, the major cases of the 1790s reflect the growing pains of the new nation. Sedition and the powers of the various branches of government are common topics of litigation during this period. State rights and civil rights issues were common in the 1860s and again 100 years later. Many cases of the late nineteenth century were concerned with child labor, unions, trust busting, and consumerism. Of course, every war in which the U.S. was engaged, from the American Revolution to Vietnam, spawned cases that resulted from protests, espionage, and treason. The 1970s saw an increasing number of cases that dealt with searches of news rooms. The 1980s unleashed an unprecedented number of libel suits, with damage awards that reached millions of dollars.

Similar to court cases, federal and state laws reflect the concerns of the American people during a given period. Laws designed to protect against subversive activity have been passed and repealed throughout our history, depending on the perceived threat. Laws both limiting and expanding the civil rights of individuals have appeared on the books of many states. Issues from gun control, the right to bear arms, the right to abortion, and gay rights have found their way into the legal system and reflect the dynamics of American society.

The law of communication is a relative newcomer to this arena. Most cases that involve judicial interpretation of the First Amendment, which guarantees freedom of speech and freedom of the press, occurred after World War I. The rapid development of mass communication in the twentieth century focused new attention on the meaning of free speech and free press.

Students studying communications law as undergraduate journalism or mass communication majors often find that they lack the proper background in the legal process to understand communications law issues. This background is necessary to comprehend the cases, statutes, and principles involved in shaping communications law and policy. Undergraduate students must realize they are studying a specialty field that would be encountered in the third year of most law schools. The remainder of this chapter is devoted to providing a point of departure for the study of communications law.

Defining the Law

Basically, *laws* may be defined as a set of rules, promulgated by government agencies with authority to do so, that attempt to guide, conduct, and subsequently provide sanctions when the rules are violated.

Sources of American Law

The foundation of the American legal system was imported from England. The jury system, development of the common law, and many statutes were adopted by the colonies and retained after the American Revolution. America expanded her legal system with the addition of the Constitution. In all, there are five sources of American law:

1. the common law
2. equity law
3. statutory law
4. constitutional law
5. administrative law

The Common Law

The roots of the common law go back to medieval England. Legal historians trace the common law to the mid-thirteenth century. It is the strongest British legacy to colonial America. In England, common law was distinguished from ecclesiastical law—the law of the Church. Ecclesiastical law used the Church as the basis for all decisions, whereas the common law looked to the people to resolve disputes. Common law is often called *discovered law*, because magistrates discovered solutions to disputes by finding out what had been done in similar situations in the past. Common law is not created by judges or legislators. Instead, a legal rule is mandated after specific cases are studied. Common law is inductive rather than deductive.

A fundamental concept of the common law is *stare decisis* or "let the decision stand." This means that judges should look to the past to resolve current problems. At first glance, this concept may give the impression that common law is also static law. After all, how can a 200-year-old decision be applied to today's disputes? And what about "bad" decisions? How does the common law keep from propagating an unfair judgment? Needless to say, many factors are taken into consideration by judges who rely on precedent. Rarely is an archaic precedent used as a basis for a judgment.

The common law is dynamic and is usually very responsive to changing times. Judges use precedent only as a guideline in reaching a decision. There is a great deal of room for interpretation and change. For example, when the Supreme Court reviews a case, it relies on previous decisions as guidelines, but many times it overrules what it considers an incorrect interpretation of the law. When this happens, a particular precedent may no longer be looked to by judges in future cases. Therefore, a "weeding out" process occurs in the application of the common law.

Theoretically, the common law offers the most equitable means of settling disputes of all forms of Anglo-American law. As Justice Oliver Wendell Holmes wrote about the common law,

> The life of the law has not been logic; it has been experience . . . . The law embodies the story of a nation's development through many centuries, and it cannot be dealt with as if it contained only the axioms and corollaries of a book of mathematics. In order to know what it is, we must know what it has been, and what it tends to become.[1]

Equity Law

Like the common law, equity law also developed in England and was imported to the colonies. Equity law emerged in the fourteenth and fifteenth centuries as a supplement to the common law and an additional means of settling disputes. The common law courts of England had become somewhat rigid by the year 1400 and many persons seeking to file grievances were turned away. Unable to obtain a hearing before a magistrate, these individuals often petitioned the king to prescribe a solution to their problem. The king's chief officer, or chancellor, set up courts of chancery to deal with these petitions. All decisions made in chancery court were made on the basis of conscience or equity—fairness. Some states still refer to equity courts as chancery courts.

Equity law retains the common law dependence on *stare decisis*. However, equity law begins where the common law stops. Child custody, divorce, property settlements, and accident claims are examples of issues taken to equity court. Equity cases are not tried before a jury and decisions are rendered in the form of discretionary orders issued by judges. Equity law provides for an injunction or restraining order, which is issued by a judge to stop someone from behaving in a manner that is deemed unfair or damaging to another. Injunctions are often sought in communications law cases.

Statutory Law

Before the Revolutionary War, Americans were bound by laws decreed by Parliament. Indeed, it was the enforcement of some of these laws that contributed to the Revolution. After the Revolution, America established her own laws in Congress and in state assemblies. These laws are statutory laws and are so named because they prescribe, by statute, the behavior of members of society. A well-constructed statute defines the behavior to be regulated and imposes sanctions for violating the statute. All statutes promulgated in the United States must not violate the U.S. Constitution. Any statute that does so is invalid *prima facie* or on its face.

Before 1825, statutory law did not play a large role in the American legal system. Most legal issues were settled via the common law. Between 1850 and 1900, however, a greater percentage of American law resulted from legislative acts rather than from common law tradition. Today, most American law is statutory. The reason for the shift from the common law to statutory law is tied to the steady growth of the United States population. Common law is most effective when dealing with the problems of individuals. Statutes are written to address the problems inherent in governing large groups.

Statutory law can anticipate social problems, but the common law cannot. While the common law is inductive, statutory law is deductive—one rule applies to many situations. All criminal law in the United States is statutory. While common law is based on precedent, statutory law is founded on various federal, state, and local codes. Ideally, statutory law leaves room for less ambiguity in interpretation than does common law. However, construction of a workable statute is often difficult. Sometimes, the application of statutory law does not take into consideration individual circumstances. For these reasons, statutes often require interpretation by judges. For example, federal and state statutes make it illegal to distribute obscene materials. However, the judge must determine what is or is not obscene. Statutory law is not always the final word.

Constitutional Law

The United States Constitution is the supreme law of the land. It provides for the organization of our government, outlines the duties and powers of the various branches of government, and guarantees United States citizens certain individual rights. The Constitution is the yardstick by which all other actions of government are measured. Any laws that conflict with the Constitution are legally unenforceable.

The student of all forms of communications law should be familiar with the Bill of Rights and subsequent amendments to the Constitution. Most, but by no means all, communications law cases stem from the interpretation of one of three amendments—the First, Sixth, and Fourteenth Amendments. The First and Sixth Amendments are a part of the original Bill of Rights, which was ratified in 1787. The

Fourteenth Amendment was ratified in 1868 and was primarily designed to limit the power of the readmitted southern states after the Civil War. The first paragraph of the Fourteenth Amendment, known as the "due process clause," has an impact on communications law.

The First Amendment states,

> Congress shall make no law respecting an establishment of religion, or prohibiting the free exercise thereof; or abridging the freedom of speech, or of the press; or the right of the people to peaceably assemble, and to petition the government for a redress of grievances.

Of major concern is the interpretation of the freedom of the press and speech clause. While written in absolute terms, most courts agree that the Founding Fathers did not mean that speech and press could never be restrained. The extent and nature of the restraint has been the subject of a plethora of litigation, most of which has taken place since 1919. Of additional concern is how the First Amendment should be applied to cases regarding the electronic media. As we shall see, the debate continues.

The Sixth Amendment states,

> In criminal prosecutions, the accused shall enjoy the right to a speedy and public trial, by an impartial jury of the State and district wherein the crime shall have been committed, which district shall have been previously ascertained by law, and to be informed of the nature and cause of the accusation; to be confronted with the witnesses against him; to have compulsory process for obtaining witnesses in his favor, and to have the Assistance of Counsel for his defense.

The Sixth Amendment guarantee of a public trial by an impartial jury sometimes conflicts with the First Amendment guarantee of freedom of the press. Sometimes, press coverage of criminal acts makes it difficult to provide a defendant with an impartial jury. The balancing of First and Sixth Amendment rights has been another major issue facing the courts.

The Fourteenth Amendment, paragraphs 1 and 5, states,

> All persons born or naturalized in the United States, and subject to the jurisdiction thereof, are citizens of the United States and of the State wherein they reside. No State shall make or enforce any law which shall abridge the privileges and immunities of citizens of the United States; nor shall any State deprive any person of life, liberty, or property, without due process of law; nor deny to any person within its jurisdiction the equal protection of the laws.
>
> The Congress shall have power to enforce, by appropriate legislation, the provisions of this article.

The First Amendment states "Congress shall make no law . . ." abridging various freedoms. It says nothing about states not making laws that limit freedoms. Consequently, many states passed statutes that limited the freedoms outlined in the

Bill of Rights. The Fourteenth Amendment applies the Bill of Rights to the states—more specifically, for students of communications law, the First Amendment is applied to the states. As we shall see, none of the freedoms implicit in the First, Sixth, and Fourteenth Amendments are absolute. States and Congress continue to pass statutes that attempt to define or limit those rights. However, the Fourteenth Amendment ensures that all statutes are in keeping with the Constitution, although their interpretation may vary according to the social climate of the day. No state can simply refuse freedom of speech to an individual or a group based on the grounds that it doesn't like what that person or group has to say.

Administrative Law

The fifth source of American law developed in the late nineteenth century as a means of coping with the growing complexity of the government. Administrative law requires knowledge of a specific industry, which is regulated by the government. The regulating body is usually an independent regulatory agency (IRA) created by Congress and staffed by members appointed by the president. The agency has legislative, executive, and judicial powers. It makes rules that apply to a particular industry, enforces those rules, and hears initial cases that involve alleged violation of those rules. The agency may levy fines or other punishments against offenders. Decisions of the agencies are checked by judicial review. A court may declare an IRA ruling unconstitutional. Regulated industries may also appeal an unfavorable decision to the U.S. Court of Appeals for the District of Columbia. As we shall see, some cases that begin with administrative agency hearings are eventually heard by the U.S. Supreme Court.

The first IRA was created by Congress in 1890 to regulate the interstate transport of natural gas through pipelines and was called the Interstate Commerce Commission (ICC). The ICC still exists and has expanded duties that include regulating interstate trucking. The ICC has been joined by a host of other such industry-specific agencies. In 1914, Congress created the Federal Trade Commission (FTC) to deal with unfair trade practices by trusts. The FTC has expanded its role to include the regulation of false and misleading advertising, and for a brief time considered the regulation of children's television advertising. The 48 IRAs operating today include the Nuclear Regulatory Commission, the Central Intelligence Agency, the Peace Corps, and the Postal Service.

Although students of communications law will encounter the FTC in their studies, the agency that most directly affects communications law is the Federal Communications Commission (FCC). Known as "the Commission" by broadcasters, the FCC began as the Federal Radio Commission (FRC) in 1927 when Congress passed the Radio Act, which authorized the five-person Commission to license radio stations in the "public interest, convenience, and necessity." The agency's role was expanded 7 years later with the passage of the Communications Act of 1934. The new act created the seven-member FCC.

Like all IRAs, FCC commissioners are appointed by the president and confirmed by the Senate. All agencies have five to seven members. No more than three or four are from the same political party. Commissioners are appointed for 7-year terms, but few serve a full term, since IRA appointments are generally thought of as stepping stones, either politically or to the industry that they regulate. Most commissioners are lawyers who, after a stint on an IRA, can build a lucrative clientele and represent the regulated industry in Washington, D.C.

Congress controls an IRA's budget and, as previously stated, agency rulings are subject to judicial review. This series of checks and balances is supposed to ensure that agencies are insulated from the political process—hence the term *independent agencies*. In reality, Republican presidents tend to appoint Republican commissioners and Democrats tend to appoint Democrats. If an agency gets too tough on a regulated industry, it may find its purse strings tightened by members of Congress under pressure from special interest groups.

The statutes and rules promulgated by IRAs can be found in the *Code of Federal Regulations*. All IRA procedures are governed by the Administrative Procedure Act of 1946, which requires that all IRA actions (including new rulings) be published in the *Federal Register*. Any new rules or changes to existing agency rules must be published as a *Notice of Proposed Rule Making*. Interested persons and parties can file comments with an IRA regarding a particular rule. The IRA is then supposed to consider these comments before implementing the rule (see Figure 1.1).

If an IRA is concerned about a particular issue, such as the effect of children's television advertising on the well-being of juveniles, it publishes a *Notice of Inquiry*. Again, interested persons or parties (usually the affected industry) file comments. A hearing before the Commission is also guaranteed. The IRA then issues a policy statement, called *Report and Order*, that deals with the issue or the proposed rule. All of these actions become part of the Code of Federal Regulations and are enacted into laws when they are ruled on by a court.

How the FCC Conducts Business

When the FCC was created in 1934 it consisted of seven members. In 1982, Congress reduced the number of members to five. As previously noted, commissioners are appointed by the president, confirmed by the Senate, and serve 5-year terms. No more than three members may be from the same political party and terms are staggered so that no two terms expire in the same year. The chairperson of the FCC is chosen by the president and is responsible for setting the agenda of the FCC. The chairperson plays a major role in FCC actions. For example, under the chairmanship of Mark Fowler (1981–1987) and Dennis Patrick (1987–1989) much of the

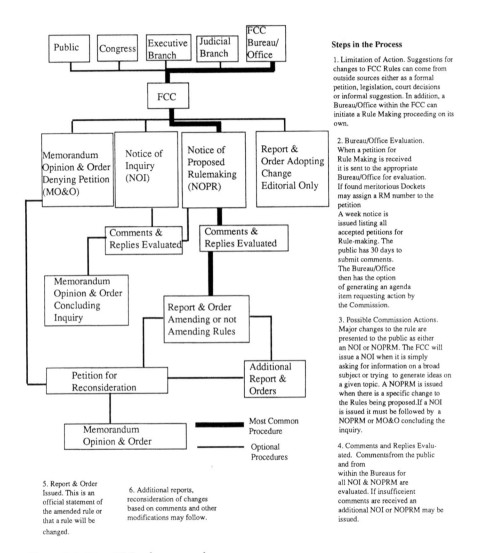

Steps in the Process

1. Limitation of Action. Suggestions for changes to FCC Rules can come from outside sources either as a formal petition, legislation, court decisions or informal suggestion. In addition, a Bureau/Office within the FCC can initiate a Rule Making proceeding on its own.

2. Bureau/Office Evaluation. When a petition for Rule Making is received it is sent to the appropriate Bureau/Office for evaluation. If found meritorious Dockets may assign a RM number to the petition A week notice is issued listing all accepted petitions for Rule-making. The public has 30 days to submit comments. The Bureau/Office then has the option of generating an agenda item requesting action by the Commission.

3. Possible Commission Actions. Major changes to the rule are presented to the public as either an NOI or NOPRM. The FCC will issue a NOI when it is simply asking for information on a broad subject or trying to generate ideas on a given topic. A NOPRM is issued when there is a specific change to the Rules being proposed.If a NOI is issued it must be followed by a NOPRM or MO&O concluding the inquiry.

4. Comments and Replies Evaluated. Commentsfrom the public and from within the Bureaus for all NOI & NOPRM are evaluated. If insufficeient comments are received an additional NOI or NOPRM may be issued.

5. Report & Order Issued. This is an official statement of the amended rule or that a rule will be changed.

6. Additional reports, reconsideration of changes based on comments and other modifications may follow.

Figure 1.1 How FCC rules are made.

deregulation of broadcasting and cable television was undertaken. When Alfred Sikes assumed the chair in 1989, he cut short some of the deregulatory momentum. He spearheaded a 24-hour ban on indecent programming and earned the moniker "Sikes, the Enforcer."

The FCC is organized into four bureaus—mass media, common carrier, private radio, and field operations. Each bureau is headed by a bureau chief and various branches report to the chief (see Figure 1.2).

The Mass Media Bureau

Most matters concerning radio, television, and cable are handled by the Mass Media Bureau. The Mass Media Bureau was formed in 1982 when the old Broadcast Bureau and Cable Bureau were merged. The Mass Media Bureau regulates AM and FM radio, television broadcasting, direct broadcast satellite (DBS) services, and instructional television fixed service (ITFS). The Mass Media Bureau also administers cable television rules, processes license applications and renewals, and proposes rules and regulations that pertain to the services under its jurisdiction.

The staff of the Mass Media Bureau takes action on most broadcast and cable matters. When commissioners must decide an issue, they are usually presented with alternatives recommended by the bureau staff at an open meeting (see Figure 1.3). Many legal scholars and former FCC commissioners are critical of the way the FCC conducts business and have suggested reforms designed to make the FCC more responsive to the needs of society. The following two dated, but still insightful, works are recommended to the reader: Barry G. Cole and Mal Oettinger, *Reluctant Regulators: The FCC and the Broadcast Audience* (Reading, MA: Addison-Wesley, 1978), and Nicholas Johnson and John Jay Dystel, "A Day in the Life: The Federal Communications Commission," *The Yale Law Journal* 82:8 (July 1973): 1574. For a general discussion of FCC procedures see Robert L. Hilliard, *The Federal Communications Commission: A Primer* (Boston: Focal Press, 1991).

If a matter requires a hearing, it is referred to an administrative law judge (ALJ). The ALJ is an employee of the Commission, but is not a member of a bureau staff. The ALJ may take testimony from the applicant and from the bureau, which may argue against or in favor of the applicant. Once the ALJ renders a decision, it is either accepted, or appealed by the losing party. The appealed issue may then be heard by the five FCC commissioners or by a review board. Should the decision from one of these ruling bodies not be acceptable, the applicant may appeal to the United States Court of Appeals for the District of Columbia. At this point, a general counsel represents the FCC in ensuing litigation. Eventually, decisions from the court of appeals may find their way to the Supreme Court. We will study several such landmark cases in this text.

The Common Carrier Bureau

Common carriers exercise no control over the content of what is communicated over their facilities and are not subject to content regulation. Because common carriers often enjoy near-monopoly status, rates and services are regulated. Interstate common carriers are regulated by the FCC and intrastate common carrier activities are regulated by state utility commissions.

Telephone, telegraph, and some satellites are examples of common carriers. The Common Carrier Bureau regulates rates and practices of local and regional Bell operating companies, and other companies providing long distance services. The

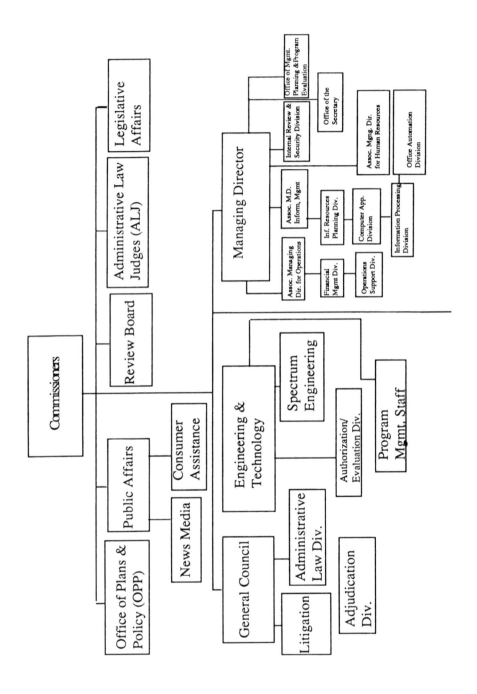

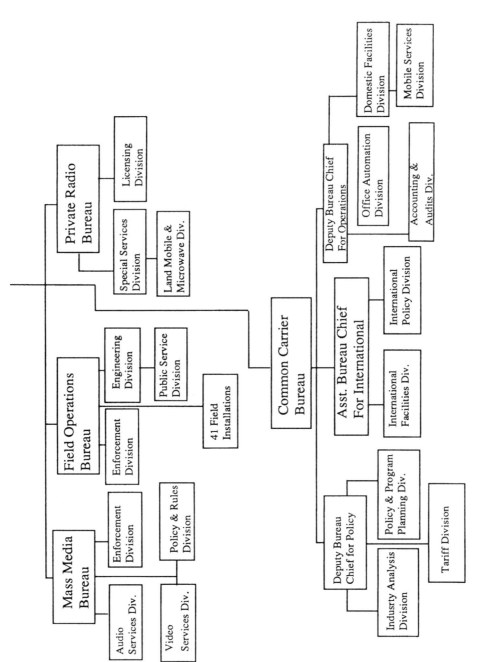

Figure 1.2 The Federal Communications Commission organizational chart.

The Federal Communications Commission held an Open Meeting Thursday June 13, 1991 at 9:30 AM in Room 856 at 1919 M Street N.W. The Commissioners sat *en banc* and considered nine items.

ITEM NO.	BUREAU	SUBJECT	TIME SPENT	VOTE
1	General Counsel, MassMedia Bureau	Notice of Rulemaking Codification of Political programming rules.	30:00	5-0
2 .	Mass Media	Adoption of Report & Order on TV satellite policy & rules	15:00	5-0
3.	Mass Media	Notice of Proposed Rulemaking regarding cable TV technical standards.	10:00	5-0
4.	Mass Media	Revision of "Effective Competition" standard for cable TV.	33:00	5-0
5.	Common Carrier	FCC declared Tennesee statute invalid as it applies to regulation of interstate rates.	7:00	5-0
6.	Common Carrier	Adopted Report & Order amending part 69 of rules relating to creation of access charge subelements for open network architecture (CC Docket No. 89-79).	20:00	5-0
7.	Private Radio	Adopted Notice of Proposed Rulemaking changing technical rules and policies regarding uses of land mobile bands below 470 MHz.	7:00	5-0
8.	Chief Engineer	Adopted a Report relating to an inquiry Relating to Preparation for the International Telecommunications Union World Administrative Conference for certain frequency allocations.	22:00	5-0
9.	Field Operations	Initiation on an Inquiry dealing with improvement of Emergency Broadcast System.	3:00	5-0

Figure 1.3 Sample of agenda and time devoted to items at FCC general meeting, June 6, 1991.

Common Carrier Bureau also administers mobile services, including cellular radio and public mobile radio.

The Private Radio Bureau

The Private Radio Bureau administers the radio services used by businesses, local government, individuals, and nonprofit organizations. Private radio includes police, fire, and emergency services; and maritime, aviation, amateur (ham operators), and citizens band (CB) radio.

Other Agencies Affecting Broadcasting and Cable

In addition to the FCC, broadcasters and cable operators must contend with other administrative agencies. The FTC was established in 1914 to regulate unfair competition in commerce. In 1938, with the passage of the Wheeler-Lea amendments, the FTC's power was expanded to include regulation of advertising to protect against unfair and deceptive advertising. Although it cannot directly fine broadcasters, the FTC can issue cease and desist orders if false and misleading advertising is suspected.

Broadcasters and cablecasters must deal with the Copyright Royalty Tribunal (CRT), which oversees the compulsory licensing scheme for cable television. The CRT also collects royalties and sets rates for musical, pictorial, and dramatic works used by radio and television stations. The CRT is discussed later in this text.

The National Telecommunications and Information Administration (NTIA) is the telecommunications policy-making and research arm of the government. It was established in 1978 as a part of the Department of Commerce. The NTIA develops policies that support the development of telecommunications, including radio, television, and cable; and also provides facilities grants to noncommercial broadcasters.

The Equal Employment Opportunity Commission (EEOC) was created by the Civil Rights Act of 1964. The charter of the EEOC is to eliminate discrimination in employment based on race, color, religion, sex, or national origin. Broadcasters must comply with EEOC and FCC guidelines to obtain or retain their license. Licensees with more than five full-time employees must present the FCC with a model EEO program when applying for a license and must provide annual updates to that program.

The Federal Aviation Administration (FAA) approves tower locations and works with the FCC to ensure that broadcast towers are painted and lighted in a manner consistent with FCC and Agency rules. Broadcasters must notify the FAA if their tower lights fail and must seek IRA approval before changing the height or location of an existing tower, or before building a new structure.

The Judiciary—An Overview

Ultimately, serious disputes involving communications law are resolved in court. Technically, there are 54 different judicial systems in the United States—one for each state, the federal court system, and the territorial district courts for Guam, Puerto Rico, and the Virgin Islands. Fortunately, although the names of the various components may differ from state to state, all courts are organized in a similar manner and owe allegiance to a single source—the Constitution.

The court system in the United States is divided into trial and appellate courts (see Figure 1.4). Each state court system is guided by a state constitution as well as the

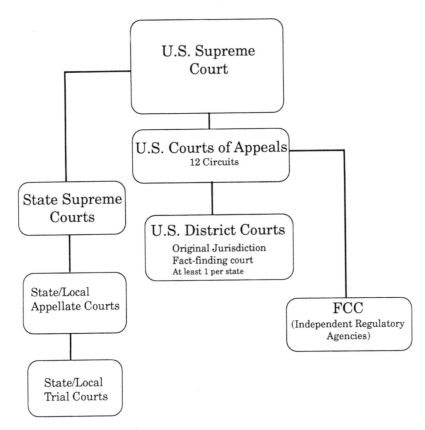

Figure 1.4 Hierarchy of the U.S. court system.

federal Constitution. Each court system is part of the third branch of the government (the legislative branch). The states have governors as chief executives and legislatures (or assemblies) who fulfill the legislative function.

Trial Courts

Trial courts are fact-finding courts. They are where most cases begin. It is the function of a trial court to determine exactly what happened in a case. These courts hear testimony from witnesses and establish a factual record of the case. Juries are present in trial courts.

Appellate Courts

After a trial court has rendered its verdict, it may be appealed to the next highest court, which is an appellate court. Appellate courts do not consider facts, they only consider law. On appeal, no more witnesses are called, no more testimony is heard, and no jury is present. A judge looks at the facts established at trial and attorneys argue whether, given the facts, the law was or was not applied properly. Should new evidence emerge, the appellate court may order a new trial.

The Supreme Court

The Supreme Court was established in 1789 and is the oldest federal court. While other federal courts are created by Congress, the Supreme Court was established by the Constitution and does not serve at the discretion of Congress or of the executive branch of the government. Supreme Court justices, like federal judges, are appointed for life. They are nominated by the president and confirmed by the Senate. Congress establishes the number of justices on the Supreme Court. This number has changed several times throughout history. The original Supreme Court, headed by Chief Justice John Jay, consisted of six justices—five associate justices and one chief justice of the United States. The total number of judges on the Supreme Court increased to seven in 1807, to nine in 1837, and to ten in 1863. Following the Civil War in 1866, the Supreme Court was reduced to seven members and then raised to its current number of nine in 1869. The most recent attempt to change the number of justices on the Supreme Court came in 1937 when President Franklin Roosevelt, frustrated by Supreme Court rulings that declared some of his New Deal programs unconstitutional, proposed that an additional justice be added for each justice reaching the age of 70 and not retiring. Roosevelt's proposal set the maximum number of justices at 15. Although Roosevelt could not persuade Congress to implement his proposal, he ultimately appointed nine men to the Supreme Court—more than any other president, except George Washington. One of Roosevelt's appointees, Justice William O. Douglas, served 36 years. This is the longest term of any Supreme Court justice. Roosevelt's New Deal influence could be felt as late as 1975, when Douglas retired.

Needless to say, a president will nominate potential justices who can steer the court in a philosophical, if not political, direction that is in step with the chief executive. Although conservative presidents tend to nominate conservative justices and liberals nominate liberals, sometimes justices don't always vote the way in which they are expected once they are on the Court. Chief Justice Earl Warren, appointed by President Eisenhower, turned out to be one of the most liberal chief justices in history. Kennedy appointee, Justice White, is more conservative than one would expect from a justice appointed by a liberal president.

President Reagan appointed three associate justices and elevated President Nixon's appointee William Rehnquist to the position of chief justice when Warren Burger retired in 1986. In 1981, Reagan's first appointee, Sandra Day O'Connor, became the first woman in history to serve on the Supreme Court. The Senate, however, exercised its right of confirmation in 1987 when it rejected the president's second choice for associate justice, Robert Bork. Bork's conservatism and controversial role in the firing of Watergate Special Prosecutor Archibald Cox in 1973 resulted in the nonconfirmation vote. Reagan's next choice, Douglas Ginsberg, admitted to smoking marijuana while a law professor at Harvard University. This admission drew such strong criticism that Ginsberg withdrew from consideration. At the time of his nomination, Ginsberg was only 41 years old and had the potential of carrying the philosophy of the Reagan years into the twenty-first century. In 1988, the Senate finally confirmed 51-year-old Anthony Kennedy as Reagan's third Supreme Court appointee.

When President Bush nominated Clarence Thomas to succeed Justice Thurgood Marshall in 1991, allegations of sexual harassment against Judge Thomas surfaced during the confirmation process. The lengthy hearings were televised and Americans were riveted to their television sets until the early hours of the morning to hear testimony. Thomas was eventually confirmed, but a heightened awareness of the nature and scope of sexual harassment in society followed him to the Court.

The Current Supreme Court

Currently there are three Reagan appointees, two Nixon appointees (one of whom was elevated to chief justice by Reagan), two Bush appointees, one Ford appointee, and one Kennedy appointee on the Supreme Court. The chief justice of the United States is

William Rehnquist, born 1924 in Virginia. Appointed as associate justice in 1972 by President Nixon. Became chief justice in 1986 when Warren Burger retired.

The associate justices of the Supreme Court are

Byron White, born 1917 in Colorado. Appointed in 1962 by President Kennedy.
Harry Blackmun, born 1908 in Minnesota. Appointed in 1970 by President Nixon.
John Paul Stevens, born 1920 in Illinois. Appointed in 1975 by President Ford.
Sandra Day O'Connor, born 1930 in Arizona. Appointed 1981 by President Reagan. Justice O'Connor is the first woman to serve on the Supreme Court.
Antonin Scalia, born 1936 in Virginia. Appointed in 1986 by President Reagan.
Anthony Kennedy, born 1936 in California. Appointed in 1988 by President Reagan.
David Souter, born 1936 in Vermont. Appointed in 1990 by President Bush.
Clarence Thomas, born 1948 in Georgia. Appointed in 1991 by President Bush. After a controversial confirmation hearing by the Senate Judiciary Committee, Justice Thomas replaced Thurgood Marshall, the first African-American justice on the Court.

How the Supreme Court Conducts Business

The Supreme Court exercises both original and appellate jurisdiction. Under original jurisdiction, the Supreme Court is the first court to hear a case. It acts like a trial court in gathering facts and deciding law. The Supreme Court rarely exercises original jurisdiction. In fact, it has done so fewer than 150 times in the last 200 years.

Much of the law in the United States comes from the exercise of the Supreme Court's appellate jurisdiction (i.e., cases are heard on appeal from a lower court). A case comes to the Supreme Court on appeal in three ways: by direct appeal, by *writ of certiorari*, and by certification.

A direct appeal may be brought to the Supreme Court from a lower federal court or from a state court that has ruled a federal law unconstitutional. The Supreme Court can turn down any appeal by simply refusing to hear the case. If that happens, the case is closed. All legal appeals have been exhausted.

A *writ of certiorari* is a discretionary order issued by the Court when it feels that an important legal question has been raised. The Court asks to hear a case, so that it may issue an opinion to be used as a precedent in similar cases. No one has a legal right to a *writ of certiorari*. The most important requirement that must be met before the Court will issue a *writ* is that all other legal remedies must be exhausted by the petitioner. This means that a case must have gone through the trial court, an intermediate appeals court, and possibly a state supreme or superior court. Then, four of the nine justices must vote in favor of hearing the case in the Supreme Court.

Very few cases reach the Supreme Court by certification. Lower federal courts are permitted to ask questions of the Court regarding matters of law that pertain to cases that the lower court may be hearing. Sometimes, the Supreme Court asks that a case be forwarded to it for the final decision.

Hearing a Case

Once the Court agrees to hear a case, the attorneys for both parties prepare their arguments. Arguing a case before the Supreme Court requires months of preparation and it is preceded by perhaps 5 years of litigation in the lower courts. When James Hill sued *Time* magazine for invasion of privacy in 1953, the case reached the Supreme Court 14 years later. In 1967, the Supreme Court ruled that if Hill wanted to collect damages from *Time*, he would have to go back to the trial court and begin again. Hill chose to drop the case.

The nine justices are provided with briefs, which are prepared by their clerks, of the case at hand. Verbal arguments are then held and each side has 30 minutes to present their arguments. In some important cases, additional arguments are heard from *amici curiae* (or friends of the court). The American Civil Liberties Union often seeks *amici curiae* status in civil rights cases.

The attorneys' arguments are carefully planned and may actually be scripted and read *verbatim*. During the presentations, the justices listen and often interrupt the attorneys to ask questions. Once the arguments have been presented, the justices move into a closed session and discuss the case. This discussion may last several days or may be relatively short.

Once a decision is reached, the justices prepare opinions. If the decision is not unanimous (and it rarely is), one justice who voted in the majority writes the opinion of the Court. If the chief justice has voted with the majority, he may write the opinion or assign it to another justice. If the chief justice did not vote with the majority, the senior associate justice who voted with the majority selects the justice to write the opinion. The opinion of the Court is then circulated among the Court for revision. This process can be time consuming. The opinion of the landmark school desegregation case *Brown v. Board of Education* circulated 2 years before it was released.

The justices who disagree with the majority opinion may draft a dissenting opinion. The dissenting opinion can be extremely important, especially in close cases. It is often the dissenting opinion that will be used as a basis for reversal in later years. Chief Justice Oliver Wendell Holmes' dissenting opinion in 1919 in *Abrams v. United States* served as the basis for clarifying the Clear and Present Danger Doctrine in later cases. This doctrine outlined conditions that justify abridging an individual's First Amendment rights. Similarly, many of Justice Douglas' dissenting opinions were later used as the basis of majority opinions as the make up and philosophy of the Supreme Court changed during his 36-year tenure.

A third opinion written by justices is the concurring opinion. Some members of the Court may concur with the majority, but disagree with certain aspects of the decision. For example, in 1957 in *Roth v. United States*, the Court agreed that the obscenity should not be afforded protection by the Constitution, but the process by which the decision was reached was disputed. In *Roth* and subsequent obscenity cases, members of the Court had difficulty applying abstract definitions of "obscene" to actual materials. Therefore, concurring and dissenting opinions were numerous in these cases.

Other Ways of Disposing of a Case

The Supreme Court may also issue a *per curiam* opinion (or a memorandum order). *Per curiam* literally means "by the court" and is an unsigned opinion drafted by the Court as their collective opinion. A memorandum order simply announces a vote, without giving an opinion. The order may cite an earlier Supreme Court decision as the reason for affirming or reversing a lower court ruling. A tie vote means that the lower court's ruling is sustained. It is rare that the Court issues this type of opinion. However, the Court issued a *per curiam* opinion in 1969 in *Brandenburg v. Ohio*, which struck down Ohio's criminal syndicalism law (i.e., teaching the necessity of or attempting to overthrow an existing government by force), and in 1971 in the famous "Penatagon Papers" case, *New York Times v. United States*.

After the Decision

The Supreme Court is not empowered to make a final judgement. The Court remands the case to the lower court for the final decision. In reality, the Court has no way to enforce a decision. This can only be done by the executive branch. Public opinion, however, helps ensure that lower courts and the executive branch abide by Supreme Court rulings.

The Federal Courts

Article III, Section I of the Constitution states that "the judicial Power of the United States shall be vested in one Supreme Court and in such inferior Courts as the Congress may from time to time ordain and establish." In other words, except for the Supreme Court, the federal courts are created by Congress.

Federal courts hear cases dealing with

- constitutional questions
- ambassadors and foreign representatives
- admiralty and maritime law
- suits against the United States government
- disputes between states
- disputes between a state and a citizen of another state
- disputes between citizens of different states

The bulk of the cases heard in federal courts involve constitutional issues or disputes between citizens of different states. Both types of cases are typical communications law situations. Many times, the case involves First and Sixth Amendment issues. Libel and invasion of privacy suits often involve citizens of different states. For example, a publication with a national circulation may originate in New York and a resident of Texas may feel libeled by material in that publication. The Texas resident would bring suit in a federal court.

Levels of Federal Courts

The lowest level federal court is the district court. There are district courts in every state and in Guam, Puerto Rico, and the Virgin Islands. Most business in the federal system begins in a district court. These courts are fact-finding courts. When there is a jury trial, it is heard in a district court. District courts also hear cases when juries are not present.

The second level in the federal court system is the court of appeals. These intermediate-level courts are sometimes called circuit courts, a term coined when judges literally rode the circuit from town to town. Now, federal appellate courts are located in major cities like Chicago, Boston, San Francisco, and Denver. They serve several states in each region and cases are tried in the city in which the court is located. There are 11 circuit courts spread across the United States. In addition, a federal circuit court, the court of appeals for the District of Columbia, and a temporary emergency court of appeals are all located in Washington, DC.

Appellate courts, as the name implies, are not trial courts. There is no jury and testimony is not taken. Cases are usually heard by a panel of three judges who review rulings that are usually forwarded from district courts. The Court of Appeals for the District of Columbia also hears appeals from IRAs, like the FCC and the FTC.

At one time, First Amendment cases were heard by a three-judge district court. This court usually consisted of two district court judges and one appellate court judge. However, in 1976 Congress limited these three-judge panels to hearing questions on activities of members of Congress and reapportionment of congressional districts. Although three-judge panels no longer hear First Amendment issues, the student of communications law may encounter decisions rendered by such a court.

Federal Judges

All federal judges are appointed by the president and must be confirmed by the Senate. Appointments are for life, but judges can be impeached if their conduct warrants impeachment. Impeachment means that charges are brought against the individual, who must be found guilty in order to be removed from office. Only ten federal judges have been impeached in the past 200 years and only five of these judges were removed from office.

The political affiliation of federal judges is an important factor considered by presidents when making appointments. After all, since a seat on the bench lasts a lifetime, the decisions coming from a federal court can steer legal interpretation of the law for a generation. It goes without saying that Democrats appoint Democrats and Republicans appoint Republicans. One of the most controversial Supreme Court nominees in recent memory was Robert Bork. Bork was a circuit court judge chosen by President Reagan to fill a vacancy on the Supreme Court in 1987. Reagan was a conservative president and therefore picked a judge whom he believed espoused views on abortion, school prayer, and rights of privacy similar to his own. Bork was not confirmed because he was perceived by the public as being out of step with mainstream American opinion on these issues.

Judicial Review

Judicial review is the right of any court in the United States to declare any law or official government action invalid because it violates a constitutional provision. The concept has its roots in the famous case of *Marbury v. Madison*, in which Chief Justice John Marshall wrote,

☐ When the Supreme Court concludes that an act of Congress, or an action of the executive, violates the Constitution, the Court can declare either null and void.[2]

Judicial review is very important in the development of the common law. When abridgments of speech or press occur, judicial review often results in the nullification of these abridgments.

The Lawsuit

In order to understand the issues that comprise communications law, the student must be familiar with the process of initiating a lawsuit and the legal names used to refer to the participants in the suit. Most communications lawsuits are civil actions, which are the result of a breach of an individual's rights or duties. Unlike criminal actions, which are punishable by a prison sentence, civil suits award monetary damages to those who win the suit.

The party who initiates a civil action is called the *plaintiff*. The person, or corporation, against whom the suit is brought is called the *defendant*. Libel, slander, invasion of privacy, and other First Amendment issues are called *torts*. A tort is a private or civil wrong done against another that results from a breach of legal duty. In a tort, a plaintiff may allege that the defendant was negligent, intended to inflict emotional distress, or a similar charge. The civil action for a tort is initiated for the sole purpose of compensating the plaintiff for damages suffered. Criminal actions, on the other hand, are concerned with punishing the wrongdoer and, generally, no compensation is offered to the victim.

Initiating the Lawsuit

To initiate a civil suit, the plaintiff chooses the proper court and presents charges against the defendant in the form of a complaint. The court then summons the defendant to answer these charges. If the defendant fails to appear in court at the designated time to respond to the charges, the plaintiff wins by default and the judge awards damages. If the defendant answers the summons, a hearing is scheduled. At the hearing, the plaintiff and defendant prepare a more detailed argument called a *pleading*. At this point, the attorneys may settle out of court. The plaintiff may settle for less money than originally asked, to avoid the cost and stress of a trial. Similarly, the defendant may compromise and the parties may reach an agreeable settlement.

Defendants may also file for demurrer, which is a motion to dismiss the complaint on grounds that the actions charged against them were not illegal. For example, defendants charged with invasion of privacy may attempt to convince the court that what they did was legal. Suppose the plaintiffs charge that the defendant took photographs of them without their consent. If the defendant can convince the judge that the photographs were taken while the individuals were on public property, no invasion of privacy occurred. If demurrer is granted, the plaintiff may appeal.

Before the trial begins, the judge may schedule another conference between the two parties in the case. At this time, the issues are focused and a settlement may be reached. If no settlement is reached, the case proceeds to trial.

If the facts in the case are agreed on by the litigants, no jury will be present. The case is heard by a judge. If the facts are disputed, a jury will be chosen. The selection of jurors varies from state to state, but most states select jurors from voter registration rolls or lists of property owners. The attorneys and the judge question prospective jurors in a process called *voir dire*. During this questioning, the suitability of jurors is determined. Attorneys attempt to expose potentially prejudiced jurors and seek to retain those who will render an impartial verdict, as required by the Sixth Amendment. Students of communications law will discover that the process of seating an impartial jury is sometimes affected by media coverage of crimes. A major communications law issue is the conflict between the press' First Amendment right to report on judicial proceedings and the defendant's right to a fair trial by an impartial jury.

The Trial

The trial itself is a rigidly structured, formal proceeding. The attorneys begin with opening statements, which are followed by the plaintiff's argument. In the case of criminal trials, the prosecution presents the state's case. Witnesses are called and testimony is taken to establish the factual record. The plaintiff's argument is followed by arguments by the defendant or, in a criminal trial, by the defense.

Once all evidence and testimony has been taken, the attorneys summarize their case in a closing argument. In criminal cases, the first closing argument is made by the counsel for the defense and is followed by the prosecutor's closing argument.

The judge may then offer instructions to the jury regarding inadmissible evidence and other legal criteria that must be considered by members of the jury as they attempt to reach their verdict. The jury then retires to a room, where it attempts to reach a verdict. Once a verdict is reached, the jury returns to court and presents its decision to the judge, who informs the litigants.

The attorney for the losing party may file a motion for appeal. If the motion is granted, the case moves to an intermediate-level or appellate court. The judge awards damages in civil suits and pronounces the sentence in criminal cases. Damages are not awarded until all appeals have been exhausted. Consequently, there are civil cases in which millions of dollars have been "won" by a plaintiff in trial court, but actually the money never changes hands because of reversals during the appeals process. In 1982, in *Pring v. Penthouse International Ltd.*, Karen Pring won a $26-million judgment against *Penthouse*, the largest libel award to that date. However, on appeal, the award was reduced to $13 million and was later reversed entirely.

The Appeals Process

When a case is appealed, the person seeking the appeal is called the *appellant*, while the other party is called the *respondent*. Appellate courts do not have juries. No new testimony is heard and a judge rules only on matters of law. For example, in a libel case, the defendant may appeal the amount of money awarded to the plaintiff. The appellate judge will then decide whether the award is justified, based on the facts established at the trial. A judge might also decide that information collected at the trial was applied incorrectly and that the defendant is not guilty of libel. If this is the case, the lower court decision may then be reversed.

After being heard in an intermediate-level court, the next higher court of appeals might be a state supreme court, state court of appeals, or, in federal cases, the U.S. Supreme Court. It is not uncommon for the higher level court to overturn the intermediate court's decision and return to the verdict reached by the trial court. Another alternative is to vacate all decisions and return the case back to a trial court for retrial.

As previously stated, the end result in a civil suit is the awarding of monetary damages. Sometimes, the amount awarded is guided by law. For example, copyright law provides damages equal to the money that would have been earned had an infringement of the copyright not occurred. Some states, like Indiana, limit libel awards to only the actual damages suffered as a result of a libel. In other states, the sky is the limit. For the most part, damages in a civil suit are determined by the amount requested by the plaintiff. Of course, judges reserve the right to reduce damage awards if they believe them to be outrageous or excessive.

The Criminal Case

A criminal case is similar to a civil suit, but instead of the plaintiff bringing suit, charges are brought against a defendant by a prosecutor on behalf of the state. The federal system requires indictment by a grand jury. A grand jury is usually comprised of 23 persons, who are summoned by the Justice Department or other appropriate federal agency to investigate a crime. The grand jury conducts hearings to determine if evidence exists to indict an individual with the alleged crime.

Defendants are arraigned after they are charged with a crime. An arraignment is a formal reading of the charge, after which the defendant pleads either guilty or not guilty. If the defendant enters a guilty plea, the judge reads the verdict of the court and may set a date for sentencing. If the defendant pleads not guilty, a trial is scheduled. In most criminal cases, except for murder and some other serious crimes, the defendant may post bail. This is money given to the court to ensure that the defendant will appear at trial. Bail is refunded when the defendant appears in court. If defendants cannot post bail, which is set by the judge, they remain in jail until the final appeals are over.

At this point, a preliminary hearing is held. The purpose of this hearing is to determine whether there is enough evidence to try the defendant on the charges that have been made. Sometimes, these hearings are called *probable cause hearings.* Probable cause hearings have been particularly troublesome in balancing First and Sixth Amendment rights. The press maintains a right to attend and report on preliminary hearings, which often generate a great deal of attention, especially when the crime under investigation is a sensational murder. At this point, although the trial has not yet begun, there are often reports of damaging testimony being made against the defendant. Some of this testimony may not be admissible in trial court, but it finds its way into newspapers and news broadcasts. This event is especially problematic, since a jury may have been exposed to biased pretrial publicity. Judges may choose to grant a change of venue, which moves the trial to a location away from where the crime was committed, so that an impartial jury can be picked from a populace less likely to have been influenced by pretrial publicity. The judge may also grant a continuance, which postpones the date of the trial in the hopes that impartial jurors will be found more easily. Following the trial, a convicted defendant may appeal the verdict.

How Cases Are Named

The name of the party initiating the lawsuit is listed first in the name of a case. For example, if Doe libels Jones and Jones files suit in 1987, the case goes to court with the name "Jones v. Doe, (1987)." The date follows the name of the case in order to clarify which Jones v. Doe case is being referred to. Jones is the plaintiff and Doe the defendant.

Suppose Doe is found guilty of libel and appeals the case. Doe is now the appellant and Jones is the respondent. If the case goes to appellate court a year later, it is named "Doe v. Jones, (1988)." If Doe wins his appeal and Jones is lucky enough to get the case heard by the Supreme Court, the case might bear the name "Jones v. Doe" again, but the date will distinguish it from the earlier case.

Interpreting Legal Citations

When discovering the common law, judges and lawyers must look to previous cases. Students of communications law must also know where to find important cases and statutes. Cases decided by the U.S. Supreme Court are fairly easy to locate by using a case reporter called the *United States Reports* or the *Supreme Court Reporter*. These multivolume works report the entire text of cases in chronological order. Each case is identified by a citation. For example, the famous libel case, *New York Times v. Sullivan*, is cited as 376 U.S. 254 (1964). This means that the text of the decision appears in volume 376 of *United States Reports*, on page 254. The case was decided in 1964.

Other case reporters use similar methods of presenting citations. Probably the most valuable case reporter for communications law students is the *Media Law Reporter*. This loose-leaf publication provides text and summaries for all cases related to media law. Cases are indexed by subject, name, or the court that decided the case. For example, the *Media Law Reporter* cites General William Westmoreland's appeal of his libel case against CBS as Westmoreland v. CBS, (CA 2, 1984) 11 Med.L.Rptr. 1013. The citation includes the case title, followed (in parentheses) by the court in which the case was decided, and the date of the decision. In this case, "CA 2" means U.S. Court of Appeals for the Second Circuit. The abbreviation "U.S.Sup.Ct" means U.S. Supreme Court and so on. Next, the volume number is noted in the citation, which in this case is 11, and is followed by the abbreviation for the reporter and the page on which the case begins. Again, other case reporters follow a similar format when citing cases.

Statutes are found in code books. All federal statutes are indexed in the *United States Code*. Rules and regulations of the IRAs are published in the *Code of Federal Regulations*. State statutes are found in state code books.

Major decisions and actions of the FCC are found in the Commission's official publications, *FCC Reports* and *FCC Record*. All material printed before 1986 is contained in *FCC Reports*. The name was changed in 1986 to *FCC Record*. FCC citations named before October 1986 are referred to by volume number, F.C.C., or F.C.C.2d. *FCC Record* cites by volume number, F.C.C.Rcd., and the page number. Actions proposed by the Commission appear in the *Federal Register* and are cited as Fed.Reg. or F.R.

An unofficial, but extremely useful source of FCC decisions is *Pike & Fischer's Radio Regulation*. Despite its name, this publication covers all activities and cases affecting radio, television, and cable communications. It is cited as *P&F Radio Reg.*

Summary

The basis of American law was imported from England to the colonies. There are five sources of the law in America: the common law, equity law, statutory law, administrative law, and constitutional law. The Constitution is the supreme law of the land and no law that violates its provisions can be enforced.

Laws in America are interpreted by the judicial branch of the government, which includes the Supreme Court which was created by the Constitution, and other federal courts created by Congress. State and local governments also provide lower courts.

Most communications law deals with civil cases (i.e., wrongs against private individuals, rather than against the state). Wrongs against the state are tried as criminal cases.

Notes/References

1. Oliver W. Holmes, *The Common Law* (Boston: Little Brown, 1881), p. 1.
2. Marbury v. Madison, 1 Cranch 137, 2 L.Ed. 60 (1803).

Cases

Abrams v. United States, 250 U.S. 616 (1919)
Brandenburg v. Ohio, 395 U.S. 444 (1969)

Brown v. Board of Education, 347 U.S. 483 (1954)
Marbury v. Madison, 1 Cranch 137, 2 L.Ed. 60 (1803)
New York Times v. United States, 403 U.S. 713 (1971)
Pring v. Penthouse International Ltd., 8 Med.L.Rptr. 2409 (1982)
Roth v. United States 354 U.S. 476 (1957)

2

□ □ □
□ □ □
□ □ □

Interpreting the First Amendment

History of Free Speech in America

The English Heritage

The development of the law of free speech and press in the United States, like most American law, has its roots in England. The British model was imported to the colonies and included a tradition that supports punishment for the publication of seditious libel. Prohibition against seditious libel began in 1275 with the enactment of *De Scandalis Magnatum*, which provided for imprisonment of anyone who disseminated false statements about the king that caused discord between the king and his subjects.

The statute of *De Scandalis Magnatum*, as eventually administered by the infamous Star Chamber, was responsible for the evolution of English censorship and seditious libel law. The original Star Chamber was part of the king's council, which sat in a chamber of stars (or *camera stellata*) at Westminster and was first called the Star Chamber during the reign of King Edward III in the fourteenth century. In 1585, the Star Chamber passed an ordinance that required all publications to be licensed and printed by the Star Chamber-sanctioned Stationer's Company. The Star Chamber controlled all printing and publishing in England until it was abolished by the Long Parliament in 1641. During this time, the Star Chamber meted out punishments to violators as it saw fit. In one case, an author who expressed a dislike for acting and actors was fined £10,000, given a sentence of life in prison, branded on his forehead, and had his nose slit and his ears cut off. The Star Chamber viewed the criticism of actors as an insult against the queen, and hence the government, who had recently taken part in a play.[1]

Although the Star Chamber ceased to exist in 1641, the English Parliament continued to harass printers and publishers through the Stationer's Company and other forms of licensing. No work could be printed legally without the approval of the stationers, who issued licenses. The stationers served as absolute censors and refused to allow publication of material deemed offensive to them. It should be noted that this concept of censorship is not limited to archaic or authoritarian governments. In spite of the First Amendment, censorship of this kind can be found as late as the 1960s in the United States. Some American cities had film licensing boards that screened motion pictures to determine their suitability for exhibition. Many of these licensing boards exercised capricious judgment and refused to grant exhibition licenses for a variety of reasons. For example, the one-person licensing board in Memphis, Tennessee, refused to allow theaters in that city to show Ingrid Bergman films, noting that her "soul was as black as the soot of hell."[2] The censor found the fact that Miss Bergman had born a child out of wedlock to be morally reprehensible.

Under the British Licensing Acts of the period, authors and printers of "obnoxious works" were hanged, quartered, mutilated, or simply fined and imprisoned "according to the temper of the judges."[3] It was in protest of this licensing act that John Milton wrote the famous *Areopagitica* in 1644. Milton's call for a free press in England is important to Americans, because his reasoning served as the philosophical basis for the marketplace of ideas theory of First Amendment interpretation. Milton wrote,

> And though all the winds of doctrine were let loose to play upon the earth, so Truth be in the field, we do injuriously by licensing and prohibiting to misdoubt her strength. Let her and Falsehood grapple; whoever knew Truth put to the worse, in a free and open encounter?[4]

The sentiments expressed by Milton in the seventeenth century found their way into American law 275 years later in the dissenting opinion of Justice Oliver Wendell Holmes in *Abrams v. United States*. In Holmes' view, truth is best attained when all ideas are free to compete in the marketplace for acceptance. Therefore, any restraints by government tend to obscure the search for truth.

The English Licensing Acts were renewed in 1662, 1685, and again in 1692. Essentially, the acts forbade all printing without a license and gave the king's agents the authority to search all houses and shops in which they suspected unlicensed books were being printed and seize them.

When the licensing acts expired in 1695, they were not renewed by the British Parliament. Although this signaled the end of press censorship in England, printers were by no means free to publish material that might be deemed seditious or treasonable. Nevertheless, newspapers began to flourish and the press became an outlet for political expression. Since this expression was often critical of those in power, the governing bodies sought new ways to silence the press. A return to licensing was proposed, but rejected. Instead, Parliament adopted a less-direct form of censorship when it passed the Stamp Act in 1712.

The Stamp Act was designed to eliminate the small newspapers that published the kind of material most disturbing to the government. The Stamp Act placed a stiff tax on newspapers, pamphlets, advertising, and on paper. The act required that publications be registered with the government, which made it easier for those in power to control the dissemination of information. This means of controlling printed material in England continued until 1855.

Punishment for seditious libel continued as common law throughout the eighteenth and the first half of the nineteenth centuries. Publishers were punished for criticizing foreign policy, the conduct of the king, or any other public official. This criticism was thought to weaken the authority of the government. The truth or falsity of the publication was immaterial. Although Fox's Libel Act of 1792 allowed a jury to acquit a publisher charged with sedition if it thought the publication was not seditious, it was not until 1843, with the passage of Lord Campbell's act, that the modern concept of freedom of the press began to formulate. This act made truth a defense in libel claims. This defense was already legal in America at the time. Twelve years later, the Stamp Act was repealed and freedom of the press was realized in England.

The American Experience

The issues of free speech and press in America essentially paralleled developments in England, but moved much more quickly. Licensing in the colonies followed the same pattern as in England. In 1662, Massachusetts appointed two licensers, without whose permission nothing could be printed. In 1664, the colony passed a law that established Cambridge as the only legal site for printing presses, which were regulated by the licensers.

The Boston *News Letter*, which was published between 1704 and 1776, carried the phrase "Published by Authority" under its nameplate. This meant that the paper contained stories approved by the colonial governor. Licensing was also the rule in Pennsylvania and Virginia, where even the laws of the colony could not be printed without a license. Between 1639 and 1776, numerous publishers and editors were prosecuted in the colonies on charges ranging from criticism of religious doctrines to seditious libel. One of the most celebrated trials was that of John Peter Zenger in New York.

Zenger was the printer of the *New York Weekly Journal*, a newspaper devoted to the opposition of controversial New York Governor William Cosby. The *Journal* was the first independent political paper published in America. Oddly enough, although the editor of the paper, James Alexander, wrote most of the material critical of the governor, Zenger, the printer, was jailed for seditious libel. Zenger was charged with printing

> . . . false news and seditious libels, both wickedly and maliciously devising the administration of His Excellency William Cosby, Captain General and Governor in Chief to traduce, scandalize and vilify both His Excellency the Governor and the ministers and officers of the king and to bring them into suspicion and the ill opinion of the subjects of the king residing within the Province . . .[5]

The *New York Weekly Journal* had been published for about 6 months before Zenger's arrest. Among the items the governor found objectionable is the following passage:

We see men's deeds destroyed, judges arbitrarily displaced, new courts created without consent of the legislature by which it seems to me trial by jury is taken away when a Governor pleases, and men of known estates denied their votes contrary of the received practice, the best expositor of any law. Who is there then in that Province that can call anything his own, or enjoy any liberty, longer than those in the administration will condescend to let them do it?[6]

Andrew Hamilton, a Quaker lawyer from Philadelphia, defended Zenger. In a suprising move, Hamilton admitted that Zenger had published the materials, but in an eloquent argument to the jury, he asserted that the statements about the governor were true. At this time, truth was not a defense in libel cases. So inspiring was Hamilton's argument, however, the jury returned a verdict of "not guilty."

The *Zenger* case helped widen the growing gap between England and the American colonies. Precedent had been set that allowed criticism of colonial governors and other authorities. As Vincent Buranelli points out in his book *The Trial of Peter Zenger*, no longer could one say that resistance to crown officials was *always* wrong.[7] America had begun to clear a path leading toward her own legal system.

In reality, the impact of *Zenger* had a more immediate effect on Britain. By 1738, accounts of Andrew Hamilton's address to the jury were apparently gaining much attention in the legal community. The major principles of the case—truth as a defense in libel actions and the jury has the right to decide both "fact" and "law"— became law in Britain in 1792 with the Fox Libel Act. America responded with a federal statute in 1798.

Another major influence on the development of American legal philosophy was the English legal authority William Blackstone. Blackstone's *Commentaries on the Laws of England* were widely read by students and barristers alike in England and in the colonies. Although dismissed by some as elementary, Blackstone's view of liberty of the press served as a benchmark for courts in Britain and America. Blackstone wrote,

> The liberty of the press is indeed essential to the nature of a free state; but this consists in laying no *previous* restraints upon publications, and not in freedom from censure for criminal matter when published. Every free man has an undoubted right to lay what sentiments he pleases before the public: to forbid this, is to destroy the freedom of the press: but if he publishes what is improper, mischievous, or illegal, he must take the consequence of his own temerity. To subject the press to the restrictive power of a licenser, as was formerly done . . . is to subject all freedom of sentiment to the prejudices of one man, and make him the arbitrary and infallible judge of all controverted points in learning, religion, and government. But to punish . . . any dangerous or offensive writings, which, when published, shall on a fair and impartial trial be adjudged of a pernicious tendency, is necessary for the preservation of peace and good order, of government and religion, the only solid foundations of civil liberty. Thus the will of individuals is still left free; the abuse only of that free will is the object of legal punishment.[8]

Blackstone wrote these words in 1769, but they are actually a fairly accurate reflection of twentieth century American interpretations of the First Amendment. In fact, the Supreme Court relied on Blackstone's concept of no "previous restraint" in the 1931 landmark case *Near v. Minnesota*. In *Near*, the Court ruled that prior or previous restraints on the press violate the First Amendment in most cases. Blackstone also espoused what would later evolve into the Clear and Present Danger Doctrine, when he noted that free speech is not protected when the "peace and good order" are threatened.

In 1791, the states ratified the first ten amendments to the new U.S. Constitution. The first amendment forbade Congress from making laws that would abridge freedom of religion, speech, and the press. Although written in absolute terms, the Supreme Court has never interpreted the First Amendment to mean that individuals have the right to say anything they please, any way they please, anywhere or under any circumstances. In fact, Congress was quick to limit freedom of speech and freedom of the press in the new nation when it passed the Sedition Act of 1798.

The Sedition Act provided punishment for the publication of false, scandalous, and malicious writings against the government, either house of Congress, or the president, if the writings were published with the intent to defame any of these groups or incite the people to rebellion. A companion law, the Alien Act, allowed the president to deport any alien judged dangerous to the security of the United States. The impact of *Zenger* and England's Fox Libel Act were felt, however, since there was precedent for using truth as a defense and the jury was empowered to determine criminality. This defense was strengthened after the expiration of the Alien and Sedition Acts during the presidency of Thomas Jefferson. Ironically, the defense of truth was used by the editor of a newspaper charged with libeling Jefferson. In another unusual twist, Alexander Hamilton, who generally opposed the First Amendment, argued brilliantly in favor of press freedoms in the case against his adversary, Thomas Jefferson.

The Sedition Act expired in March 1801 and was not renewed. Except for Lincoln's unofficial suppression of critics of his policies during the Civil War, there was no major government action raising free speech issues until the First World War.

The First Amendment in the Twentieth Century

When America entered World War I, Congress passed the Espionage Act of 1917. The Espionage Act was designed to protect against spying by foreign countries and to protect military secrets. The act was amended in 1918 to include what is commonly called the Sedition Act (not to be confused with the Sedition Act of 1798). This amendment dealt more with advocacy, speaking, teaching, printing, and inciting than did the original act. Although the Sedition Act was repealed in 1921, the Espionage Act remained in force into the 1940s.

These especially harsh restraints on press and speech freedoms were the result of internal suspicions during the war with Germany (the number of Americans with a German heritage led some to question loyalty), the controversy generated over conscription of troops, and the growing threat of Bolshevism. During this time, more than 1,900 people were prosecuted for alleged subversion and criticism of the national government.

Why was the suppression of First Amendment freedoms tolerated during this time? Legal scholar Zechariah Chafee writes that it may have been because many Americans viewed the freedoms guaranteed by the Founding Fathers as no more than abstract doctrine.

> The First Amendment had no hold on people's minds because no live facts or concrete images were then attached to it. Like an empty box with beautiful words on it, the Amendment collapsed under the impact of terror of Prussian battalions and terror of Bolshevik mobs. So the emotions generated by the two simultaneous cataclysms of war and revolution swept unchecked through American prosecutors, judges, jurymen, and legislators.[9]

It was during this tumultuous time that the initial First Amendment cases reached the Supreme Court. It was also during this time that the first serious interpretations of the meaning of the First Amendment were attempted. With the development of case law, the First Amendment took on a new character—that of living law. No longer was the First Amendment an ethereal concept untouched by the courts of the land. In *Schenck v. United States*, the Court began the arduous task of shaping concrete images from abstract doctrine.

The Clear and Present Danger Test

Schenck was the first and most influential case dealing with significant First Amendment issues to come before the Supreme Court. In this case, Justice Holmes formulated the "clear and present danger" test for determining when an individual's First Amendment rights may be abridged. Schenck had been charged with violating the Espionage Act of 1917, because he distributed leaflets that urged men not to register for the draft during World War I. Justice Holmes delivered the following opinion of the Court:

☐ **Schenck v. United States (1919)**
This is an indictment in three counts. The first charges a conspiracy to violate the Espionage Act of June 15, 1917 . . . by causing and attempting to cause insubordination &c., in the military and naval forces of the United States, and to obstruct the recruiting and enlistment service of the United States, when the United States was at war with the German Empire, to wit, that the defendants wilfully conspired to have printed and circulated

to men who had been called and accepted for military service . . . a document set forth and alleged to be calculated to cause such insubordination and obstruction. The count alleges overt acts in pursuance of the conspiracy, ending in the distribution of the document set forth. The second count alleges a conspiracy to commit an offence against the United States, to wit, to use the mails for the transmission of matter declared to be non-mailable by title 12, section 2, of the Act of June 15, 1917 . . . The document in question upon its first printed side recited the first section of the Thirteenth Amendment, said that the idea embodied in it was violated by the Conscription Act and that a conscript is little better than a convict. In impassioned language it intimated that conscription was despotism in its worst form and a monstrous wrong against humanity in the interest of Wall Street's chosen few. It said "Do not submit to intimidation," but in form at least confined itself to peaceful measures such as a petition for repeal of the act. The other and later printed side of the sheet was headed "Assert Your Rights." It stated reasons for alleging that any one violated the Constitution when he refused to recognize "your right to assert your opposition to the draft," and went on "If you do not assert and support your rights, you are helping to deny or disparage rights which it is the solemn duty of all citizens and residents of the United States to retain." It described the arguments on the other side as coming from cunning politicians and a mercenary capitalist press, and even silent consent to the conscription law as helping to support an infamous conspiracy. It denied the power to send our citizens away to foreign shores to shoot up people of other lands, and added that words could not express the condemnation such cold blooded ruthlessness deserves . . . winding up "You must do your share to maintain, support and uphold the rights of the people of this country."

Of course the document would not have been sent unless it had been intended to have some effect, and we do not see what effect it could be expected to have upon persons subject to the draft except to influence them to obstruct the carrying of it out. The defendants do not deny that the jury might find against them on this point.

But it is said, suppose that was the tendency of this circular, it is protected by the First Amendment to the Constitution. Two of the strongest expressions are said to be quoted respectively from well-known public men. . . . We admit that in many places and in ordinary times the defendants in saying all that was said in the circular would have been within their constitutional rights. But the character of every act depends on the circumstances in which it is done. . . . The most stringent protection of free speech would not protect a man in falsely shouting fire in a theatre and causing a panic. It does not even protect a man from an injunction against uttering words that may have all the effect of force. . . . The question in every case is whether the words used are used in such circumstances and are of such a nature as to create a *clear and present danger* that they will bring about the substantive evils that Congress has a right to prevent. [Emphasis added by the author.]. . . When a nation is at war many things that might be said in time of peace are such a hindrance to its effort that their utterance will not be endured so long as men fight and that no Court could regard them as protected by any constitutional right. It seems to be admitted that if an actual obstruction of the recruiting service were proved, liability for words that produced that effect might be enforced.[10]

Schenk was found guilty of violating the Espionage Act. Justice Holmes articulated the Clear and Present Danger Doctrine as a means of setting the limits of First Amendment rights. In essence, speech could be punished if the utterance of words might bring about "evils that Congress has a right to prevent." Interpretation of clear and present danger was still not absolutely clear. In fact, Justice Holmes found himself on the dissenting side of a similar case shortly after *Schenck*. Holmes disagreed with the majority of the Court's application of the doctrine in *Abrams v. United States*. Abrams and four other Russian-born aliens living in the United States were convicted of violating the Espionage Act. These self-admitted revolutionists were critical of President Wilson's policies and called for the "workers of the world" to rise and put down capitalism. The Supreme Court saw this call as a clear and present danger intended to incite an uprising against the government of the United States. Justice Holmes disagreed.

☐ **Abrams v. United States**

Mr. Justice Holmes dissenting:

This indictment is founded wholly upon the publication of two leaflets.

. . . The first of these leaflets says that the President's cowardly silence about the intervention in Russia reveals the hypocrisy of the plutocratic gang in Washington.

. . . The other leaflet, headed "Workers—Wake Up," with abusive language says that America together with the Allies will march for Russia to help the Czecko-Slovaks [sic] in their struggle against the Bolsheviki, and that this time the hypocrites shall not fool the Russian emigrants and friends of Russia in America. It tells the Russian emigrants that they must now spit in the face of the false military propaganda . . . and further, "Workers in the ammunition factories, you are producing bullets, bayonets, cannon to murder not only Germans, but also your dearest, best, who are in Russia fighting for freedom." It then appeals to the same Russian emigrants at some length not to consent to the "inquisitionary expedition in Russia," . . . The leaflet winds up by saying "Workers, our reply to this barbaric intervention has to be a general strike! . . . Woe unto those who will be in the way of progress. Let solidarity live! [signed] The Rebels."

No argument seems to be necessary to show that these pronounciamentos in no way attack the form of government of the United States. . . .

I do not doubt for a moment . . . the United States constitutionally may punish speech that produces or is intended to produce a clear and imminent danger . . . The power undoubtedly is greater in time of war than in time of peace because war opens dangers that do not exist at other times.

But as against dangers peculiar to war, as against others, the principle of the right of free speech is always the same. It is only the present danger of immediate evil or an intent to bring it about that warrants Congress in setting a limit to the expression of opinion where private rights are concerned. Congress certainly cannot forbid all effort to change the mind of the country.[11]

Holmes applied the marketplace of ideas concept in *Abrams*. Borrowing from Milton's *Areopagitica* and nineteenth century philosopher John Stuart Mill's essay *On Liberty*, Holmes wrote,

☐ the best test of truth is the power of the thought to get itself accepted in the competition of the market, and that truth is the only ground upon which their wishes can be safely carried out.[12]

The marketplace of ideas theory assumes that all ideas, regardless of how loathesome they may be, should be heard. While Milton might assume that truth will triumph over falsity and that "good" will prevail over "evil," neither Mill nor Holmes are so naive. Both accept the fact that truth may not triumph, but in the words of Mill,

. . . [T]he peculiar evil of silencing the expression of an opinion is, that it is robbing the human race; posterity as well as the existing generation; those who dissent from the opinion, still more than those who hold it.[13]

In Holmes' view, the only time government should intervene in the process is when these opinions

☐ imminently threaten immediate interference with the lawful and pressing purposes of the law that an immediate check is required to save the country.[14]

Applying the First Amendment to the States

Six years after *Abrams*, the Supreme Court decided *Gitlow v. People of New York*. In *Gitlow*, the Court upheld the conviction of Benjamin Gitlow for violating the New York Criminal Anarchy Statute. Although a majority of the Court found New York's law to be reasonable, even the dissenters, Holmes and Brandeis, agreed on the principle that the First Amendment was binding on the states through the Fourteenth Amendment. They disagreed as to *how* it should be applied.

Gitlow v. People of State of New York (1925)
Justice Sanford delivered the opinion of the Court:

☐ ... For present purposes we may and do assume that freedom of speech and of the press—which are protected by the First Amendment from abridgement by Congress—are among the fundamental personal rights and "liberties" protected by the due process clause of the Fourteenth Amendment from impairment by the States.[15]

Justice Holmes, dissenting, wrote,

☐ Justice Brandeis and I are of the opinion that this judgement should be reversed. The general principle of free speech, it seems to me, must be taken to be included in the Fourteenth Amendment, in view of the scope that has been given to the word "liberty" as there used.[16]

The Balancing Test

Sometimes the courts must balance First Amendment interests against conflicting social and personal interests. In these situations, the court must determine which interest should receive the greater protection. The balancing test was articulated by the Supreme Court in *American Communications Association v. Douds*.

The Fighting Words Doctrine

Although the Clear and Present Danger Doctrine and the balancing test offer methods of adjudicating First Amendment disputes, they are by no means the only methods employed by the courts. Different First Amendment conflicts require different solutions. Therefore, the common sense approach of what was to become the Fighting Words Doctrine evolved in the 1940s. The Fighting Words Doctrine says that words directed at an average person that may provoke a fight are not protected by the First Amendment. The rationale is that a breach of the peace should be avoided over the protection of an individual's right to utter hostile words. The Fighting Words Doctrine stems from *Chaplinsky v. New Hampshire*, a case that involved a Jehovah's Witness and his activities on a street corner in Rochester, New Hampshire.

☐ **Chaplinsky v. New Hampshire (1942)**
... Chaplinsky was distributing the literature of his sect on the streets of Rochester on a busy afternoon. Members of the local citizenry complained to the City Marshal ... that Chaplinsky was denouncing all religion as a

"racket." The Marshal told them that Chaplinsky was lawfully engaged and warned Chaplinsky that the crowd was getting restless. . . . Chaplinsky made the following remarks to the Marshal outside City Hall: "You are a God-damned racketeer and a damned Fascist and the whole government of Rochester are Fascists or agents of Fascists."

Chaplinsky . . . asked the Marshal to arrest those responsible for the disturbance. But the Marshal, according to Chaplinsky, instead cursed him and told Chaplinsky to come along with him. Chaplinsky was prosecuted under a New Hampshire statute, part of which forbade "addressing any offensive, derisive or annoying word to any other person who is lawfully in any street or other public place."

. . . The statute, as construed, does no more than prohibit the face-to-face words plainly likely to cause a breach of the peace by the speaker—including "classical fighting words," words in current use less "classical" but equally likely to cause violence, and other disorderly words, including profanity, obscenity and threats. . . . Argument is unnecessary to demonstrate that the appellations "damned racketeer" and "damned Fascist" are epithets likely to provoke the average person to retaliation and thereby cause a breach of the peace.[17]

In the years following *Chaplinsky*, the Fighting Words Doctrine was seriously weakened. Many state laws were struck down on the grounds that they were overbroad—and that, as constructed, they not only prohibited fighting words, but other expression as well. In *Gooding v. Wilson*, a Georgia statute prohibiting the use of "opprobrious words or abusive language tending to breach the peace" was struck down as unconstitutionally vague and overbroad under the First and Fourteenth Amendments.[18]

Citing *Chaplinsky*, the Supreme Court defined "fighting words" as those having a "direct tendency to cause acts of violence by the person to whom, individually, the remark is addressed."[19] This means that the doctrine is not applied when groups of people are provoked.

In *Lewis v. City of New Orleans*, the Court also struck down a New Orleans ordinance making it unlawful to "curse or revile or to use obscene or opprobrious language toward or with reference to" a police officer on duty.[20] The New Orleans ordinance was found to have a "broader sweep" than the constitutional definition of fighting words.

Offensive or indecent words, in and of themselves, are not necessarily fighting words. When Paul Robert Cohen walked into the Los Angeles County Courthouse in April of 1968 wearing a jacket with "Fuck the Draft" printed on it, he was arrested for disturbing the peace. Even though he made no physical disturbance, he was convicted on grounds that the writing on his jacket might provoke others to acts of violence. In *Cohen v. California*, the Supreme Court overturned his conviction and stated that the four-letter word displayed by Cohen in relation to the draft was not directed to any one person.

☐   . . . No individual actually or likely to be present could reasonably have
regarded the words on the appellant's jacket as a direct personal insult. . . . There is . . . no showing that anyone who saw Cohen was in fact
violently aroused or that the appellant intended such a result.[21]

The display was protected by the First Amendment, as it was Cohen's opinion of
the Vietnam War and the draft.

In 1977, the American Nazi Party was denied a parade permit by village officials
in Skokie, Illinois, because they feared that the sight of Nazi symbols, such as the
swastika, might trigger violence and trauma based on the vulnerability of Holocaust
survivors to symbolic reminders of past persecution. In April 1977, an injunction
prohibiting the Nazi demonstration was obtained and in the following weeks three
ordinances were passed that required permits for which the American Nazis could
not qualify. The Nazis obtained the assistance of the American Civil Liberties Union
and filed suit against the town on grounds that the ordinances violated the First
Amendment. After a lengthy struggle in the courts in *Village of Skokie v. National
Socialist Party*, the Nazis finally won the right to demonstrate.

☐   **Village of Skokie v. National Socialist Party (1978)**
Plaintiff urges and the appellate court has held, that the exhibition of the
Nazi symbol, the swastika, addresses to ordinary citizens a message
which is tantamount to fighting words. Plaintiff further asks this court to
extend *Chaplinsky*, which upheld a statute punishing the use of such
words, and hold that the fighting-words doctrine permits a prior restraint
on defendant's symbolic speech. In our judgement we are precluded from
doing so. . . .

   . . . The display of the swastika, as offensive to the principles of a free
nation as the memories it recalls may be, is symbolic political speech intended to convey to the public the beliefs of those who display it. It does
not, in our opinion, fall within the definition of "fighting words" and that
doctrine cannot be used here to overcome the heavy presumption against
the constitutional validity of a prior restraint. . . . We do not doubt that the
sight of this symbol is abhorrent to the Jewish citizens of Skokie, and that
the survivors of the Nazi persecutions, tormented by their recollections,
may have strong feelings regarding their display. . . . In summary, as we
read the controlling Supreme Court opinions, use of the swastika is a symbolic form of free speech entitled to First Amendment protections. Its display on uniforms or banners by those engaged in peaceful demonstrations
cannot be totally precluded because that display may provoke a violent
reaction by those who view it. Particularly . . . where . . . there has been
advance notice by the demonstrators of their plans so that they have become . . . "common knowledge" and those to whom sight of the swastika
banner or uniforms would be offensive are forewarned and need not view

them. A speaker who gives prior notice of his message has not compelled a confrontation with those who voluntarily listen.[22]

Although they won a legal victory, the Nazis eventually cancelled their plan to march in Skokie. According to Professor Donald Downs, the leader of the National Socialist Party, Frank Collin, decided against the march because he knew his group would make easy targets for counterdemonstrators.

Probably no case involving the First Amendment so tests the fabric of the marketplace of ideas theory as does the *Skokie* case. The parameters of the conflict give new life to Justice Douglas' resurrection of the concept in his dissent in *Dennis v. United States:*

☐ Full and free discussion even of ideas we hate encourages the testing of our own prejudices and preconceptions. Full and free discussion keeps a society from becoming stagnant and unprepared for the stresses and strains that work to tear all civilizations apart.[23]

Speech and Action

Courts have experienced difficulty in cases involving both verbal and nonverbal elements. When David Paul O'Brien burned his draft card on the steps of the South Boston Courthouse, he said he did so in protest of the war in Vietnam. Although draft card mutilation was a violation of the Military Training and Service Act of 1948, O'Brien maintained that the draft card burning was "symbolic speech" and was therefore protected by the First Amendment. In *United States v. O'Brien*, the Supreme Court disagreed. Justice Warren wrote,

☐ This Court has held that when "speech" and "nonspeech" elements are combined in the same course of conduct, a sufficiently important governmental interest in regulating the nonspeech element can justify incidental limitations on First Amendment freedoms. . . . The many functions performed by Selective Service certificates establish beyond doubt that Congress has a legitimate interest in preventing their wanton and unrestrained destruction and continuing their availability by punishing people who knowingly and willfully destroy or mutilate them.[24]

O'Brien could have burned "symbolic" draft cards, but not the real item.

The Supreme Court reached a different decision one year later. Students in Des Moines wore black arm bands to school to protest the Vietnam War. The Des Moines school system had specifically prohibited the wearing of arm bands. Seven of the 18,000 students enrolled in the system wore arm bands and no disruption of school operations occurred. In *Tinker v. Des Moines Independent School District*, the Court held that the wearing of arm bands was a "symbolic act" protected by the First Amendment.

Twenty years later, a badly divided Supreme Court (5 to 4) ruled that burning the American flag may be symbolic speech. In *Texas v. Johnson*, Justice Brennan delivered the opinion of the Court:

☐ **Texas v. Johnson (1989)**

. . . While the Republican National Convention was taking place in Dallas in 1984, respondent Johnson participated in a political demonstration . . . . the purpose of this event was to protest the policies of the Reagan administration and of certain Dallas-based corporations. The demonstrators marched through the Dallas streets, chanting political slogans and stopping at several corporate locations to stage "die-ins" intended to dramatize the consequences of nuclear war . . . . [Johnson] . . . did . . . accept an American flag handed him by a fellow protestor who had taken it from a flag pole outside one of the targeted buildings.

The demonstration ended in front of Dallas City Hall, where Johnson unfurled the American flag, doused it with kerosene, and set it on fire. While the flag burned, the protestors chanted, "America the red, white and blue, we spit on you." After the demonstrators dispersed, a witness to the flag burning collected the flag's remains and buried them in his backyard.

Of the approximately 100 demonstrators, Johnson alone was charged with a crime. The only criminal offense with which he was charged was the desecration of a venerated object in violation of Tex. Penal Code Ann . . . . After a trial, he was convicted, sentenced to one year in prison, and fined $2000. The Court of Appeals for the Fifth District of Texas at Dallas affirmed Johnson's conviction, but the Texas Court of Criminal Appeals reversed . . .

Johnson was convicted of flag desecration for burning the flag rather than for uttering insulting words. This fact somewhat complicates our consideration of his conviction under the First Amendment . . . .

Texas conceded that Johnson's conduct was expressive conduct. Johnson burned an American flag as part—indeed, as the culmination—of a politcal demonstration that coincided with the convening of the Republican Party and its renomination of Ronald Reagan for President. The expressive, overtly political nature of this conduct was both intentional and overwhelmingly apparent . . . .

Texas claims that its interest in preventing breaches of the peace justifies Johnson's conviction for flag desecration. However, no disturbance of the peace actually occurred or threatened to occur because of Johnson's burning of the flag . . . . The State's position, therefore, amounts to a claim that an audience that takes serious offense at particular expression is necessarily likely to disturb the peace and that the expression may be prohibited on this basis. Our precedents do not countenance such a presumption.

On the contrary, they recognize that a principal "function of free speech under our system of government is to invite dispute." ...

Nor does Johnson's expressive conduct fall within that small class of "fighting words" that are "likely to provoke the average person to retaliation, and thereby cause a breach of the peace." *Chaplinsky v. New Hampshire* 315 U.S. 568 (1942) ...

The State also asserts an interest in preserving the flag as a symbol of nationhood and national unity ... If there is a bedrock principle underlying the First Amendment, it is that the Government may not prohibit the expression of an idea simply because society finds the idea itself offensive or disagreeable.

We have not recognized an exception to this principle even where our flag has been involved .... In short, nothing in our precedents suggests that a State may foster its own view of the flag by prohibiting expressive conduct relating to it ....

To conclude that the Government may permit designated symbols to be used to communicate only a limited set of messages would be to enter territory having no discernible or defensible boundaries. Could the Government, on this theory, prohibit the burning of state flags? Of copies of the Presidential seal? Of the Constitution? In evaluating these choices under the First Amendment, how could we decide which symbols were sufficiently special to warrant this unique status? To do so, we would be forced to consult our own political preferences, and impose them on the citizenry, in the very way that the First Amendment forbids us to do so.

There is, moreover, no indication—either in the text of the Constitution or in our cases interpreting it—that a separate judicial category exists for the American flag alone ....

We are fortified in today's conclusion by our conviction that forbidding criminal punishment for conduct such as Johnson's will not endanger the special role played by our flag or the feelings it inspires.

... The way to preserve the flag's special role is not to punish those who feel differently about these matters. It is to persuade them that they are wrong ....[25]

In October 1989, President Bush signed into law the Flag Protection Act. This law provides for penalites of up to 1 year in jail and a $1000 fine for those who desecrate the American flag.

Prior Restraint

Prior restraint means censoring or preventing material from being broadcast or published. While the presumption against prior restraint in Anglo-American law may be traced back to Blackstone's *Commentaries,* the first major

American case did not reach the Supreme Court until 1931. *Near v. Minnesota* involved a Minnesota newspaper called *The Saturday Press*.

A Minnesota statute allowed local prosecutors to enjoin publications judged "malicious, scandalous and defamatory." The county attorney of Hennepin County brought such an action against *The Saturday Press*. It seems that the paper had accused the law enforcement officials in Minneapolis of failing to punish gambling, bootlegging, and racketeering activities. The paper also charged that law enforcement was controlled by a "Jewish gangster."

The state trial court found that the *Press* had violated the Minnesota public nuisance statute and "perpetually enjoined" publication of the paper. The Supreme Court reversed the ruling, finding the Minnesota statute unconstitutional. States are free to provide for punishment *after* publication, but the Court stressed that freedom to publish must be guarded. In *Near*, the Supreme Court noted that although there was a heavy presumption against prior restraints, there may be times when such action is justified.

> No one would question but that a government might prevent actual obstruction to its recruiting service or the publication of sailing dates of transports or the number and location of troops. On similar grounds, the primary requirements of decency may be enforced against obscene publications. The security of community life may be protected against incitements to acts of violence and the overthrow by force of orderly government.[26]

The Doctrine of Prior Restraint was tested again in 1971 in what has become known as the Pentagon Papers Case. The *New York Times* was restrained from publishing 36 classified papers outlining how America became involved in the Vietnam War. The papers had been obtained from Dr. Daniel Ellsberg, a former Pentagon employee who had become disenchanted with the war.

A temporary restraining order was issued against the *Times*, but when the United States government requested a permanent injunction, Judge Gurfein of the Federal District Court for the Southern District of New York refused to grant one. The U.S. Court of Appeals for the Second Circuit reversed, calling for further hearings on the matter. In the meantime, the temporary injunction remained in effect.

Next, the *Washington Post* obtained the papers and planned to publish them. The government, once again, requested a restraining order. Judge Gerhard Gesell of the U.S. District Court for the District of Columbia refused to issue the order and the *Post* was free to publish, while the *Times* could not. The Supreme Court eventually ruled in favor of the *Times*, noting that,

> Any system of prior restraints of expression come to this Court bearing a heavy presumption against its constitutional validity . . . . The government "thus carries a heavy burden of showing justification for the enforcement of such a restraint." . . . The District Court for the Southern District of New

York in the *New York Times* case and the District Court for the District of Columbia and the Court of Appeals for the District of Columbia Circuit in the *Washington Post* case held that the government had not met that burden. We agree.[27]

In the fall of 1990, the Cable News Network (CNN) planned to cablecast tapes of jail telephone call conversations between deposed Panamanian dictator Manuel Noriega and his attorneys. Miami, Florida, District Court Judge William Hoeveler issued a temporary injunction against CNN on the grounds that Noriega's Sixth Amendment right to a fair trial may be jeopardized. In spite of the injunction, CNN did cablecast one of the conversations, but eventually turned the tapes over to the court for fair trial consideration. CNN was threatened with contempt charges for the cablecast. On November 18, 1990, the Supreme Court refused to schedule arguments on the merits of the injunction and also refused to give CNN permission to air the taped conversations. On November 28, 1990, Judge Hoeveler lifted the restraining order, saying that after viewing the tapes he had concuded that Noriega's right to a fair trial would not be impaired.

Clear and Present Danger Doctrine Revisited

After *Schenck* and *Abrams*, the Clear and Present Danger Doctrine fell into disuse. It did not reappear until 1951 and then in a somewhat altered form. In *Dennis v. United States*, the Supreme Court upheld the conviction of Eugene Dennis and ten other persons for violating the Smith Act. The Smith Act made it a crime to conspire to teach and advocate the overthrow of the United States government by force. In a 6–2 decision, the Court convicted the petitioners for conspiracy and advocacy—not for actual violence. A majority of the Court held that the state cannot be expected to wait until violence is imminent before acting. The justices noted that obstructions to free speech and press might be necessary in order to prevent an even greater evil to society. Hence, Dennis presented a clear and present danger.

The doctrine reached its apex with *Dennis*. An individual's First Amendment rights could be abridged for merely *teaching* the necessity of overthrowing the government. However, the pendulum quickly began to swing the other way. In spite of the fact that the government brought many prosecutions under the Smith Act after *Dennis*, by 1957 the act had been overruled. With McCarthyism on the wane, the Supreme Court, in *Yates v. United States*, made a distinction between advocacy of direct action and advocacy of abstract doctrine. The latter, said the Court, was protected by the First Amendment.

The Clear and Present Danger Doctrine was finalized in *Brandenburg v. Ohio*, when the Supreme Court held that advocacy may not be banned unless it is directed to inciting or producing imminent lawless action and is likely to incite or produce such action.

The First Amendment and Broadcasting

As we shall study in later chapters, material broadcast over the air is not afforded the same First Amendment protection as printed matter. The underlying assumption of broadcast regulation originally rested on the premise that broadcasters used a scarce public resource—the electromagnetic spectrum. In theory, because there are a limited number of broadcast frequencies available, the FCC was charged with choosing the best applicant from those who applied for a broadcast license. The FCC developed criteria for making that choice, all of which are under the umbrella of the "public interest standard." Unlike newspapers, broadcasters were "public trustees." While the First Amendment protected publishers, the Supreme Court ruled in *Red Lion v. FCC*, that

☐   . . . Because of the scarcity of radio frequencies, the Government is permitted to put restraints on licenses in favor of others whose views should be expressed on this unique medium. But the people as a whole retain their interest in free speech by radio and their collective right to have the medium function consistently with the ends and purposes of the First Amendment. *It is the right of the viewers and listeners, not the right of the broadcasters which is paramount.* [Emphasis added by the author.] It is the purpose of the First Amendment to preserve an uninhibited marketplace of ideas in which truth will ultimately prevail, rather than to countenance monopolization of that market, whether it be by the Government itself or by private licensee . . . . It is the right of the public to receive suitable access to social, political, esthetic, moral and other ideas and experiences which is crucial here.[28]

In spite of the fact that "scarcity" is a creation of the frequency allocation process and that even the FCC has questioned its validity, concern over fairness remains.[29]

The FCC is prohibited from censoring program content. Newspapers and magazines are legally free to publish almost any material that has not been judged by a court to be obscene. Broadcasters do not have that freedom. Because of the pervasive nature of the broadcast media, certain material may not be broadcast over the air, as ruled in *FCC v. Pacifica Foundation*. The courts and the FCC have ruled that because broadcasting comes into the home, sometimes "uninvited," consideration for the make up of the audience is in order. Cable operators are not subjected to these restrictions on content.

Unlike newspapers, broadcasters must provide equal time to political candidates and the rates at which this time can be sold is governed by the Communications Act. Any legislation suggesting that newspapers or magazines be subjected to the same standards would surely violate the First Amendment, which was the case in *Miami Herald Publishing Co. v. Tornillo* (1974).

Many in the industry see these regulations as unfair burdens that hinder the ability to compete in the marketplace. Others in society believe that regulation enhances the number of voices given access to the marketplace of ideas. The regulation of over-the-air broadcasting and cable, and their respective First Amendment freedoms, has evolved in very different directions. New challenges are presented by emerging technologies. It is this dynamism that will engage us throughout the rest of this text.

Summary

The major cases that dealt with interpretations of the First Amendment did not occur until the twentieth century. While the First Amendment is written in absolute terms, the courts have developed guidelines that indicate the limitations of freedom of speech and freedom of the press. The interpretations of the First Amendment given by the courts have varied over the years, depending on the philosophical bent of the justices hearing the cases.

Because broadcast media are licensed to serve the public interest and use space on the electromagnetic spectrum, they are held to a stricter standard under the First Amendment than publishers or cable television operators.

Notes/References

1. Edward G. Hudon, *Freedom of Speech and Press in America* (Washington, D.C.: Public Affairs Press, 1963), 11.
2. Donald M. Gillmor and Jerome A. Barron, *Mass Communication Law*, 4th ed. (St. Paul: West Publishing Co., 1984), 738.
3. Ibid.
4. John Milton, *Areopagitica and Of Education*, ed. George H. Sabine (New York: Appleton-Century-Crofts, 1951), 50.
5. Vincent Buranelli, *The Trial of Peter Zenger* (Washington Square: New York University Press, 1957), 95.
6. Ibid., 97.
7. Ibid., 62.
8. William Blackstone, *Commentaries on the Laws of England*, ed. Charles M. Haar (Boston: Beacon Press, 1962), 161–62.
9. Zechariah Chafee Jr., *Thirty-Five Years with Freedom of Speech* (New York: Roger N. Baldwin, Civil Liberties Foundation, 1952), 4.
10. Schenck v. United States, 249 U.S. 47 (1919).
11. Abrams v. United States, 250 U.S. 616 (1919).
12. Abrams v. United States, 250 U.S. 616 (1919).

13. J.S. Mill, *On Liberty Etc.* (London: Oxford University Press, 1969), 24.
14. Abrams v. United States, 250 U.S. 616 (1919).
15. Gitlow v. People of State of New York, 268 U.S. 652, 45 S.Ct. 625, 69 L.Ed. 1138 (1925).
16. Ibid.
17. Chaplinsky v. New Hampshire, 315 U.S. 568, 62 S.Ct. 766, 86 L.Ed. 1031 (1942).
18. Gooding v. Wilson, 405 U.S. 518 (1972).
19. Ibid.
20. Lewis v. City of New Orleans, 408 U.S. 913 (1972) and Lewis v. City of New Orleans, 415 U.S. 130 (1974).
21. Cohen v. California, 403 U.S. 15 at 20 (1971).
22. Village of Skokie v. National Socialist Party, 373 N.E. 2d 21 (Ill. 1978).
23. Dennis v. United States, 341 U.S. 494 (1951).
24. United States v. O'Brien, 391 U.S. 367 (1968).
25. Texas v. Johnson, Slip op. 88–155 (U.S. June 21, 1989).
26. Near v. Minnesota, 283 U.S. 697 (1931).
27. New York Times v. United States, 403 U.S. 308 (1971).
28. Red Lion v. FCC, 395 U.S. 367 (1969).
29. For additional information regarding this issue, see the *Fairness Report of 1985*, 102 F.C.C.2d 143, 58 R.R.2d 1137 (1985) and "Fairness Doctrine Legislation Re-Emerges," *Broadcasting* (January 12, 1991): 43.

Cases

Abrams v. United States, 250 U.S. 616 (1919)

American Communications Association v. Douds, 339 U.S. 382 (1950)

Brandenburg v. Ohio, 395 U.S. 444 (1969)

Chaplinsky v. New Hampshire, 315 U.S. 568, 62 S.Ct. 766, 86 L.Ed. 1031 (1942)

Cohen v. California, 403 U.S. 15 at 20 (1971)

Dennis v. United States, 341 U.S. 494 (1951)

FCC v. Pacifica Foundation, 438 U.S. 726 (1978)

Gitlow v. People of State of New York, 268 U.S. 652, 45 S.Ct. 625, 69 L.Ed. 1138 (1925)

Gooding v. Wilson, 405 U.S. 518 (1972)

Lewis v. City of New Orleans, 408 U.S. 913 (1972)

Lewis v. City of New Orleans, 415 U.S. 130 (1974)

Miami Herald Publishing Co. v. Tornillo, 418 U.S. 241 (1974)

Near v. Minnesota, 283 U.S. 697 (1931)

New York Times v. United States 403 U.S. 713 (1971)

Red Lion Broadcasting Co., Inc. v. FCC, 395 U.S. 367 (1969)
Schenck v. United States, 249 U.S. 47 (1919)
Texas v. Johnson, Slip op. 88–155 (U.S. June 21, 1989)
Tinker v. Des Moines Independent School District, 393 U.S. 503 (1969)
United States v. O'Brien, 391 U.S. 367 (1968)
Village of Skokie v. National Socialist Party, 373 N.E.2d 21 (Ill., 1978)
Yates v. United States, 354 U.S. 298 (1957)

3

□ □ □
□ □ □
□ □ □

The Rationale
of Broadcast Regulation

*I think this is probably the only industry of the United States
that is unanimously in favor of having itself regulated.*[1]

When Commerce Secretary Herbert Hoover made this statement at the Third National Radio Conference in 1924, he was describing a chaotic industry. The number of radio stations on the air continued to increase, while few frequencies had been allocated for broadcast use. Hoover had designated 833 kHz for broadcast use in 1921 and added 750 kHz in 1922. By 1923, the band was expanded to include frequencies from 550 kHz to 1350 kHz. Every channel was filled and there was considerable interference among stations.

Even to an ardent believer of free enterprise like Hoover, it seemed that the only solution to the problem of radio interference was stricter government regulation. Hoover had already established the groundwork for government intervention into broadcasting when he established frequency allocations, power regulations, and operating schedules. The Commerce Department's authority to regulate radio was the Radio Act of 1912. This act provided for government regulation of the maritime industry, spurred largely by the *Titanic* disaster. Although the Radio Act of 1912 was weak and did not anticipate commercial radio broadcasting as it was to develop in the 1920s, it served as the only radio regulatory legislation passed by Congress until 1927.

Using the 1912 Act as the basis of his authority, Hoover called a series of four radio conferences between 1922 and 1925. Originally, he hoped that the radio industry could work out its problems without government controls. But with each conference, that possibility appeared more remote. In 1922, only 22 broadcasters attended the radio conference. By 1925, more than 400 were in attendance. Each year the industry called for the government to step in and straighten out the mess.

Despite the overt cries from the industry for regulation, and the obvious need for some form of control over the burgeoning broadcast industry, enacting regulatory measures did not come easily.

When Representative Wallace H. White of Maine sponsored legislation in 1922 authorizing Hoover to act as "traffic cop of the air," it was voted down by Congress. In 1923, when Hoover attempted to reduce the overcrowding of the airwaves, the U.S. Court of Appeals for the District of Columbia ruled in *Hoover v. Intercity Radio Co. Inc.* that Hoover had exceeded his authority. The final blow to Commerce Department regulation of radio came in 1926 when a series of court rulings denied Hoover the authority to regulate frequencies, power, or operating hours. This case, *United States v. Zenith Radio Corp. et al.*, led directly to the passage of the Radio Act of 1927 and ultimately to the Communications Act of 1934.

United States v. Zenith Radio Corp. *et. al.* (1926)

After the Fourth National Radio Conference in 1924, the Zenith Radio Corporation applied to the Commerce Department for a permit to build a radio station. A license was granted and Zenith was authorized to operate WJAZ radio on a frequency of 930 kHz. WJAZ was also required to share this frequency with several other stations. Time sharing was common during this period and served as a somewhat less than optimal solution to the overcrowding problem. Zenith found the 2 hours per week it was permitted to broadcast to be overly restrictive and applied for a license to broadcast on 910 kHz. This frequency was not available for use by American stations. An agreement between the United States and Canada had limited 910 kHz to Canadian use. Zenith's application for the frequency was denied, but Zenith defiantly changed frequencies anyway. After Zenith "jumped frequency," other stations announced their intention to do the same. The Commerce Department took Zenith to court, but an Illinois federal district court found that the Radio Act of 1912 gave the Commerce Department no authority to establish radio regulations. Therefore, the Commerce Department was powerless to stop Zenith from broadcasting on any frequency it chose.

Judge Wilkerson wrote,

☐   . . . There is no express grant of power in the act to the Secretary of Commerce to establish regulations.

The fifteenth regulation prohibits a private or commercial station not engaged in the transmission of bona fide commercial business by radio communication or in experimentation in connection with the development and manufacture of radio apparatus for commercial purposes from using a wave length exceeding 200 meters except by special authority of the Secretary of Commerce. Defendant's license authorizes the use of wave length 332.4 meters on Thursday night from 10 to 12 PM *when use of this period is not desired by the General Electric Company's Denver station.*

Each of the acts of the defendant, relied upon by the United States as the basis of prosecution, is within the prohibition of the fifteenth regulation. Each count of the information covers broadcasting on a wave length of 329.5 meters at a time not covered by the authority in the license. Section 4 contains a special provision for penalties for violations of regulations as follows:

For a violation of any of these regulations, subject to which a license under sections one and two of this act may be issued, the owner of the apparatus shall be liable to a penalty of one hundred dollars, which may be reduced or remitted by the Secretary of Commerce . . . and for repeated violations . . . the license may be revoked.

Does the operation of the station upon any wave length at any other time than from 10 to 12 PM on Thursday constitute a violation of section 1? The license provides:

This station to be operated only on Thursday nights from 10 to 12 PM Central Standard Time and then only when use of this period is not desired by the General Electric Company's Denver station.

The provision in section 2 as to stating in the license the hours for which the station is licensed must be read and interpreted in its relation to the entire act.

The Secretary of Commerce is required to issue the license subject to the regulations in the act. The Congress has withheld from him the power to prescribe additional regulations. If there is a conflict between a provision in the license and the regulations established by Congress, the latter must control . . .[2]

The *Zenith* case leaves no doubt that it is Congress that must establish regulatory procedures to be applied to radio. By 1927, Congress had passed the Radio Act designed to do just that.

The Radio Act of 1927 was signed into law by President Coolidge on February 23, 1927. The act created a temporary, five-member Federal Radio Commission (FRC). The commissioners remained in power from year to year through various acts of Congress. The 1927 act was eventually superseded by the Communications Act of 1934. The 1934 act created the FCC, which was a permanent regulatory agency.

An important feature of the 1927 act was the establishment of the "public interest, convenience, and necessity" phrase as the standard for licensing radio stations. The somewhat slippery phrase was borrowed from public utility legislation and was incorporated into the 1934 act as well. The ambiguity of the public interest standard has served as the basis for much of the litigation surrounding broadcast law. Since the phrase was incorporated into the Communications Act of 1934, it has been and still is a source of controversy.

While the Radio Act of 1927 brought an end to the chaos of radio by creating an agency to oversee the development of broadcasting, the act left some aspects of radio and all interstate and foreign wire communication under the control of other federal agencies. The Communications Act of 1934 brought wire and wireless communication under the control of the Commission. The essence of broadcast regulation remained the same, because much of the Radio Act was imported to the Communications Act. Although there have been numerous amendments over the years and several attempts at rewriting the 1934 act, today's broadcast stations are essentially regulated under many of the same provisions that were part of the 1927 act.

The FCC began formal operation on July 11, 1934. The Commission was created by the Roosevelt administration as an independent regulatory commission, like the Interstate Commerce Commission and the Federal Trade Commission. Like the FRC before it, the FCC based its authority to regulate broadcasting on the nebulous "public interest" concept. The phrase "public interest, convenience, and necessity" was borrowed from an 1887 Illinois railroad statute and was later adopted in the Federal Transportation Act of 1920. Legal scholar Don Le Duc wrote,

> Yet, whereas it would seem relatively easy to decide when the extension of a rail line or an increase in shipping tariffs might ultimately serve the needs or interests of its customers, it was far more complex and less precise in outcome to make a similar determination, in terms of audience requirements about factors as sophisticated as subtle programming balance or local orientation.[3]

The Communications Act of 1934

The Communications Act sets the parameters within which the FCC functions. It stipulates the organization of the Commission, outlines the procedures to be followed, defines terms, and states the "charge" of the FCC. The act was originally made up of six "titles." In 1984, Congress passed the Cable Communications Policy Act, so that currently there are seven titles:

Title I—Definition of Terms; Provisions Setting up the Commission
Title II—Common Carriers (Telephone and Telegraph)
Title III—General Powers of the Commission, Licensing, Administrative
    Sanctions, Public Broadcasting
Title IV—Hearings and Appeals of Commission Decisions
Title V—Penal Provisions and Forfeitures
Title VI—Cable Television (added in 1984)
Title VII—Miscellaneous Provisions, War Powers of the President

Each of these titles is comprised of sections and paragraphs. Some sections of the Communications Act have become so well known that they are referred to by number. For example, Section 315 is the equal time provision, which applies to candidates for public office. Section 326 contains the no censorship clause. It is essential for the student of the law of electronic media to become familiar with these and other provisions of the Communications Act.

Title III, Part I, Sec. 301

It is the purpose of this Act, among other things, to maintain the control of the United States over all the channels of interstate and foreign radio transmission; and to provide for the use of such channels, but not the ownership thereof, by persons for limited periods of time, under licenses granted by Federal authority, and no license shall be construed to create any right beyond the terms, conditions, and period of the license.[4]

Title III, Part I, Sec. 302

(a) The Commission may, consistent with the public interest, convenience, and necessity, make reasonable regulations governing the interference potential of devices which in their operation are capable of emitting radio frequency energy.[5]

Title III, Part I, Sec. 303

Except as otherwise provided in this Act, the Commission from time to time, as public convenience, interest, or necessity requires shall—

(a) Classify radio stations;

(b) Prescribe the nature of the service to be rendered by each class of licensed stations and each station within any class;

(c) Assign bands of frequencies to the various classes of stations, and assign frequencies for each individual station and determine the power which each station shall use and the time during which it may operate;

(d) Determine the location of classes of stations or individual stations;

(f) Make such regulations not inconsistent with law as it may deem necessary to prevent interference between stations and to carry out the provisions of this Act . . .

(l) (1) Have authority to prescribe the qualifications of station operators . . .

(n) Have authority to inspect all radio installations associated with stations required to be licensed . . . to ascertain whether in construction, installation, and operation they conform to the requirements of the rules and regulations of the Commission . . .

(o) Have authority to designate call letters of all stations . . .

(r) Make such rules and regulations and prescribe such restrictions and conditions, not inconsistent with law, as may be necessary to carry out the provisions of this Act . . .[6]

Title III, Part I, Sec. 312

The Commission may revoke any station license or construction permit—

(1) for false statements knowingly made either in the application or in any statement of fact which may be required pursuant to section 308;

(2) because of conditions coming to the attention of the Commission which would warrant it in refusing to grant a license or permit on an original application;

(3) for willful or repeated failure to operate substantially as set forth in the license;

(4) for willful or repeated violation of, or willful or repeated failure to observe, any provision of this Act or any rule or regulation of the Commission authorized by this Act or by a treaty ratified by the United States;

(5) for violation of or failure to observe any final cease and desist order issued by the Commission under this section;

(6) violation of section 1304, 1343, or 1464[7] of Title 18 of the United States Code; or

(7) for willful or repeated failure to allow reasonable access to or permit purchase of reasonable amounts of time for the use of a broadcasting station by a legally qualified candidate for Federal elective office on behalf of his candidacy.

Title III, Part I, Sec. 315

(a) If any licensee shall permit any person who is a legally qualified candidate for any public office to use a broadcasting station, he shall afford equal opportunities to all other such candidates for that office in the use of such broadcasting station: *Provided,* that such licensee shall have no power of censorship over the material broadcast under the provisions of this section. No obligation is imposed under this subsection upon any licensee to allow the use of its station by any such candidate. Appearance by a legally qualified candidate on any—

(1) bona fide newscast,

(2) bona fide news interview,

(3) bona fide news documentary (if the appearance of the candidate is incidental to the presentation of the subject or subjects covered by the news documentary), or

(4) on-the-spot coverage of bona fide news events (including but not limited to political conventions and activities incidental thereto),

shall not be deemed to be use of a broadcasting station within the meaning of this subsection. Nothing in the foregoing sentence shall be construed as relieving broadcasters, in connection with the presentation of news-casts, news interviews, news documentaries, and on-the-spot coverage of news events, from the obligation imposed upon them under this Act to operate in the public interest and to afford reasonable opportunity for the discussion of conflicting views on issues of public importance.[8]

(b) The charges made for the use of any broadcasting station by any person who is a legally qualified candidate for any public office in connection with his campaign for nomination, or election to such office shall not exceed—

   (1) during the forty-five days preceeding the date of the primary runoff election and during the sixty days preceeding the date of a general or special election in which a person is a candidate, the lowest unit charge of the station for the same class and amount of time for the same period; and

   (2) at any other time, the charges made for comparable use of such station by other users thereof.

(c) No station licensee may make any charge for the use of such station by or on behalf of any legally qualified candidate for Federal elective office (or for nomination to such office) unless such candidate (or a person specifically authorized by such candidate in writing to do so) certifies to such licensee in writing that the payment of such charge will not violate any limitation . . . of the Campaign Communications Reform Act . . .[9]

Title III, Part I, Sec. 326

Nothing in this Act shall be understood or construed to give this Commission the power of censorship over the radio communications or signals transmitted by any radio station, and no regulation or condition shall be promulgated or fixed by the Commission which shall interfere with the right of free speech by means of radio communication.[10]

The U.S. Criminal Code

Originally, the prohibition against broadcasting obscene or indecent language was part of Section 326 of the Communications Act. In 1948, the prohibition was removed and made part of the U.S. Criminal Code. Title 18, U.S.C. 1464 states,

Whoever utters any obscene, indecent, or profane language by means of radio communication shall be fined not more than $10,000 or imprisoned not more than two years or both.[11]

These issues are discussed in greater depth in Chapter 5.

Evolution of FCC Authority

Although the Communications Act seems to guarantee broadcasters protection under the First Amendment, application of that right took a peculiar turn. Freedom of speech was to apply to speech deemed to be in the public interest. It was not that the speech of broadcasters was to be protected, as much as it was the right of the radio audience to be protected from certain forms of speech. In *KFKB Broadcasting v. Federal Radio Commission*, the Commission revoked the license of the station featuring programs by Dr. J. R. Brinkley. Brinkley answered medical questions on the air and dispensed his medicines, for which he received a fee. The Commission denied renewal to KFKB on grounds that it had not operated in the "public interest." The FRC denied that it had exceeded its jurisdiction and engaged in censorship and the court agreed.

In *Trinity Methodist Church, South v. Federal Radio Commission*, the Commission expanded this doctrine further. Associate Justice Groner wrote,

☐   Appellant, Trinity Methodist Church, South, was the lessee and operator of a Radio Broadcasting station at Los Angeles, Cal., known by the call letters KGEF. The station had been in operation for several years. The Commission, in its findings, shows that, though in the name of the church, the station was in fact owned by the Reverend Doctor Shuler and its operation dominated by him. Dr. Shuler is the minister in charge of Trinity Church. The station was operated for a total of 23 1/4 hours each week.

In September, 1930, appellant filed an application for renewal of station license. Numerous citizens of Los Angeles protested, and the Commission, being unable to determine that the public interest, convenience, and necessity would be served, set the application down for hearing before an examiner . . . upon consideration of the evidence, the examiner's report, the exceptions, etc., the Commission denied the application for renewal upon the ground that the public interest, convenience and/or necessity would not be served by the granting of the application. Some of the things urging it to this conclusion were that the station had been used to attack a religious organization, meaning the Roman Catholic Church; that the broadcasts by Dr. Shuler were sensational rather than instructive; and that in two instances Shuler had been convicted of attempting in his radio talks to obstruct the orderly administration of public justice . . .

. . . The basis for this appeal is that the Commission's decision is unconstitutional, in that it violates the guaranty [sic] of free speech, and also that it deprives appellant of his property without due process of law. It is further insisted that the decision violates the Radio Act because it is not supported by substantial evidence, and therefore is arbitrary and capricious.

. . . [I]t is generally regarded that freedom of speech and press cannot be infringed by legislative, executive, or judicial action, and that the constitutional guarantee should be given liberal and comprehensive construction. It may therefore be set down as a fundamental principle that under these constitutional guarantees the citizen has in the first instance the right to utter or publish his sentiments, though, of course, upon condition that he is responsible for any abuse of that right . . . But this does not mean that the government, through agencies established by Congress, may not refuse a renewal of license to one who has abused it to broadcast defamatory and untrue matter. In that case there is not a denial of the freedom of speech, but merely the application of the regulatory power of Congress in a field within the scope of its legislative authority.

. . . This is neither censorship nor previous restraint, nor is it a whittling away of the rights guaranteed by the First Amendment or an impairment of their free exercise. Appellant may continue to indulge his strictures upon the characters of men in public office. He may just as freely as ever criticize religious practices of which he does not approve. He may even indulge private malice or personal slander—subject, of course, to be required to answer for the abuse thereof—but he may not, as we think, demand of right the continued use of an instrumentality of commerce for such purposes, or any other, except in subordination to all reasonable rules and regulations Congress, acting through the Commission, may prescribe.[12]

The first broadcasting case to reach the Supreme Court was decided in 1943. Again, the essence of the case questioned the scope of FCC regulatory power. The NBC case is worthy of study because it resulted in a greatly expanded role for the FCC in the regulation of broadcast content. It also outlined major issues in broadcast regulation. Along with the public interest standard and the limited broadcast spectrum, issues like multiple ownership, network dominance over programming, antitrust considerations, and economic impact would continue to dot the regulatory landscape, long after the Chain Broadcasting Regulations had disappeared.

National Broadcasting Co., Inc., *et al.* v. United States *et al.* (1943)

In the late 1930s, the FCC became concerned over the power that the national radio networks exercised over local stations. The Commission perceived that the public interest was not being served because NBC, CBS, and mutual radio networks demanded much of the affiliate stations' time. The principal of localism, among other things, was not being adhered to when a station obtained and broadcast a high percentage of its programming from New York. Of additional concern was the nature of the affiliate agreements. The FCC was concerned that these agreements forced stations to give up control of programming to the networks.

Although the FCC had no direct jurisdiction over the networks themselves, the agency chose a "back door" approach to regulating network affiliate agreements and ultimately to regulating programming. The Commission proposed the Chain Broadcasting Regulations.

Justice Frankfurter delivered the opinion of the Court.

☐   ... These suits were brought October 30, 1941 to enjoin the enforcement of the Chain Broadcasting Regulations promulgated by the Federal Communications Commission on May 2, 1941, and amended on October 11, 1941.

... On March 18, 1938, the Commission undertook a comprehensive investigation to determine whether special regulations applicable to radio stations engaged in chain broadcasting were required in the "public interest, convenience, or necessity." The Commission's order directed that inquiry be made ...

... The Commission found at the end of 1938 there were 660 commercial stations in the United States, and that 341 of these were affiliated with national networks. 135 stations were affiliated exclusively with the National Broadcasting Company, Inc., known in the industry as NBC, which operated two national networks, the "Red" and the "Blue." NBC was also the licensee of 10 stations, including 7 which operated on so-called clear channels with the maximum power available, 50 kilowatts, under management contracts with their licensees. 102 stations were affiliated exclusively with the Columbia Broadcasting System Inc., which was also the licensee of 8 stations, 7 of which were clear-channel stations operating with the power of 50 kilowatts. 74 stations were under exclusive affiliation with the Mutual Broadcasting System, Inc. In addition, 25 stations were affiliated with both NBC and Mutual, and 5 with both CBS and Mutual. These figures, the Commission noted, did not accurately reflect the relative prominence of the three companies, since the stations affiliated with Mutual were, generally speaking, less desirable in frequency, power, and coverage. It pointed out that the stations affiliated with national networks utilized more than 97% of the total nighttime broadcasting power of all the stations in the country. NBC and CBS together controlled more than 85% of the total nighttime wattage, and the broadcast business of the three national network companies amounted to almost half of the total business of all stations in the United States.

The Commission recognized that network broadcasting had played and was continuing to play an important part in the development of radio ... The Commission's duty under the Communications Act of 1934 is not only to see that the public receives the advantages and benefits of chain broadcasting, but also, so far as its powers enable it, to see that practices which adversely affect the ability of licensees to operate in the public interest are eliminated ...

The Commission found that eight network abuses were amenable to correction within the powers granted it by Congress:

Regulation 3.101—Exclusive affiliation of station. . . . The effect of this provision was to hinder the growth of new networks, to deprive the listening public in many areas of service to which they were entitled, and to prevent station licensees from exercising their statutory duty of determining which programs would best serve the needs of their community.

. . . Accordingly, the Commission adopted Regulation 3.101, providing as follows:

No license shall be granted to a standard broadcast station having any contract, arrangement, or understanding, express or implied, with a network organization under which the station is prevented or hindered from, or penalized for, broadcasting the programs of any other network organization.

Regulation 3.102—Territorial exclusivity. . . . The effect of this provision, designed to protect the affiliate from the competition of other stations serving the same territory, was to deprive the listening public of many programs that might otherwise be available . . . Regulation 3.102, promulgated to remedy this particular evil, provides as follows:

No license shall be granted to a standard broadcast station having any contract, agreement, or understanding, express or implied, with a network organization which prevents or hinders another station serving substantially the same area from broadcasting the network's programs not taken by the former station, or which prevents or hinders another station serving a substantially different area from broadcasting any program of the network organization. This regulation shall not be construed to prohibit any contract, arrangement, or understanding between a station and a network organization pursuant to which the station is granted the first call in its primary service area upon the programs of the network organization.

Regulation 3.103—Term of affiliation. . . . The Commission, relying upon 307(d) of the Communications Act of 1934, under which no license to operate a broadcast station can be granted for a longer term than three years, found the five-year affiliation term to be contrary to the policy of the Act . . .

. . . Accordingly, the Commission adopted Regulation 3.103:

No license shall be granted to a standard broadcast station having any contract, agreement, or understanding, express or implied, with a network organization which provides, by original term, provisions for renewal, or otherwise for the affiliation of the station with the network organization for a period longer than two years: *Provided,* that a contract, arrangement, or understanding for a period up to two years, may be entered into within 120 days prior to the commencement of such period.

Regulation 3.104—Option time. The Commission found that network affiliation contracts usually contained so-called network optional time clauses. Under these provisions the network could upon 28 days' notice call upon its affiliates to carry a commercial program during any of the hours specified in the agreement as "network optional time." For CBS affiliates "network optional time" meant the entire broadcast day . . . In the Commission's judgement these optional time provisions, in addition to imposing serious obstacles in the path of new networks, hindered stations in developing a local program service. The exercise by the networks of their options over the station's time tended to prevent regular scheduling of local programs at desirable hours . . .

. . . The text of the Regulation follows:

No license shall be granted to a standard broadcast station which options for network programs any time subject to call on less than 56 days' notice, or more time than a total of three hours within each of four segments of the broadcast day . . .

Regulation 3.105—Right to reject programs. The Commission found that most network affiliation contracts contained a clause defining the right of the station to reject network commercial programs . . .

. . . While seeming in the abstract to be fair, these provisions, according to the Commission's finding, did not sufficiently protect the "public interest." As a practical matter, the licensee could not determine in advance whether the broadcasting of any particular network program would or would not be in the public interest.

. . . The Commission undertook in Regulation 3.105 to formulate the obligations of licensees with respect to supervision over programs:

No license shall be granted to a standard broadcast station having any contract, agreement, or understanding, express or implied, with a network organization which (a) . . . hinders the station from rejecting or refusing network programs which the station reasonably believes to be unsatisfactory or unsuitable; or which (b) . . . prevents the station from rejecting or refusing any program which, in its opinion, is contrary to the public interest, or from substituting a program of outstanding local or national importance.

Regulation 3.106—Network ownership of stations. The Commission found that NBC, in addition to its network operations, was the licensee of 10 stations, 2 each in New York, Chicago, Washington, and San Francisco, 1 in Denver, and 1 in Cleveland. CBS was the licensee of 8 stations, in each of these cities: New York, Chicago, Washington, Boston, Minneapolis, St. Louis, Charlotte, and Los Angeles. These 18 stations owned by NBC and CBS, the Commission observed, were among the most powerful and desirable in the country, and were permanently inaccessible to competing networks.

. . . Regulation 3.106 reads as follows:

No license shall be granted to a network organization, or to any person directly or indirectly controlled by or under common control with a network organization, for more than one standard broadcast station where one of the stations covers substantially the service area of the other station, or for any standard broadcast station in any locality where the existing standard broadcast stations are so few or of such unequal desirability (in terms of coverage, power, frequency, or other related matters) that competition would be substantially restrained by such licensing.

Regulation 3.107—Dual network operation. This regulation provides that: "No license shall be issued to a standard broadcast station affiliated with a network organization which maintains more than one network . . .

Regulation 3.108—Control by networks of station rates. The Commission found that NBC's affiliation contracts contained a provision empowering the network to reduce the station's network rate, and thereby to reduce the compensation received by the station, if the station set a lower rate for non-network national advertising than the rate established by the contract for the network programs. Under this provision the station could not sell time to a national advertiser for less than it would cost the advertiser if he bought the time from NBC . . .

The Commission concluded that "it is against the public interest for a station licensee to enter into a contract with a network which has the effect of decreasing its ability to compete for national business . . ."

Accordingly, the Commission adopted Regulation 3.108, which provides as follows:

No license shall be granted to a standard broadcast station having any contract, arrangement, or understanding, express or implied, with a network organization under which the station is prevented or hindered from, or penalized for, fixing or altering its rates for the sale of broadcast time for other than the network's programs.

The appellants attack the validity of these Regulations along many fronts. They contend that the Commission went beyond the regulatory powers conferred upon it by the Communications Act of 1934 . . .

The Act itself establishes that the Commission's powers are not limited to the engineering and technical aspects of regulation of radio communication. Yet we are asked to regard the Commission as a kind of traffic officer, policing the wave lengths to prevent stations from interfering with each other. But the Act does not restrict the Commission merely to the supervision of traffic. It puts upon the Commission the burden of determining the composition of that traffic. The facilities of radio are not large enough to accommodate all who wish to use them. Methods must be devised for choosing from among the many who apply. And since Congress itself could not do this, it committed the task to the Commission.[13]

The *NBC* case attempts to clarify the FCC's role in defining the "public interest" standard. Since the case was the first broadcasting case to come before the Supreme Court, it broke entirely new ground for the emerging industry. The nation's highest court had recognized broadcasting as a social institution worthy of its attention.

Justice Frankfurter articulates the limits of the First Amendment rights of broadcasters. He reminds the networks of the "limited spectrum" and the obligation to serve the public interest. These arguments serve as the basis for the regulation of the electronic media. Throughout the years, courts and the Commission have assigned varying degrees of importance to the fundamental arguments, but nonetheless, they remain just that—fundamental.

Another result of the *NBC* case was the creation of the American Broadcasting Company in 1945. In 1943, NBC sold the less profitable Blue Network, which then became ABC.

The Supreme Court next considered the FCC's power in 1969. In the intervening years, the Commission's foray into program regulation continued. In 1946, the FCC issued the controversial "Blue Book," so named because of the color of its binding. The Blue Book was officially titled *Public Service Responsibility of Broadcast Licensees* and essentially chastised the industry for failing to provide local programs, for providing an overabundance of commercials, and for the general failure of most programming to serve the "public interest." Although the measures were never really enforced, the report concluded with ways the FCC would enforce higher programming standards. For example, the FCC urged broadcasters to devote more time to local programming and to sustaining programs. Sustaining programs were programs without commercial sponsorship.

The Rise and Fall of the Fairness Doctrine

From its earliest days, the Commission believed that broadcasters should be fair in their presentation of public issues. As early as 1929, the FRC noted that,

☐ It would not be fair, indeed it would not be good service to the public to allow a one-sided presentation of the political issues of a campaign. In so far as a program consists of discussion of public questions, public interest requires ample play for the free and fair competition of opposing views, and the commission believes that the principle applies not only to addresses by political candidates but to all discussions of issues of importance to the public.[14]

The concern with fairness was the subject of various FCC cases. In 1940, in *Mayflower*, the Commission prohibited broadcasters from editorializing. In 1949, the Commission issued a report called *In the Matter of Editorializing by Broadcast Licensees*. The report reversed the FCC's policy on editorializing set forth in *Mayflower* and outlined the new Fairness Doctrine by stating,

☐ ... [U]nder the American system of broadcasting the individual licensees of radio stations have the responsibility for determining the specific program material to be broadcast over their stations. The choice, however, must be exercised in a manner consistent with the basic policy of the Congress that radio be maintained as a medium of free speech for the general public as a whole rather than as an outlet for the purely personal or private interests of the licensee. This requires that licensees devote a reasonable percentage of their broadcasting time to the discussion of public issues of interest in the community served by their stations and that such programs be designed so that the public has a reasonable opportunity to hear different opposing positions on the public issues of interest and importance in the community.[15]

In 1959, Section 315 of the Communications Act was amended. The addition of the statement requiring broadcasters to "afford reasonable opportunity for the discussion of conflicting views on issues of public importance" (see section 315, paragraph (a)(4)) appeared to codify the Fairness Doctrine. In 1986, a court ruled that this was not the case. The ruling in *Telecommunications Research and Action Center v. Federal Communications Commission* (TRAC v. FCC) played an important part in the demise of the Fairness Doctrine.

The wording of the 1959 statement still remained vague and in 1964 the Commission issued what it called a "Fairness Primer," which was titled *Applicability of the Fairness Doctrine in the Handling of Controversial Issues of Public Importance*. In the primer, the FCC attempted to clarify fairness and delineate it from the "equal opportunites" requirement in Section 315. The Commission provided examples of possible "controversial issues," such as the nuclear test ban treaty, Communism, and civil rights. The FCC offered this additional advice:

☐ While Section 315 thus embodies both the "equal opportunies" requirement and the fairness doctrine, they apply to different situations and in different ways. The "equal opportunites" requirement relates solely to use of broadcast facilities by candidates for public office ...

   The fairness doctrine deals with the broader question of affording reasonable opportunity for the presentation of contrasting viewpoints on controversial issues of public importance. Generally speaking, it does not apply with the precision of the "equal opportunities" requirement.[16]

In 1967, the Commission added two more aspects to the Fairness Doctrine—the personal attack rules and political editorializing. Before the end of the decade, the issue of fairness in broadcasting would come before the Supreme Court in *Red Lion*. At issue was not only the validity of the Fairness Doctrine, but also the extent of the Commission's power.

Red Lion Broadcasting Co. Inc. *et al.* v. Federal Communications Commission *et al.* (1969)

Justice White delivered the opinion of the Court.

☐ The Red Lion Broadcasting Company is licensed to operate a Pennsylvania radio station, WGCB. On November 27, 1964, WGCB carried a 15-minute broadcast by the Reverend Billy James Hargis as part of a "Christian Crusade" series. A book by Fred J. Cook entitled "Goldwater—Extremist on the Right" was discussed by Hargis, who said that Cook had been fired by a newspaper for Communist-affiliated publication; that he defended Alger Hiss and attacked J. Edgar Hoover and the Central Intelligence Agency; and that he had now written a "book to smear and destroy Barry Goldwater" ... When Cook heard of the broadcast he concluded that he had been personally attacked and demanded free reply time, which the station refused. After an exchange of letters among Cook, Red Lion and the FCC, the FCC declared that the Hargis broadcast constituted a personal attack on Cook; that Red Lion had failed to meet its obligation under the fairness doctrine ... to send a tape, transcript, or summary of the broadcast to Cook and offer him reply time; and that the station must provide reply time whether or not Cook would pay for it. On review in the Court of Appeals for the District of Columbia Circuit, the FCC's position was upheld as constitutional and otherwise proper. 127 U.S.App. D.C. 129, 381 F.2d 908 (1967).

    ... Not long after the *Red Lion* litigation was begun, the FCC issued a Notice of Proposed Rule Making ... with an eye to making the personal attack aspect of the fairness doctrine more precise and more readily enforceable ... the regulations read as follows:

    "Personal attacks; political editorials.

    (a) When, during the presentation of views on a controversial issue of public importance, an attack is made upon the honesty, character, integrity or like personal qualities of an identified person or group, the licensee shall, within a reasonable time and in no event later than 1 week after the attack, transmit to the person or group attacked (1) notification of the date, time and identification of the broadcast; (2) a script or tape (or an accurate summary if a script or tape is not available) of the attack; and (3) an offer of a reasonable opportunity to respond over the licensee's facilities ...

Believing that the specific application of the fairness doctrine in *Red Lion*, and promulgation of the regulations . . . are both authorized by Congress and enhance rather than abridge the freedoms of speech and press protected by the First Amendment, we hold them valid and constitutional . . .

It is the right of the viewers and listeners, not the right of broadcasters, which is paramount. . . . It is the purpose of the First Amendment to preserve an uninhibited marketplace of ideas in which truth will ultimately prevail, rather than to countenance monopolization of that market, whether it be by the Government itself or a private license . . . In view of the scarcity of broadcast frequencies, the Government's role in allocating those frequencies, and the legitimate claims of those unable without governmental assistance to gain those frequencies for the expression of their views, we hold the regulations and ruling at issue here are both authorized by statute and constitutional.[17]

The Supreme Court upheld both the Fairness Doctrine and personal attack rules. The latter are not applied to attacks on foreign groups, or individuals, or to statements made by legally qualified candidates for public office. Other exemptions are similar to those found in Section 315 such as bona fide newscasts, news interviews, and so forth. (See 47 C.F.R 73.123 for the complete text of the personal attack rules.)

In *Red Lion*, the court relied on the "spectrum scarcity" rationale to base its decision. That is, because there are a finite number of broadcast channels available, those granted a broadcast license must operate in the public interest. The FCC was to act as proxy for those who would present different views by giving them access to broadcast facilities through the Fairness Doctrine. Broadcast licensees had an affirmative duty to seek out these contrasting viewpoints.

Application of the Fairness Doctrine after *Red Lion*

The first station after *Red Lion* to have license renewal denied for failure to adhere to the Fairness Doctrine was WXUR. In 1972, in *Brandywine-Main Line Radio Inc. v. Federal Communications Commission*, the court upheld the Commission's decision to deny renewal based on Fairness Doctrine violations and lack of candor. The operator of WXUR was the Faith Theological Seminary. The Reverend Carl McIntire presided over the seminary. In 1965, a group headed by McIntire applied for transfer of control of WXUR and the application was opposed by community groups. The FCC approved the transfer only after the McIntire group pledged they would provide opportunity for the expression of opposing viewpoints on controversial public issues.

At license renewal time, citizens groups decided that McIntire had not honored his pledge. The station manager was finally fired as a result of anti-Semitic remarks that had been made on the air. Other personal attacks had been made and WXUR had established no guidelines for providing notice and response as required by the *Red Lion* ruling. The license renewal was denied by the FCC.

Commercials

The Fairness Doctrine played a major part in the congressional ban of cigarette advertising from the airwaves. In 1967, the FCC held that, because of the health concern involved, cigarette smoking constituted a controversial issue of public importance. Therefore, the broadcast of cigarette advertisements were affected by the Fairness Doctrine. Broadcasters were required to devote time to opposing viewpoints. In 1968, in *Banzhaf v. Federal Communications Commission*, the Commission ruled that equal time was not required for anti-smoking spots, but balanced coverage was expected. In 1969, the FCC proposed to ban cigarette ads from radio and television completely.

Broadcasters, led by the NAB, favored a gradual phasing out of cigarette ads. They argued that self-regulation was the most effective way of dealing with the issue. Congress beat the Commission to the punch. In 1970, cigarette broadcast advertising was banned by statute. The law went into effect January 2, 1971. In 1986, Congress banned smokeless tobacco products, such as snuff and chewing tobacco, from the airwaves in the Comprehensive Smokeless Tobacco Health Education Act of 1986. Cigars and pipe tobacco are not included in the ban.

The FCC would have preferred to treat cigarette ads as a special situation and not apply the Fairness Doctrine to advertising. In *Friends of the Earth v. Federal Communications Commission*, the Commission refused to require broadcasters to present contrasting views in response to automobile ads. The petitioners argued that gasoline and high-powered engines contributed to air pollution and therefore were within the definition of a "controversial issue." They argued that these ads were in the same vein as cigarette ads. The U.S. court of appeals agreed and ordered the FCC to be consistent.

Faced with the possibility of a staggering number of fairness complaints, the Commission modified its policy. The FCC applied the Fairness Doctrine to advocacy or editorial advertisements, but not to product ads. It left the regulation of deceptive advertisements to the Federal Trade Commission. The reversal of the policy was challenged by public interest groups, but was upheld by a federal court in 1975 in *Public Interest Research Group v. Federal Communications Commission*.

Political Campaigns

Section 315 of the Communications Act was designed to cover appearances of political candidates, but did not address appearances of a candidate's supporters. This was left to be addressed in the Fairness Doctrine. In a "Letter to

Nicholas Zapple," the Commission noted that the 1959 amendment to Section 315 recognized that the Fairness Doctrine applied when a candidate's own appearance was exempt from Section 315. This letter is the basis of the Zapple Doctrine, which states that if broadcasters give or sell time to supporters of one political candidate, they must do the same for supporters of the opposing candidates for the same office. The Zapple Doctrine remains in effect today.

The Supreme Court ruled in *CBS v. Democratic National Committee* that there is no First Amendment right of access to broadcast facilities. The Fairness Doctrine no longer applied to editorial advertising, but the Cullman Doctrine might apply.

Abolition of the Fairness Doctrine

Although the Fairness Doctrine was held to be constitutional in *Red Lion*, the policy was not without its critics. Many believed that the doctrine did not promote the discussion of conflicting viewpoints as intended, but rather inhibited that discussion. In 1985, the Commission issued a report that concluded the Fairness Doctrine was no longer justified. The *1985 Fairness Report* stated that the diversity of opinions sought by the doctrine was being served by the "multiplicity of voices in the marketplace."[18]

The report concluded that the Fairness Doctrine actually inhibited robust discussion of ideas and restricted the journalistic freedom of broadcasters. The Commission was concerned that it was too involved in evaluating viewpoints and that continued enforcement of the doctrine increased government interference in the editorial process of broadcast journalists. The FCC noted that a large percentage of its staff time was needed to deal with fairness complaints and noted that it had received more than 6700 complaints in 1984. The Commission argued that the costs associated with enforcement were unnecessary, because the tremendous increase in information sources had made the doctrine obsolete.

The scarcity rationale used as the basis of *Red Lion* was also attacked. The Commission stated that dramatic increase in the number of radio and television outlets since *Red Lion* had made that argument moot. Again, the FCC relied on the marketplace to ensure that the public was exposed to controversial issues of public importance.

The Commission did not act to eliminate the Fairness Doctrine, preferring to wait until Congress had the opportunity to respond to the *1985 Fairness Report*. In the meantime, the Commission announced that it would continue to enforce the Fairness Doctrine.

In 1984, the Commission ruled that the Meredith Corporation's WTVH had violated the Fairness Doctrine. The station had presented a series of commercials discussing a proposed nuclear power plant. The FCC found that the station failed to present balanced coverage with contrasting points of view. The Meredith Corporation appealed the Commission's ruling and relied heavily on the *1985 Fairness Report* as a defense. In *Meredith Corp. v. Federal Communications Commission,* Circuit Judge Silberman maintained,

☐   ... The Commission's *1985 Fairness Report* quite clearly determined that the Fairness Doctrine as embodied in its regulations no longer serves the statutory public interest Congress charges the Commission with advancing and further states that if it were up to the Commission it would hold the Doctrine unconstitutional ... An agency is not required to reconsider the merits of a rule each time it seeks to apply it. ... Here, however the Commission itself has already largely undermined the legitimacy of its own Rule. ... "If time and changing circumstances reveal that the "public interest" is not served by the application of such regulations, it must be assumed that the Commission will act in accordance with its statutory obligations."[NBC] ... Accordingly we remand the case to the FCC with instructions to consider the Petitioner's constitutional arguments.[19]

The court tossed the issue back into the lap of the Commission, where it might have lagged if not for the *TRAC* decision. In this case, the court of appeals found that the 1959 amendment to Section 315(a) did not codify the fairness doctrine:

☐   We do not believe the language adopted in 1959 made the fairness doctrine a binding statutory obligation; rather, it ratified the Commission's longstanding position that the public interest standard authorizes the fairness doctrine. ... The words employed by Congress also demonstrate that the obligation recognized and preserved was an administrative construction, not a binding statutory directive.[20]

At this point, the FCC could have avoided the constitutional question by simply deciding that the Fairness Doctrine was no longer in the public interest, but it chose a different approach. Instead, the FCC reversed its decision in *Meredith* and declared its belief that the Fairness Doctrine was not in the public interest and was unconstitutional.

The Syracuse Peace Council appealed the Commission's decision. In *Syracuse Peace Council v. Federal Communications Commission,* the court of appeals issued an opinion supporting the FCC's refusal to enforce the Fairness Doctrine, but refused to make a determination of the doctrine's constitutionality. Circuit Judge Williams maintained,

☐   Under the "fairness doctrine," the Federal Communications Commission has, as its 1985 Fairness Report explains, required broadcast media licensees (1) "to provide coverage of vitally important controversial issues of interest in the community served by the licensees," and (2) "to provide a reasonable opportunity for the presentation of contrasting viewpoints on such issues." ... In adjudication of a complaint against Meredith Corporation, licensee of station WTVH in Syracuse, New York, the Commission concluded that the doctrine did not serve the public interest and was unconstitutional. Accordingly it refused to enforce the doctrine against Meredith. Although the Commission somewhat entangled its public interest and constitutional findings, we find that the Commission's public interest determination was an independent basis for its decision and was supported by the record. We uphold that determination without reaching the constitutional issue.[21]

Following the court of appeals decision in *Syracuse Peace Council,* some members of Congress drafted a bill designed to codify the Fairness Doctrine. The bill, called the Fairness in Broadcasting Act of 1987, was vetoed by President Reagan.

Further discussion of the elements that remain in force may be found in Chapter 5, including the personal attack rules, the political editorializing rule, and the Zapple Doctrine.

Reasonable Access to Broadcast Media for Political Candidates

As noted earlier, in *CBS v. Democratic National Committee,* the Supreme Court held that a network policy refusing to sell time to political groups for the discussion of social and political issues was not a violation of the First Amendment. In 1981, however, the Court added a twist to the matter of access. It might appear that *CBS v. Democratic National Committee* and *CBS v. FCC* deal with identical issues, and that the Court was inconsistent. In *CBS v. FCC,* the Court was dealing with a statutory right conferred by Section 312(a)(7) of the Communications Act. For the Court to rule against the general network policy that resulted in *CBS v. Democratic National Committee,* it would have required a determination that the First Amendment had been violated.

Enforcement Powers of the Commission

Stations that are found to be in violation of FCC rules or policies may suffer a variety of different punishments. Since the FCC does not monitor programming, nontechnical violations come to its attention via listener and viewer complaints. When a complaint is received, the FCC will ask the broadcaster to respond in writing. The reply is examined. If the FCC is satisfied, the matter may go no further. If the Commission decides to pursue the issue, the broadcaster may be required to rectify the situation in some way. Perhaps an apology to offended parties may be necessary. In more serious cases, the Commission may issue a letter of reprimand to the station. This "wrist slapping" usually does not require payment of a fine, but it serves to officially put the station "on notice" to not repeat the transgression. In still more serious cases, a cease and desist order may be issued. This is a legal notice that requires the licensee to stop a specified activity. Failure to obey such an order carries a fine. The FCC may also fine broadcasters. This is called a *forfeiture* and may carry a fine of as much as $2000 per day, but not more than $20,000 per offense (see Figure 3.1). In 1990, the FCC fined Infinity Broadcasting $6000 for a shock-jock Howard Stern broadcast transmitted on three Infinity stations.

The FCC may consider the past record of licensees at license renewal time and may issue a short-term renewal if it finds a station's performance to be below par. The station is given a period of time to clean up its act, after which time the license may be renewed for the full term or revoked. Indiscretions by the president of a Boston television station resulted in several short-term renewals for WHDH-TV in the 1950s and 1960s. In a case that spanned 15 years, the station eventually lost its license.

The "death sentence" for broadcasters is license revocation. This occurs primarily at license renewal. The ultimate penalty is reserved for those who have engaged in the most egregious practices. Lying to the Commission or "lack of candor," failure to observe the Fairness Doctrine, conviction of drug offenses by station owners, and lack of licensee control of station operations have all been reasons for license revocation.

Regulation of Cable Television

The rationale of broadcast regulation rests on the theory of the limited broadcast spectrum. Broadcasters are required to operate in the public interest because they are public trustees of the airwaves. Throughout the 1930s and 1940s,

Violation	Fine	Violation	Fine
Misrepresentation or lack of candor	$20,000	Use of unauthorized equipment	$10,000
Inadequate tower lighting and marking	$20,000	Violations of children's TV rules	$10,000
Construction or operation without Authorization	$20,000	Violation of main-studio rule	$10,000
Unauthorized substantial transfer of control	$20,000	Operation at unauthorized location	$10,000
False distress broadcasts	$20,000	Inadequate frequency coordination	$10,000
Misuse of distress and safety frequencies	$20,000	Failure to file information	$7,500
Refusal to permit inspection	$18,750	Failure to maintain public files	$7,500
Malicious interference	$17,500	Failure to properly identify sponsors	$6,250
Failure to respond to FCC communications	$17,500	Violations of rules governing lotteries	$6,250
Exceeding authorized antenna height	$15,000	Failure to maintain technical logs	$5,000
Exceeding power limits	$12,500	Failure to maintain time-brokerage files	$5,000
Unauthorized emissions	$12,500	Broadcasting telephone calls	
Using unauthorized frequency	$12,500	without permission	$5,000
EBS equipment not installed or operational	$12,500	Failure to make measurements and monitor	
	$2,500		
Broadcast of indecent programming	$12,500	Violations of enhanced underwriting	
Failure to comply with EEO obligations	$12,500	requirements	$2,500
Violations of political broadcasting rules	$12,500	Failure to identify station on air	$2,500
Unauthorized discontinuance of services	$10,000	Failure to maintain records	$2,500
		Unauthorized pro forma transfer of control	
	$2,500		
		Miscellaneous violations	$1,250

The amounts in the right-hand columns are the "base" fines for the given violations. They are subject to adjustments up or down by between 20% and 90% based on specific criteria. The "upward" criteria (and adjustment range): 1) egregious misconduct (50%-90%); 2) ability to pay (50%-90%); 3) intentional violation (50%-90%); 4) substantial harm (40%-70%); 5) prior violation of same rule (40%-70%); 6) substantial economic gain (20%-50%); and 7) repeated or continuous violation (varies).
The "downward" criteria: 1) minor violation (50%-90%); 2) good faith or voluntary disclosure (30%-60%); 3) history of overall compliance (20%-50%); and 4) inability to pay (varies).

Figure 3.1 The FCC's revised forfeiture schedule. Reprinted with permission from *Broadcasting Magazine*, August 5, 1991, p. 24.

broadcasters and the FCC developed a working relationship with one another. The tensions between the two fostered a certain elasticity as broadcasters tested the limits of the regulatory system. Eventually, the FCC and broadcasters became partners in the regulatory process. The well-being of all parties was intertwined. The economic interests of broadcasters became a concern of the Commission. Put simply, if broadcasting did not exist, neither would the Commission. In the early 1950s, this delicate balance began to shift with the advent of cable television.

Cable television was not originally intended as a means of providing programming to individual households. Coaxial cable was perfected in the 1930s at Bell Labs. "Coax" is capable of delivering a number of different signals within a single wire. Coaxial cable was first used in broadcasting as a means of interconnecting the television networks and their affiliate stations. It was the failure of the FCC to redraw its flawed UHF television allocation scheme of 1952 that led to the use of cable as a means of delivering TV signals to individual homes. In short, the Commission allocated UHF stations to markets too small to support network affiliates. The Commission's goal was to establish a nationwide system of local TV stations. Instead, it created the perfect conditions for an alternative distribution system.

The first cable systems were called community antenna television (or CATV) operations. Early CATV systems developed in mountainous areas of Pennsylvania and Oregon. Their primary purpose was to provide quality television service to areas not served by TV.

In the early 1950s, cable TV was viewed as a temporary solution to the problem of poor television reception. It was assumed that the FCC would allocate more stations to areas that were underserved and reallocate those frequencies unable to support quality operations. By the mid 1950s, it became obvious that this was not to be. As late as 1958, 34% of American homes could receive only one television channel.

CATV came to the rescue of both the viewing public and TV broadcasters by using microwaves to link the missing network signals to underserved areas. Broadcasters did not perceive cable as a threat, because CATV expanded the television audience at no cost to the stations or networks. The only FCC interest in cable stemmed from the need for Commission approval of the microwave relay systems used in importing the broadcast signals. This approval was routinely granted and the FCC stated in 1959 that it had no interest in regulating CATV. It was not until cable systems began competing with over-the-air broadcasters that the FCC changed its mind about regulation.

Eventually, cable systems began to import television signals from distant cities. These signals were often in direct competition with the local television stations. Smaller markets were hurt most by this practice. For example, given a choice of a small, local television station and an imported signal from a station in a larger city, viewers often chose to watch the latter. Of course, this had a detrimental economic impact on the smaller station and eventually these stations complained to the Commission. After several years of agitation by broadcasters, the FCC decided that it would regulate cable television. The basis for the regulation rested on the premise that the economic impact of cable television on broadcasting may not be in the public interest. Specifically, economic injury to small, local broadcasters did not foster the FCC's policy of localism. Therefore, it was not in the public interest. Of additional concern was the fact that cable operators paid nothing for the programs they carried. The Commission thought that this gave cable operators an unfair economic advantage over broadcasters.

In the mid-1960s, the FCC developed a series of regulations designed to prevent cable television from effectively competing with over-the-air broadcasters. In 1965, the Commission implemented the must-carry rule, which requires cable systems to carry all local broadcast signals. The FCC also restricted the importation of distant television signals by cable systems. In *United States v. Southwestern Cable Co.*, this regulation was challenged and resulted in a Supreme Court decision to uphold the FCC's authority to regulate cable under the mandate in the Communications Act, which required regulation of all wire and radio communication. The Court also based its decision on the premise that cable systems threatened the growth of local over-the-air television services and therefore could threaten the public interest. FCC regulation would ensure that this did not happen.

The *Southwestern Cable* case established only that the FCC could assert jurisdiction over cable, but it did not outline the limits of this authority. By the late 1960s, the Commission had promulgated rules that required large cable systems to originate local programming. In *United States v. Midwest Video Corp.*, the Supreme Court upheld these rules, but noted that the FCC had "strained the outer limits" of its authority to regulate cable. Two years later, the FCC repealed the local origination rule, but issued new rules that required new cable systems to allocate channels for public access. In *United States v. Midwest Video Corp.*,[22] the Supreme Court held that the FCC had exceeded its authority by promulgating the access rule. The Court held that the access rules imposed a common carrier obligation on cable operators—something that Congress did not intend. Local municipalities were still allowed to air public access channels as part of the franchising process.

In the late 1970s and early 1980s, the FCC eliminated many of the rules affecting cable television. The Copyright Act of 1976 provided a means for compensating broadcasters for carrying cable programming. This act eliminated one of the original bases of regulation. The addition of satellite-delivered cable programming services in the late 1970s, such as Home Box Office, reduced the demand for broadcast programming.

The Cable Communications Policy Act of 1984

In late 1984, Congress enacted the Cable Communications Policy Act of 1984. The act codified many of the cable regulations that had been developed during the period beginning in the 1960s. The Cable Act amended the Communications

Act of 1934 and gave the FCC jurisdiction over cable television. As a result, the FCC no longer had to justify its regulation of cable television because of cable TV's interface with broadcasting. Significant provisions of the act are presented on the following pages:

Section 521

The purposes of this title are to

1. establish a national policy concerning cable communications;
2. establish franchise procedures and standards which encourage the growth and development of cable systems and assure [sic] that cable systems are responsive to the needs and interests of the local community;
3. establish guidelines for the exercise of Federal, State, and local authority with respect to the regulation of cable systems;
4. assure [sic] and encourage that cable communications provide and are encouraged to provide the widest possible diversity of information sources and services to the public;
5. establish an orderly process for franchise renewal which protects cable operators against unfair denials of renewal where the operator's past performance and proposal for future performance meet the standards established by this title; and
6. promote competition in cable communications and minimize unnecessary regulation that would impose an undue economic burden on cable systems.[23]

Section 541

. . . (c) Any cable system shall not be subject to regulation as a common carrier or utility by reason of providing any cable service.[24]

Section 559

Whoever transmits over any cable system any matter which is obscene or otherwise unprotected by the Constitution of the United States shall be fined not more than $10,000 or imprisoned not more than two years or both.[25]

Franchises

The Cable Communications Policy Act gives state and local governments the power to award franchises and to determine the qualifications necessary for systems to be awarded local franchises. Section 541 of the act requires cable systems to obtain a franchise. In *City of Los Angeles v. Preferred Communications Inc.*,[26] the Supreme Court ruled that as long as utilities are adequate, a city cannot deny a franchise to more than one cable company. "Adequate," in this case, means that rights-of-way are available to support an additional cable system.

Section 622 limits the amount that may be charged for a franchise fee. Section 533 prohibits broadcast and cable cross-ownership in overlapping markets, nor may a common carrier own a cable system in its service area. The FCC has been reconsidering this restriction.

Just as broadcasters must obtain renewal of their licenses by the FCC, cable operators are subject to the franchise renewal process by local municipalities. Like broadcasters, cable systems are fearful of nonrenewal. Section 626 of the act requires that a denial of franchise renewal must be based on a finding that the cable operator failed to comply substantially with the franchise agreement. In addition, denial must be predicated on the fact that the cable operator provided inferior service to the community, is legally or technically unqualified, or cannot possibly meet the future needs of the community. Like broadcasters, there is a strong renewal expectancy for existing franchises.

Section 543 provides for the regulation of basic cable rates in the absence of effective competition. Otherwise, cable operators are free to charge whatever the market will bear. This provision has led to charges that cable is a monopoly and should be subjected to more stringent rate regulation. The subject of cable franchising is discussed in detail in Chapter 8.

Programming

Although the Cable Act prohibits the broadcast of obscene programming, the act does not regulate programming services. Unlike over-the-air broadcasters, cable operators appear to be given First Amendment protection for program content. Cable franchises may specify the number and types of channels, and mandate public access, but they may not require specific program services. For example, the franchise may call for an all news channel but it may not require a cable operator to choose CNN.

Two areas related to programming are the syndicated exclusivity and must-carry rules. The syndicated exclusivity rule (Syndex) requires that cable systems "black out" syndicated programs carried on a distant station if the same program (or series) is being carried by a local station. The Syndex rule was originally passed in 1972 and then abolished by the FCC in 1980. The rule was restored in 1990 and is applied to all cable systems with more than 1000 subscribers.[27]

The must-carry rules required cable systems to carry all local television signals. In 1985, a federal court found the rules, as written, to be a violation of cable operators' First Amendment right of editorial discretion.[28]

In the fall of 1990, a bill before Congress was defeated that would have restored a rewritten form of the must-carry rules and other substantial cable regulations. It is expected that Congress will reconsider the regulation of cable in the 1990s. Issues of concern continue to be the monopolistic nature of franchising, the possible ownership of cable systems by telephone companies, and rate regulation.

Deregulation of Broadcasting and Cable Television

The Communications Act of 1934 was a product of New Deal legislation and of the social forces of the Great Depression. The mid-1970s saw a change in social attitudes toward the role of government in the way it affected our nation. Between 1934 and 1975, the FCC had steadily promulgated more regulations that affected broadcasters. Many of these regulations resulted in a great deal of paperwork and were only marginally effective, if at all. Deregulation began as early as 1972 under FCC Chairman Richard Wiley. Wiley called his policy "reregulation" and planned to reregulate the industry by eliminating burdensome administrative procedures.[29] During the Carter administration, FCC chairman Charles Ferris made deregulation the official policy. It was under his chairmanship that radio was deregulated and the Commission began to deregulate television.[30]

During the Reagan administration and under the FCC chairmanship of Mark Fowler, the Commission began to dismantle much of the monitoring and enforcement structure that had evolved over the years. Fowler's policy of "unregulation" made good on President Reagan's pledge to "get government off the backs of the people" or, in this case, off the backs of the broadcasters. The only area of broadcast regulation essentially untouched was the public interest responsibility guaranteed by the Communications Act, although it came under much reinterpretation.

The deregulators preferred to allow the marketplace to satisfy most regulatory goals. Many minor "underbrush" regulations were eliminated in the 1970s and major rules, like formal community ascertainment and the Fairness Doctrine, fell out of use during the 1980s.

The FCC began deregulating radio in 1981. First the Commission eliminated rules that required formal ascertainment of community needs. No longer were radio stations required to survey the general public and community leaders in their city of license and generate programming that met community needs. Radio was only required to have general knowledge of these needs. The FCC also eliminated the requirement to keep program logs, guidelines for nonentertainment programming, and guidelines for the amount of commercial time. Deregulation of television and noncommercial broadcasting followed in 1984.

The deregulatory trend produced major changes in the rules governing radio, broadcast television, and cable television. The FCC increased the term of a license from 3 years to 7 years for radio and from 3 years to 5 years for television (1981). The Commission increased the number of stations that one person or group could own from 21 to 36 stations (1985) and dropped the requirement that they must be held for at least 3 years (1982). The Commission reversed its stance on the long-cherished Fairness Doctrine (1985) and virtually dropped most of its cable rules, including the must-carry rules (1985 to 1987), after the rules were declared unconstitutional—twice. The FCC even relinquished leadership in the area of technical standards when it eliminated the classes of engineering licenses (1981), and relaxed station engineering requirements and failed to specify a standard for AM stereo (1982), deferring to marketplace forces.

This list of deregulations is by no means exhaustive, but by 1987 there was evidence that the pendulum was beginning to swing back. Although the FCC had never intended to eliminate all regulation of broadcast and cable, in theory it hoped to eliminate those regulations that affected how broadcasters conducted their business. Rules affecting program types and content were primary targets. Rules designed to preserve competition in the marketplace should, ideally, be left in place.

Unfortunately, this theoretical model did not hold up well in practice. As the 1980s drew to a close, the Commission, responding again to public pressure, undertook a series of attempts at reregulating program content and types. The FCC had moved away from its policy of "channeling" indecent programming and by early 1990 had proposed a 24-hour ban on indecent programs. In October 1990, Congress passed a bill that required television stations to serve the "educational and informational needs of children" and placed limits on the length and types of advertisements that could be used during these programs. Cable TV was the subject of a reregulatory attempt in late 1990. Amid these new constraints, FCC Chairman Alfred Sikes called for an "attic-to-basement" review of broadcast regulations in 1991. The goal of this review is to study the continued need for certain regulations in today's multichannel video environment.

After nearly two decades of deregulation, there have really been very few substantial modifications to the legal obligations facing broadcast licensees. In spite of attempts by Congress to rewrite the Communications Act, the act of 1934 still stands in essentially the same form. While the FCC can modify its rules and policies, it cannot alter the substance and the charge of the Communications Act. Only Congress can release the Commission from its duty to regulate broadcasting—something that is not likely to occur. Because the Communications Act still stands, it is possible that a future administration could reregulate broadcasting and related industries.

Summary

The rationale for the regulation of broadcasting is based on the notion of spectrum scarcity. Broadcasters are licensed to serve the public interest as public trustees. For this reason, broadcasters are treated differently under the First Amendment than publishers or cable operators.

In the 1920s, the secretary of commerce acted as a "traffic cop of the air" to sort out growing technical interference between radio stations. In 1927, Congress passed the Radio Act, which created the Federal Radio Commission. The FRC was supplanted in 1934 when passage of the Communications Act created the Federal Communications Commission. Both agencies were charged with regulating broadcasting and ensuring that the public interest standard was met. In the 1960s, the Supreme Court held that the Communications Act gave the FCC jurisdiction over cable television.

Deregulation of broadcasting began in the late 1970s and continued throughout the 1980s. Although many rules and regulations were removed or modified, the public interest standard mandated by Congress in the Communications Act of 1934 remains in effect today.

Notes/References

1. Erwin G. Krasnow and Lawrence D. Longley, *The Politics of Broadcast Regulation*, 2nd ed. (New York: St. Martin's Press, 1978), 9.
2. United States v. Zenith Radio Corp. et al., 12 F.2d 614 (N.D. Ill., 1926)
3. Don R. Le Duc, *Beyond Broadcasting: Patterns in Policy and Law* (New York: Longman, 1987), 10.
4. 47, U.S.C.A., title III, section 301.
5. *Ibid.*, section 302.
6. *Ibid.*, section 303.
7. Section 1304 pertains to the broadcast of lottery information. Section 1343 prohibits fraud by wire, radio, or television. Section 1464 prohibits broadcasting obscene, indecent, or profane language.
8. This section was part of a 1959 amendment to the Communications Act and served as the basis of the Fairness Doctrine. The Doctrine was repealed by the FCC in 1987, but remains a "live" issue to many in Congress.
9. 47 U.S.C.A. Section 315(c).
10. 47 U.S.C.A. Section 326.
11. 18 U.S.C., 1464.
12. Trinity Methodist Church, South v. Federal Radio Commission, 62 F.2d 850 (D.C. Cir.Ct., 1932), cert. denied 288 U.S. 599 (1933)
13. National Broadcasting Co., Inc., et al. v. United States et al., 319 U.S. 190 (1943).
14. In Re-application of Great Lakes Broadcasting Co., FRC Docket 4900, 3 F.R.C.Ann.Rep. 32 (1929).
15. In the Matter of Editorializing by Broadcast Licenses, 13 FCC 1246 (1949) at 21.
16. Applicability of the Fairness Doctrine in the Handling of Controversial Issues of Public Importance, 29 Fed.Reg. 10415, July 25, 1964.
17. Red Lion Broadcasting Co., Inc., et al. v. FCC et al., 395 U.S. 367 (1969).
18. Inquiry into Section 73.1910 of the Commission's Rules and Regulations Concerning the General Fairness Obligations of Broadcast Licensees, 102 F.C.C.2d 143, 58 R.R.2d 1137 (1985).
19. Meredith Corp. v. Federal Communications Commission, (DC CA, 1987) 13 Med.L.Rptr. 1993.
20. Telecommunications Research and Action Center v. Federal Communications Commission, 801 F.2d 501, 61 R.R.2d 330, 13

Med.L.Rptr. 1881, rehearing denied 806 F.2d 1115, 61 R.R.2d 1342, 13 Med.L.Rptr. 1896 (D.C.Cir. 1986), certiorari denied 482 U.S. 919 (1987).
21. Syracuse Peace Council v. Federal Communications Commission (DC CA, 1989) 16 Med.L.Rptr. 1225, cert. denied Jan. 8, 1990.
22. 440 U.S. 689 (1979).
23. 47 U.S.C.A., Title VI, 521.
24. *Ibid.*, 541.
25. *Ibid.*, 559.
26. 476 U.S. 488 (1986).
27. C.F.R. 47 Parts 76.151 through 76.163.
28. Quincy Cable TV v. FCC, 768 F.2d 1434, 58 RR2d 977 (DC Cir.1985).
29. "Making Life a Bit Easier; Reregulation Gets Under Way," *Broadcasting*, November 6, 1972, p. 19.
30. "The Laissez Faire Legacy of Charles Ferris," *Broadcasting*, January 19, 1981, p. 37.

Cases

Banzhaf v. Federal Communications Commission, 405 F.2d 1082, 14 R.R.2d 2061, (D.C.Cir., 1968) 1 Med.L.Rptr. 2037, cert. denied 396 U.S. 842 (1969)
Brandywine-Maine Line Radio Inc. v. Federal Communications Commission, 473 F.2d 16, 25 R.R.2d 2010, (DC Cir., 1972) 1 Med.L.Rptr. 2067, cert. denied 412 U.S. 922 (1973)
CBS v. Democratic National Committee, 412 U.S. 94 (1973)
City of Los Angeles v. Preferred Communications Inc., 476 U.S. 488 (1986)
Friends of the Earth v. Federal Communications Commission, 449 F.2d 1164, 22 R.R.2d 2145 (DC Cir., 1971)
Hoover v. Intercity Radio Co. Inc., 286 F. 1003 (DC Cir., 1923)
In the Matter of Editorializing by Broadcast Licensees, 13 F.C.C. 1246 (1949)
In the Matter of the Mayflower Broadcasting and the Yankee Network Inc. (WAAB), 8 F.C.C. 333 (1941)
In Re-Application of Great Lakes Broadcasting Co., FRC Docket 4900, 3 F.R.C.Ann.Rep. 32 (1929)
KFKB Broadcasting v. Federal Radio Commission, 47 F.2d 670 (DC Cir., 1931)
Meredith Corp. v. Federal Communications Commission (DC CA, 1987) 13 Med.L.Rptr. 1993
National Broadcasting Co., Inc., et al. v. United States et al., 319 U.S. 190 (1943)
Public Interest Research Group v. Federal Communications Commission, 522 F.2d 1060, 34 R.R.2d 1375 (1st Cir., 1975), cert. denied 424 U.S. 965 (1976)
Red Lion Broadcasting Co., Inc., et al. v. FCC et al., 395 U.S. 367 (1969)

Syracuse Peace Council v. Federal Communications Commission (DC CA, 1989) 16 Med.L.Rptr. 1225, cert. denied Jan. 8, 1990

Telecommunications Research and Action Center v. Federal Communications Commission, 801 F.2d 501, 61 R.R.2d 330, 13 Med.L.Rptr. 1881, rehearing denied 806 F.2d 1115, 61 R.R.2d 1342, (DC Cir., 1986) 13 Med.L.Rptr. 1896, cert. denied 482 U.S. 919 (1987).

Trinity Methodist Church, South v. Federal Radio Commission, 62 F.2d 850 (DC Cir.Ct., 1932), cert. denied 288 U.S. 599 (1933)

United States v. Midwest Video Corp., 406 U.S. 649 (1972)

United States v. Southwestern Cable Co., 392 U.S. 157 (1968)

United States v. Zenith Radio Corp. et al., 12 F.2d 614 (N.D. Ill., 1926)

4

Licensing Broadcast Stations

In previous chapters, we discussed the development of broadcast and cable regulation. We now turn to the pragmatic task of applying those regulations to the daily operation of commercial broadcast and cable facilities. We will look at the process of obtaining and renewing a license. We will not deal with engineering and technical regulations, except as they interface with the issues related to licensing broadcast stations. It is essential that students of broadcast law and regulation become familiar with Title 47 of the Code of Federal Regulations as it applies to broadcasting. Rules that affect daily broadcast operation can be found in Title 47. Students should also check the *Federal Register* for Notices of Proposed Rule Making and other FCC actions that affect broadcasters and cable operations.

The Process of Obtaining a Broadcast License

There are, essentially, two ways that a broadcast license may be obtained. A license may be sought for a new facility or for an existing facility. The latter case is certainly the most common. However, from time to time, the FCC allows for the construction of new stations. Recent examples include the expansion of the AM band by 10 kHz, the authorization of low-power television, and the creation of several Docket 80–90 class A FM stations. In any case, potential applicants must show that they are legally, technically, and financially qualified to hold a broadcast license.

Qualifications of Licensees

The Communications Act requires that any grant of a broadcast license must be in the public interest. Section 308(b) also states,

All applications for station licenses, or modifications or renewals thereof, shall set forth such facts as the Commission by regulation may prescribe as to the citizenship, character, and financial, technical and other qualifications of the applicant to operate the station . . .[1]

The basic qualifications for broadcast ownership are grouped into five categories: legal, technical, financial, character, and adherance to EEO practices.

Legal Qualifications

Section 310 of the Communications Act requires that holders of broadcast licenses be U.S. citizens. Section 313 prohibits the granting of a license to any applicant whose license has previously been revoked for an antitrust violation. Section 312 applies to holders of construction permits (CPs) and licenses and provides for administrative sanctions against those who violate FCC rules or the U.S. Criminal Code. The U.S. Criminal Code prohibits the broadcast of obscene materials and certain lottery information. Violations of FCC rules or failure to meet the standards set forth in the Communications Act render an applicant legally unqualified to hold a broadcast license. This means that a license may be initially denied, not renewed, or revoked.

Technical Qualifications

Potential broadcast licensees must comply with a myriad of technical requirements developed by the Commission. These requirements are designed to minimize interference between stations and increase the operating efficiency of all stations. The technical qualifications also ensure that a certain quality of service is available to the population. Potential broadcast licensees must assure the FCC that audio and video quality, coverage area, and tower and transmission systems all meet Commission standards.

Financial Qualifications

The FCC requires that new broadcast license applicants have enough funds to operate the proposed station for 3 months without advertising revenue. This is to ensure that the station has adequate time to take root in the community and serve the public interest. This rule also discourages quick turnaround in the sale of broadcast properties.

Character Qualifications

For many years, character issues played a very important role in determining the fitness of broadcast applicants. Then, in keeping with the deregulatory trend of the 1970s and 1980s, the Commission eliminated many of the criteria it previously mandated. In 1986, the FCC redefined its interest in character to take into account misconduct involving violations of FCC rules or the Communications

Act, misrepresentations or "lack of candor" (i.e., lying) before the Commission, and fraudulent programming.[2] In 1990, the FCC reconsidered its policy and expanded its character inquiry to include any felony conviction involving an owner or manager. This policy reversal came after the Commission was criticized for renewing the license of WKSP-AM in Kingtree, South Carolina, whose owner had received a drug conviction. In January 1991, FCC Adminisrative Law Judge Joseph Chachkin revoked WSKP's license, citing the 1987 drug-trafficking conviction of the station's owner. The Commission also considers licensee convictions for antitrust or anti-competitive activity concerning any area of mass communication.

Equal Employment Opportunity

The FCC requires broadcast licensees to afford equal employment opportunity to all qualified persons and refrain from discrimination on the basis of race, color, religion, national origin, or sex. Stations planning to employ five or more full-time employees must establish a program designed to ensure equal employment opportunity for women and minority groups. The Commission defines minority groups as Blacks not of Hispanic origin, Asian or Pacific Islanders, American Indians, Alaskan Natives, and Hispanics. If minority group representation in the available labor force is less than 5%, a program for minorities is not required. Because women always comprise a significant portion of the available workforce, a program for women is required unless the station employs fewer than five full-time employees.

Other Considerations

The FCC also attempts to determine how the grant of a broadcast license to an applicant will serve the public interest. Indeed, the Commission must decide whether the public interest might be better served if the channel were left vacant.

Diversification of Media

Multiple Ownership Rules

In the case of new applicants, the FCC will consider whether a grant of the license will violate the multiple ownership rules, as stipulated in 47 CFR 73.3555(d)(1)(i) and 76.501 as applied to cable systems.

The number of stations that can be owned by a single group or individual has steadily increased over the years. In 1953, the FCC limited ownership of stations to 7 AM, 7 FM and 7 television stations, two of which had to be UHF. When Storer Broadcasting applied for a sixth VHF station, the Commission dismissed the application. In *United States v. Storer Broadcasting Co.*, the Supreme Court upheld the FCC's authority to set limits on the number of stations any one individual or group could own. The "rule of sevens" remained in effect until 1985, when it was revised in *Multiple Ownership (12–12–12 Reconsideration)* to permit ownership of 12 AM, 12

FM, and 12 TV stations. In 1992, the radio portion of the rule was revised again to permit ownership of 18 AM and 18 FM stations. After 1994, broadcasters may be permitted to own 20 AM stations and 20 FM stations. At this writing, no party may own more than 12 television stations. However, action by the FCC in raising this cap is expected during 1992. Currently, no group-owned television stations may reach more than 25% of the television households in the country. UHF stations are assessed at 50% of their market's television households to encourage purchases of these facilities.

For example, Capital Cities/ABC presently owns eight television stations that reach 24.4% of the nation's TV households. Although Capital Cities/ABC does not own 12 television stations, they are prohibited from acquiring another. When Capital Cities Communications and ABC merged in 1985, the new organization had to sell WKBW-TV in Buffalo and WTNH-TV in New Haven in order to meet the 25% rule.

According to a study conducted by the National Association of Broadcasters in 1990, none of the largest group owners held their complement of television properties. The nine NBC-owned stations reached 22.18% of the nation's households, with five CBS stations attaining 20.82%. Fox Broadcasting's seven stations covered 17.31% of American TV households. The same study noted that, overall, there are about 207 groups who have some interest in 843 broadcast stations. The average number of television stations owned by any one group is four.

An exception to the "rule of twelves" applies if at least two of the stations are minority controlled (i.e., 50% of the station's interest is owned by members of a minority group). If this is the case, that individual may own up to 14 stations and reach up to 30% of the television households.

The duopoly rule prohibits ownership of more than one TV station in the same market. The FCC began to liberalize this rule for radio in 1989 and relaxed the rule even further in 1992 per 73.3555(a)(3)(ii). Under current rules, a single owner may operate as many as four stations in markets having more than 14 radio stations. These four stations, 2 AM and 2 FM, are subject to a 25% audience share cap. In other words, the combined audience share of the four stations must be less than 25%.

In markets with 7 to 14 radio stations, a single owner may operate three stations, provided they are not all AM or FM. Owners in smaller markets may own one AM and one FM radio station.

It should be noted that local management agreements (LMAs)—contractual arrangements in which one licensee allows the licensee of another broadcast facility to operate a station in return for a share of the profits—are considered "ownership" under the rules. Therefore, a broadcaster in a market with 15 stations, who already owns three stations in the market, may enter into an LMA with only one other station.

The one-to-a-customer rule prohibits ownership of more than one AM, FM, and VHF station in the same market, per 73.3555(a). There is an exception for UHF and radio stations. The Commission considers these applications on an ad hoc basis. When the rule was promulgated in 1970, UHF stations were treated on an individual basis because, at that time, UHF was the weaker of the television services. Any AM/FM/VHF combinations existing before the rule went into effect were "grandfathered" (i.e., allowed to continue until such time as the stations were sold). At that point, the rule would be enforced.

In 1989, the Commission announced that it would be receptive to AM/FM/TV combinations in the top 25 markets as long as there were at least 30 separately owned stations in the market. The FCC granted Capital Cities/ABC a waiver in *Capital Cities/ABC, Inc.*, when the 1989 merger creating that company produced AM/FM/TV combinations in Chicago, New York, and Los Angeles, and an AM/FM combination in San Francisco.

Cross-ownership Rules

Since 1975, the FCC has prohibited common ownership of broadcast stations and daily newspapers. This policy is designed to foster diversification of media voices. The rationale behind this policy is based on the theoretical assumption that media audiences will be exposed to more than one opinion on issues of public importance.

When the Commission enacted the newspaper/broadcast cross-ownership rule in *Second Report and Order*, it allowed many existing newspaper/broadcast corporations' cross-ownerships to continue until the corporation sold the broadcast station.

As in the case of *Policy Research Group v. FCC*, when a tranfer of a license results in a violation of the cross-ownership rules, the FCC often grants a temporary waiver, giving the new licensee 2 years in which to divest the property.

FCC v. National Citizen's Committee
for Broadcasting (1978)
Justice Marshall delivered the opinion of the Court.

☐ . . . In setting its licensing policies, the Commission has long acted on the theory that diversification of mass media ownership serves the public interest by promoting diversity of program and service viewpoints, as well as by preventing undue concentration of economic power. . . .

Diversification of ownership has not been the sole consideration thought relevant to the public interest, however. The Commission's other, and sometimes conflicting, goal has been to ensure "the best practicable service to the public." . . . Moreover, the Commission has given considerable weight to a policy of avoiding undue disruption of existing service. As a result, newspaper owners in many instances have been able to acquire broadcast licenses for stations serving the same communities as their newspapers, and the Commission has repeatedly renewed such licenses on findings that continuation of the service offered by the common owner would serve the public interest.

. . . Against this background, the Commission began the instant rulemaking proceeding in 1970 to consider the need for a more restrictive policy toward newspaper ownership of radio and television broadcast stations. . . . Citing studies showing the dominant role of television stations and daily newspapers as sources of local news and other information . . . the notice of rulemaking proposed adoption of regulations that would eliminate all newspaper-broadcast combinations serving the same market, by prospectively banning formation or transfer of such combinations and requiring dissolution of all such existing combinations within five years. . . . At the same time, however, the Commission expressed "substantial concern" about the disruption of service that might result from divestiture of existing combinations. . . .

. . . While recognizing the pioneering contributions of newspaper owners to the broadcast industry, the Commission concluded that changed circumstances made it possible, and necessary, for all new licensing of broadcast stations to "be expected to add to local diversity." . . . In reaching this conclusion, the Commission did not find that existing co-located newspaper-broadcast combinations had not served the public interest. . . .

. . . The Commission concluded that . . . divestiture was warranted only in "the most egregious cases," which it identified as those in which a newspaper-broadcast combination has an "effective monopoly" in the local "marketplace of ideas as well as economically."

. . . The Order identified 8 television-newspaper and 10 radio-newspaper combinations meeting the divestiture criteria. . . . Waivers of the divestiture requirements were granted *sua sponte* to 1 television and 1 radio combination, leaving a total of 16 stations subject to divestiture. The Commission explained that waiver requests would be entertained in the latter cases, but absent waiver, either the newspaper or the broadcast station would have to be divested by January 1, 1980. . . .

. . . [T]he Court of Appeals affirmed the prospective ban on new licensing of co-located newspaper-broadcast combinations, but vacated the limited divestiture rules, and ordered the Commission to adopt regulations requiring dissolution of all existing combinations that did not qualify for a waiver under the procedure outlined in the order. . . . The court was also unable to find a rational basis for distinguishing between the 16 egregious cases that had to be divested and the remaining grandfathered combinations. . . .

. . . In concluding that the Commission acted unreasonably in not extending its divestiture requirement across-the-board, the Court of Appeals apparently placed heavy reliance on a "presumption" that existing newspaper-broadcast combinations "do not serve the public interest." . . . But the weighing policies under the "public interest" standard is a task that Congress has delegated to the Commission in the first instance, and we are unable to find anything in the Communications Act, the First Amendment, or the Commission's past or present practices that would require the Commission to "presume" that its diversification policy should be given controlling weight in all circumstances.[3]

The Cable Communications Act of 1984 bars cable and over-the-air television cross-ownership in the same market. Cable systems are also enjoined from carrying the signal of any broadcast station if the station owns a national television network, such as ABC, CBS, or NBC, as stipulated in 76.501(a). However, in mid-1992, the FCC considered relaxing the cable/network cross-ownership rules.

The Application Process: Filing the Right Forms

The FCC is a bureaucracy and by nature is dependent on procedure. It is imperative that anyone dealing with the Commission file the proper forms. The forms should be up-to-date and filled in completely. Blanks or partially answered questions can lead to long delays in the processing of an application. Filing an obsolete or improper form can result in the entire application being returned to the applicant.

FCC forms can be obtained from the Commission in Washington, DC, or from a local FCC field office. Forms may also be obtained by calling 202–632–FORM, 24 hours a day, or by filling out FCC Form 207, Form Order Card, and mailing it to the Commission.

Authority to Construct or Make Changes in an Existing Station

When applying for a new station, applicants file FCC Form 301 with the Mass Media Bureau to request the authority to construct a new broadcast station or to make changes in an existing facility. Applicants ask the Commission to grant a CP to build or modify a facility.

Form 301 requires applicants to provide information designed to allow the FCC to determine the applicant's qualifications to hold a broadcast license. The form asks for information about citizenship, character, financial status, other media interests, and sources of capital. Applicants are also required to submit information about the proposed programming of the station and address how that programming will serve the community of license. The form also requires applicants to submit an elaborate engineering study including estimated coverage area, height of the tower, and coordinates of the antennna. Stations having more than five full-time employees are required to submit a detailed EEO plan.

If a CP is granted, the operator of a television station has 2 years in which to complete construction (a radio station has 18 months) or they risk forfeiture. Stations may file for an extension of the CP by filing Form 307, per CFR 73.3534.

Upon completion of construction, the applicant must apply for a license. This is done by completing Form 302 (see Appendix 2). On this form, applicants must show compliance with the terms outlined in the CP. Assuming there are no extenuating circumstances, the license is routinely granted by the Commission.

Buying or Selling a Station

Buyers of broadcast properties must receive FCC approval before the sale can be closed. The proper forms must be filed with the Commission at least 45 days before the proposed sale. Form 314 is used when requesting consent to assign assets associated with a CP or broadcast license. Form 315 is used when requesting approval to transfer control of a corporation holding a CP or license—that is, when the parent company has been sold. Form 316 is the short version of Forms 314 and 315. It is used when there is no "substantial change" in the licensee's control. For example, assignment from a corporation to its individual stockholders without changing the disposition of their interests would qualify for Form 316. Low-power television stations and translator stations seeking assignment of their license fill out Form 345.

Sellers of broadcast properties are required to publish notice of the proposed sale in local newspapers and broadcast a notice over the station per 47 CFR 73.3580(d)(3). Low-power television stations and FM translator stations are exempt from this requirement.

The Licensing Process

In routine situations, the staff of the Mass Media Bureau handles the licensing process. Section 73.3591 of the FCC Rules provides,

In the case of any application for an instrument of authorization, other than a license pursuant to a construction permit, the FCC will make the grant if it finds (on the basis of the application, the pleadings filed or other matters which it may officially notice) that the application presents no substantial and material question of fact and meets the following requirements:

1. There is not pending a mutually exclusive application filed in accordance with paragraph (b) of this section;
2. The applicant is legally, technically, financially, and otherwise qualified;

3. The applicant is not in violation of provisions of law or the FCC rules, or established policies of the FCC; and

4. A grant of the application would otherwise serve the public interest, convenience and necessity.[4]

In other words, if there is no one else applying for the same frequency, and the applicant meets basic qualifications and can reasonably establish that the public interest will be served, the license will be granted. Of course, if the Commission cannot act on an application because it does not meet the stipulated requirements, the FCC may designate a hearing. The hearing is conducted by an ALJ. This individual functions very much like a regular court judge, but there is no jury present at the hearing and the issues of the case are determined by the FCC.

Hearings

A hearing will be conducted if two or more parties file for use of the same or interfering frequencies. In 1965, the Commission issued the *Policy Statement on Comparative Broadcast Hearings* and outlined eight factors it would consider when deciding between mutually exclusive applications. The FCC's description of the hearing process and the eight factors outlined in the statement remain important to this day.

☐ **Policy Statement on Comparative Broadcast Hearings (1965)**
One of the Commission's primary responsibilities is to choose among qualified new applicants for the same broadcast facilities. . . . This commonly requires extended hearings into a number of areas of comparison. The hearing and decision process is inherently complex, and the subject does not lend itself to precise categorization or to the clear making of precedent. The various factors cannot be assigned absolute values, some factors may be present in some cases and not in others, and the differences between applicants with respect to each factor are almost infinitely variable.

Furthermore, membership on the Commission is not static and the views of individual Commissioners on the importance of particular factors may change. For these and other reasons, the Commission is not bound to deal with all cases at all times as it has done in the past that seem comparable . . . and changes of viewpoint, if reasonable, are recognized as both inescapable and proper . . .

All this being so, it is nonetheless important to have a high degree of consistency of decision and of clarity in our basic policies. It is also obviously of great importance to prevent undue delay in the disposition of comparative hearing cases. A general review of the criteria governing the disposition of comparative broadcast hearings will, we believe, be useful to parties appearing before the Commission. . . . Our purpose is to promote stability of judgement without foreclosing the right of every applicant to a full hearing.

We believe that there are two primary objectives toward which the process of comparison should be directed. They are, first, the best practicable service to the public, and second, a maximum diffusion of control of the media of mass communications. . . .

Several factors are significant in the two areas of comparison mentioned above, and it is important to make clear the manner in which each will be treated.

1. *Diversification of control of the media of mass communications.* Diversification is a factor of primary significance since, as set forth above, it constitutes a primary objective in the licensing scheme.

   As in the past, we will consider both common control and less than controlling interests in other broadcast stations and other media of mass communications. The less the degree of interest in other stations or media, the less will be the sigificance factor. Other interests in the principal community proposed to be served will normally be of most significance, followed by other interests in the remainder of the proposed service area . . . and, finally, generally in the United States. . . . The number of other mass communication outlets of the same type in the community proposed to be served will also affect to some extent the importance of this factor in the general comparative scale . . .

2. *Full-time participation in station operation by owners.* We consider this factor to be of substantial importance. It is inherently desirable that legal responsibility and day-to-day performance be closely associated. In addition, there is a likelihood of greater sensitivity to an area's changing needs, and of programming designed to serve those needs, to the extent that the station's proprietors actively participate in the day-to-day operation of the station. This factor is thus important in securing the best practicable service. . . . It also frequently complements the objective of diversification, since concentrations of control are necessarily achieved at the expense of integrated ownership . . .

   Past participation in civic affairs will be considered as a part of a participating owner's local residence background, as will any other local activities indicating a knowledge of and interest in the welfare of the community . . . No credit will be given either the local residence or experience of any person who will not put his knowledge of the community (or area) or experience to any use in the operation of the station.

3. *Proposed program service.* . . . The importance of program service is obvious. The feasiblity of making a comparative evaluation is not so obvious . . .

The basic elements of an adequate service have been set forth in our July 29, 1960 "Report and Statement of Policy Re: Commission *en banc* Programming Inquiry," 25 F.R. 7291, 20 Pike & Fischer, R.R. 1901, and need not be repeated here.... And the applicant has the responsibility for a reasonable knowledge of the community and area, based on surveys or background, which will show that the program proposals are designed to meet the needs and interests of the public in that area ... Contacts with local civic and other groups and individuals are also an important means of formulating proposals to meet an area's needs and interests. Failure to make them will be construed as a serious deficiency, whether or not the applicant is familiar with the area.

... The Commission expects every licensee to carry out its proposals, subject to factors beyond its control, and subject to reasonable judgement that the public's needs and interests require a departure from original plans....

4. *Past broadcast record.* ... We are interested in records which, because either unusually good or unusually poor, give some indication of unusual performance in the future ... [A]n extraordinary record compiled while the owner fully participated in operation of the station will not be accorded full credit where the party does not propose similar participation in the operation of the new station for which he is applying.

5. *Efficient use of frequency.* ... [T]he possible variations of situations in comparative hearings are numerous. Therefore, it is not feasible here to delineate the outlines of this element, and we merely take this occasion to point out that the element will be considered where the facts warrant.

6. *Character.* The Communications Act makes character a relevant consideration in the issuance of a license. See Section 308(b), 47 U.S.C. 308(b). Significant character deficiencies may warrant disqualification, and an issue will be designated when appropriate.... In the absence of a designated issue, character evidence will not be taken...

7. *Other Factors.* As we stated at the outset, our interest in the consistency and clarity of decision and in expedition of the hearing process is not intended to preclude the full examination of any relevant and substantial factor. We will thus favorably consider petitions to add issues when, but only when, they demonstrate that significant evidence will be adduced ...[5]

Commissioners Hyde and Bartley wrote dissenting statements to this 1965 policy statement and Commissioner Lee wrote a reluctant concurring statement. These statements make interesting reading for the student wishing to pursue the topic further.

In accordance with FCC rule 47 CFR 73.3593, if an application is designated for a hearing, the Commission must "notify the applicant and all known parties in the interest of such action and the grounds and reasons therefore." The applicant must give public notice of the hearing by publishing such notice in a local newspaper and broadcasting it, if possible, per 47 CFR 73.3594(a). Notice must be given at least twice a week for two consecutive weeks within the 3-week period immediately following the release of the FCC's order of a hearing. The notice must specify the time and commencement of the hearing, and must appear in a general circulation paper published in the community in which the station is proposed.

If the application designated for a hearing involves the change in location of a station, the notice must be given in both the present and proposed communities of license, per 73.3594(3).

If an existing station seeks license modification, renewal, assignment, or transfer and the application is designated for a hearing, the station must broadcast notice over its own facilities per 73.3594 (3)(b). This requirement does not apply to international broadcast, low-power TV, TV translator, FM translator, or FM booster stations.

If the station is the only operating station in its broadcast community or if it is a noncommercial educational station, it is exempt from the requirement to publish hearing information in a local newspaper. Broadcasting the information is usually sufficient. Noncommercial educational stations not on the air during the period in question must still publish the notice, per 47 CFR 73.3594(4)(c).

The FCC is very specific about the time and manner that applicants must fulfill this obligation. Again, the notice must detail the time and place of the hearing. Specific text is provided in CFR 73.3594 (4)(d)(1):

(1) The name of the applicant or applicants designated for hearing.

(2) The call letters, if any, of the station or stations involved, and the frequencies or channels on which the station or stations are operating or proposed to operate.

(3) The time and place of the hearing.

(4) The issues in the hearing as listed in the FCC's order or summary of designation for hearing.

(5) A statement that a copy of the application, amendment(s), and related material are on file for public inspection at a stated address in the community in which the station is located or is proposed to be located.

(e) Per 73.3594, when an application for renewal of license is designated for a hearing, the notice shall contain the following additional statements:

(1) Immediately preceding the listing of issues in the hearing:

The application of this station for a renewal of its license to operate this station in the public interest was tendered for filing with the Federal Communications Commission on (date). After considering this application, the FCC has determined that it is necessary to hold a hearing to decide the following questions: . . .

(2) Immediately following the listing of the issues in the hearing:

The hearing will be held at (*place of hearing*) commencing at (*time*), on (*date*). Members of the public who desire to give evidence concerning the foregoing issues should write to the Federal Communications Commission, Washington, DC 20554 not later than (*date*). Letters should set forth in detail the specific facts concerning which the writer wishes to give evidence. If the FCC believes that the evidence is legally competent material, and relevant to the issues, it will contact the person in question. . . .[6]

Commercial and educational television stations must broadcast the notice verbally, with a camera focused on an announcer. The notice must be broadcast between 7:00 P.M. and 10:00 P.M. by commercial stations. Educational stations have the same requirement, but are not required to broadcast the notice during times that they are not normally on the air.

The 1990 Revamp of the Comparative Hearings Process

In December 1990, the FCC streamlined the comparative hearings process with the hope of shortening the time for disposing of a comparative case from 3 years to just 1 year. The Commission eliminated policies that permitted applicants acquiring licenses through settlements to renege on integration or divestiture requirements, set procedural dates for hearings in the designation order, and limited time for discovery to 60 days. The FCC will also encourage more and earlier settlements through earlier payment of the hearing fee.

"Standing" before the Commission

Outside parties have a right to participate in the licensing process and are afforded "standing" before the FCC or the ALJ during a hearing. Originally, other broadcasters could object to the granting of a license on grounds of economic injury, as provided for in the Carroll Doctrine.

In 1988, however, the FCC eliminated the Carroll Doctrine. Instead, it proposed a three-part test to determine when economic injury may be considered in granting a new license. The FCC required hard evidence that such a grant would have a detrimental effect on the service to the public. It also required challengers to address whether the revenue potential of the market was so small that an existing station would lose significant income, whether that loss of income would force the existing station to curtail public service programming, and whether this loss of programming would be offset by nonnetwork programming to be offered by the new station. All three items must be addressed by stations opposing grants on economic grounds.

In 1966, citizens groups were given official standing in broadcast proceedings. While citizens groups are most active in license renewal situations, they may also provide input during initial licensing. Matters of character, financial stability, and proposed program service are areas that citizens groups may address. Citizens groups and broadcasters may enter into agreements specifying how the broadcaster will serve the community during the license period. The FCC will consider these agreements at renewal time.

The License Renewal Process

Radio licenses are issued for 7 years and television licenses are granted for 5 years. All radio or television licenses in a single state come up for renewal in the same year. Originally, the license term was 3 years for both radio and television, but Congress modified the term in 1981.

Before the deregulation of the 1980s, the paperwork associated with license renewal was substantial. Not only were stations required to fill out a lengthy form, but at varying times in history broadcasters were required to submit a "composite week" of program logs to the Commission and results of formal community ascertainment-of-needs studies were to be placed in their public files. Stations were measured against the yardstick of "promise versus performance"—Did you program what you said you would when you applied for the license?

Stations are no longer required to keep program logs and deregulation has eliminated much of the paperwork to be submitted to the Commission during the renewal period. The "promise versus performance" policy was deleted in 1983, but broadcasters still must serve the communities in which they are licensed.

In the year of license renewal, commercial broadcasters receive the postcard renewal form from the FCC. For most stations, this is the extent of their contact with the FCC during renewal. For approximately 4% of the stations up for renewal, a random visit by an inspector from the Field Operations Bureau may occur. The inspector checks to be sure the public inspection file is in order and that the station is in compliance with technical standards.

The Public Inspection File

The license renewal form requires broadcasters to ensure that the public file is complete. Therefore, before completing the renewal application, licensees must be sure that the file contains all the necessary materials. Rule 47 73.3536 outlines the materials to be included in the public file for commercial stations and 47 73.3527 lists the requirements for noncommercial stations. Essentially, the public file must contain the following:

Materials pertaining to applications and forms filed with the Commission must be included in the public file. This includes applications for CPs, license renewal, transfer of license, and lists of anyone who filed a petition to deny against any of these applications. All related supporting documents must also be in the file.

All ownership materials, including the Annual Ownership Report (Form 323) and management agreements with nonemployees and employees (if the agreement involves profit sharing), must be in the public file.

Annual employment reports (Forms 395 or 395-B) must be in the public file.

A quarterly issues/programs list must be included. The list should include the issues examined and a narrative that explains how each issue was addressed by the station. The list must include the time, date, and length of each broadcast, as well as the title and program type (documentary, news, interview, etc.).

Agreements between citizens groups and the station must be placed in the public file.

These materials must be retained for a period of 7 years. Other materials kept in the file (such as the following) must be retained for varying periods of time:

Requests for air time by political candidates and disposition of the request, including charges, must be in the file.

Any free time given within 72 hours of the election must be part of the file.

A list of chief executive officers of any organization that sponsors or provides free information for political programs dealing with controversial issues of public importance must be in the public file.

These last three items must be retained for a period of 2 years. Requests for time by political candidates must be updated daily.

Letters received from members of the public must be retained for 3 years.

The Public and Broadcasting—A Procedure Manual is a 1974 publication, but is still required to be in the file. It must be retained indefinitely.

Noncommercial stations must also place a list of donors supporting specific programs aired on the station in the file.

The public file must be a located at the main studio location or other location accessible to the general public. Individuals must be allowed access to the file during normal business hours. A station must make copies of documents in the public file, but may charge a "reasonable fee" to anyone requesting copies.

The Postcard Renewal Form

The Commission sends Form 303-S (see Appendix 2) to a station approximately 7 months before the expiration of its license. During this period, the station ensures that the public file is in order and gathers information that will be a part of the renewal application.

Prefiling and Postfiling Announcements

At each license renewal, the licensee must broadcast an announcement over the station that informs the public that the license is up for renewal. The station must also invite comments from the public in prefiling and postfiling announcements (see Figures 4.1 and 4.2). Since citizens groups have legal standing before the FCC in license renewal matters, this is extremely important. FCC rules require that these announcements begin 2 months before the station files for renewal and continue for 3 months after the application has been filed, per 73.3580(d)(4).

Stations must file for renewal 4 months before the expiration date of the license. Therefore, the first prefiling announcement must be broadcast 6 months before the license expires. Both prefiling and postfiling announcements must be broadcast on the first and sixteenth days of the month. Commercial radio stations must make two prefiling and three postfiling announcements between 7 A.M. and 9 A.M., and/or 4 P.M. and 6 P.M. If a station is not on the air during these times, the announcement must be made during the first two hours of operation. Noncommercial radio stations must adhere to the same guidelines, but are not required to broadcast an announcement in any month that it does not regularly operate, per 73.3580(A).

Commercial television stations must broadcast at least two of the prefiling and three of the postfiling announcements between 6 P.M. and 11 P.M. Eastern and Pacific time (between 5 P.M. and 10 P.M. Central and Mountain time). They must also use visuals with the licensee's and the FCC's addresses when the announcement is being presented verbally by an announcer.

On *(date of last renewal grant) (station call letters)* was granted a license by the Federal Communications Commission to serve the public interest as a trustee until *(expiration date)*. Our license will expire on *(date)*. We must file an application for renewal with the FCC on or before *(first day of fourth full calendar month prior to expiration date)*. When filed, a copy of this application will be available for public inspection during our regular business hours. It contains information concerning this station's performance during the last *(period of time covered by the application)*.

Individuals who wish to advise the FCC of facts relating to our renewal application and to whether this station has operated in the public interest should file comments and petitions with the FCC by *(first day of last full calendar month prior to the month of expiration)*.

Further information concerning the FCC's broadcast license renewal process is available at *(address of location of the station's public inspection file)* or may be obtained from the FCC, Washington, D.C. 20554.

Figure 4.1 Text of prefiling announcement.

On *(date of last renewal grant) (station call letters)* was granted a license by the Federal Communications Commission to serve the public interest as a public trustee until *(expiration date)*. Our license will expire on *(date)*. We have filed an application for license renewal with the FCC.

A copy of this application is available for public inspection during our regular business hours. It contains information concerning this station's performance during the last *(period of time covered by application)*.

Individuals who wish to advise the FCC of facts relating to our renewal application and to whether this station has operated in the public interest should file comments and petitions with the FCC by *(first day of last full calendar month prior to the month of expiration)*.

Further information concerning the FCC's broadcast license renewal process is available at *(address of location of the station's public inspection file)* or may be obtained from the FCC, Washington, D.C. 20554.

Figure 4.2 Text of postfiling announcement.

If an emergency precludes the airing of an announcement at its scheduled time, stations must broadcast the announcement on the day after the emergency has ended, at the time the announcement would have originally been broadcast.

Within 7 days after fulfilling the obligation to broadcast these announcements, stations must place a certificate of compliance in the public file. This document indicates the dates and times of each announcement, the text, and any variations from the prescribed FCC schedule.

After the Renewal Application Is Filed

After the renewal application is filed, the Commission staff reviews the applicant's record of compliance with FCC regulations and the Communications Act. It is at this point that members of the public can file a petition to deny. Competitors may also file a competing application. The petition to deny asks the FCC to deny license renewal on grounds that the applicant has not met its public interest responsibilities. A competing application most often alleges that the applicant failed to meet certain licensee obligations and that a competing applicant promises to do a better job of meeting these obligations than the current licensee. If the Commission decides that there are serious concerns addressed by a petition to deny or a competing application, it will designate a hearing. The FCC will also identify the issues to be discussed in that hearing. The Ashbacker Doctrine, which resulted from *Ashbacker Radio Corp. v. FCC*, guarantees a hearing when mutually exclusive applications are filed.

Barring a challenge from the public or a competitor, most broadcast licenses are renewed provided the applicant meets basic licensing qualifications, is not in violation of the law, and the FCC believes the grant to be in the public interest.

Comparative Proceedings and Renewal Expectancy

When a comparative hearing is granted in a renewal situation, the incumbent enjoys an advantage over the challenger. The policy of renewal expectancy grew out of *Hearst Radio Inc. (WBAL)*. In this case, the Commission ruled in favor of the incumbent, noting:

☐ . . . The determining factor in our decision is the clear advantage of continuing the established and excellent service now furnished by WBAL and which we find to be in the public interest, when compared to the risks attendant on the execution of the proposed programming service of Public Service Radio Corporation, excellent though the proposal may be.[7]

Renewal expectancy is not automatic; it must be earned and is based on the record of the incumbent. This rather straightforward policy began a long period of varied interpretations in *Greater Boston Television Corp. v. FCC*, which dragged on for 15 years.

In 1954, four mutually exclusive applicants applied for Channel 5 in Boston. After holding hearings, in 1957 the Commission awarded the license to WHDH Inc., a wholly owned subsidiary of the *Boston Herald-Traveler* newspaper. The competing applicants appealed the FCC award. However, WHDH began operation as the appeal was filed. During the appeals process, it was alleged that WHDH president, Robert Choate, had improperly met with with the FCC Chairman. Choate was accused of attempting to influence the Commission. The FCC revoked WHDH's construction permit, granted the station a special temporary license, and reopened the comparative proceeding.

In 1960, the FCC once again selected WHDH over competing applicants. This time, however, WHDH was given a four-month license because of the alleged indiscretions of Choate. When WHDH filed for renewal, competing applications were again filed.

In 1966, the Commission found WHDH's performance to be "average" and therefore not entitled to special credit. It also found that WHDH was below average on "diversification of media" grounds, because of the newspaper cross-ownership. In 1969, in *In the Matter of WHDH Inc.*, the FCC took the license of WHDH, primarily citing the cross-ownership issue.

The court of appeals upheld the Commission's grant of the license to challenger Better Boston Incorporated (BBI). The court noted that because of WHDH's earlier difficulties with the Commission, renewal expectancy was not granted.

The broadcast industry followed the *WHDH* case closely. As might be expected, many in the industry were concerned that an existing license could be given to a challenger. After all, station owners invest capital in equipment and resources, and tend to become skittish when faced with the possibility of losing that investment each time license renewal comes up.

Broadcasters began lobbying Congress to pass legislation protecting their investment. In late 1969, Senator John Pastore, Chairman of the Senate Subcommittee on Communications, drafted a bill amending Section 309 of the Communications Act to require that the FCC "may not consider the application of any other person for facilities for which renewal is sought." The Commission compromised and adopted what has become known as the 1970 Policy Statement, which was the result of the *Policy Statement on Comparative Hearings Involving Regular Renewal Applicants.* The Pastore bill was withdrawn.

The policy statement provided that in a hearing between an incumbent and a challenger, the incumbent is preferred, provided that past performance does not contain serious deficiencies.

The 1970 Policy Statement was challenged by citizens groups as a violation of the Ashbacker Doctrine. Recall that the Ashbacker Doctrine guarantees a full hearing when mutually exclusive applications are filed. In *Citizens Communications Center v. FCC*, the court found that the policy did violate the Ashbacker Doctrine and Section 309(e) of the Communications Act. The court added that the FCC could consider superior performance of an incumbent and that the challenger has the burden of proof to show why the existing license should be displaced. The 1970 Policy Statement was abandoned, but no clear standard to replace it was proposed.

Throughout the 1970s, the issue of renewal expectancy remained unclear. For the most part, license renewals were granted unless evidence of serious deficiencies became evident. The Commission had essentially been unable or unwilling to distinguish between "superior" performance and "average" performance. Critics argued that, in practice, the FCC was abiding by the defunct 1970 Policy Statement.

When Cowles Florida Broadcasting Inc. applied for renewal of its Daytona Beach television station, the renewal application was challenged by Central Florida Enterprises. After much deliberation and questionable procedures, the Commission awarded the license to the incumbent. During the course of the proceedings Cowles' performance was upgraded from "thoroughly acceptable" to "superior." The Commission also disregarded Cowles' violation of main studio location rules and mail fraud allegations in reaching its decision (see Commissioner Robinson's dissent in *Cowles Florida Broadcasting Inc.*).

Central Florida Enterprises appealed the decision and the Court of Appeals for the District of Columbia reversed the renewal. In *Central Florida Enterprises, Inc. v. FCC,* the court remanded to the Commission and instructed the FCC to consider its procedures for granting renewal when a hearing is conducted.

When the case was remanded to the Commission, the FCC again awarded renewal. Central Florida appealed again and the issue returned to the Court of Appeals for the District of Columbia, which rendered the following decision:

☐   . . . For some time now the FCC has had to wrestle with the problem of how it can factor in some degree of "renewal expectancy" for a broadcaster's meritorious past record, while at the same time undertaking the required comparative evaluation of the incumbent's probable future performance versus the challenger's. As we stated in *Central Florida I*, "the incumbent's past performance is some evidence, and perhaps the best evidence, of what its future performance would be." And it has been intimated—by the Supreme Court in *FCC v. National Citizen's Committee for Broadcasting (NCCB)* and by this court in *Citizens Communications Center v. FCC* and *Central Florida I*—that some degree of renewal expectancy is permissible. But *Citizens* and *Central Florida I* also indicated that the FCC has in the past impermissibly raised renewal expectancy to an irrebuttable presumption in favor of the incumbent. . . .

   . . .The new policy, as we understand it, is simply this: renewal expectancy is to be a factor weighed with all other factors, and the better the past record, the greater the renewal expectancy "weight" . . . We are relying, then, on the FCC's commitment that renewal expectancy will be factored in for the benefit of the public, not for incumbent broadcasters.[8]

In 1989, the FCC issued a proposed rule designed to clarify its policy of renewal expectancy. The document was titled, *Formulation of Policies and Rules Relating to Broadcast Renewal Applicants, Competing Applicants, and Other Participants to the Comparative Renewal Process and to the Prevention of Abuses of the Renewal Process.* The Commission proposed that an incumbent in a renewal proceeding be granted a rebuttable presumption that it has provided meritorious service sufficient to warrant renewal expectancy. The burden of proof would shift to the challenger. At this point, the incumbent would be required to present evidence in the form of the issues/programs list showing how it provided substantial service to the community. The challenger could rebut the presumption by showing that the incumbent did not broadcast the programs listed on the issues/programs list or that the programs were not responsive to the issues of concern in the community of license. At the time of this writing, the Commission has not taken formal action on this proposal.

The RKO Case

The *RKO* case makes the *WHDH* case pale in its complexity. The strange series of events that led, ultimately, to RKO's loss of all 16 of its broadcast licenses, began in 1966.

When RKO's Los Angeles television station, KHJ, applied for renewal in 1966, the renewal was challenged by Fidelity Television Inc. The hearing examiner denied renewal of KHJ on grounds that the station had not responded to community criticism of excessive violence in its programming and that the station relied too heavily on old movies as a programming staple. The Commission reversed the decision and granted renewal. The FCC concluded that while KHJ's programming was not "superior," neither was it "unusually poor." The FCC concluded that the two applicants were essentially "equal" and that, in such cases, continuation of existing service would be in the public interest.

Fidelity appealed and although the court of appeals merely found KHJ's performance "average," the renewal was upheld in *Fidelity Television Inc. v. FCC.*

Meanwhile, the licenses of two other RKO stations were challenged when they applied for renewal. In 1969, two challengers filed for RKO's Boston television station, WNAC-TV, Channel 7. In 1974, RKO's New York City station, WOR-TV, Channel 9, was challenged.

The challengers of the Boston license alleged that RKO and its parent company, General Tire and Rubber Co., had knowingly violated the FCC's sponsorship identification rules and had engaged in anticompetitive practices, contrary to the sponsorship identification rules stipulated in CFR 73.1212. Things began to go down hill very quickly for RKO and General Tire.

In 1975, the Securities and Exchange Commission (SEC) began an investigation of General Tire and Rubber Co. on grounds that the company had bribed officials in Chile, Morocco, and Romania. Later in the same year, the challengers of WNAC-TV's license filed a petition with the FCC to enlarge the parameters of their challenge. They now alleged that General Tire had engaged in unethical conduct in and out of the United States and that RKO had "exhibited a lack of candor" by failing to disclose information about the investigation of General Tire by the SEC to the FCC.

In 1976, the SEC found several indications of misconduct by General Tire. Many of these items were as alleged in the WNAC-TV challengers' petition a year earlier. Still, RKO had not offically advised the FCC of the SEC investigation. It was only after General Tire had entered into a consent decree with the SEC, which prohibited concealment of alleged misconduct, that RKO finally advised the FCC of the ongoing SEC investigation. The consent decree also provided for a special review committee that was charged with investigating the situation further.

The FCC took no futher action against RKO or in the WNAC-TV license renewal challenge, preferring to wait on the report by the special review committee. In the meantime, however, more information damaging to RKO surfaced.

It appeared that RKO had failed to complete the barter and trade portion of FCC Form 324, the Annual Financial Report, for the years 1972 to 1976. The WNAC-TV challengers filed an additional petition with the FCC noting this fact.

The special review committee filed its report in July 1977 and it confirmed the allegations about General Tire. But before the FCC took action on the WNAC-TV renewal, the challengers (Dudley Station Corporation and Community Broadcasting of Boston) merged and petitioned to *purchase* WNAC-TV from RKO for $54 million. The transfer was contingent on FCC renewal of WNAC-TV's license to RKO. The Dudley/Community petition was opposed by Fidelity TV and Multi-State Communications—the challengers for KHJ in Los Angeles and WOR-TV in New York City.

In 1980, in *RKO General Inc.* (1980), the FCC denied RKO's application for renewal of WNAC-TV, thereby scuttling the proposed transfer. The Commission cited RKO's lack of candor and General Tire's anticompetitive trade practices as the basis of the decision. The FCC also denied RKO's renewal applications for the Los Angeles and New York stations, citing the company as unfit to hold those licenses.

In *RKO v. Federal Communications Commission*, the court upheld the denial of renewal of WNAC-TV. The court would not allow the FCC to deny renewal of the stations in New York and Los Angeles, and noted that the Commission would have to deal with each renewal in separate proceedings. The FCC began to do just that.

While the comparative renewal proceedings regarding WOR-TV, New York, were pending, Congress amended the Communications Act section 331 to require that the FCC renew the license of any VHF station willing to relocate to a state without a commercial VHF station. The measure was sponsored by New Jersey Senator Bill Bradley, whose state had no commercial VHF stations. In 1982, RKO notified the Commission that it would move WOR-TV from New York City to Secaucus, New Jersey. The license was automatically renewed. The move temporarily took care of the WOR-TV challenge, but KHJ in Los Angeles and the remaining RKO stations remained a target for the FCC.

In 1982, RKO still owned 15 broadcast properties—3 television and 12 radio stations. In February 1983, acting under a court order, the FCC began accepting competing applications for the other 13 RKO stations. In 1985, the FCC began the comparative proceedings.

In 1984, RKO admitted that two of its radio networks were guilty of overbilling and also admitted to allegations of fraud. Network fraud became an issue in the KHJ case. Then, in 1985, Westinghouse Broadcasting and Cable sought to purchase KHJ-TV from RKO. The plan called for a complex series of events, including a promise by RKO to withdraw its renewal application for KHJ-TV. Because Fidelity Television had filed a competing application, the license would be awarded to Fidelity. Fidelity would then sell KHJ-TV to Westinghouse. Westinghouse would then pay Fidelity's debts incurred in the matter.

The FCC did not approve the matter and Westinghouse withdrew its offer. In the aftermath, the FCC suggested that RKO dispose of all its broadcast properties by simply selling them to the competing applicants. The proceedings were suspended pending the outcome of negotiations of sales. After a period of time, no major settlements resulted, so the Commission reinstituted the proceedings.

In 1987, in *RKO General, Inc. (KHJ-TV)* (1987), an administrative law judge found RKO unfit to hold a broadcast license and ordered RKO to sell the remaining licenses—for substantially less than full value. In 1988, the FCC approved the transfer of KHJ-TV to Disney Co., but did not rule on the "fitness" of RKO as a licensee. In a dissenting opinion in *RKO General, Inc.* (1988), Commissioner Dennis noted that failure to rule on "fitness" sends the wrong signal to station licensees. It took until 1991 for the last RKO property to be sold. In March of that year, the FCC approved the transfer of KFRC-AM, San Francisco, to South Jersey Radio, Inc. It was agreed that South Jersey would sell the station to Bedford Broadcasting for $8 million. RKO received slightly more than $4 million of the proceeds.

Program Format and Renewal Questions

The FCC has been confronted with a variety of petitions requesting that license renewals and transfers be denied on grounds that the station has changed format and no longer serves the audience it once did, such as *Citizens Committee to Preserve Voice of the Arts in Atlanta v. FCC, Citizens for Jazz on WRVR, Inc. v. FCC,* and *Save WEFM v. FCC.*

In *Citizens Committee to Save WEFM-FM v. FCC,* the court gave the Commission authority to consider a station's format in deciding whether license renewal or transfer would be in the public interest. In this case, the Commission decided that the format change issue should not be considered. The issue later reappeared and ultimately found its way to the Supreme Court.

Federal Communications Commission v. WNCN Listeners Guild (1981)
Justice White delivered the opinion of the Court.

☐   . . . The issue before us is whether there are circumstances in which the Commission must review past or anticipated changes in a station's entertainment programming when it rules on an application for renewal or transfer of a radio broadcast license. The Commission's present position is that it may rely on market forces to promote diversity in entertainment programming and thus serve the public interest.

This issue arose when, pursuant to its informal rulemaking authority, the Commission issued a "Policy Statement" concluding that the public interest is best served by promoting diversity in entertainment formats through market forces and competition among broadcasters and that a change in entertainment programming is therefore not a material factor that should be considered by the Commission in ruling on an application for license renewal or transfer. Respondents, a number of citizens groups interested in fostering and preserving particular entertainment formats, petitioned for review in the Court of Appeals for the District of Columbia

Circuit. That court held that the Commission's Policy Statement violated the Act. We reverse the decision of the Court of Appeals.

I

Beginning in 1970, in a series of cases involving license transfers, the Court of Appeals for the District of Columbia Circuit gradually developed a set of criteria for determining when the "public interest" standard requires the Commission to hold a hearing to review proposed changes in entertainment. Noting that the aim of the Act is to "secure the maximum benefits of radio to all people of the United States," . . . the Court of Appeals ruled in 1974 that preservation of a format [that] would otherwise disappear, although economically and technologically viable and preferred by a significant number of listeners, is generally in the public interest."

. . . In January 1976, the Commission responded to these decisions by undertaking an inquiry into its role in reviewing format changes . . .

Following public notice and comment, the Commission issued a Policy Statement pursuant to its rulemaking authority under the Act. The Commission concluded in the Policy Statement that review of format changes was not compelled by the language or history of the Act, would not advance the welfare of the radio-listening public, would pose substantial administrative problems, and would deter innovation in radio programming. In support of its position, the Commission quoted from FCC v. Sanders Brothers Radio Station, 309 U.S. 470, 475 (1940): "Congress intended to leave competition in the business of broadcasting where it found it, to permit a licensee . . . to survive or succumb according to his ability to make his programs attractive to the public." The Commission also emphasized that a broadcaster is not a common carrier and therefore should not be subjected to a burden similar to the common carrier's obligation to continue to provide service if abandonment of that service would conflict with public convenience or necessity.

The Commission also concluded that practical considerations as well as statutory interpretation supported its reluctance to regulate changes in formats. Such regulation would require the Commission to determine whether a change in format had occurred; to determine whether the prior format was "unique"; and to weigh the public detriment resulting from the abandonment of a unique format against the public benefit resulting from that change. . . .

Finally, the Commission explained why it believed that market forces were the best available means of producing diversity in entertainment formats. First, in large markets, competition among broadcasters already produced "an almost bewildering array of diversity" in entertainment formats. Second, format allocation by market forces accommodates listeners' desires for diversity within a given format and also produces a variety of formats. Third, the market is far more flexible than governmental regulation and responds more quickly to changing public tastes . . .

The Court of Appeals . . . held that the Commission's policy was contrary to the Act as construed and applied in the court's prior format decisions . . .

IV

Respondents contend that the Court of Appeals judgement should be affirmed because . . . the Policy Statement conflicts with the First Amendment rights of listeners to "receive suitable access to social, political, esthetic, moral and other ideas and experiences." . . . Although observing that the interests of the people as a whole were promoted by debate of public issues on the radio, we did not imply that the First Amendment grants individual listeners the right to have the Commission review the abandonment of their favorite entertainment programs. The Commission seeks to further the interests of the listening public as a whole by relying on market forces to promote diversity in radio entertainment formats and to satisfy the entertainment preferences of radio listeners. This policy does not conflict with the First Amendment.

Contrary to the judgement of the Court of Appeals, the Commission's Policy Statement is not inconsistent with the Act. It is also a constitutionally permissible means of implementing the public interest standard of the Act. Accordingly, the judgement of the Court of Appeals is reversed, and the case is remanded for further proceedings consistent with this opinion.[9]

Equal Employment Opportunity (EEO) Practices and Renewal

The FCC has concluded that discrimination on the basis of race, sex, color, religion, or national origin by broadcast stations is not in the public interest. Therefore, applicants for license renewal having five or more full-time employees must complete Form 396, an Equal Employment Opportunity Program, with the license renewal form (see Appendix 2). In addition, all stations are required to file an Annual Employment Report (Form 395-B) by May 31st of each year (see Appendix 2). Stations having fewer than five full-time employees do not complete the entire form. The Annual Employment Report provides the FCC with a profile of the station staff and is useful in determining EEO compliance.

The Commission periodically reviews broadcasters' EEO materials and reviews the entire record at the time of license renewal. If the FCC finds that a station's records are below par, action may be taken in the form of forfeitures, short-term renewals, or nonrenewal. The early 1990s saw the Commission cracking down on EEO violations. In February 1991, WWGS and WCUP-FM in Tipton, Georgia, were granted short-term renewals and fined $10,000 for EEO violations. An investigation by the FCC did not reveal evidence of discrimination that required a hearing, but the

Commission did find a record of inadequate EEO efforts. Although the stations did attract and hire a few minority employees during the license term, the licensee's overall efforts in minority recruitment were inadequate.[10]

Summary

In order to obtain a broadcast license, applicants must demonstrate that they meet legal, technical, financial, and character qualifications. They must also agree to adhere to EEO guidelines. When determining who will receive a broadcast license, the FCC also considers statements by applicants that detail how they will serve the public interest. Applicants must adhere to multiple and cross-ownership rules. Mutually exclusive applications are designated for a hearing to determine who will be awarded the license.

Broadcast licenses are granted for a limited, renewable term. Television station licenses are issued for five years and radio licenses are issued for a 7-year term. A license may be revoked if licensees violate Commission rules or the terms of the license. Other options available to the FCC when dealing with rule offenders include short-term renewal and nonrenewal of licenses. Lesser offenses may result in fines.

Notes/References

1. 47 U.F.C. Sec. 308(b) (1989).
2. See *Character Qualifications in Broadcast Licensing,* 102 F.C.C.2d 1179, 59 R.R.2d 801 (1986).
3. FCC v. National Citizens Committee for Broadcasting, 436 U.S. 775 (1978).
4. 47 CFR., 73.3591.
5. Policy Statement on Comparative Broadcast Hearings, 1 F.C.C.2d 393 (1965).
6. 47 CFR 73.3594(4)(d)(1).
7. Hearst Radio Inc. (WBAL), 15 F.C.C. 1149, 6 R.R. 994 (1951).
8. Central Florida Enterprises, Inc. v. FCC, U.S. Ct.App. D.C. Cir., 683 F.2d 503, R.R.2d 1045 (1982), cert. denied 460 U.S. 1084 (1983).
9. Federal Communications Commission v. WNCN Listener's Guild, 450 U.S. 582 (1981).
10. "EEO Forfeitures and Short Term License Renewals Continue," *Haley, Bader & Potts Information Memorandum* 16 (February 14, 1991): 6.

Cases

Ashbacker Radio Corp. v. FCC, 326 U.S. 327, 66 S.Ct. 148, 90 L.Ed. 108 (1945)

Capital Cities/ABC, Inc., 66 R.R.2d 1146 (1989)

Central Florida Enterprises, Inc. v. FCC, 598 F.2d 37, 44 R.R.2d 345 (DC Cir., 1978)

Central Florida Enterprises, Inc. v. FCC, U.S. Ct.App. DC Cir., 683 F.2d 503, 51 R.R.2d 1045 (1982), cert. denied 460 U.S. 1084 (1983)

Citizens Committee to Preserve Voice of the Arts in Atlanta v. FCC, 141 U.S. Ct.App. DC 109, 436 F.2d 263 (DC Cir., 1970)

Citizens Committee to Save WEFM-FM v. FCC, 165 U.S. App. DC 185, 506 F.2d 246 (DC Cir., 1970)

Citizens Communications Center v. FCC, 447 F.2d 1201 (DC Cir., 1971)

Citizens for Jazz on WRVR, Inc. v. FCC, 755 F.2d 392, 59 R.R.2d 249 (DC Cir., 1985)

Committee to Save WEFM v. FCC, 808 F.2d 113, 61 R.R.2d 1444 (DC Cir., 1986)

Cowles Florida Broadcasting Inc., 60 F.C.C.2d 372, 37 R.R.2d 1487, 1555–56 (1976)

FCC v. National Citizen's Committee for Broadcasting, 436 U.S. 775 (1978)

Federal Communications Commission v. WNCN Listener's Guild, 450 U.S. 582 (1981)

Fidelity Television Inc. v. FCC, 515 F.2d 684, 32 R.R.2d 1607, rehearing denied 34 R.R.2d 419 (DC Cir., 1975), cert. denied 423 U.S. 926 (1975)

Greater Boston Television Corp. v. FCC, U.S. Ct.App., DC Cir., 444 F.2d 841 (1970), cert. denied 403 U.S. 923 (1971)

Hearst Radio Inc. (WBAL), 15 F.C.C. 1149, 6 R.R. 994 (1951)

In the Matter of WHDH Inc., 16 F.C.C. 1 (1969)

Multiple Ownership (12–12–12 Reconsideration), 100 F.C.C.2d 74, 75 R.R.2d 967 (1985)

Policy Research Group v. FCC, 807 F.2d 1038, 61 R.R.2d 1450 (DC Cir., 1986)

Policy Statement on Comparative Broadcast Hearings, 1 F.C.C.2d 393 (1965)

Policy Statement on Comparative Hearings Including Regular Renewal Applicants, 22 F.C.C.2d 424 (1970)

RKO v. Federal Communications Commission, U.S. Ct.App. DC Cir., 670 F.2d 215, 50 R.R.2d 821 (1981), cert. denied 457 U.S. 1119 (1982)

RKO General, Inc., 78 F.C.C.2d 1 (1980)

RKO General, Inc. (KHJ-TV), 63 R.R.2d 866 (A.L.J., 1987)

RKO General, Inc. (KHJ-TV), 3 F.C.C.Rcd. 5057, 65 R.R.2d 192 (1988)

Second Report and Order, Docket 18110, 50 F.C.C.2d 1046 (1975)

U.S. v. Storer, 351 U.S. 192 (1956)

5

□ □ □
□ □ □
□ □ □

Regulation of Broadcast Programming

Nothing in this Act shall be understood or construed to give the Commission the power of censorship over the radio communications or signals transmitted by any radio station, and no regulation or condition shall be promulgated or fixed hereby the Commission which shall interfere with the right of free speech by means of radio communication. [1]

Although the Communications Act prohibits outright censorship of broadcast programming by the FCC, this does not mean that broadcasters have escaped Commission action in this area. Indeed, as we read in Chapter 3, throughout the years the Commission has retained varying degrees of interest in the regulation of broadcast programming content. The Commission's concern stemmed from enforcement of the public interest standard. Based on this standard, policies were developed, including localism, network affiliation rules, "promise versus performance," and the Fairness Doctrine. The policy of "promise versus performance" called for the actual programming broadcast to be in line with what was stated on the FCC application. The policy was unevenly enforced and was ultimately eliminated in 1985. The FCC required stations to keep program logs and, as previously stated, at one point compelled stations to submit a "composite week" of program logs to the Commission during the license renewal process. One by one, many of these rules and policies disappeared, and Commission program regulation was returned to the original congressional mandate—to ensure that stations serve the public interest.

Development of Programming Policy

The Blue Book of 1946 marked the Commission's first serious attempt to regulate program content (see Chapter 3). Policies developed from this document shaped program regulation in various forms until the 1980s.

Ascertainment of Community Needs

Since broadcasters were charged with serving their community of license, it stood to reason that they should be familiar with the problems and needs affecting that community. Indeed, the FCC expected broadcasters to program *to* those needs. The policy of community ascertainment developed from this expectation. Although community service was always expected, the policy of formal ascertainment for commercial stations was instituted in 1971 in *Primer on Ascertainment of Community Problems*. Beginning in 1975, noncommercial stations were required to conduct formal ascertainment.

Formal ascertainment consisted of four major steps. First, broadcasters were required to conduct a survey of the general public in the community of license. The survey was to be designed to allow the broadcaster to determine the major issues and problems facing the community. Second, a survey of community leaders was to be conducted. The FCC provided guidelines that indicated that the leaders must come from areas such as business, education, religion, agriculture, etc. The bulk of the community leaders survey was to be conducted by station management—not the clerical staff or an outside firm. Next, the results of the surveys were to be analyzed and a list of ten major problems facing the community was to be generated. Initially, this list was to be submitted to the FCC, but later the list was to be placed in the station's public file. Finally, the station was expected to propose and actually broadcast programming designed to meet the needs and problems identified in the ascertainment process.

As one might expect, this process involved considerable personnel hours and paperwork. In 1981, the Commission began reducing the requirements of the formal ascertainment process. The general public and community leaders surveys were simplified and stations were required to generate a list of five to ten issues that the station covered during the course of the year. This list was to be kept in the public file. The FCC retained the right to question stations about the programming aired at license renewal. By 1984, formal ascertainment had been eliminated. However, due to *Federal Communications Commission, Deregulation of Radio* and *Deregulation of Commercial Television*, a variation on the significant issues list remained in the form of the quarterly programs/issues list.

The Quarterly Programs/Issues List

When formal ascertainment procedures were eliminated, stations were required to identify five to ten issues of importance to their communities and place this list in the public file. Stations were also expected to provide examples of programming broadcasts that addressed those issues. This policy evolved into the present requirement, which calls for broadcasters to prepare quarterly lists of community issues and to show how those issues were addressed on the air (Figure 5.1). There is no minimum or maximum number of issues to be addressed. In *Deregulation of Radio*, the FCC did suggest, however, that stations identifying a minimum of five issues would probably be in compliance with the spirit of the rule.

Each quarterly list must identify the issue and include the program title, a narrative description of the program, the program's length, and time and date of airing. The programming can be almost any kind of nonentertainment program, including public service announcements. The programs need not be locally produced, but they must deal with issues of importance to the local community.

The quarterly lists must be placed in the public inspection file by the tenth of the month following the end of the quarter. In other words, the lists must be in the file by January 10th, April 10th, July 10th, and October 10th of each year. The quarterly reports are extremely important and may be used by the FCC at license renewal to determine whether the station has operated in the public interest. In February 1991, the Commission sanctioned the Arkansas Educational Television Commission for failure to place an issues/programs list in its public file on a quarterly basis. The FCC noted that failure to place the list in the public file is not simply a record-keeping error, but a major part of the license renewal process.

While 5 issues are listed in this example, stations should place all issues given significant treatment in their public file.

Issue	Title	Description	Time	Date	Duration
Poor Roads	Five part series following evening newscast	The series documents state of local and state highways and what has been planned to improve them	6:24 PM	M-F 2/1-2/4	Four minutes per segment
	"The Mayor's Hotline"	A call-in program featuring the mayor Viewers discuss the issue with the mayor.	12:30 PM	Friday 2/12	15:00
Aids Awareness	"Healthline"	Doctors and Health officials discuss the issue on camera.	9:30PM	Sunday 3/19	30:00
Military Base Closings locally	"Say Goodnight..."	A documentary on the effects of base closing on the local economy.	7:30 PM	Tuesday 3/22	30:00
Local police community/ relations.	"In-Focus"	A discussion with police and community leaders	10:00AM	Sunday 3/19	30:00
Local enconomic development	"In Focus"	Conversation with city planners and developers about downtown revitalization project.	10:00AM	Sunday 3/36	30:00

Figure 5.1 Sample quarterly issues/programs list.

Control of Political Programming

As was discussed in Chapter 3, Section 315 of the Communications Act affords candidates for public office equal opportunities in the use of broadcast facilities.

(a) If any licensee shall permit any person who is a legally qualified candidate for any public office to use a broadcasting station, he shall afford equal opportunities to all other such candidates for that office in the use of such broadcasting station: *provided*, that such licensee shall now have power of censorship over the material broadcast under the provisions of this section. No obligation is imposed under this subsection upon any licensee to allow the use of its station by any such candidate. Appearance by a legally qualified candidate on any—
   (1) Bona fide newscast,
   (2) Bona fide news interview,
   (3) Bona fide news documentary (if the appearance of the candidate is incidental to the presentation of the subject or subjects covered by the news documentary), or
   (4) On-the-spot coverage of bona fide news events (included but not limited to political conventions and activities incidental thereto),
   shall not be deemed to be the use of a broadcasting station within the meaning of this subsection. Nothing in the foregoing sentence shall be construed as relieving broadcasters, in connection with the presentation of newscasts, news interviews, news documentaries, and on-the-spot coverage of news events, from the obligation imposed upon them under this Act to operate in the public interest and to afford reasonable opportunity for the discussion of conflicting views on issues of public importance.

(b) The charges made for the use of any broadcast station by any person who is a legally qualified candidate for any public office in connection with his campaign for nomination for election, or election, to such office shall not exceed—
   (1) During the 45 days preceding the date of a primary or primary runoff election and during the 60 days preceding the date of a general or special election in which such a person is a candidate, the lowest unit charge of the station for the same class and amount of time for the same period; and
   (2) At any other time, the charges made for comparable use of such station by other users thereof.

(c) For the purposes of this section:
   (1) The term "broadcasting station" includes a community antenna television system.

(2) The terms "licensee" and "station licensee" when used with respect to a community antenna television system, mean the operator of such system.

(d) The Commission shall prescribe appropriate rules and regulations to carry out the provisions of this section.[3]

Who Is a Legally Qualified Candidate?

Section 315 of the Communications Act only applies to legally qualified candidates for public office. Section 73.1940 of the FCC rules defines a legally qualified candidate as

... [A]ny person who:
(i) has publicly announced his or her intention to run for nomination or office;
(ii) is qualified under the applicable local, state or federal law to hold the office for which he or she is a candidate; and,
(iii) has met the qualifications set forth in either subparagraphs (2), (3) or (4), below. ...

(2) A person seeking election to any public office including that of President or Vice President of the United States, or nomination for any public office except that of President or Vice President, by means of a primary, general or special election, shall be considered a legally qualified candidate if, in addition to meeting the criteria set forth in subparagraph (1) above, that person:
(i) has qualified for a place on the ballot, or
(ii) has publicly committed himself or herself to seeking election by the write-in method and is eligible under applicable law to be voted for by sticker, by writing in his or her name on the ballot or by other method, and makes a substantial showing that he or she is a bona fide candidate for nomination or office. Persons seeking election to the office of President or Vice President of the United States shall, for the purposes of the Communications Act and the Rules thereunder, be considered legally qualified candidates only in those states or territories (or the District of Columbia) in which they have met the requirements set forth in paragraph (a)(1) and (2) of this Rule: Except, that any such person who has met the requirements set forth in paragraph (a)(1) and (2) in at least 10 states (or nine and the District of Columbia) shall be considered a legally qualified candidate for election in all states, territories and the District of Columbia for purposes of this Act.

(3) A person seeking nomination to any public office, except that of President or Vice President of the United States, by means of a convention, caucus

or similar procedure, shall be considered a legally qualified candidate if, in addition to meeting the requirements set forth in paragraph (a)(1) above, that person makes a substantial showing that he or she is a bona fide candidate for such nomination: Except, that no person shall be considered a legally qualified candidate for nomination by the means set forth in this paragraph prior to 90 days before the beginning of the convention, caucus or similar procedure in which he or she seeks nomination.

(4) A person seeking nomination for the office of President or Vice President of the United States shall, for the purposes of the Communications Act and the rules thereunder, be considered a legally qualified candidate only in those states or territories (or the District of Columbia) in which, in addition to meeting the requirements set forth in paragraph (a)(1) above.

   (i) he or she, or proposed delegates on his or her behalf, have qualified for the primary or Presidential preference ballot in that state, territory or the District of Columbia, or

   (ii) he or she has made a substantial showing of bona fide candidacy for such nomination in that state, territory or the District of Columbia; except that any such person meeting the requirements set forth in paragraphs (a)(1) and (4) in at least ten states (or nine and the District of Columbia) shall be considered a legally qualified candidate for nomination in all states, territories and the District of Columbia for purposes of this Act.[4]

Retention of Political Broadcast Information

(d) See §§73.3526 and 73.3527. Records, inspection. Every licensee shall keep and permit public inspection of a complete record (political file) of all requests for broadcast time made by or on behalf of candidates for public office.[5]

Time Limitations for Equal Opportunities Requests

(e) Time of Request. A request for equal opportunities must be submitted to the licensee within one week of the day on which the first prior use giving rise to the right of equal opportunities occurred: provided, however, that where the person was not a candidate at the time of such first prior use, he shall submit his request within one week of the first subsequent use after he has become a legally qualified candidate for the office in question.

(f) Burden of Proof. A candidate requesting equal opportunities of the licensee, or complaining of noncompliance to the Commission shall have the burden of proving that he and his opponent are legally qualified candidates for the same public office.[6]

Applications of Section 315

Section 315 of the Communications Act has been modified a number of times throughout the years. Prior to 1959, stations were liable for remarks made on the air by candidates, even though broadcasters were forbidden from censoring potentially litigious remarks. In *Farmers Educational Cooperative Union v. WDAY Inc.* (1959) the Supreme Court ruled in a 5–4 decision that broadcasters could not be held liable in defamation suits brought as a result of candidates' remarks. It should be noted that candidates themselves are still liable for potentially defamatory statements.

Another content-related problem of Section 315 occurred in 1984 when *Hustler* magazine publisher Larry Flynt announced that he would run for President. Flynt said that he would take advantage of his status as a candidate and the Commission's "no censorship" provision by running sexually explicit "announcements" over broadcast television. Legislation was introduced in Congress that was designed to allow broadcasters to refuse to air pornographic materials under Section 315. The FCC indicated that the "no censorship" clause of Section 315 would not apply to obscene or indecent political announcements. In an unrelated incident, Flynt was shot and subsequently withdrew as a presidential candidate before the FCC had to deal with the question of sexually explicit political broadcasts.

The Problem of Debates

In 1960, when presidential candidates Richard Nixon and John F. Kennedy planned a series of broadcast debates, Congress suspended Section 315. This questionable application of policy occurred so that the debate would be limited to appearances by Nixon and Kennedy—freezing out any minority candidates. While this suspension made the debates practical, the move certainly questioned the spirit of Section 315 altogether. One might ask that if Section 315 could be suspended, why was it necessary in the first place?

In 1962 the Commission decided that debates by major candidates sponsored by the news media did not qualify as a "bona fide news event" and was, therefore, subject to Section 315.[7] There were no presidential debates broadcast again until 1976. In that year, the FCC ruled that broadcast coverage of a debate by presidential candidates was a news event under Section 315 if it was broadcast live in its entirety and not sponsored or controlled by the broadcaster or the candidate. The Carter-Ford debates were sponsored by the League of Women Voters and were covered live by the networks.

In 1980, the third-party candidacy of John Anderson complicated the broadcast debate process. The League of Women Voters planned a series of debates that included Republican nominee Ronald Reagan, incumbent Jimmy Carter, and challenger Anderson. Carter refused to debate with Anderson. The networks covered the event as a news event. Later, the League sponsored a broadcast debate between Carter and Reagan. The League withdrew its sponsorship of presidential debates in 1988, citing demands by candidates for too much control of the debate.

This move was of little importance to the future of presidential debates, however, for in 1983, the FCC reversed its policy and allowed broadcasters to sponsor debates between political candidates without the obligation of providing free time to all qualified candidates. In petitions of *Henry Geller et. al.,*, the Commission noted that broadcaster-sponsored debates may benefit the public by increasing the number of these events.

Other changes in the FCC policy on debates and political programs included a redefintion of the phrase "on-the-spot" news contained in Section 315. This was originally interpreted as "live" coverage. In *United Church of Christ v. FCC* (1978) the FCC allowed a broadcaster to tape a political program and air it within 24 hours. This rule was relaxed further in the *Geller* case when the Commission indicated that broadcasters may use their judgment in deciding how long to hold a taped political program before airing it.

Use by Supporters—The Zapple Doctrine

The Zapple Doctrine (or quasi-equal opportunities), which was the result of the *Nicholas Zapple* decision, requires a station that makes time available to supporters or to a spokesperson for a candidate to make time available to supporters or a spokesperson for the opposing candidate.

As discussed in Chapter 3, the Zapple Doctrine does not apply outside campaign periods, nor does it apply to minor candidates. It applies to major party candidates only.

Nonpolitical Appearance by Candidates

It is generally accepted that all appearaces by political candidates fall within the definition of "use" in Section 315. Local air personalities running for office must usually leave the air during their candidacy or risk providing regular "free time" to their opponent. When Ronald Reagan ran for the Republican nomination in 1976, the Broadcast Bureau ruled in *Adrian Weiss* that stations showing old Reagan films were obligated to provide as much time to his opponent—Gerald Ford.

In 1985, California journalist William H. Branch, who was running for office, challenged the validity of applying Section 315 each time he appeared on the air reporting a news story. Branch argued that the equal time provision should not be applied each time he appeared on camera, because he was reporting a news story and not making a political announcement. He contended that his appearance was part of a "bona fide news event" as defined in Section 315.

In *Branch v. Federal Communications Commission* (1987) Judge Bork, writing on behalf of the Court of Appeals for the District of Columbia noted that,

☐ When a broadcaster's employees are being sent out to cover a news story involving other persons, therefore, the "bona fide news event" is the activity engaged in by those other persons, not the work done by the employees covering the event . . . There is nothing at all "newsworthy" about the work being done by the broadcaster's own employees, regardless of whether any of those employees happens also to be a candidate for public office.[8]

Lowest Unit Rate

Under Section 315(b), broadcasters are required to charge political advertisers no more than the stations "most favored commercial advertisers" would be charged for comparable time. This means that political advertisers may not be charged more than the lowest rate charged for the same class and amount of time for the same period. Recently, the FCC held that preemptible spots and runs of schedule spots constitute a separate class of time for purposes of Section 315. The lowest unit rate is in effect 45 days preceding a primary or primary runoff election and 60 days preceding a general or special election. Recently, the FCC has stepped up enforcement of this provision. In May 1990, the Commission levied a record $10,000 fine against WXIN-TV in Indianapolis for repeated violations of the lowest unit charge requirements.

The "comparable use" rule applies when the lowest unit rate rule does not. This rule provides that charges for use of a station by a legally qualified candidate may not exceed charges made for comparable use of the station by other advertisers.

Reasonable Access

Section 312(a)(7) of the Communications Act requires broadcasters to provide "reasonable access to or to permit purchase of reasonable amounts of time" by candidates for federal elective office. Although Section 312(a)(7) applies only to federal candidates, a 1971 FCC ruling states that broadcasters have a public interest obligation to make some time available to non-federal candidates.[9]

CBS Inc. v. FCC (1981)

In 1981, the issue of reasonable access reached the Supreme Court in *CBS Inc. v. FCC*. In December 1979, the Carter-Mondale campaign asked to purchase 30 minutes of air time on the three major television networks. CBS offered to sell 10 minutes of time, in 5-minute segments. ABC said that it would not sell political time until January and NBC denied the request completely. The Carter campaign committee complained to the FCC, which found the network owned and operated stations (O&Os) in violation of Section 312(a)(7). The court of appeals and the Supreme Court agreed. Chief Justice Burger delivered the opinion of the Court.

☐   Broadcasters are free to deny the sale of air time prior to the commencement of a campaign, but once a campaign has begun, they must give reasonable and good faith attention to access requests from "legally qualified candidates" for federal elective office. Such requests must be considered on an individualized basis, and broadcasters are required to tailor their responses to accommodate, as much as reasonably possible, a candidate's stated purposes in seeking air time.

. . . The Commission has concluded that, as a threshold matter, it will independently determine whether a campaign has begun and the obligations imposed by § 312(a)(7) have attached. . . . Petitioners assert that, in undertaking such a task, the Commission becomes improperly involved in the electoral process and seriously impairs broadcaster discretion.

However, petitioners fail to recognize that the Commission does not set the starting date for a campaign. Rather, on review of a complaint alleging denial of "reasonable access," it examines objective evidence to find whether the campaign has already commenced . . .

. . . [P]etitioners assert that § 312(a)(7) as implemented by the Commission violates the First Amendment rights of broadcasters by unduly circumscribing their editorial discretion. . . . Petitioners are correct that the Court has never approved a *general* right of access to the media . . . Nor do we do so today . . .

Nevertheless, petitioners ABC and NBC refused to sell the Carter-Mondale Presidential Committee any time counteroffers, but adopted "blanket" policies refusing access despite the admonition against such an approach. . . . Likewise, petitioner CBS, while not barring access completely, had an across-the-board policy of selling only 5-minute spots.

. . . Section 312(a)(7) represents an effort by Congress to assure [sic] that an important resource—the statutory right of access, as defined by the Commission and applied in these cases, properly balances the First Amendment rights of federal candidates, the public and broadcasters.[10]

Policies Carried Over from the Fairness Doctrine

The Fairness Doctrine is no longer in effect at this writing; however, the FCC still enforces the political editorial and personal attack rules.

The Political Editorializing Rule — Section 73.1930

The political editorializing rule requires broadcasters to notify legally qualified candidates if they editorialize against the candidate. The broadcaster must provide a transcript of the editorial and offer reply time. If the broadcaster endorses a candidate, the notification and offer of reply time must be sent to all other legally qualified candidates for that office. If a broadcaster opposes a candidate, notification and an offer of reply time must be afforded to that candidate.

The broadcaster has 24 hours to notify the candidate, unless the editorial occurs within 72 hours of the election. If that is the case, the candidate must be given notice far enough in advance, so that the candidate has sufficient time to respond.

The Personal Attack Rules — Section 73.1920

Originally, the personal attack rules were an outgrowth of the *Red Lion* case (see Chapter 3). If a broadcaster attacks the character, honesty, integrity, or similar personal qualities of an identifiable person or group, during the presentation of a controversial issue of public importance, the rules take effect. Within one week of the broadcast the station must:

notify the person of the date, time, and identification of the broadcast
provide a script or tape (or an accurate summary, if a script or tape is not available) of the attack
offer the individual or group attacked a reasonable opportunity to respond over the licensee's facilities

The personal attack rules do not apply to the following situations and categories:

personal attacks on foreign groups or foreign public figures
personal attacks that occur during broadcast use by legally qualified candidates
personal attacks made by legally qualified candidates or their spokespersons in broadcasts deemed not to be "use" under Section 315
bona fide newscasts, news interviews, and on-the-spot coverage of news events, including commentary or analysis

The Zapple Doctrine and Fairness

Also carried over from the Fairness Doctrine is the Zapple Doctrine. As noted earlier in this chapter, the Zapple Doctrine states that stations giving or selling time to supporters or spokespersons of candidates during election campaigns must provide comparable time to supporters or spokespersons for an opponent. Although the Zapple Doctrine applies to supporters of political candidates, it emerged as part of the Fairness Doctrine.

Indecent, Suggestive, or Offensive Material

Obscenity versus Indecency

Title 18, Section 1464 of the Federal Criminal Code prohibits broadcasting "obscene, indecent or profane language" and provides punishments of $10,000 in fines, 2 years imprisonment, or both for violation of the code. Recall that Section 326 of the Communications Act prohibits censorship by the FCC. These contradictory laws help make FCC regulation of obscenity and indecency a difficult area. As the adage goes, one person's pornography is another person's art, as witnessed by the controversy surrounding the exhibition of Robert Mapplethorpe's photographs in 1990.

What can be said with certainty is that obscene materials have no First Amendment protection. Obscenity is a legal term applied by a court. For material to be declared obscene, it must meet criteria set forth in *Miller v. California* (1973). In this case, the Supreme Court developed what has become known as the LAPS test. LAPS is an acronym for literary, artistic, political, or scientific value—the standards that emerged under *Miller* for determining obscenity. Under the LAPS test a work may be judged obscene if the average person, applying contemporary community standards, finds that the work, when taken as a whole, appeals to prurient interest and describes, in a patently offensive way, sexual conduct specifically defined by applicable state law, and lacks serious literary, artistic, political, or scientific value. Needless to say, this test is very difficult to apply.

In *In the Matter of Enforcement of Prohibitions Against Broadcast Obscenity and Indecency*, "indecency" has been defined by the FCC to include "language that describes, in terms patently offensive as measured by contemporary community standards for the broadcast medium, sexual or excretory activities and organs."[11] Indecency, while not devoid of First Amendment protection, has been determined by the FCC to be unsuitable for the broadcast media. Cable and print media are not subjected to this form of content regulation.

FCC Authority in Regulating Obscene, Indecent, and Offensive Material

Originally, the prohibition against broadcasting obscene, indecent, or profane matter was contained in the Communications Act. In 1948, it was removed from the act and made a part of the U.S. Criminal Code. Sections 312 and 503 of the Communications Act give the FCC the authority to order a broadcaster to cease and desist from broadcasting indecent or obscene material. The Commission may also impose fines of up to $2000 per day, per offense, and may revoke or deny renewal of the station license. These punishments are in addition to the sanctions provided in Section 1464 of the Criminal Code.

Development of FCC Policy

In 1964, the FCC responded to complaints received during license renewal against several stations owned by the Pacifica Foundation in *In re Pacifica Foundation*. The subjects of the complaints included the broadcast of poetry readings by Lawrence Ferlinghetti, a broadcast of Edward Albee's *The Zoo Story*, and a program entitled "Live and Let Live," during which eight homosexuals discussed their attitudes and problems. The Commission upheld the license renewal of the Pacifica stations noting,

☐ We recognize that as shown by the complaints here, such provocative programming as here involved may offend some listeners. But this does not mean that those offended have the right, through the Commission's licensing power, to rule such programming off the airwaves. Were this the case, only the wholly inoffensive, the bland, could gain access to the radio microphone or camera.[12]

In *Pacifica I* (1964), the FCC came down squarely on the side of freedom of expression. The remedy for those offended was to turn off the program. Six years later the Commission took a different view.

In 1970, WUHY-FM, a noncommercial station, broadcast a taped interview with Jerry Garcia, guitarist and singer for the cult rock group, the Grateful Dead. Garcia was joined by an individual known only as "Crazy Max." Garcia discussed music, politics, philosophy, and presented his opinions on the state of society. Crazy Max warned that computers would soon take over society. Throughout the interview, Garcia used numerous expletives. More specifically, his comments were frequently interspersed with the words "fuck" and "shit," used as adjectives or simply as stand-alone introductions to a phrase.

In response to complaints to the FCC, WUHY argued that the Garcia interview dealt with important topics of the day and since the program was designed to reach an "underground" audience, Garcia's language was acceptable. The Commission disagreed.

☐ **Eastern Educational Radio (WUHY-FM) (1970)**

The issue in this case is not whether WUHY-FM may present the views of Mr. Garcia or "Crazy Max" on ecology, society, computers and so on. Clearly that decision is a matter solely within the judgement of the licensee. . . . Further we stress, as we have before, the licensee's right to present provocative or unpopular programming which may offend some listeners. . . . Rather the narrow issue is whether the licensee may present previously taped interview or talk shows where the persons intersperse or begin their speech with expressions like, "Shit, man . . . ," ". . . and shit like that," or ". . . 900 fucking times," etc. . . . [I]f WUHY can broadcast an interview with Mr. Garcia where he begins sentences with "Shit, man" or uses "fucking" before word after word, just because he talks that way, so can any other person on radio. Newscasters or disc jockeys could use the same expressions, as could other persons . . . on the ground that that is the way they talk and it adds flavor and emphasis to their speech. But the consequences of any such widespread practice would be to undermine the usefulness of radio to millions of others. For, these expressions are patently offensive to millions of listeners.[13]

The FCC fined WUHY, a student-run noncommercial station, $100 and told them not to do it again.

In the early 1970s, a radio format developed that has been dubbed "topless radio." These programs were usually midday, call-in shows targeted to women. The topics discussed were sexual in nature. The host, though tame by today's "shock jock" standards, tended to include sexual innuendos in his conversations with callers. The FCC ruled in *Sonderling Broadcasting Corp. (WGLD-FM)* (1973) that WGLD-FM in Oak Park, Illinois, had violated both the obscenity and indecency standards of Section 1424. The program in question was the February 23 broadcast of "Femme Forum," the topic of which was oral sex. The FCC stressed that it was not the topic itself that was offensive, but rather the way in which the topic was presented. The FCC objected to the program host's "leering innuendo" when discussing sexual topics. The Commission added that "Gresham's Law" is at work in this case.

☐ If broadcasters can engage in commercial exploitation of obscene or indecent material . . . an increasing number will do so for competive reasons, with spiraling adverse effects upon millions of listeners.[14]

Sonderling was fined $2000 for the offense.

Channeling Offensive Material

Another theme that reoccurs in the Commission's indecency policy is that of keeping indecent or offensive material away from children who may be in the audience. In *WUHY* and *Sonderling*, the Commission touched on the pervasive nature of broadcast media. Unlike print, which is selected by the reader, the FCC and others worried that radio and television may intrude uninvited into the home, bringing with it unwanted offensive material, at best. At its worst, it may even be harmful to children in the audience.

Rationalizing this view in light of the First Amendment proved perplexing. After all, unless a broadcast was determined to be obscene under the *Miller* standard, it retained a certain amount of First Amendment protection. Obscenity cases are rare in broadcasting. It is doubtful that *Sonderling* would be declared obscene today. The FCC did find some assistance in dealing with the problem of keeping broadcast indecency away from children in the audience while protecting the First Amendment rights of those wishing to receive such programs. In *Young v. American Mini Theatres Inc.* (1976) the Supreme Court held that cities could zone sexually explicit movie theaters and bookstores and confine them to specific parts of town. Provided an ordinance was carefully drawn, zoning itself would not run afoul of the First Amendment. The FCC used a similar tactic in suggesting that stations "channel" potentially indecent programs to portions of the broadcast day when children were less likely to be in the audience.

FCC v. Pacifica Foundation (1978)

This case evolved as a result of the broadcast by noncommercial WBAI, New York, of a 12-minute monologue by humorist George Carlin. The monologue, entitled "Filthy Words," was taken from a Carlin record album called "Occupation: Foole." In the monologue, Carlin satirizes the way we use words and how we give them meaning. He includes his version of the "seven words you can never say on TV." The "heavy seven," as he calls them, are *shit, piss, fuck, cunt, cocksucker, motherfucker,* and *tits.* Carlin says in the monologue, "These are the words that will curve your spine, grow hair on your hands and, God help us, bring peace without honor." He then discussed each word individually in a humorous, yet satiric manner. The broadcast was part of an overall program aired on WBAI on the uses of language in society. Other speakers were part of the program and a warning was broadcast before the Carlin routine aired at around 2:00 P.M.

A man and his young son were driving in their car and inadvertently tuned in to the broadcast. The listener was offended and complained to the FCC. His was the only complaint about the broadcast.

The FCC ruled that Pacifica, the owner of WBAI, was subject to administrative sanction, but imposed no formal sanction. The Commission placed the order in a file in the event other complaints were received.

The FCC cited four reasons for treating broadcasting differently from other media:

1. access by unsupervised children
2. since radio receivers are in the home, privacy interests are entitled to extra deference
3. unconsenting adults may tune in without warning that offensive language is being used
4. scarcity of sepctrum space requires the government to license in the public interest

The Court of Appeals for the District of Columbia overturned the FCC decision, but the Supreme Court upheld the Commission's position and opened the door to the concept of "channeling" broadcast programming.

☐ The Commission characterized the language used in the Carlin monologue as "patently offensive," though not necessarily obscene, and expressed the opinion that it should be regulated by principles analogous to those found in the law of nuisance where the "law generally speaks to *channeling* behavior more than actually prohibiting it. . . . [T]he concept of 'indecent' is intimately connected with the exposure of children to language that describes, in terms patently offensive as measured by contemporary community standards for the broadcast medium, sexual or excretory activities and organs at times of the day when there is reasonable risk that children may be in the audience." 56 FCC 2d, at 98. . . .

. . . It is appropriate . . . to emphasize the narrowness of our holding. This case does not involve a two-way radio conversation between a cab driver and a dispatcher, or a telecast of an Elizabethan comedy. We have not decided that an occasional expletive in either setting would justify any sanction or, indeed, that this broadcast would justify criminal prosecution. The Commission's decision rested entirely on a nuisance rationale under which context is all important. . . . The time of day was emphasized by the Commission. The content of the program in which the language is used will also affect the composition of the audience, . . . and differences between radio, television and perhaps closed-circuit transmissions may also be relevant. As Mr. Justice Sutherland wrote, a "nuisance may merely be the right thing in the wrong place—like a pig in the parlor instead of the barnyard." . . . We simply hold that when the Commission finds that a pig has entered the parlor, the exercise of its regulatory power does not depend on proof that the pig is obscene.[15]

Keep in mind that Section 326 of the Communications Act prohibits censorship by the FCC. In *Pacifica*, channeling indecent material does not represent censorship in the eyes of the Supreme Court, since the material may still be broadcast and receives some First Amendment protection.

Commission Policy After Pacifica II

Between 1975 and 1987, the FCC found no other broadcasters guilty of indecent programming. During this time, the FCC tried to assure broadcasters that it would only be concerned with the "seven dirty words," as defined by Carlin, and, then, only if they were used repeatedly. In 1987, sparked by complaints from the public, the FCC embarked upon a new indecency policy.

The 1987 Revised Indecency Standard

In 1987, the Commission took action against three broadcast stations and one amateur radio facility for indecency in *Pacifica Foundation Inc., The Regents of the University of California*, and *Infinity Broadcasting Corp. of Pennsylvania*. The broadcast stations were WYSP-FM in Philadelphia, Pacifica's KPFK-FM in Los Angeles, and the University of California at Santa Barbara's KCSB-FM.

KFPK had broadcast excerpts from the play *Jerker*, which consists of telephone conversations of two homosexuals dying of AIDS. The offensive programming that aired on KFPK included such phrases as "suck ass," "suck my balls," and "drink piss from his cock."

The complaint against the University of California station was based on offensive lyrics in a song by the Pork Dukes called "Making Bacon." The lyrics included, "Come here baby; make it quick; kneel down there and suck on my dick."

The offensive material broadcast on WYSP involved "shock jock" Howard Stern. The Commission noted that Stern's program regularly dwelled on sexual and excretory matters in a way that was patently offensive as measured by contemporary community standards for the broadcast medium. Specifically, the Commission was concerned about expressions like "I didn't see any penis on that sock" and "limp dick."

Because the indecency provisions of Section 1464 had been applied for the first time in many years, all of the above stations escaped with only a warning, but a major Commission policy change began to take shape. In 1987, the FCC issued a document entitled *New Indecency Enforcement Standards to Be Applied to All Broadcast and Amateur Radio Licensees* 2 FCCRcd. 2726 (1987).

The revised standard no longer limited itself to Carlin's seven dirty words. The Commission applied the broad definition of indeceny as approved by the Supreme Court in *Pacifica II*. Indecency was defined as "language or material that depicts or describes, in terms patently offensive as measured by contemporary community standards for the broadcast medium, sexual or excretory activities or organs."[16]

Responding to pressure from broadcasters and other organizations in November 1987, the Commission created a "safe harbor" between midnight and 6 A.M. for the broadcast of programming that might otherwise be banned as indecent. The "safe harbor" was a variation on the "later evening day parts" concept espoused in *Pacifica*. Even during these hours, broadcasters were required to provide a warning that offensive material might be contained in a given program. Under the policy, indecent speech was to be channeled to day parts, when children were not likely to be listening or viewing. In December 1988, the FCC adopted a 24-hour ban on indecent programming shortly after Congress, led by North Carolina Senator Jesse Helms, passed a law requiring the FCC to act. The 24-hour ban was stayed by the Court of Appeals for the District of Columbia in January 1989. In spite of all this activity, only one enforcement action was taken. That action involved a fine against KZKC-TV in Kansas City for a May 26, 1987, prime time broadcast of the movie "Private Lessons."

Building Support for a Proposed 24-Hour Ban

In 1989, shortly after Alfred Sikes replaced Dennis Patrick as Chairman of the FCC, the Commission stepped up its indecency enforcement again. In August 1989, the FCC initiated action against three more radio stations for airing indecent programs. This time, the action involved "Morning Zoo" personalites at WFBQ in Indianapolis, WLUP in Chicago, and KSJO in San Jose. Chairman Sikes also asked the court of appeals to remand the stay of the 24-hour ban to the FCC so that the Commission could build a record supporting the ban.

In October 1989, the FCC fined WLLZ-FM in Detroit $2000 for the broadcast of an off-color song "Walk with an Erection." The song, a parody of the Bangles hit "Walk Like an Egyptian," contained lyrics like, "He puts Penthouse in his desk/He's got big muscles in his wrist/He holds his organ in his fist/He gives his pink dolphin a mighty twist . . . All the girls in the office they say 'Hard-on, hard-on, beg my pardon.'/Walk with an erection."[17]

In the fall of 1989, the FCC asked for comments from broadcasters to assist the agency in building support for the 24-hour ban of indecent programming. Not surprisingly, only one broadcaster, Bonneville International Corporation, submitted comments favorable to the proposal. The opposition to the total ban on indecent programming was led by a group of 17 media organizations, including the National Association of Broadcasters and the three major television networks. The group argued that the FCC's total ban failed to meet the constitutional test of the least restrictive means of advancing a compelling government interest.

In July of 1990, the FCC adopted a report recommending a 24-hour ban on indecent programs. The Commission concluded that prohibition of indecent broadcasts did not violate the First Amendment because it was "narrowly tailored." Chairman Sikes noted that indecent materials were available to those wishing to receive them, through means other than the broadcast medium. The FCC was concerned that the prevalence of children in the broadcast audience made the proposed ban feasible. The Commission concluded that children are in the broadcast audience for both radio and television at all times, both day and night. The FCC also concluded that channeling and technological devices attached to receivers were not effective in protecting these children from exposure to potentially harmful, indecent programming.

The modified enforcement policy provided stations with the opportunity to demonstrate that children are not present in the broadcast audience during the time potentially indecent programming is aired. When Infinity Broadcasting was fined $6000 for a December 1988 broadcast of the Howard Stern show, it vowed to fight the sanction. Infinity argued that the results of a Gallup study demonstrated that no children 12 and younger listen to the Stern show on an unsupervised basis.

Still, the FCC pressed for a 24-hour ban on indecency. The proposed ban continued to come under fire from a federal appeals court judge, as well as from the industry.

In April of 1991, the FCC and the U.S. Department of Justice entered a Memorandum of Understanding concerning the resolution of complaints about indecent or obscene programming. Under the agreement, the Justice Department and the FCC have independent jurisdiction over complaints involving the broadcast of allegedly obscene or indecent material. The Department of Justice indicated that it would forward all complaints to the FCC for consideration under FCC rules after evaluating each complaint to determine whether criminal action should be taken. The FCC will continue to process complaints it receives, but may refer complaints to the Justice Department for criminal prosecution.

Shortly after this agreement, the FCC took action against KCNA in Cave Junction, Oregon, and WVIC-FM in East Lansing, Michigan. KCNA was fined $4000 for material broadcast in two segments of the Guy Kemp Morning Show. The material in question included a taped phone argument between Kemp and former KCNA news director Michael Perry. Kemp used the word "fuck" six times, as well as "shit" and "bullshit." The same show featured a caller who twice said "fuck you," "mother-fucker," "ass wipe," and "dick shit." Kemp also told an off-color joke. Michael Perry filed the complaint with the FCC.

The East Lansing station was fined $2000 for a September 1989 portion of the "Michaels in the Morning" show. The issue centered around a news story about a man who lost a testicle in a hot tub drain while on his honeymoon. Callers were asked to provide headlines for the item. Suggestions included, "Drain Sucks Off Man" and "Man Falls Victim to Ball Sucker." The FCC found the remarks to be patently offensive.

The 24-Hour Ban Is Struck Down— The Safe Harbor Returns

In *Action for Children's Television v. FCC*, the U.S. court of appeals ruled that the proposed 24-hour ban on indecent programming was unconstitutional. In *Sable Communications v. FCC*, the FCC prohibition against the interstate trans-mission of indecent, but not obscene, "dial-a-porn" messages was struck down as unconstitutional. The Commission had promulgated dial-a-porn rules in response to a congressional amendment to Section 223(b) of the Communications Act that prohibited indecent as well as obscene telephone communications directed at people regardless of their age. The same fate awaited the 24-hour indecency ban. A three-judge panel unanimously ordered the FCC to establish a "safe harbor," permitting the broadcast of indecent material. The judges upheld the Commission's definition of indecency and left room for the FCC to regulate indecent material when there is a liklihood that children are present in the audience. The Commission is in the process of drafting rules that reflect the safe harbor ruling. Until such rules are developed, indecency is banned between the hours of 6 A.M. and 8 P.M.

Song Lyrics

Concern over the lyrics to popular songs has been a growing issue since the 1950s. The link between broadcasting and the music industry continues to draw broadcasters into the fray. When Elvis Presley first appeared on the "Ed Sullivan Show" in 1956, camera operators were told to refrain from showing Elvis' gyrating hips. A decade later, the Rolling Stones were required to sing "let's spend some *time* together" instead of "let's spend the *night* together" on another Sullivan show. Jim Morrison and the Doors were asked to delete the word "higher" from their 1967 hit "Light My Fire" when they appeared on the program. They didn't and never came back. The Doors were later to become the first rock group to be prosecuted for obscenity, as a result of a concert in Miami.

In the mid-70s, Rod Stewart's "Tonight's The Night" drew the ire of those fearful that the lyrics might nudge underage girls into having sex. Today, that same song can be heard on "lite rock" stations and background music services. In the early 80s,

Sheena Easton's "Sugarwalls" and Prince's "Little Red Corvette" spawned similar concerns. In 1985, the Parents Music Resource Center (PMRC), headed by Tipper Gore, lobbied for voluntary labeling of records containing sexually explicit or violent material. Many record companies began labeling their products. But in spite of the labels, the controversy continues. The music and performances of Madonna and 2 Live Crew remain controversial. At the heart of the matter is a balancing of the First Amendment right of free expression against the concern of potentially harmful material being made available to children.

In the early 1970s, the Commission became concerned with drug-oriented music aired on some radio stations. The Commission issued a notice that required broadcasters to be aware of the content of the music to be aired. Specifically, the FCC suggested broadcasters could prescreen material, monitor selections while they are being played, or consider and respond to complaints made by members of the public. In *Yale Broadcasting Co. v. FCC* (1973), the court ruled that the Commission's order did not violate the First Amendment. The court noted that in order for a licensee to serve the public interest, it must have knowledge of what it is broadcasting. The order did not prohibit stations from playing drug-oriented material *per se*, but stations were required to take reasonable measures to be aware that they had done so.

This list of examples is not exhaustive, but it serves to illustrate the symbiotic relationship between popular music and broadcasting. Radio and television programmers strive to provide audiences with the music they want to hear and performances that will garner viewers. Increasingly, however, the music contains lyrics that, while acceptable on records, may skirt the boundaries of indecency for broadcast matter. Indeed, the material of the rap group 2 Live Crew was found obscene by a Florida district court. The case outlines the parameters of the issue facing society.

☐ **Skyywalker Records Inc. v. Navarro (1990)**

Gonzalez, J.:

This is a case between two ancient enemies: Anything Goes and Enough Already.

Justice Oliver Wendell Holmes, Jr. observed in *Schenck v. United States*, 249 U.S. 47 (1919), that the First Amendment is not absolute and that it does not permit one to yell "Fire" in a crowded theater. Today, this court decides whether the First Amendment absolutely permits one to yell another "F" word anywhere in the community when combined with graphic sexual descriptions.

Two distinct and narrow issues are presented: whether the recording *As Nasty As They Wanna Be (Nasty)* is legally obscene; and second, whether the actions of the defendant Nicholas Navarro . . . as Sheriff of Broward County Florida, imposed an unconstitutional prior restraint upon the plaintiffs' right to free speech.

THE FACTS

The recording *As Nasty As They Wanna Be* was released to the public by 2 Live Crew in 1989. To date, public sales have totalled approximately 1.7 million copies. . . . 2 Live Crew has also produced a recording entitled *As Clean As They Wanna Be (Clean)* which has sold approximately 250,000 copies. . . . [I]t apparently contains the same music as *Nasty* but without the explicit sexual lyrics.

In mid-February 1990, the Broward County Sheriff's office began an investigation of the *Nasty* recording. The investigation began in response to complaints by South Florida residents.

Broward County Deputy Sheriff Mark Wichner was assigned to the case. On February 26, 1990, he traveled to Sound Warehouse . . . and purchased the *Nasty* recording. The tape was purchased from an open display rack marked "Rap Music," easily accessible to all of Sound Warehouse's customers regardless of age.

Deputy Wichner listened to the *Nasty* recording, had six of the eighteen songs transcribed, and prepared an affidavit detailing these facts requesting that the Broward County Circuit Court find probable cause that the *Nasty* recording was legally obscene. . . .

On March 9, Judge Grossman issued an order after reviewing the *Nasty* recording "in its entirety." The judge . . . found probable cause to believe this recording was obscene under section 847.011 of the Florida Statutes. . . .

The Broward County Sheriff's office received and copied the order and distributed it countywide to retail establishments that might be selling the *Nasty* recording. . . .

Thereafter, Deputy Wichner revisited the store where he had purchased the original recording plus another Sound Warehouse and a store called Uncle Sam's Records. On these visits, the deputy wore a jacket marked "Broward County Sheriff" and displayed his badge in plain view. He spoke with a manager in each of the three stores, provided them with a copy of Judge Grossman's order, and told them, in a friendly and conversational tone, that they should refrain from selling the *Nasty* recording. The managers were warned that further sales would result in arrest and if convicted, the penalty for selling to a minor was a felony, and a misdemeanor if sold to an adult. . . .

The Sheriff's office warnings were very effective. Within days, all retail stores in Broward County ceased offering the *Nasty* recording for sale. . . . Some stores continued to sell the *Clean* recording. *Nasty* was no longer sold, even by stores having a policy of specially marking the recording with a warning and of not selling it to minors.

On March 16, 1990, the plaintiffs filed this action in federal district court. On March 27, 1990, Sheriff Nicholas Navarro filed an *in rem* proceeding in Broward County Circuit Court against the *Nasty* recording seeking a judicial determination that it was obscene under state law.

This is . . . not a case about whether the group 2 Live Crew or any of its music is obscene. The third element of the *Miller* test focuses upon the social value of the particular work, not its creators. The fact that individuals of whom we approve hold objectionable ideas or that people of whom we do not approve hold worthy ideas does not affect judicial review of the value of the ideas themselves. . . .

Finally, this court's role is not to serve as a censor or an art or music critic. If the *Nasty* recording has serious literary, artistic, political, or scientific value, it is irrelevant that the work is not stylish, tasteful, or even popular.

The plaintiffs themselves testified that neither their music nor their lyrics were created to convey a political message.

The only witness testifying at trial that there was political content in the *Nasty* recording was Carlton Long, who was qualified as an expert on the culture of black Americans. This witness first stated that the recording was political because the 2 Live Crew, as a group of black Americans, used this medium to express themselves. While it is doubtless true that *Nasty* is a product of the group's background, including their heritage as black Americans, this fact does not convert whatever they say, or sing, into political speech . . .

In terms of science, Professor Long also suggested that there is cultural content in 2 Live Crew's recording which rises to the level of serious sociological value. According to this witness, white Americans "hear" the *Nasty* recording in a different way than black Americans because of their frames of reference. Long identifies three cultural devices evident in the work here: "call and response," "doing the dozens," and "boasting." The court finds none of these arguments persuasive.

The only examples of "call and response" in the *Nasty* recording are portions where males and females yell in repetitive verse, "Tastes Great— Less Filling" . . . The phrases alone have no significant artistic merit nor are they examples of black American culture . . . this is merely a phrase lifted from a beer commercial.

The device of "doing the dozens" is a word game composed of a series of insults escalating in their satirical content. The "boasting" device is a way for persons to overstate their virtues as sexual prowess.

While this court does not doubt that both "boasting" and "doing the dozens" is commonly found in the culture of black Americans, these devices are also found in other cultures. . . .

The plaintiffs stress that the *Nasty* recording has value as comedy and satire. Certainly, people can and do laugh at obscenity. The plaintiffs point to the audience reaction at trial when the subject recording was played in open court. The audience giggled initially, but the court observed that after the initial titillation, all fell silent. . . .

It cannot be reasonably argued that the violence, perversion, abuse of women, graphic depictions of all forms of sexual conduct, and microscopic descriptions of human genitalia contained on this recording are comedic art.

The *Nasty* recording is not comedy, but is first and foremost, music. . . .

. . . Musical works are obscene if they meet the *Miller* test . . . The focus of the *Nasty* recording is predominately on the lyrics. . . .

. . . 2 Live Crew has "borrowed" components called "riffs" from other artists. Taking the work in its entirety, the several riffs do not lift *Nasty* to the level of serious artistic work. Once the riffs are removed, all that remains is the rhythm and the explicit sexual lyrics which are without any redeeming social value.

Obscenity is not a required element for socially valuable "rap" or "hip-hop" music. 2 Live Crew proved this point by its creation of the *Clean* recording. . . .

. . . The recording *As Nasty As They Wanna Be*, taken as a whole, is legally obscene.[18]

The court also found the actions of the Broward County Sheriff's Department in threatening retail stores with arrest for selling the *Nasty* recording before the judgment to be an unconstitutional prior restraint. The court issued a permanent injunction against Sheriff Navarro and his agents, prohibiting future such action.

Audience Harm by Broadcast Programming

One of the earliest concerns over the direct harmful effects of broadcast programming is certainly the 1938 "War Of The Worlds" broadcast. Even though Orson Welles and the Mercury Theater actors issued a disclaimer before and during the broadcast, the realistic (for 1938) broadcast format caused many to believe that an invasion from Mars was real.

The pervasive nature of the broadcast media makes it impossible to accurately predict how messages will be interpreted by listeners and viewers. Advertisers strive to capture interest and attention. They hope to motivate individuals in the audience to purchase their products. Broadcast news has worked to combine credibility with an attractive format designed to hold the attention of the audience. Sometimes, these factors have unintended effects. Should the broadcaster be held legally responsible when members of the audience misinterpret messages and behave in an antisocial manner? The courts have ruled that broadcasters are rarely liable for such behavior. Only if broadcasters actively encourage harmful behavior are they to be blamed.

In *Weirum v. RKO General* (1975), the court found that a radio station promotion was responsible for causing a fatal accident. The station promotion offered a cash prize for the first listener to find the location of a disk jockey (DJ), who was driving to various points in a station vehicle. Two teenagers arrived at the correct location, but failed to win the prize because they were not the first on the scene. They followed the DJ to his next location, hoping to be the first to arrive. While speeding to the location on a crowded freeway, they caused a fatal accident. The court held that the station promoted reckless driving by requiring potential winners to hurry to the next location of the DJ.

In most other major cases, the broadcast media fared better. In *Olivia v. NBC* (1981) the California court of appeals dealt with a made-for-television movie, starring *The Exorcist's* Linda Blair. The program contained a scene depicting a broom handle rape in a state-run girls home. The plaintiff was the victim of a similar crime in real life, said to have been inspired by the movie. The court held that NBC had not met the "incitement" test. At no time did the network overtly suggest to viewers that they "copy" this crime.

In 1982, a segment on the *Tonight Show Starring Johnny Carson* spawned *DeFilippo v. NBC* (1982). A professional stunt man appeared on the program, explaining how certain apparently dangerous movie stunts were accomplished. Johnny Carson announced that following the commercial break, he would drop through a trap door with a noose around his neck. The man warned the audience that this was a dangerous stunt and not to try it at home. After the commercial break Carson did the stunt and emerged unscathed. Several hours after the broadcast, the plaintiff's 13-year-old son, Nicky, was found hanging in front of the television set, which was still tuned to WJAR-TV, the NBC affiliate.

Once again, the court ruled that no incitement had occurred, since no one else emulated the action and the program took action to prevent emulation by warning viewers not to try the stunt.

In *Zamora v. CBS*, a teenager named Ronny Zamora blamed television for having caused him to commit murder. Zamora claimed that TV incited him to duplicate atrocities he saw in TV programs. The district court did not buy the argument.

Similar rulings were reached in cases involving suicides and heavy metal music. In *McCollum v. CBS Inc.* (1988), the California Court of Appeals for the Second District held that the death of a 19-year-old who repeatedly listened to Ozzy Osbourne albums before taking his own life was not caused by the records. The boy had a history of alcohol abuse and other emotional problems. Even though the content of the songs on the Osbourne records emphasized death, suicide, and other antisocial activities, *incitement* was not present.

In a comparable case, *Vance v. Judas Priest* (1990), a Nevada district court held that subliminal messages and "back-mastered" lyrics on the album "Stained Glass," urging "do it," did not incite two teenaged boys to shoot themselves.

The court did note that subliminal messages, because they cannot be detected by the listener, have no First Amendment protection. The Nevada district court based the decision on the assumption that subliminal speech does not advance any purposes of free speech, there is a First Amendment right to be free from unwanted speech, and the listener's right of privacy outweighs the speaker's right of free speech. When a person is exposed to subliminal messages, that person is deprived of the constitutional right to choose which speech to listen to. The court added that hidden messages also violate the right to privacy.

Contests and Promotions

Broadcast stations regularly run contests in order to boost audiences. Station-sponsored contests are legal, as long as they are not fraudulent, are not broadcast only during ratings periods, and do not disturb the public safety.

Section 73.1216 of the FCC rules also regulates contests:

A licensee that broadcasts or advertises information about a contest it conducts shall fully and accurately disclose the material terms of the contest, and shall conduct the contest substantially as announced or advertised. No contest description shall be false, misleading or deceptive with respect to any material term.

For the purpose of this rule:

(a) A contest is a scheme in which a prize is offered or awarded, based upon chance, diligence, knowledge or skill, to members of the public.

(b) Material terms include those factors which define the operation of the contest and which affect participation therein. Although the material terms may vary widely depending upon the exact nature of the contest, they will generally include: how to enter or participate; eligibility restrictions; entry deadline dates; whether prizes can be won; when prizes can be won; the extent, nature and value of the prizes; basis for valuation of the prizes; time and means of selection of winners; and/or tie breaking procedures.[19]

Stations also schedule stunts and promotional events as audience-building and -retaining devices. While the FCC is lenient in allowing most stunts and promotions, stations should exercise care when these activities might cause adverse community action or result in public injury.

Hoaxes

While not technically a "promotion," a St. Louis radio station suffered a $25,000 fine as a result of the broadcast of a false nuclear attack. On January 29, 1991, KSHE-FM aired a phony announcement that the U.S. had come under nuclear attack. The broadcast was complete with the Emergency Broadcasting System (EBS) tone and sound effects of exploding bombs. The broadcast occurred in the midst of the Gulf War. The stunt evoked more than 100 calls to the station and complaints were filed to the FCC. KSHE's morning personality John Ulet said he initiated the false broadcast to demonstrate the seriousness of nuclear war.

The *KSHE* decision crossed the line into what FCC Mass Media Bureau and Enforcement Division Chief Chuck Kelly called a "War of the Worlds" situation. NAB Deputy General Counsel Barry Umansky noted,

> A station is responsible for all its on-air programming . . . At license renewal time, if there were to be a finding that the station's programming led to injuries or some development where the station was sued, it would constitute a major black mark against the station.[20]

In April 1991, the FCC began investigating KROQ-FM, Pasadena/Los Angeles, for the broadcast of a false murder confession on the station's morning drivetime show. The morning team at the Infinity station, Kevin Ryder and Gene (Bean) Baxter, had developed a bit called "Confess Your Crime." Listeners were encouraged to call the program and reveal personal "crimes" on the air. One of the callers claimed to have killed his girlfriend. The story was picked up by TV's *Unsolved Mysteries*, which aired a segment on October 19, 1990.

The "confessed killer" was actually Doug Roberts, another DJ working in Arizona—a friend of Ryder and Baxter. The hoax began to unravel after Roberts came to work for KROQ and the similarity between Roberts' voice and the "killer" was noticed. When Infinity began an internal investigation, the DJs admitted the hoax. Infinity suspended the DJs involved and KROQ-FM broadcast several apologies. The station also cooperated with police and made an offer of restitution. The FCC sent Infinity a letter to determine whether the company acted "responsibly and effectively" once it learned that the broadcast was a hoax.

In 1992 the FCC enacted a rule prohibiting the broadcast of hoaxes that may be harmful to the public.

Children's Television Programming

In the early days of television, local children's programs became a staple of the broadcast day. Indeed, the FCC expected broadcasters to program to the needs and interests of children, as stipulated in *Report and Statement of Policy re: Commission en banc Programming Inquiry*. Gradually, economic changes in the industry forced the demise of local children's programs and the task of children's programming fell on the networks. What emerged was a block of animated, made-for-TV series that aired primarily on Saturday mornings. Responding to pressure from groups like Action for Children's Television, in 1974 the FCC issued a policy statement as a result of *Children's Television Report and Policy Statement*, urging broadcasters to increase the amount of children's programming offered and to schedule it throughout the week. The FCC also suggested that this programming contain informational and educational material, in addition to pure entertainment. The Commission also expressed concern over the commercial practices used in existing programs. Of special concern was the concept of "host selling," where the cartoon character appears in commercials during the program.

In 1979, the Commission examined the effect of the 1974 Policy Statement and concluded in *Children's Television Programming and Advertising Practices (1979)* that the policy had little effect on children's programming in most areas. However, the FCC did not act until 1984. Then, the FCC, in keeping with the deregulatory spirit of the Reagan years, abandoned the 1974 Policy Statement, preferring to allow the marketplace to respond to children's needs. The Commission no longer expected broadcast stations to provide *any* children's programming. The FCC noted in *Children's Television Programming and Advertising Practices (1984)* that the emergence of new technologies (VCRs and cable television) would also help meet the programming needs of children. In *Action for Children's Television v. FCC* (1985), the Commission policy was upheld. Two years later, in *Action for Children's Television v. FCC* (1987), the court concluded that the FCC had failed to sufficiently justify its deregulatory approach in regard to commercial practices in children's television programs. The court remanded the case back to the Commission for further study. It is at this point that the FCC considered creating new rules for children's TV.[21]

After 3 years and a veto by outgoing President Reagan, Congress finally passed the Children's Television Act of 1990. The Commssion adopted rules implementing the act in April, 1991, and the rules went into effect on January 1, 1992.

The 1991 Children's Television Rules

The 1991 Children's Television Rules limit commercial time in children's programming to 10.5 minutes per hour on weekends and 12 minutes per hour on weekdays. These rules apply to programs originally produced and broadcast primarily for persons 12 years of age and younger. The rules also apply to cable television.

Commercial television stations are required to air some programming that meets the educational and informational needs of children. Noncommercial stations are exempt from this requirement. The Commission defines educational and informational programming as "furthering the positive development of the child in any respect, including the child's cognitive/intellectual or emotional/social needs."[22] The FCC cited programs like "Fat Albert and the Cosby Kids," "CBS Schoolbreak Specials," "Winnie the Pooh and Friends," and "Life Goes On" (because of it's positive subject matter) as meeting this requirement.

The Commission requires licensees to place, in their public files, a summary of programming, nonbroadcast efforts and other ways the educational and informational needs of children have been served.

The FCC also prohibits program-length commercials in children's programs. The Commission defined program-length commercials as "associated with a product, in which commercials for that product are aired."[23]

The Prime-time Access Rule

The Prime-time Access Rule (PTAR) grew out of the FCC's concern over the major networks' control over the schedule of local stations. The PTAR, as it exists today, has been in effect since 1975. The original rule was promulgated in 1970 in *Competition and Responsibility in Network Television Broadcasting*. When it was modified in 1973, it was struck down by the court, in *National Association of Independent Television Producers and Distributors v. FCC*, on a technicality. The PTAR was rewritten in 1975. The PTAR, as excerpted below, does not apply to noncommercial television stations.

> § 73.658(k) Effective September 8, 1975, commercial television stations owned or affiliated with a national television network in the 50 largest television markets . . . shall devote, during the four hours of prime time (7–11 P.M. E.T. and P.T., 6–10 P.M. C.T. and M.T.), no more than three hours to the presentation of programs from a national network, programs formerly on a national network (off-network programs) other than feature films, or on Saturdays, feature films; PROVIDED, HOWEVER, that the following categories of programs need not be counted toward the three-hour limitation: . . .
>
> (1) On nights other than Saturdays, network or off-network programs designed for children, public affairs programs or documentary programs . . .
>
> (2) Special news programs dealing with fast-breaking news events, on-the-spot coverage of news events or other material related to such coverage, and political broadcasts by or on behalf of legally qualified candidates for public office. . . .
>
> (3) Regular network news broadcasts up to the half hour, when immediately adjacent to a full hour of continuous locally produced news or locally produced public affairs programming. . . .
>
> (4) Runovers of live network broadcasts of sporting events, where the event has been reasonably scheduled to conclude before prime time or occupy only a certain amount of prime time, but the event has gone beyond its expected duration due to circumstances not reasonably forseeable by the networks or under their control. This exemption does not apply to post-game material. . . .
>
> (5) In the case of stations in the Mountain and Pacific time zones, on evenings when network prime time programming consists of a sports event or other program broadcast live and simultaneously throughout the contiguous 48 states, such stations may assume that the network's schedule that evening occupies no more of prime time in these zones than it does in the Eastern and Central time zones. . . .
>
> (6) Network broadcasts of an international sports event (such as the Olympic Games), New Year's Day college football games, or any other network programming of a special nature other than motion pictures or other

sports events, when the network devotes all of its time on the same evening to the same programming, except brief incidental fill material. . . .[24]

The FCC hoped that by giving an additional hour of prime time back to the network affiliates, more local programming would result. Indeed, owners of some larger stations, like the Group W, began producing programs for the stations they owned, featuring local talent and local issues. Group W stations ran a program called *Evening Magazine*. The program worked so well in "access," that it was syndicated as *PM Magazine* to more that 100 affiliates across the country. The program featured local hosts, some local stories, and a pool of features produced as part of a cooperative from affiliates.

Other access programs developed, like *Wheel of Fortune*, an evening version of *Jeopardy*, and, eventually, numerous made-for-access magazine shows, like *Hard Copy*, *Entertainment Tonight*, and *A Current Affair*. Syndicators also began producing made-for-access situation comedies, like *Charles In Charge* and *Mama's Family*.

PTAR became a boost for some program syndicators, but it has not been effective in stimulating local programming by affiliate stations. Attempts by program syndicators and producers to have the rule eliminated have not been met with favor by the FCC.

The Financial and Syndication Rules

The financial and syndication (fin-syn) rules are related to PTAR in that these rules also seek to limit the control the major networks exercise over broadcast programming. The FCC defines a "network" as follows:

> § 73.658(j)(4) . . . [T]he term network means any person, entity or corporation which offers an interconnected program service on a regular basis for 15 or more hours per week to at least 25 affiliated television licensees in 10 or more states; and/or any person, entity or corporation controlling, controlled by or under common control with such person, entity or corporation.[25]

The fin-syn rules were implemented in the 1970s, before cable television and alternative video systems eroded the traditional networks' share of the viewing audience. The fin-syn rules limit the amount of programming the networks can produce and regulate the syndication of network programming. Until 1991, the networks were prohibited from syndicating programs they produced in the United States, nor could they distribute programs internationally that they did not produce, as stipulated in 47 CFR Section 73.658(j)(l)(i). Throughout the 1980s, the networks argued that the fin-syn rules were overly restrictive and, in the changing market, were actually contributing to the demise of the networks. In 1990, the emerging Fox Network, also a major program syndicator, sought an exemption from the fin-syn rules in order to increase its programming hours. Fox argued that a permanent exemption was warranted to further network diversity. On May 4, 1990, Fox Broadcasting was granted a one-year waiver of the rules that allowed them to program 18.5 hours per week without running afoul of the fin-syn rules.

When Alfred Sikes became chairman of the FCC, he promised to review the fin-syn rules. In April 1991, they were modified. The rules that resulted, however, were far from the major relaxation expected by the networks. Indeed, the FCC itself was split 3–2 on the decision to adopt new rules.

The new rules allow networks to produce, own, and sell 40% of the shows on their prime-time schedules. The networks will also be permitted to own a portion of the shows produced by others as long as they promise some financial rights to the producers.

The networks and Hollywood producers both reacted negatively to the revised rules and planned to appeal the FCC decision. The three major networks discussed the possibility of cutting their prime-time offerings back to 15 hours per week in order to escape the FCC's definition of a network. Such a move would allow networks to engage in domestic and foreign syndication.

Lotteries

Section 73.1211 of the FCC rules prohibits the broadcast of most lottery information. Exceptions include state lotteries,[26] certain fishing contests when all receipts defray the actual costs of operation,[27] certain gaming conducted by Indian Tribes,[28] lotteries conducted by certain "not-for-profit" organizations,[29] and contests conducted as a promotional activity by a commercial organization that is clearly occasional and incidental to the primary business of that organization.[30]

State-sanctioned Lotteries

Broadcasters may advertise state-sanctioned lotteries, provided they are licensed to markets within states operating those lotteries. If a state does not have a state-sanctioned lottery, then stations licensed to markets within that state may not advertise any other state's lottery. If a state has a sanctioned lottery, then stations licensed to markets within that state may advertise adjacent state's sanctioned lotteries. The same applies to live lottery drawings.

The Elements of a Lottery

The elements of a lottery are chance, consideration, and prize. Unless all three of these elements are present, there is no lottery.

Chance
The element of chance is present if no skill is required to win a prize or other consideration. Spinning a wheel, drawing numbers or names from a jar,

random numbers generated by a computer, or being the third caller to a radio station are all elements of chance. Guessing the number of beans in a jar is also chance, since there is no skill involved in deriving the answer.

Chance may also be present in a contest that initially involves skill. For example, suppose a station contest required a listener to name the number one song for the week of May 3, 1986. If two listeners called with the right answer (Robert Palmer's "Addicted To Love"), the tie must be broken by another means involving skill. The station could not simply flip a coin to decide the winner.

Consideration

Consideration means exchanging something of value in order to win a prize or participate in a game, contest, or other promotional arrangement. Examples of consideration include the payment of an entry fee, a required purchase, a test drive to enter a contest (which is a consideration because time and effort are required to win the prize), or receiving a discount after purchase.

Requiring an individual to be present to win is not consideration, nor is requiring listeners to call the station after hearing their name broadcast over the air. Age and eligibility requirements are not consideration.

It is important to remember that consideration must flow to the promoter and/or copromoters. In *Greater Indianapolis Broadcasting Co. Inc. (WXLW)*, the Commission held that a radio station-sponsored golf contest in which the winner was determined by a random drawing of score cards was not a lottery. Entrants paid a greens fee to play a round of golf, but they paid no money to place their score card in the drawing. The money to play the round of golf did not go to WXLW, nor was the golf course a cosponsor of the contest. Had this been the case, the event would have been a lottery.

Prize

A prize is anything of value offered to a contestant. It can be in the form of goods, money, services, discounts, or refunds. In short, it can be worth a million dollars or one penny. The prize is the primary element in a lottery, for without a prize, a lottery does not exist.

Sanctions and Broadcasters' Responsibility

If radio or television stations broadcast a lottery, they may face a fine or other difficulty at license renewal time. Broadcasters cannot escape penalty by claiming that they didn't know that a commercial, promotion, or other program actually constituted a lottery. Stations must exercise diligence in identifying a potential lottery.

Summary

Section 326 of the Communications Act prohibits FCC censorship of broadcast programming. The Commission may set guidelines that affect programs that are broadcast to ensure that stations are operating in the public interest. The political broadcasting rules, in Section 315 of the Communications Act, are one example of this kind of regulation. Channeling of certain kinds of programs, such as indecency, is another means of program content regulation without direct FCC censorship.

Diversity of program sources is a policy that the FCC has attempted to foster with regulations like the financial and syndication rules, the syndicated exclusivity rule, and the prime-time access rule.

Broadcast stations are prohibited from advertising or promoting lotteries. Exceptions to this rule include the broadcast of state-run lotteries. Stations licensed to markets within a state sponsoring such a lottery may broadcast that lottery information. In states where there is a state-sanctioned lottery, broadcasters may transmit information about state-sanctioned lotteries in adjacent states.

Notes/References

1. 47 U.S.C. Sec. 326 (1989).
2. See Programming Information in Broadcast Applications, 65 R.R.2d 397 (1988) for additional information.
3. 47 U.S.C.A. Sec. 315.
4. 47 CFR Section 73.1940.
5. 47 CFR Section 73.1940 4(d).
6. Ibid. 4(e)(f).
7. 24 R.R. 401 (1962).
8. Branch v. Federal Communications Commission, 824 F.2d 37, 63 R.R.2d 826, 14 Med.L.Rptr. 1465 (1987).
9. For a detailed discussion of nonfederal candidate obligation see *Nab Legal Guide*, pp.56–57.
10. CBS Inc. v. FCC, 453 U.S. 367 (1981).
11. *In the Matter of Enforcement of Prohibitions Against Broadcast Obscenity and Indecency*, 18 U.S.C. 1464, Order FCC 88–416 (Dec. 19, 1988), 53(249) F.R. 52425 (Dec. 28, 1988).
12. *In re Pacifica Foundation*, 36 FCC 147 (January 22, 1964).
13. *Eastern Educational Radio (WUHY-FM)*, 24 F.C.C.2d 408 (1970).
14. Sonderling Broadcasting Corp. (WGLD-FM), 27 R.R.2d 285 (FCC 1973).
15. FCC v. Pacifica Foundation, 438 U.S. 726 (1978).
16. Ibid.

17. "FCC Fines Detroit Station for Indecency," *Broadcasting* (October 9, 1989): 41.
18. *Skyywalker Records Inc. v. Navarro*, 17 Med.L.Rptr. 2073 (DC So.Fla., 1990).
19. 47 CF4, Section 73.1216.
20. "Station Stunts Tread Fine Line of Humor and Hoax." *Broadcasting* (April 8, 1991): 55.
21. See Revision of Programming and Commercialization Policies, Ascertainment Requirements, and Program Log Requirements for Commercial Television Stations, MM Docket No. 83–670 and Further Notice of Proposed Rulemaking/Notice of Inquiry, FCC 87–338, R.R.2d, Current Service, 53:365 (1987).
22. Public Law No. 101–437 (October 18, 1990).
23. "New Children's Television Rules Adopted," *Pike & Fischer's Broadcast Rules Service* No. 27 (March/April, 1991): 2.
24. 47 CFR 73.658.
25. Ibid.
26. This provision went into effect May 7, 1990, as a result of the Charity Games Advertising Clarification Act of 1988. See 18 USC § 1307(a); 102 Stat. 3205.
27. See USC § 1305.
28. See Indian Gaming Regulatory Act, 25 USC § et. seq.
29. See 18 USC § 1307; 102 Stat 3205. "Not-for-profit" organizations are defined as those that qualify as tax exempt under Section 501 of the Internal Revenue Code of 1986.
30. See 18 USC § 1307(a); 102 Stat 3205.

Cases

Action for Children's Television v. FCC, 756 F.2d 899 (DC Cir., 1985)
Action for Children's Television v. FCC, 821 F.2d 741 (DC Cir., 1987)
Action for Children's Television v. FCC, (CA DC, 1991) 18 Med.L.Rptr. 2153
Adrian Weiss, 58 F.C.C.2d 342, 36 R.R.2d 292 (1976)
Branch v. Federal Communications Commission, 824 F.2d 37, 63 R.R.2d 826, 14 Med.L.Rptr. 1465 (1987)
Broadcast of Station Contests, 37 R.R.2d 260 (FCC, 1976)
CBS v. FCC, 453 U.S. 367 (1981)
Children's Television Programming and Advertising Practices, 75 F.C.C.2d 138 (1979)
Children's Television Programming and Advertising Practices, 96 F.C.C.2d 634 (1984)

Children's Television Report and Policy Statement, 50 F.C.C.2d 1 (1974)

Competition and Responsibility in Network Television Broadcasting, 23 F.C.C.2d 382 (1970)

DeFilippo v. NBC, (CA, RI) 8 Med.L.Rptr. 1872 (1982)

Deregulation of Commercial Television, 98 F.C.C.2d 1076, 56 R.R.2d 1005 (1984), 60 R.R.2d 526 (1986)

Deregulation of Radio, 104 F.C.C.2d. 505, note 8 (1986)

Eastern Educational Radio (WUHY-FM), 24 F.C.C.2d 408, 18 R.R.2d 860 (1970)

Farmers Educational Cooperative Union v. WDAY Inc., 360 U.S. 525 (1959)

FCC v. Pacifica Foundation, 438 U.S. 726 (1978)

FCC Sanctions Noncommercial Licensee for Failure to Prepare and Maintain Issues/Programs List in Public File; Haley, Bader & Potts Information Memorandum 21:1 (February 28, 1991)

Federal Communications Commission, Deregulation of Radio, 84 F.C.C.2d 968, 49 R.R.2d 1 (effective April 3, 1981), 53 R.R.2d 805, 53 R.R.2d 1371, affirmed 706 F.2d 1224, 53 R.R.2d 1501, 707 F.2d 1413, 53 R.R.2d 1371, 719 F.2d 407, 54 R.R.2d 811, 1151 (DC Cir., 1983)

Greater Indianapolis Broadcasting Co. Inc. (WXLW), 44 F.C.C. 2d 37 (1973)

Henry Geller et. al., F.C.C.2d 1236, 54 R.R.2d 1246 (1983)

In the Matter of Enforcement of Prohibitions Against Broadcast Obscenity and Indecency, 18 U.S.C. 1464, Order FCC 88–416 (Dec. 19, 1988), 53 (249) F.R. 52425 (Dec. 28, 1988)

In re Pacifica Foundation, 36 F.C.C. 147 (January 22, 1964)

Infinity Broadcasting Corps of Pennsylvania, 2 F.C.C.Rcd. 2705, 62 R.R.2d 1202 (1987)

McCollum v. CBS Inc., (CA Cal. 2 Cir., 1988) 15 Med.L.Rptr. 2001

Miller v. California, 413 U.S. 15 (1973)

National Association of Independent Television Producers and Distributors v. F.C.C., 502 F.2d 249 (2d Cir., 1974), 50 F.C.C.2d at 852

Nicholas Zapple, 23 F.C.C.2d 707, 19 R.R.2d 421 (1970)

Olivia v. NBC, 7 Med.L.Rptr. 2359 (1981)

Pacifica Foundation Inc., 2 F.C.C.Rcd. 2698, 62 R.R.2d 1191 (1987)

Primer on Ascertainment of Community Problems (1971); revised, 74 F.C.C. 942, 39 F.R. 32288 (1974)

The Regents of the University of California, 2 F.C.C.Rcd. 2703, 62 R.R.2d 1199 (1987)

Report and Statement of Policy re: Commission *en banc* Programming Inquiry, 25 F.R. 7291 (July 29, 1960)

Sable Communications v. FCC, (CA DC, 1989) 16 Med.L.Rptr. 1961

Skyywalker Records Inc. v. Navarro, (DC So.Fla., 1990) 17 Med.L.Rptr. 2073

Sonderling Broadcasting Corp. (WGLD-FM), 27 R.R.2d 285 (FCC, 1973)

United Church of Christ v. FCC, (DC Cir., 1978) 4 Med.L.Rptr. 1410

Vance v. Judas Priest, (DC 2 Nev., 1990) 15 Med.L.Rptr. 2010

Weirum v. RKO General, 15 Cal.3d 40 (1975)

William H. Branch, 101 F.C.C.2d 901 (1985)

Yale Broadcasting Co. v. FCC, U.S. Ct.App. DC, 478 F.2d 594 (1973), cert. denied 414 U.S. 914 (1973)

Zamora v. CBS, (DC Fla., 1979) 5 Med.L.Rptr. 2109

6

□ □ □
□ □ □
□ □ □

Regulation of
Commercial Practices

The Development
of Commercial Regulation

The regulation of commercial content in the United States emerged early in the twentieth century as a result of excesses spawned by *laissez faire* capitalism. Muckraking journalists fueled the passage of regulations like the Pure Food and Drug Act of 1906, which prohibited misrepresentation of cures and required that all ingredients be identified on the product label.

The Federal Trade Commission

Congressional concern over enforcement of the Sherman Antitrust Act and the Clayton act led to the 1914 Federal Trade Commission Act. This act created the FTC, an independent regulatory agency originally charged with regulating unfair competition. In *FTC v. Winstead Hosiery Co.*, the Supreme Court upheld the FTC's authority to regulate exaggerated advertising claims. In 1938, the Wheeler-Lea amendment to the FTC Act expanded the FTC's power to include the regulation of false and deceptive advertising. Congress also allowed the FTC to issue cease and desist orders and levy fines for violation of those orders. The Wheeler-Lea amendment was passed as a result of *FTC v. Raladam Co.*, in which the Supreme Court ruled that the Commission could not ban false advertising unless it could be shown that it was a form of "unfair competition."

In 1975, Congress passed the Magnuson-Moss Act, which gave the FTC authority over local as well as national advertising.

The FTC is organized very much like the FCC. It has five commissioners who are appointed by the president. No more than three commissioners may belong to the same political party. At this writing, the chairwoman of the FTC is Janet Steiger. The FTC has three bureaus—the Bureau of Consumer Protection, the Bureau of Competition, and the Bureau of Economics. The Bureau of Consumer Protection is most concerned with advertising and it is through this bureau that investigations are initiated.

In spite of legislation giving the FTC enforcement powers, the agency was viewed as a paper tiger until the consumer movements of the 1960s and 1970s. At one point in the late 1970s, under the chairmanship of Michael Pertschuk, the FTC became so active in the area of children's television advertising that Congress threatened to cut off funding, because many powerful advertisers, with friends in Congress, felt threatened by FTC actions. In the 1980s, the FTC's power declined as the Reagan administration drastically reduced the agency's budget for regulating deceptive advertising. In the 1990s, under the direction of Chairwoman Janet Steiger, the FTC stepped up enforcement practices. Of special interest to the FTC were competition in cable television issues, children's advertising, and program length commercials often dubbed "infomercials."[1]

Enforcement Powers of the FTC

Consent Decrees

If the FTC determines that advertising is deceptive, it notifies the offender and asks that a consent decree be signed. In signing a consent decree, the advertiser agrees that it will stop the deceptive ads, but admits no guilt. Failure to adhere to the consent decree may result in a $10,000-a-day fine.

Cease and Desist Orders

If an advertiser chooses not to sign a consent decree, the FTC may issue a cease and desist order. The cease and desist order is heard by an administrative law judge before becoming final. Advertisers may appeal the order to the FTC and then to a federal appellate court. Acting on a cease and desist order can be a time-consuming process. For example, the FTC began a proceeding against the makers of Carter's Little Liver Pills in 1943. The complaint revolved around the use of the word "liver." The pills in question are a laxative and have nothing to do with the liver. *Carter Products Inc. v. FTC* was finally resolved in 1959, with the word "liver" being removed from the product title.

Corrective Advertising

If the FTC determines that an advertisement has created a false impression in the minds of the public, it may require corrective advertising. In 1971, the FTC required the makers of Profile Bread to issue corrective ads to change public misconception that the bread was lower in calories than other breads. In reality, the slices of Profile were smaller, but contained the same number of calories based on overall weight.

In 1975 in *Warner-Lambert Co. v. Federal Trade Commission*, the FTC required Warner-Lambert, the makers of Listerine, to include a statement in their advertising that corrected the misconception that Listerine prevented colds or lessened the severity of sore throats. Warner-Lambert was required to run the corrective until the company spent $10 million on ads. This was roughly the amount spent on creating the false impression.

Advertising and the First Amendment

Until the mid-1970s, commercial speech was not protected by the First Amendment. In fact, the Commercial Speech Doctrine that emerged from the Supreme Court in 1942, in *Valentine v. Chrestensen*, stated that speech promoting goods and services is less deserving of constitutional protection than speech promoting other ideas.

The Commercial Speech Doctrine rested on the premise that advertising served no important social function. Advertising was viewed as self-serving, with little or no benefit transferred to the receiver of such communication. This assumption began to change in 1975. In *Bigelow v. Virginia*, the Supreme Court held that an advertisement in a Virginia newspaper for a New York abortion referral service was protected by the First Amendment. Abortions were legal in New York, but illegal in Virginia. The Court found that Virginians had a First Amendment right to receive information about a legal service. Additionally, the state of Virginia was not able to demonstrate sufficient reason for prohibiting the ad.

The Commercial Speech Doctrine fell the following year in *Virginia State Bd. of Pharmacy v. Virginia Citizens Consumer Council Inc.* (1976). The Supreme Court struck down a Virginia statute prohibiting the advertising of prescription drug prices. The basis of the decision, like that of *Bigelow*, was the public's right to receive information about a service. The Court added:

> Advertising, however tasteless and excessive it may seem, is nonetheless dissemination of information as to who is producing and selling what product, for what reason, and at what price. So long as we preserve a predominantly free enterprise economy, the allocation of our resources in large measure will be made through numerous private economic decisions. It is a matter of public interest that those decisions, in the aggregate, be intelligent and well informed. To this end, the free flow of commercial information is indispensable. And if it is indispensable to the proper allocation of resources in a free enterprise system, it is also indispensable to the formation of intelligent opinions as to how that system ought to be regulated or altered. Therefore, even if the First Amendment were thought to be primarily an instrument to enlighten public decision-making in a democracy, we could not say that the free flow of information does not serve that goal.[2]

The Court added that this decision did not mean commercial speech could not be regulated. The ruling left room for governments to draft carefully constructed commercial speech regulations designed to deal with specific problems and concerns associated with advertising. For example, false and misleading ads and advertisements for illegal products might easily be regulated.

The revised Commercial Speech Doctrine was clarified in *Central Hudson Gas & Electric Corp. v. Public Service Commission* (1980). In this case, the Supreme

Court developed a four-part test to help determine whether a particular commercial expression is protected by the First Amendment. For commercial speech to be protected it must meet the following criteria:

1. It must concern lawful activity and cannot be misleading.
2. The asserted government interest in regulating the speech must be substantial.
3. Regulation of the commercial speech must further the government's goals.
4. If the first three parts of the test are met, the proposed regulation must not be more extensive than necessary to further the government's interest.

Children's TV Advertising

Time Standards

As noted in Chapter 5, the deregulation of television by the FCC included the elimination of commercial time guidelines for children's television programs. Action for Children's Television (ACT) appealed this decision and in *Action for Children's Television v. FCC* (1987), the court of appeals remanded the case to the FCC for further consideration of the issue. In 1987, the FCC issued a Further Notice of Proposed Rule Making, requesting comments from the public to assist the agency in developing a children's television commercial policy.[3] Specifically, the Commission sought to determine whether market forces were sufficient to regulate commercial time in children's television programming or whether additional government regulation was required.

In July 1990, the Senate passed a children's television bill that provided for commercial time limits during programs primarily aimed at children. The bill limited commercial time during children's programs to 10.5 minutes on weekends and 12 minutes on weekdays. The House accepted these guidelines in a compromise bill that was passed on October 2, 1990. The bill became law on October 17, 1990, without the signature of President Bush. The House legislation removed a Senate provision requiring a national endowment to support public broadcasting. The commercial time limits apply in programs directed primarily to children 12 years of age and younger. The rules apply to over-the-air and cable programs, but not to low-power television stations.

Program-length Commercials

The FCC has defined program-length commercials as programs associated with a product in which commercials for that product are aired.[4]

ACT filed a complaint with the FCC in 1983 alleging that programs like "He Man," "Thunder Cats," and "Masters of the Universe" violated FCC policies against directing program-length commercials to children. ACT argued that these animated programs promoted products or services under the guise of entertainment. The characters in the programs were marketed as plastic toys that are available to children. ACT contended that these programs should have been logged as commercial time.

In *Action for Children's Television* (1985) the FCC dismissed ACT's complaint, noting that there was no evidence that program-length commercials were harmful to children in the audience and that there was no evidence in this case showing an intermingling of commercial and program material. The Commission ruling was appealed by the National Association for Better Broadcasting (NABB) in 1985 in *National Association for Better Broadcasting v. FCC.* The court of appeals reversed and remanded *NABB v. FCC* back to the FCC. The Commission denied NABB's complaint on grounds that the programs in question were bartered and thereby did not trigger the sponsorship identification requirements.

ACT remains concerned over the FCC's definition of program-length commercials. In 1986, ACT requested the Commission to require programs depicting products that are toys to carry announcements that the program material is designed to promote the sale of the product in the story. The following year, ACT filed another petition asking the FCC to rule that children's programs that carry an inaudible signal that interacts with certain toys be in violation of the public interest. The FCC did not act specifically on these recommendations, but included a prohibition against program-length commercials in the 1991 children's television rules.

ACT filed a petition with the FCC in May 1991, contending that the Commission erred in failing to define program-length commercials in terms of the public interest. ACT noted that the FCC definition is currently limited to shows associated with a product in which commercials for that product are aired. ACT argued that this definition failed to address public interest issues and that Commission action was arbitrary and unlawful.

Liquor and Wine Ads on Radio, TV, and Cable

There is currently no federal prohibition against advertising legal alcoholic beverages on radio, television, or cable. Traditionally, broadcasters have exercised self-restraint in accepting alcoholic beverage ads. They have generally refused advertisements for hard liquor and have refrained from showing individuals engaged in excessive consumption. States, on the other hand, may restrict alcoholic beverage advertising in over-the-air broadcast media. However, states may not prohibit cable systems from retransmitting out-of-state signals that contain alcoholic beverage commercials. When Oklahoma attempted to apply its statewide ban on alcoholic beverage advertising to signals imported by cable systems, the Supreme Court ruled in *Capital Cities v. Crisp* that authority over out-of-state signals was part of FCC jurisdiction and therefore subject to federal law.

In February 1985, Senate hearings were conducted that considered legislative restrictions on beer and wine advertising on radio and television. The Senate Sub-committee sought evidence to determine whether advertising caused nondrinkers to become drinkers and whether ads caused drinkers to increase consumption. The results were inconclusive. In May 1985, the House Subcommittee on Telecommunications, Consumer Protection, and Finance addressed the relationship between beer and wine ads, and abuse of those products. Again, no conclusive evidence was produced and eventually congressional interest in the topic waned. In 1990, Senator Al Gore (D. Tenn.) and Representative Joe Kennedy (D. Mass.) introduced the Sensible Advertising and Family Education Act of 1990 (the SAFE Act). The bill called for health warnings on all advertisements for alcoholic beverages, including print, broadcast, and cable. The legislation was not passed.

Cigarette and Tobacco Products Advertising

The congressional ban on cigarette and smokeless tobacco products advertising on broadcast and cable originated from the Fairness Doctrine. As evidence mounted in the mid-1960s that indicated that cigarette smoking was a health hazard, individuals became increasingly concerned over the plethora of ads for cigarettes on television. Indeed, cigarettes had been a major sponsor of network programs since the early days of the "Camel News Caravan with John Cameron Swayze." Even the animated *Flintstones* were sponsored by Winston cigarettes. Television personalities like Edward R.Murrow, Jack Paar, and Andy Griffith smoked during the course of their programs. Cigarettes were touted as "refreshing."

Applying the Fairness Doctrine to Advertising Cigarettes

In December 1966, an attorney named John Banzhaf asked WCBS-TV in New York for reply time to respond to cigarette commercials. He based his request on the Fairness Doctrine. His rationale was that smoking cigarettes posed a potential health hazard. Therefore, he argued that the discussion of cigarette smoking fell into the category of a "controversial issue of public importance," triggering the Fairness Doctrine. There was precedence in FCC case law in the *Petition of Sam Morris*, which extended the concept of "fairness" to advertising.

When WCBS-TV refused to allow Banzhaf time to rebut the cigarette ads it had broadcast, Banzhaf filed a complaint with the FCC. In *WCBS-TV*, the Commission ordered WCBS-TV to grant reply time. The decision was upheld by the U.S. court of appeals in *Banzhaf v. FCC*. The *Banzhaf* decision attempted to limit the application of the Fairness Doctrine to cigarette advertising only. The court of appeals held that cigarette ads had to be counter-balanced by expression devoted to pointing out the hazards of cigarette smoking.

Although *Banzhaf* tried to limit the application of the Fairness Doctrine to advertising, the cat had been let out of the bag. In *Friends of the Earth v. FCC,* a citizens group argued that free time should be made available to antipollution groups wishing to respond to automobile advertisements. The rationale behind their argument was that cars pollute the air—a controversial issue of public importance. The FCC refused to order counter ads in this case, but the court of appeals reversed the Commission ruling.

As a result of the *Friends of the Earth* case, the FCC issued the *1974 Fairness Report.*[5] In this report, the FCC states that product commercials do not trigger the "controversial issue of public importance" test required to induce a Fairness Doctrine complaint. In short, the Commission developed a new policy that refused to apply the Fairness Doctrine to product advertising. Fairness still applied to editorial advertising.

The Congressional Ban of Cigarette and Smokeless Tobacco Ads

Congress passed the Federal Cigarette Labeling and Advertising Act in 1965. The act required cigarette packages and advertisements to display the statement "Caution: Cigarette Smoking May Be Hazardous To Your Health." In 1969, the Public Health Cigarette Smoking Act was enacted. This legislation beefed up the warning required on cigarette packages and ads to "Warning: Excessive Cigarette Smoking Is Dangerous To Your Health." The act also banned cigarette advertising from the airwaves after January 1, 1971.

In 1986, the Comprehensive Smokeless Tobacco Health Education Act extended the broadcast and cable advertising ban to smokeless tobacco products such as snuff and chewing tobacco.

Self-regulation and the NAB Codes

Broadcasters and cablecasters exercise self-regulation in the area of advertising. The networks, Multiple System Owners (MSOs), and individual stations and franchises have adopted standards for acceptible advertising. All must be within the bounds of the law, but some are more restrictive than others. Through self-regulation, the industry hopes to stave off additional regulation by Congress through the FCC. This regulation is usually the result of a widespread public outcry that manifests itself in the form of pressure on congresspeople. Congress, in turn, pressures the FCC. Examples of regulatory measures, both sucessful and unsuccessful, include the Children's Television Act, the proposed 24-hour ban on indecency, and renewed efforts to reregulate cable television.

The National Association of Broadcasters (NAB) developed advertising codes for radio advertising in 1929 and for television advertising in 1952. The codes were voluntary guidelines set up to ward off government regulation. The NAB codes suggested that radio stations broadcast no more than 18 minutes of commercial time per hour and that television stations limit commercials to 14 minutes per hour.

In 1979, the Justice Department brought suit against the Television Code, alleging that the code violated antitrust laws. Television stations were suspected of artificially limiting advertising and depriving advertisers of the benefits of open competition. In 1982, the NAB voluntarily dissolved the radio and television codes.

Summary

The FTC is empowered to regulate false and misleading advertising. While the FTC may order a broadcaster to stop airing an ad that is deemed deceptive, the FTC cannot revoke a broadcast license. Advertising now receives some protection under the First Amendment, although that protection is limited.

One of the FCC's major concerns is the advertising in children's television programs. The Commission limits the amount of commercial time in children's programs and prohibits host selling.

Cigarettes and smokeless tobacco product advertisements are the only legal products specifically banned from the airwaves by Congress. Liquor and wine ads and other personal products are voluntarily excluded by broadcasters. This is an example of self-regulation.

Notes/References

1. See "Janet Steiger: The FTC's Vigilant Enforcer," *Broadcasting* (February 5, 1990): 76; "FTC Takes Action on 'Infomercials,'" *Electronic Media* (May 21, 1990): 32.
2. *Virginia State Bd. of Pharmacy v. Virginia Citizens Consumer Council Inc.*, 425 U.S. 748 (1976).
3. See *Further Notice of Proposed Rule Making/Notice of Inquiry*, MM Docket No. 83–670, F.C.C. 87–338, 2 F.C.C. Rcd. 6822 (1987).
4. MM Docket 90–570, FCC 90–373.
5. See *In the Matter of the Handling of Public Issues Under the Fairness Doctrine and the Public Interest Standards of the Communications Act*, 48 F.C.C.2d 1 (1974).

Cases

Action for Children's Television, 58 R.R.2d 61 (1985)
Action for Children's Television v. FCC, 821 F.2d 741 (DC Cir., 1987)
Banzhaf v. FCC, 405 F.2d 1082 (DC Cir., 1968)

Bigelow v. Virginia, 421 U.S. 809 (1975)

Capital Cities Cable v. Crisp, (U.S. Sup.Ct., 1984) 10 Med.L.Rprt. 1873

Carter Products Inc. v. FTC, 268 F.2d 461 (9th Cir., 1959), cert. denied 361 U.S. 884 (1959)

Central Hudson Gas & Electric Corp. v. Public Service Commission, 447 U.S. 557 (1980)

Friends of the Earth v. FCC, 449 F.2d 1164 (DC Cir., 1971)

FTC v. Raladam Co., 283 U.S. 643 (1931)

FTC v. Winsted Hosiery Co., 258 U.S. 483 (1922)

National Association for Better Broadcast v. FCC, U.S. Court of Appeals, DC, Court Case No. 89–1462 (1989)

National Association for Better Broadcasting v. FCC, 830 F.2d 270 (DC Cir., 1986)

Petition of Sam Morris, 11 F.C.C. 197 (1946)

Valentine v. Chrestensen, 316 U.S. 52 (1942)

Virginia State Bd. of Pharmacy v. Virginia Citizens Consumer Council Inc., 425 U.S. 748 (1976)

Warner-Lambert Co. v. Federal Trade Commission, 562 F.2d. 749 (DC Cir., 1977), cert. denied 435 U.S. 958 (1978)

WCBS-TV, 8 F.C.C.2d 381 (1967), 9 F.C.C.2d 921 (1967)

7 ⬜⬜⬜
⬜⬜⬜
⬜⬜⬜

Noncommercial Educational Broadcasting

The Rationale of Noncommercial Service

Noncommercial educational broadcasting has developed alongside the commercial service in the United States. Noncommercial radio and television have been the focus of regulatory attention since the 1920s. Some of the regulations applied to this service were designed to protect what many believed to be a necessary counterpart to commercial broadcasting. Much of the regulatory activity has been the result of the Commission's failure to adequately plan for the development of a viable noncommercial service. A brief historical view of noncommercial educational broadcasting is necessary to understand the regulatory activity and development of policy.

The Development of Educational Broadcasting

As early as 1897, institutions of higher education began experimenting with radio transmission. These early stations were usually located in physics and engineering departments, where the concern was with hardware—not programming. By 1920, some educational stations, like WHA at the University of Wisconsin, began broadcasting local weather reports to farmers. By 1924, 100 educational stations were offering this service in cooperation with the U.S. Department of Agriculture and agricultural schools.

Some schools brought microphones into the classroom and broadcast lectures on history, government, economics, psychology, and foreign languages. These classroom and agricultural uses of radio, although pioneering the use of the medium, were met with a great deal of criticism. The broadcasts were condemned for their boring content and lack of institutional follow-up of the broadcast's impact.

The educational experimentation with radio took place against the backdrop of the Commerce Department's attempt to develop an efficient spectrum management policy. In addition, it was not yet clear if radio would evolve into a commercial service, a sustaining service (noncommercial), or a common carrier. Tensions between sup-porters of each model grew in the early and mid-1920s. However, it soon became clear that noncommercial educational broadcasting would take a back seat to more powerful interests.

"Squeezing" the Educational Stations

Commerce Secretary Herbert Hoover called a series of four Radio Conferences between 1922 and 1925. The purpose of the conferences was to develop a policy that would chart the direction of broadcasting in the United States. The commercial broadcast model, as we know it today, emerged dominant. Noncom-mercial interests remained silent until the Fourth Conference. The number of non-commercial stations on the air had begun to decline. The year 1925 marked the first year that the number of noncommercial licenses lost was more than the number granted. It was also becoming evident that commercial interests coveted the valuable spectrum space occupied by the noncommercial stations and that pressure would be exerted on the Commerce Department to free up that space for commercial expansion.

At the Fourth Radio Conference, a resolution was issued that called for the reservation of some channels for noncommercial educational use. The resolution was not adopted and noncommercial educational broadcasting fell into a long period of decline. Gradually, the FRC and, later, the FCC developed rules and policies that favored the growth of commercial broadcasters and effectively "squeezed out" the faltering noncommercial stations. The rationale for the commercial preference by the FRC was that the noncommercial stations were inferior in coverage area and quality. The FRC noted that commercial stations offered free or cost-of-operation time to educational interests, but most noncommercial interests had refused the time. The FRC concluded that educational programs could be provided by existing commercial broadcasters. In the meantime, the number of unrenewed noncommercial licenses continued to rise.

The FCC continued the policy of "squeezing out" noncommercial stations. This policy was supported by the fact that NBC and CBS had agreed to present sustaining programs of an educational nature. The Commission saw little need to assign spec-trum space to noncommercial interests. NBC broadcast a music appreciation pro-gram called the *RCA Hour* from 1928 until 1940. CBS broadcast *The American School of the Air* from 1930 until 1940.

Reserving Educational Channels

There was an attempt to build the reservation of noncommercial channels into the Communications Act of 1934. The move came in the form of the Wagner-Hatfield amendment, which proposed that the newly formed FCC set aside

25% of all channels for educational and nonprofit organizations. The amendment was defeated 42 to 23.

Although the Wagner-Hatfield amendment was defeated, it provided the impetus for later attempts at channel reservation. By the late 1930s the technology of FM broadcasting had been fully developed, but American broadcasters were not ready economically to scrap the existing AM system in favor of the new technology. Commercial broadcasters opposed educational channel reservation on the AM band, because they needed those channels for expansion of the current system. The FM band, on the other hand, was not in the immediate commercial game plan. When the FCC opened up space in the VHF spectrum in 1938, they received little opposition to the reservation of channels in the 41–42-MHz band for educational use. The allocation was virtually useless from a practical standpoint, but a precedent had been set. The VHF allocation was still AM, but educational stations went on the air in New York and Cleveland.

The initial channel reservation was short-lived. In 1940, the FCC moved the educational allocation to 42–43 MHz and switched the mode of transmission from AM to FM. By 1941, seven noncommercial stations were operating on the new FM channels. Unfortunately, the lack of FM receiver penetration once again made the channel reservation a hollow victory.

Musical Chairs with the FM Band

In 1941, with the onset of World War II, the Defense Communications Board banned the use of certain critical materials, which resulted in a "freeze" of further radio or television development. This meant that FM radio growth was halted.

After the war, FM frequencies were changed again, making the commercial viability of FM difficult. In 1945, the FCC shifted the FM band to the current 88–108 MHz, because of the "possibility of serious skywave interference nullifying to a great extent the possibilities of interference-free reception of FM."[1]

Since FM was not commercially viable, the FCC received little opposition to its reservation of the 20 channels between 88 and 92 MHz, which were for noncommercial use. In spite of channel reservation, noncommercial FM did not flourish.

Noncommercial Television Channels

In 1952, the FCC issued its *Sixth Report and Order*, which ended the 4-year freeze on the assignment of television channels and provided for the use of the UHF band. The Commission reserved 242 channels nationwide for noncommercial use. Eighty of these channels were VHF and 162 were UHF. It should be remembered that most television receivers were incapable of tuning in UHF broadcasts. In fact, it was not until 1962 that television set manufacturers were required to include UHF tuners on the sets. This factor, coupled with the poor reception associated with UHF, made the service slow in developing. Noncommercial stations had difficulty acquiring an audience and, with no national network connection and erratic schedules, often provided an inferior service.

The Carnegie Commission and the Public Broadcasting Act

By the mid-1960s, both noncommercial radio and television were dying. Stations were underfunded and seldom watched or listened to. In 1965, a report by the Carnegie Commission recommended a number of changes designed to give noncommercial broadcasting a much-needed boost.

The Carnegie Commission coined the term "public" broadcasting to disassociate noncommercial stations from the boring and motionless image associated with "educational" broadcasting. The Carnegie Commission also recommended that new sources of funding be established to support noncommercial, "public," broadcasting.

In 1967, Congress implemented many of the Carnegie Commission recommendations by passing the Public Broadcasting Act. The act was incorporated into the Communications Act, as Part IV, beginning with Section 390.

The Public Broadcasting Act provided for the creation of a quasi-governmental, nonprofit corporation called the Corporation for Public Broadcasting (CPB). The CPB is made up of 15 members, who are appointed by the president with the advice and consent of the Senate. The goal of the CPB is to encourage the growth and development of noncommercial radio and television. The CPB is not a program source, but is a clearinghouse for funding program producers and qualified stations.

Public Versus Noncommercial Educational Broadcasting

All public broadcasting stations are classified as noncommercial educational (NCE) stations. However, all NCE stations are not necessarily public stations. Public stations are those that qualify for funds from the CPB. CPB-qualified stations meet certain minimum staffing requirements and maintain a minimum operating schedule established by the CPB. For example, CPB-qualified public radio stations must maintain a staff of five full-time employees and broadcast at least 18 hours a day, 365 days a year. In turn, the CPB provides funding and access to high-quality programming, such as that available from National Public Radio (NPR).

The majority of NCE stations are not CPB-qualified stations. The FCC does not require that these stations adhere to a minimum operating schedule or have any full-time staff. The Commission does require that NCE stations be licensed to a not-for-profit organization, such as a school or community group.

Rules Applied to NCE Stations

Many of the same rules that apply to commercial stations apply to NCE stations. Political broadcasting rules (Section 315) requirements for maintaining the public file and quarterly program lists are examples of similarly applied rules, although the "lowest unit rate" is inapplicable. Multiple ownership, duopoly, fin-syn rules, and the PTAR do not apply to NCE stations. NCE broadcasters also file slightly different forms with the FCC. For example, instead of filing Form 301 to make a major change in a facility, NCE broadcasters file Form 340. NCE broadcasters are also given wider latitude in prefiling and postfiling announcements during license renewal. The FCC recognizes that NCE stations may have limited schedules, so the stations are not required to broadcast an announcement at any time they are not regularly on the air.

Licensing Requirements

NCE stations may be licensed to nonprofit educational organizations. The term *educational organization* has been interpreted loosely by the Commission so that, essentially, four classes of licensees have developed over the years—educational institutions such as colleges, universities, and high schools; nonprofit educational organizations qualifying for tax exemption under IRS Code Section 501(c)(3) (many of which operate public radio and television stations as "community licensees"); municipal corporations independent of an educational institution; and state public broadcasting authorities. State public broadcasting agencies commonly operate one major production center and provide service statewide with a series of repeater stations. Kentucky, Alabama, Arkansas, and Mississippi operate like this.

Religious organizations may operate NCE stations, but only to the extent that the operation of the station is for educational, rather than religious, purposes.

Noncommercial Program Service

NCE stations are required to furnish a nonprofit and noncommercial broadcast service. While NCE stations may not broadcast any promotional announcements on behalf of a commercial entity, acknowledgments of contributions may be made. These acknowledgments may not interrupt regular programming (see Figure 7.1).

In the *Second Report and Order*, the FCC relaxed certain restrictions on fundraising and language permitted in acknowledging donations. The Commission amended Section 73.503 (for NCE radio) and Section 73.621 (as applied to NCE TV) of the FCC rules to allow public broadcasters to air promotional announcements when they are in the public interest and when no consideration for airing the announcements is received. The FCC defined consideration as "anything of value given

Text continues on page 163.

Before the
Federal Communications Commission
Washington, D.C. 20554

In the Matter of

Petition of XAVIER UNIVERSITY

Licensee of Noncommercial
Radio Station WVXU (FM),
Cincinnati, OH

for Reconsideration of
Letter of Admonition

MEMORANDUM OPINION AND ORDER

Adopted: March 28, 1990:   Released: March 30, 1990

1.   The Commission has under consideration: (1) a letter of admonition to Xavier University ("Xavier"), license of noncommercial radio station WVXU (FM), Cincinnati, OH, issued November 14, 1989, by the Chief, Complaints and Investigations Branch, Enforcement Division, Mass Media Bureau, for apparent violations of Section 73.503(d) of the Commission's Rules and Section for 399B of the Communications Act of 1934, as amended; and (2) Xavier's petition for reconsideration dated December 11, 1989, requesting that the admonition be rescinded and that the station's files be cleared of any adverse action in regard to the underwriting credits at issue therein. The Mass Media Bureau has referred the petition to the Commission for action pursuant to Section 1.104 of the Commission's Rules.

2.   The letter of admonition (LOA) was issued as a result of an August 23, 1989, complaint alleging that WVXU (FM) had been airing advertisements or promotional material inappropriate for broadcast on a noncommercial station. As examples, the complaint submitted audio tapes containing the six specific announcements cited in the LOA and demonstrating that WVXU (FM) had broadcast them during its "Morning Edition" program between 7:00 a.m. and 9:00 a.m. on various days in August 1989.

3.   The LOA determined that the following material from six of WVXU's announcements was inconsistent with the requirements of Section 73.503 (d) [Footnote 1] of the Commission's Rules and Section 399B of the Communications Act. [Footnote 2]

Figure 7.1   FCC reconsideration of admonition to WVXU for "commercial practices."

-- "This WVXU traffic watch update is brought to you by Jiffy Lube now offering a discount on air conditioner recharge with a Penzoil oil change and 14-point lube check."

-- "Morning Edition is brought to you in part by Ametury (sic) and Associates offering creative services for advertising, marketing and training."

-- "The Choice is Yours is pleased to sponsor programming on WVXU. A health food store and restaurant. The Choice is Yours is located at 821 Delta, on Mount Lookout Square...Fresh and original foods are the speciality."

-- "Programming on WVXU is made possible in part by the new Meritan Gallery...featuring art expressing timeless traditional truths in contemporary visual vocabulary."

-- "Morning Edition is made possible in part by a grant from Arthur Anderson and Company and Anderson Consulting, servicing accounting and audit, tax and management information consulting needs for over 75 years."

-- "Morning Edition is made possible in part by Strauss and Troy, a Cincinnati based law firm in its 36th year."

The LOA found that the word "discount" was comparative and provided price information, that the words "creative," "fresh and original," and those describing the Meritan Gallery's art, were qualitative and promotional in the context of the foregoing announcements, and that specifying a company's number of years in business was qualitative and impliedly comparative.

4.   Xavier argues that any sanctions are unwarranted in the above cases. It explains that, shortly after the subject Jiffy Lube announcement was aired (in August), it determined that the language in the announcement (created by "the Traffic Watch") exceeded station underwriting policies and it discontinued such broadcast. Moreover, Xavier instituted a policy requiring that Traffic Watch provide advance FAX notification of any tag lines for review by station personnel, and in September 1989 a four-member underwriting screening committee began to review the FAX submissions on a daily basis. Because of corrective action, all of which occurred well before the initiation of any Commission action, the licensee asks that the admonishment be rescinded with respect to this violation.

Figure 7.1 *(continued)*

5. Further, Xavier explains its reasoning in concluding that the phrasing in the other five announcements was within the bounds of our rules and policies governing underwriting credits on noncommercial broadcast stations. For example, regarding the description of Amateuli & Associates' produce or service listing Xavier states that Amateuli offers "creative original material for their clients," "creative material" being the stock in trade of fall ad agencies. Mention of the health food store/restaurant's "fresh and original foods," the licensee argues, is a statement identifying a product offered by the underwriter comparable to "French food, or homemade food, or fast food," and describes the underwriter's practice of bringing in foods "right from the farm" and creating "its own totally original menu entrees." Reference to the longevity of business underwriters, the licensee maintains, describes what the firms have to offer in the way of experience and is not claims to have received from Commission personnel. Xavier urges that its reasonable, good faith judgement in these situations, rather than fine semantic distinction, should be given more weight and that the admonition should be rescinded.

6. As the Commission stated in COMMISSION POLICY CONCERNING THE NONCOMMERCIAL NATURE OF EDUCATIONAL BROADCASTING STATIONS, 90 FCC 2d 895 (1982), "We recognize that it may be difficult to distinguish at times between announcements that promote and those that identify. We only expect our public broadcast licensees to exercise their reasonable, good faith judgement in this regard." [Footnote 3] We are persuaded that the language at issue in the latter five announcements listed at Paragraph 3, above, is not clearly reasonable, good faith judgement regarding the language in the five disputed announcements describing its underwriters' produce lines and services. Accordingly we find that the broadcast of these announcements is not a violation of Section 73.503 (d) of the Commission's Rules or Section 399B of the Communications Act, and that no sanctions should have been issued.

7. With respect to the other announcements, which mentioned a discount being offered by Jiffy Lube, the underwriter, we find that under the totality of circumstances WVXU should not be admonished. In this case, the licensee immediately took action to correct this isolated lapse well before the Commission issued the LOA. Such action included deleting the questionable announcement and instituting review procedures to prevent airing similar announcements in the future. Moreover, it certainly is not as egregious as the promotional announcements that triggered previous enforcement actions. See i.g., Public Notice, "In the Matter of Commission Policy Concerning the Noncommercial Nature of Educational Broadcasting Stations." FCC 86-161 at a5 n. 3, April 11, 1986.

Figure 7.1 *(continued)*

8.   In light of the foregoing, we believe it appropriate to rescind the November 14, 1989, letter of admonition. Accordingly, the subject petition for reconsideration filed by Xavier University on December 11, 1989, IS HEREBY GRANTED.

FEDERAL COMMUNICATIONS COMMISSION

Donna R. Searcy

FOOTNOTES

1.   Each [noncommercial education FM broadcast] station shall furnish a nonprofit and noncommercial broadcast service..No promotional announcements on behalf of for profit entities shall be broadcast at any time in exchange for the receipt in whole or in part, of consideration to the licensee, its principals or employees...47 C.F.R. 47.503 (d)

2.   (a) For purposes of this section, the term "advertisement" means any message or other programming material which is broadcast or otherwise transmitted in exchange for any remuneration, and which is intended...to promote any service, facility or product offered by any person who is engaged in such offering for profit.

(b) (2) No public broadcast station may make its facilities available to any person for the broadcasting of any advertisement. 47 U.S.C. 399B

3.   90 FCC 2d at 911. See also Public Notice, "In the Matter of Commission Policy Concerning the Noncommercial Nature of Education Broadcasting Stations,": FCC 86-161, April 11, 1986.

Figure 7.1 *(continued)*

in exchange for something else of value."[2] The FCC also eliminated the name-only requirement for donor announcements and allows stations to broadcast informational messages, including the donor's name, logo, location, and product lines. These announcements may not contain value judgments about the donor's product or service (i.e., "best hamburgers in town" or "friendliest service" would not be allowed.)

The *Second Report* reflected the FCC's desire to balance the financial needs of NCE stations against the obligation to provide a noncommercial broadcast service. The *Second Report* suggests eliminating time and frequency restrictions on donor announcements, but in 1982 the FCC reconsidered this measure. In a *Memorandum Opinion and Order* (1982), the FCC stated,

☐   To recapitulate, public broadcasters may broadcast: (1) donor acknowledgements which inform but do not promote (i.e., the donor's logogram, may include a general description of product lines or services, as well as the donor's location); (2) announcements which promote the goods, services or activities of profit entities deemed in the public interest for which no consideration is received; and (3) announcements which promote the goods, services or activities of non-profit organizations, whether or not consideration is received. However, public broadcasters may not schedule announcements so as to interrupt regular programming.

. . . The *Second Report* is thus interpreted as prohibiting the broadcast of any direct fundraising activity, in the form of brief announcements as well as suspended programming, which inures to the benefit of any individual, organization or entity other than the licensee.[3]

Editorializing

Originally, noncommercial educational broadcasters were prohibited by Section 399 of the Communications Act from editorializing. The rationale was that, as an educational service, they should not espouse any one particular point of view. Additionally, a statutory ban made it easier for stations to resist suggestions by donors that they favor an issue in exchange for a contribution.

In 1984, the Supreme Court found that the ban on editorializing violated the First Amendment. In *FCC v. League of Women Voters of California* (1984), the Court allowed noncommercial stations to air editorials, but refused to allow stations to support or oppose candidates for political office.

Summary

Noncommercial educational broadcasting is the official title of the class of service designated by the FCC to be licensed to nonprofit foundations and educational institutions. Many of the rules and regulations that apply to commercial broadcasters apply to noncommercial stations as well. There are some notable exceptions, including a prohibition on the broadcast of commercial advertisements. However, these stations may broadcast underwriting announcements to acknowledge funds raised to support programming. Public radio and televison stations are noncommercial educational stations that are qualified to receive funds from the CPB.

Notes/References

1. Federal Communications Commission, *Annual Report, 1945* (Washington, DC: U.S. Government Printing Office, 1946), 20.
2. Second Report and Order, 86 F.C.C.2d 141 (1981) at 142.

3. Memorandum Opinion and Order, supra. at 903, 905. See also
   Memorandum and Opinion and Order, Docket 21136, 49 FR 13534, April
   5, 1984.

Cases

FCC v. League of Women Voters of California, 468 U.S. 364 (1984)
Memorandum Opinion and Order, Docket 21136, 49 FR 13534, April 5, 1984
Second Report and Order, 86 F.C.C.2d 141 (1981)

8

□ □ □
□ □ □
□ □ □

The Regulation
of Cable Television

As noted in Chapter 3, the FCC's authority for jurisdiction over cable television originally stemmed from cable's retransmission of over-the-air broadcast signals. In the mid-1950s, broadcasters, concerned with potential harm to over-the-air TV, asked the FCC to regulate cable as a common carrier. In *Frontier Broadcasting v. Collier*, the FCC held that cable was not a common carrier and therefore was outside the Commission's jurisdiction. By the early 1960s, however, the Commission changed its mind and indicated concern with the potential economic injury to broadcasters posed by cable television. This concern was the impetus to regulation. In 1965, the FCC promulgated rules regulating cable TV. The original rules required cable systems to carry all television stations that placed a grade B signal over a community. The rules also prohibited importation of a distant signal if the same program was available at the same time on a local channel. Finally, in *First Report and Order* and *Second Report and Order*, the FCC required cablecasters who wished to import a distant signal into one of the top 100 markets to show that the importation would serve the public interest. In *United States v. Southwestern Cable Co.*, the Supreme Court upheld the Commission's rules and its authority to regulate cable. The Court noted that the Commission's authority emanated from Section 152 of the Communications Act, which empowers the FCC to regulate all interstate communication by wire or radio.

Protecting Broadcasters—The 1970s

After *Southwestern*, the FCC placed a freeze on the importation of distant signals by cable companies. The freeze was instituted to allow the Commission time to develop new cable rules, which culminated in a *Notice of Proposed Rulemaking and Notice of Inquiry*.

During the 1970s, the FCC developed a number of rules regulating cable. Again, the underlying premise of most of the rules was the protection of broadcasters. For example, the FCC established franchising standards and required systems in major television markets to have a minimum of 20 channels, two-way capability, public access channels, and program origination.

In 1975, the FCC adopted antisiphoning rules designed to keep cable from taking sports and movie programming away from broadcasters. In *Home Box Office Inc. v. FCC* (1977), the court ruled that the FCC had exceeded its authority and the anti-siphoning rules were repealed. This decision paved the way for the growth of cable movie channels, which spearheaded cable's growth in the 1980s.

In 1977, the FCC began to relax cable regulations. In *Economic Relationship Between TV Broadcasting and CATV*, the FCC found that deregulation of cable would have no serious economic effect on broadcasting.

Cable in the '80s—A Period of Growth and Deregulation

In the 1980s, cable was substantially deregulated, which allowed the medium to enjoy tremendous growth. Also during this decade, Congress gave the FCC specific authority to regulate cable television. The 1984 Cable Communications Policy Act established a national policy for cable television.

As the decade closed and cable threatened to unseat traditional broadcasting in the United States, many argued for reregulation of cable. As in the past, the economic impact on broadcasters provided a major impetus for cable regulation. Critics charged that cable systems had become unresponsive to the public and enjoyed monopolies, charging outrageous rates for inferior services. Broadcasters argued for a "level playing field," which would allow them to more effectively compete with cable. Broadcasters watched their shares of the viewing audience dwindle from 90% to slightly under 60% between 1970 and 1991. In July 1991, the FCC Office of Plans and Policy (OPP) issued a report, referred to as the "Pepper Report" after OPP Chief Robert Pepper. The report predicts that increased cable penetration throughout the decade will lead to the demise of all but the healthiest broadcast stations located in the larger markets. FCC Chairman Alfred Sikes, in response to the "Pepper Report," called for further relaxation of regulations restraining broadcast stations economically. Sikes told *Broadcasting*, "The transmission medium that had been dominant is now secondary. Broadcasting has been eclipsed by cable."[1] As part of a planned "attic-to-basement" review of broadcast regulations, the FCC issued a Notice of Inquiry inviting broadcasters to submit wish lists of agency rules they would like to see changed.

The cable industry, on the other hand, worried about a different kind of threat—the entry of telephone companies (telcos) into the video delivery business. Cable feared that if telcos offered a "video dial tone" on fiber optic cable, with the potential of 108 channels in a true common carrier environment, cable television would suffer the same economic woes that they had inflicted on broadcasters.

It is within this framework that the regulation and proposed reregulation of cable television developed over the past decade. New communications technologies threaten to change the landscape drastically before the end of the century. High-definition television (HDTV); direct broadcast satellites (DBS); telco fiber optics; laser disks; multichannel, multipoint distribution services (MMDS); and other developments must be factored into the regulatory equation. When these new technologies clash with the archaic regulatory machinery of the FCC, it is certain that an interesting, if not always equitable, result will occur. Let us now turn to the issues and policy questions influencing the regulation of cable television.

Franchising/Overbuilding

The 1984 Cable Communications Policy Act establishes local franchising procedures. Because local governments control the rights of way and utility poles, local franchise authorities are usually municipalities or state agencies. The franchise authority grants a cable company use of the "rights of way" for a specific period of time, provided certain conditions are met. The franchise agreement will specify the number of channels to be provided by the cable operator, including any local access channels.

In the early 1980s, competition for cable franchises was fierce. Cable companies often made grandiose promises to municipalities in order to obtain the exclusive franchise. Assurances of numerous access channels, two-way communications, rapid wiring of the area, and other public service activities were made. Unfortunately, once the franchise was granted, many cable companies forgot their promises.

The process of choosing between applicants for a franchise triggers First Amendment issues. By selecting one applicant over another, the franchise authority effectively denies the community the programming offered by the rejected applicant. In *Group W Cable Inc. v. Santa Cruz*, the District Court for the District of Northern California ruled that if exclusive franchises are granted, the franchising authority must demonstrate that cable has some unique characteristic that justifies some exception to the rule prohibiting government intrusion into the functioning of the media. Santa Cruz violated the First Amendment because it failed to show that existing physical structures could not accommodate all cable operators who sought access. The issue raised is that of overbuilding—that is, allowing a second (or more) cable company to serve an area already served by cable.

The clash between the exclusive awarding of franchises and the First Amendment reached the Supreme Court when Preferred Communications sued the city of Los Angeles.

City of Los Angeles *et al.* v. Preferred Communications Inc. (1986)
Justice Rehnquist delivered the opinion of the Court.

☐ Respondent Preferred Communications, Inc. sued petitioners City of Los Angeles (City) and the Department of Water and Power (DWP) in the

United States District Court for the Central District of California. The complaint alleged a violation of the respondent's rights under the First and Fourteenth Amendments, and under §§1 and 2 of the Sherman Act, by reason of the City's refusal to grant respondent a cable television franchise and of DWP's refusal to grant access to DWP's poles or underground conduits used for power lines. The District Court dismissed the complaint for failure to state a claim upon which relief could be granted. . . . The Court of Appeals for the Ninth Circuit affirmed with respect to the Sherman Act, but reversed as to the First Amendment claim. . . . We granted certiorari with respect to the latter issue. . . .

Respondent asked Pacific Telephone and Telegraph (PT&T) and DWP for permission to lease space on their utility poles in order to provide cable television service in the south central area of Los Angeles. . . . These utilities responded that they would not lease space unless respondent first obtained a cable television franchise from the City. . . . Respondent asked the City for a franchise, but the City refused to grant it one stating that respondent had failed to participate in an auction that was to award a single franchise in the area. . . . The complaint further alleged that cable operators are First Amendment speakers . . . that there is sufficient excess physical capacity and economic demand in the south central area of Los Angeles to accommodate more than one cable company . . . and that the City's auction process allowed it to discriminate among franchise applicants based on which one it deemed to be the "best." . . . Based on these and other factual allegations, the complaint alleged that the City and DWP had violated the Free Speech Clause of the First Amendment, as made applicable to the States by the Fourteenth Amendment . . .

The City did not deny that there was excess physical capacity to accommodate more than one cable television system. But it argued that the physical scarcity of available space on public utility structures, the limits of economic demand for the cable medium, and the practical and esthetic disruptive effect that installing and maintaining a cable system has on the public right-of-way justified its decision to restrict access to its facilities to a single cable television company. . . .

The Court of Appeals for the Ninth Circuit . . . upheld the conclusion that petitioners were immune from liability under federal antitrust laws. . . . But it reversed the District Court's dismissal of the First Amendment claim, and remanded for further proceedings. . . . It held that, taking the allegations in the complaint as true. . . . the City violated the First Amendment by refusing to issue a franchise to more than one cable company when there was sufficient excess physical and economic capacity to accommodate more than one. . . . The Court of Appeals expressed the view that the facts alleged in the complaint brought respondent into the ambit of cases such as *Miami Herald Publishing Co. v. Tornillo*, 418 U.S. 241 (1974), rather than of cases such as *Red Lion Broadcasting Co. v. FCC*, 395 U.S. 367 (1969) . . .

We agree with the Court of Appeals that respondent's complaint should not have been dismissed, and we therefore affirm the judgment of that court; but we do so on a narrower ground than the one taken by it. The well-pleaded facts in the complaint include allegations of sufficient excess physical capacity and economic demand for cable television operators in the area which respondents sought to serve. The City, while admitting the existence of excess physical capacity on the utility poles, the rights-of-way, and the like, justifies the limit on franchises in terms of minimizing the demands that cable systems make on public property. The City characterizes these uses as the stringing of "nearly 700 miles of hanging and buried wire and other appliances necessary for the operation of the system" . . . The City also characterizes them as "a permanent visual blight," . . . Respondent in its turn replies that the City does not "provide anything more than speculations and assumptions," and that the City's "legitimate concerns are easily satisfied without the need to limit the right to speak to a single speaker."

. . . We are unwilling to decide the legal questions posed by the parties without a more thoroughly developed record of proceedings in which the parties have an opportunity to prove those disputed factual assertions upon which they rely.

We do think that the activities in which the respondent allegedly seeks to engage plainly implicate First Amendment interests. Respondent alleges:

> *"The business of cable television, like that of newspapers and magazines, is to provide its subscribers with a mixture of news, information and entertainment. As do newspapers, cable television companies use a portion of their available space to reprint (or retransmit) the communications of others, while at the same time providing some original content."* . . .

Thus, through original programming or by exercising editorial discretion over which stations or programs to include in its repertoire, respondent seeks to communicate messages on a wide variety of topics and in a wide variety of formats . . . Cable television partakes of some of the aspects of speech and the communication of ideas as do the traditional enterprises of newspaper and book publishers, public speakers, and pamphleteers. Respondent's proposed activities would seem to implicate First Amendment interests as do the activities of wireless broadcasters . . . Moreover, where speech and conduct are joined in a single course of action, the First Amendment values must be balanced against competing societal interests. See e.g., *Members of City Council v. Taxpayers for Vincent, 466 U.S. 789 (1984), at 805–807; United States v. O'Brien, 391 U.S. 367, 376–377 (1968).* We do not think, however, that it is desirable to express any more detailed views on the proper resolution of the First Amendment claim raised by respondent's complaint and the City's responses to it without a fuller development of the disputed issues in the case . . . This Court "may not simply assume that the ordinance will always advance the asserted state interests sufficiently to justify its abridgement of expressive activity." *Taxpayers for Vincent, 466 U.S. at 803, n.22; Landmark Communications, Inc. v. Virginia, 435 U.S. 829, 843–44 (1978).*

We affirm the judgment of the Court of Appeals reversing the dismissal of respondent's complaint by the District Court, and remand the case to the District Court so that petitioners may file an answer and the material factual disputes between the parties may be resolved.[2]

Preferred essentially says that provided utilities are adequate, a city cannot arbitrarily deny a franchise to more than one cable company. The Supreme Court did not definitively answer the question of overbuilding. If evidence can be presented that shows that a cable company is a natural monopoly in a given market, then permission to overbuild can be denied, as evidenced in *Central Telecommunications v. TCI Cablevision, Inc.* For a natural monopoly to occur, it must be demonstrated that no willing competitors exist. At this writing, *Preferred* is winding its way back to the Supreme Court. It is currently being heard in the ninth circuit.

Leased Access

The 1984 Cable Act did not mandate that local franchises set aside channels for public, educational, and government (PEG) access. The act did mandate that systems with more than 35 channels provide commercial, leased access channels. Systems having 36 to 54 channels must set aside 10% of their activated channels for commercial leased access. Stations with more than 54 channels must set aside 15% of active channels for commercial leased access. In calculating the number of active channels, the cable company cannot deduct retransmitted over-the-air channels. The statute provides a deduction for the number of channels the federal law requires systems to carry.

The Cable Act relieves cable operators of any liability for libel and other content-related suits filed as a result of material transmitted on a leased access channel. Liability is assumed by the program producer. The cable operator may prohibit the transmission of potentially obscene or indecent programming.

The act also allows local cable companies to set the rates and conditions for leased access. This means that the cable company can take into account whether a leased access program will adversely compete with other channels on the system or whether a leased access program will add to the diversity. While leased access has not been used on a national scale by program producers denied a channel on a cable system, the Playboy Channel has purchased leased access in some markets.

Public, Educational, and Government Channels

The local franchising authority is empowered by Section 531(a) of the Cable Act to establish PEG channel access. PEG channels are noncommercial in nature and vary in number and form according to the requirements stipulated by the franchise agreement. It must be remembered that cable stations are not required by the act to provide PEG channels. Cable stations are required to provide leased access channels. However, the local community may require PEG channels before a franchise will be awarded.

Federal, State, and Local Relationships

The franchising authority may regulate the rates of a local cable system if the cable system is not subjected to effective competition. Effective competition, as defined by the FCC, exists if either of the following two conditions are met:

(1) Six unduplicated over-the-air broadcast television signals are available in the entire cable community; or
(2) an independently owned, competing multichannel video delivery service is available to 50 percent of the homes passed by the incumbent cable system, and subscribed to by at least 10 percent of the homes passed by the incumbent cable system.[3]

In determining effective competition, the Commission counts all unduplicated over-the-air broadcast services available to the community. This includes all full-service commercial and noncommercial stations, as well as satellite stations, translators, and low-power television stations.

In applying the multichannel competitor test in communities lacking six broadcast channels, the FCC will consider a second cable service, satellite master antenna television (SMATV), home satellite dishes, multichannel multipoint distribution services (MMDS), and direct broadcast satellite (DBS) availability.

Rate Regulation

The FCC requires that when franchising authorities regulate cable rates, they allow cable operators to earn a fair return on their investment. The Cable Act provides for an automatic 5% annual increase in rates. Any additional rate regulation would be applied after the initial 5% and then only in the absence of effective competition, as stipulated in CFR 47, Section 543 (a)(e)(1)(2).

Technical Standards

Cable systems are required to deliver an acceptable signal to the homes of subscribers. Technical standards are regulated by the FCC and may be found in CFR, Subpart K, Section 76.601 to Section 76.619. Federal guidelines supersede local franchising authority in this area. The Supreme Court upheld FCC authority in this area in *New York City v. FCC*. The Court ruled that the Cable Act implied preemption of state and local technical standards by the Commission.

Signal Carriage Rules

The Must-Carry Rules

As noted in Chapter 3, the FCC first promulgated must-carry rules for cable in 1965. The rules required cable systems to carry the signals of all local television stations. The intent of the rules was to ensure that "free TV" was not undermined by cable. In the early development of cable, the must-carry rules benefited both broadcasters and cablecasters. UHF broadcasters in particular reaped positive benefits. Carriage of their signals on cable helped them overcome some of the transmission and channel positioning problems that had plagued UHF in an effort to compete with VHF signals. Cablecasters benefited from the must-carry rules, because they were given a free source of quality programming, much of it from the major networks. This lent a legitimacy to the enterprise.

As cable penetration increased and more viable sources of programming became available to cable systems, must-carry rules became more of a burden to cable operators. Many felt that they should not be forced to tie up channels with the signals of marginal local stations when more lucrative choices were available. In 1980, Turner Broadcasting System filed a petition with the FCC asking that the agency repeal the must-carry rules. The Turner Petition argued that the rules violated the First and Fifth Amendment rights of cable operators and programmers. In *Turner Broadcasting System, Inc. v. FCC*, the FCC rejected Turner's argument and the rules remained.

In 1980, Quincy Cable TV dropped two signals it carried under the must-carry rules without FCC approval. Quincy's rationale for dropping the channels was that the stations did not carry programming of interest to the community. Quincy replaced the dropped channels with stations it believed to be of more interest to the community. The FCC fined Quincy Cable $5000 for the rule infraction.

Quincy Cable and the Turner Broadcasting System appealed their cases to the U.S. Court of Appeals for the District of Columbia. In *Quincy Cable TV, Inc. v. FCC*, the court found the must-carry rules, as drafted, to be in violation of the First Amendment and outside the scope of the FCC's regulatory authority.

☐ **Quincy Cable TV, Inc. v. FCC (1985)**

. . . Almost from the beginning, the must carry rules were a centerpiece of the FCC's efforts to actively oversee the growth of cable television. . . . Then, as now, the applicability of the rules varied according to such factors as the quality of the broadcast signal available in the community. In general, however, the rules required cable operators, upon request, to carry any broadcast signal considered local under the Commission's complex formula. . . .

. . . Although the economic analysis initially advanced in support of the must-carry rules was somewhat complicated, the Commission's general objective was straightforward: to assure [sic] that the advent of cable technology did not undermine the financial viability of free, community oriented television.

. . . At the time of the initial promulgation of the rules, the Commission acknowledged that it had insufficient data to "predict with reliability" the extent of the risk posed by cable. *First Report and Order*, 38 FCC at 711. *See also Second Report and Order*, 2 FCC 2d at 744–745.

. . . By forcing cable systems to carry local and significantly viewed broadcast signals, the Commission sought to channel the growth of cable in a manner consistent with the public's interest in the preservation of local broadcasting.

. . . On several occasions, the Supreme Court has addressed questions concerning the breadth of the FCC's jurisdiction over cable television. *See United States v. Southwestern Cable*, 392 U.S. at 178. . . . However in marked contrast to the extensive First Amendment jurisprudence developed in the context of the broadcast media . . . the Court has never confronted a challenge to the constitutional validity of the must-carry rules or any other regulation affecting cable television. . . .

In the lower federal courts, questions concerning the constitutionality of various cable regulations arose almost from the first moment the Commission asserted its regulatory jurisdiction over the industry.

. . . The most common approach was simply to treat cable and broadcast television as indistinguishable for purposes of First Amendment analysis. Because it was well established that broadcast media could be subject to regulation far more intrusive than the First Amendment would tolerate in other contexts, it naturally followed for these courts that cable regulation, a variant on the same theme, should be subject to no more exacting scrutiny . . . Other courts undertook a somewhat more discriminating analysis. They upheld the regulations only after concluding that the restraint on speech was no greater than was reasonably required to serve the important interest of preserving local broadcasting. . . .

In recent years, the lower federal courts have subjected FCC regulation of cable television to a far more rigorous constitutional analysis. *It is*

now clearly established, for example, that cable operators engage in con-
duct protected by the First Amendment. [Emphasis added by the author.]

. . . [I]n *Home Box Office* this court noted that earlier cases that had
considered the intersection of the First Amendment and cable television
regulations had incorrectly relied on Supreme Court precedent developed
in the context of regulation of the broadcast media . . .

At issue in *Home Box Office* were a number of FCC regulations limiting the programming fare a cablecaster . . . could offer its subscribers. The
Commission defended the rules by suggesting that they were necessary
to assure [sic] that the various forms of pay television, including cable, not
degrade the quality of programming on conventional broadcast television.
As in the present controversy, the Commission suggested that the competitive injury to broadcasters would be felt most acutely by those who
could not afford the more expensive video services.

The court rejected the FCC's argument and sustained the First
Amendment challenge. Concluding that the regulation should be treated
as an incidental burden on speech, the court applied the test announced
by the Supreme Court in *United States v. O'Brien*, 391 U.S. 367, 377 (1968).
Thus the regulations would be valid only if they served a substantial governmental interest and were no more intrusive than necessary to serve
that interest. . . .

. . . We begin by evaluating whether First Amendment principles governing regulation of the broadcast media should also apply to the regulation of cable television. Concluding that cable television warrants a standard of review distinct from that applied to broadcasters, we next
consider whether the must-carry rules merit treatment as an "incidental"
burden on speech and therefore warrant analysis under the balancing test
set out in *United States v. O'Brien, supra*, 367 U.S. at 199. Although our
review leaves us with serious doubts about the appropriateness of invoking *O'Brien's* interest-balancing formulation, we conclude that the rules so
clearly fail under that standard that we need not resolve whether they
warrant a more exacting scrutiny.

. . . In short, our examination of the purposes that underlie the must-
carry rules, the nature and degree of the intrusions they effect, and prior
judicial treatment of analogous regulations leaves us with serious doubts
about the propriety of applying the standard of review reserved for incidental burdens on speech. Although the goal of the rules—preserving local broadcasting—can be viewed as unrelated to the suppression or protection of any particular set of ideas, the rules nonetheless profoundly
affect values that lie near the heart of the First Amendment. They favor
one group of speakers over another. They severely impinge on editorial
discretion. And, most importantly, if a system's channel capacity is substantially or completely occupied by mandatory signals, the rules prevent

cable programmers from reaching their intended audience even if that result directly contravenes the preference of cable subscribers.

. . . Regulation of emerging video technologies requires a delicate balancing of competing interests . . .

When the Commission strikes this balance in favor of regulations that impinge on rights protected by the First Amendment, it assumes a heavy burden of justification . . .

After extensive examination of the purposes and effects of the must-carry rules, we have concluded that the Commission has failed to carry this heavy burden . . .

We stress that we have not found it necessary to decide whether any version of the mandatory carriage rules would contravene the First Amendment. We hold only that in their current form they can no longer stand.[4]

The Interim Must-Carry Rules of 1987

The FCC did not wait long before promulgating new must-carry rules. In 1987, the Commission developed rules that were the product of a compromise between broadcaster and cablecasters. Small cable systems were exempt from the new rules, while larger systems were granted more leeway in determining which stations they would be required to carry. Only those broadcast stations within 50 miles of a cable system, capable of delivering a high-quality signal to the cable system, would be considered for carriage. In addition, commercial stations were required to demonstrate significant viewership if they wanted carriage. Cable systems were not required to carry stations that duplicated programming, such as network affiliates.

In order to ensure that viewers had easier access to the broadcast signals not carried by cable systems, the FCC required cable companies to sell and install A/B switches in subscribers homes. An A/B switch enabled subscribers to switch between cable and off-air signals.

Finally, the new rules also required cable systems to carry at least one public television station, regardless of distance or signal quality.

The must-carry rules and the A/B box requirement were to expire after 5 years. This provision assumed that 5 years was sufficient time for subscribers to be properly "educated" in the method of switching between cable and over-the-air broadcasting.

The interim must-carry rules were challenged based on the First Amendment and *O'Brien*. In 1987, the District of Columbia court of appeals struck down the rules in *Century Communications Corp. v. FCC*. The Supreme Court refused to review the case.

☐ **Century Communications Corp. v. FCC (1988)**

. . . In the aftermath of *Quincy Cable TV*, the FCC immediately suspended enforcement of the must-carry rules. Four months later, it announced its intention to undertake rulemaking proceedings . . . and eventually, in

November 1986, 16 months after *Quincy* had been handed down, the agency released a new, more limited set of must-carry rules designed to accommodate *Quincy Cable TV's* concerns . . .

The most salient feature of the new rules was that the Commission substantially altered its stated justification for imposing must-carry rules at all. No longer did the Commission argue, as it had prior to the *Quincy Cable TV* decision, that the rules were needed for the indefinite future to ensure the viewer access to local broadcast stations. Rather, the Commission now argued that must-carry rules were needed to guarantee such access during a shorter-term transition period during which viewers could become accustomed to an existing and inexpensive but largely unknown piece of equipment known as the "input-selector device."

Such devices, if hooked up to a television, allow viewers at any given time to select, simply by flicking a switch, between shows offered by their cable system and broadcast television shows offered off-the-air. These devices, the most common of which is known in the cable industry as an "A/B switch," are about the size of a standard lightswitch, and work by being hooked up to a roof-top, attic or television-top antenna . . .

The Commission estimated that it would take approximately five years for the public to become acclimated to the existence of these switches, and accordingly, its interim rules should be in place for that same five years . . .

The FCC, however, adduces scant evidence for its judgement of a widespread "misperception" among cable subscribers that the only means of access to off-the-air signals is through cable service. It puts forth no attitudinal surveys, or polls, suggesting the likely pace of consumer adaptation to the A/B switch technology . . .

Additionally, we are skeptical—and the FCC's report says nothing to relieve this skepticism—that any consumer education campaign will have much impact so long as viewers can continue to rely on must-carry to get their fix of local broadcasts . . .

Our decision is a narrow one. We hold simply that, in the absence of record evidence in support of its policy, the FCC's reimposition of must-carry rules on a five-year basis neither clearly furthers a substantial governmental interest nor is of brief enough duration to be considered narrowly tailored so as to satisfy the *O'Brien* test for incidental restrictions on speech. . . . Accordingly, we have no choice but to strike down this latest embodiment of must-carry.[5]

The court did not say that must-carry was, in itself, an unconstitutional concept. It merely found that the FCC had not justified the reason for implementing the rules sufficiently. The FCC began, at the request of Congress, to collect data useful in determining the impact of the demise of must-carry rules on broadcasters. Since

Century, cable legislation has been introduced with must-carry as a part of the package. At this writing, this legislation has not been passed.

Among the options that have been discussed as a compromise to must-carry is the concept of "retransmission consent." Under a bill brought before the Senate in the summer of 1991, broadcasters could choose between traditional must-carry or file for retransmission consent. Retransmission consent would allow broadcasters to negotiate with local cable operators in order to work out terms under which the broadcast station's signal could be transmitted.

Program Exclusivity

The FCC adopted new program exclusivity rules, which became effective on January 1, 1990. These rules are the syndicated exclusivity (Syndex) and network nonduplication rules. Recall that the Commission abolished similar rules in 1980 as part of the deregulation of cable (See Chapter 3). In *United Video Inc. v. FCC* (1989), the court ruled that the program exclusivity rules did not violate the First Amendment. The court based the decision on the assumption that no First Amendment right exists to make use of others' copyrighted programs.

Syndicated Exclusivity Rules

The Syndex rules protect local broadcasters from distant signal importation of syndicated programs that are broadcast locally. In other words, if a local station buys the rights to a syndicated program such as *Oprah*, a cable system may be prohibited from importing *Oprah* from a station outside the market. If *Oprah* has been purchased on a market-exclusive basis, the local station can require the local cable company to refrain from transmitting the signal of the distant station at times when that station broadcasts *Oprah*, as stipulated in CFR, Sections 76.151–76.113. The geographic area protected by Syndex is dependent on the terms negotiated between the program supplier and the program purchaser. The contract must contain specific language invoking Syndex. The FCC requires the following language:

> [T]he licensee (or substitute name) shall, by the terms of this contract, be entitled to invoke the protection against duplication of programming imported under the Compulsory Copyright License, as provided in § 76.151 of the FCC rules ("or as provided in the FCC's syndicated exclusivity rules").[6]

Network Nonduplication Rules

Section 76.92 of the FCC rules allows networks and affiliates to enter into agreements that prohibit cable systems from duplicating network signals in a single market. The nonduplication rule applies to stations within 35 miles of a cable system in the top 100 markets and within 55 miles of a cable system in markets larger than 100.

Broadcasters who wish to invoke the nonduplication rules must notify the cable system of their intent to do so within 60 days of signing a nonduplication contract with a network. No specific language is required in the contract, like that required to invoke Syndex.

Copyright and Cable

In *Fortnightly Corp. v. United Artists Television Inc.* (1968), the Supreme Court ruled that cable systems could retransmit the signals of local broadcast stations without incurring liability under the Copyright Act of 1909. Six years later, in *Teleprompter Corp. v. CBS*, the Court extended the same protection for the retransmission of distant signals. The rationale for the Court's decision in both cases was that cable retransmission was not a "performance" of a copyrighted work and therefore not subject to liability under the Copyright Act.

Broadcasters and program producers felt that this interpretation of the law was inequitable and when Congress began a revision of the Copyright Act, they argued that cable ought to pay copyright owners for retransmission.

Congress believed it impractical for each cable system to negotiate directly with copyright owners to obtain retransmission rights, so it created a compulsory license for cable television.

The compulsory license provides for semiannual royalty payments by cable operators to the Copyright Royalty Tribunal, which was created as part of the 1976 Copyright Act. Every 6 months, cable operators must provide the Copyright Office with information about retransmitted broadcast signals, the system's gross subscriber receipts, and receipts from secondary retransmission of local and distant broadcast signals. Royalty payments are established in the Copyright Act of 1976 and may be adjusted from time to time by the CRT.

The compulsory license has many critics. Broadcasters, copyright owners, cablecasters, and members of Congress have called for its repeal. The critics charge that copyright owners are not being fairly compensated and that the compulsory license does not accomplish what it is supposed to do.

The cable reregulation bill before the Senate in the summer of 1991, sparked additional concerns over the compulsory license. If retransmission consent becomes reality, the Copyright Office expressed the opinion that the compulsory licensing scheme is no longer valid.

Indecency and Cable

The Cable Act prohibits the transmission of obscene material by cable systems. Section 559 provides for a $10,000 fine or 2 years imprisonment, or both, for transmission of material "unprotected by the Constitution." Indecency has constitutional protection and is, therefore, not prohibited by the Cable Act. The courts have struck down local ordinances designed to prohibit indecency on cable.

The City of Miami passed an ordinance prohibiting the transmission of obscene and indecent material on cable systems. The ordinance was not challenged on its definition of "obscene," nor on the right to prohibit such material. The ordinance was challenged on First Amendment grounds. It was argued that because "indecent" material is not void of First Amendment protection, it cannot be completely prohibited.

In deciding *Cruz v. Ferre*, the U.S. Court of Appeals for the Eleventh Circuit distinguished between cable and broadcasting. The court noted that while broadcast signals are pervasive and may "intrude" on the privacy of the home, cable is invited in.

☐ The Cablevision subscriber must affirmatively elect to have cable service come into his home. Additionally, the subscriber must make the additional affirmative decision whether to purchase any "extra" programming services, such as HBO . . .

However noble may have been the city's intentions, we are constrained to recognize the limitations imposed by the Constitution and the opinions of the Supreme Court. The city's attempt through the challenged ordinance to regulate indecency on its cable television system exceeds these limitations.[7]

In *Jones v. Wilkinson* (1986), the U.S. Court of Appeals for the Tenth Circuit struck down the Utah Cable Television Programming Decency Act. The act authorized nuisance actions against cable systems in Utah that transmitted indecent programming. The court ruled that the Utah statute was preempted by the Cable Communications Policy Act, which limits state authority over cable program content to the prosecution of obscenity and material not protected by the Constitution.

Antisiphoning Rules

In the 1970s, the FCC became concerned that cable TV would "siphon" programs from over-the-air TV. Of special concern were the rights to sports and feature films. After running in the theater, many films would find their way, often in edited form, to network television. Cable networks like Home Box Office would run these films uncut, which provided an attractive alternative for program distributors.

The FCC promulgated rules that prohibited cable systems from showing films less than 3 years old. Cable systems were also barred from devoting more than 90% of their schedules to films or sports. In *Home Box Office Inc. v. FCC* (1977), the court overturned the antisiphoning rules and held that the rules were outside the FCC's jurisdiction over cable television and a violation of the First Amendment.

Sports Blackouts

Section 76.67 of the FCC rules prohibits a cable system from carrying a live sporting event if that event is not being broadcast by a station carried on the cable system. In order to invoke prohibition, the broadcast station must request that the event not be carried on the cable system. If a cable system is required to delete a sports program, it may substitute a program from another television station, rather than simply go to black, as stipulated in FCC Rules, Section 76.67(1)(d).

Rules Common to Broadcasting and Cable

Equal Opportunity Employment

Like broadcasters, cable companies are required to adhere to EEO guidelines. Cable companies must file an annual employment report (FCC Form 395A) on or before May 1st of each year, as stipulated in FCC Rules, Section 76.77(a). The FCC uses Form 395A to determine whether cable systems are in compliance with EEO guidelines. Section 76.77(c) requires that the FCC investigate each cable system at least once every 5 years.

Records Available for Public Inspection

Cable systems must also make certain records available for public inspection. Annual employment reports and complaint reports filed with the Commission (including exhibits and letters that are part of these reports) must be available for public inspection at each cable office that has five or more full-time employees, as stipulated in Section 76.79(a)(b). These documents must be maintained for 5 years.

Cablecasts by Candidates for Public Office and Personal Attack Rules

Cablecasters are subjected to the same "equal time" and "lowest unit rate" requirements as broadcasters. The Fairness Doctrine was applied to cable and, like broadcasters, the personal attack rules, political editorializing rule, and Zapple Doctrine are applicable, as stipulated in FCC Rules, Section 76.209.

Cross-ownership, Multiple Ownership, and Fin-Syn

In 1992 the FCC voted to allow the three networks (ABC, CBS, and NBC) to own cable systems and vice versa. Television networks may acquire cable systems serving up to 10% of homes passed nationwide and up to 50% of homes passed in the market. The 50% cap will be waived in situations where the network-owned system is in competition with an existing cable system.[8] The multiple ownership and financial and syndication rules do not apply to cable.

Summary

The FCC's authority to regulate cable stems from the Communications Act, which empowers the Commission to regulate all interstate wire and radio communication. The Cable Televsion Act of 1984 outlines the scope of the Commission's authority over cable. Although cable television has been substantially deregulated, the Commission places some programming and ownership restrictions on the industry. Cable is not subjected to the same public interest standard as over-the-air broadcasters.

Notes/References

1. "Sikes Looks To Strengthen Broadcasters' Hand," *Broadcasting* (July 8, 1991): 23.
2. City of Los Angeles et al. v. Preferred Communications Inc., 476 U.S. 488 (1986).
3. *FCC Redefines Effective Competition for Cable; Seeks Comment on Mandatory Signal Carriage Requirements*, MM Docket 90–4, (June 13, 1991).
4. *Quincy Cable TV, Inc. v. FCC*, U.S. Ct.App.D.C., 768 F.2d 1434 (1985), cert. denied 476 U.S. 1169 (1986).
5. *Century Communications Corp. v. FCC*, 835 F.2d 292 (D.C. Cir. 1987), cert. denied 108 S.Ct. 2014 (1988).
6. 47 CFR Section 76.159.
7. *Cruz v. Ferre*, U.S. Ct.App. 11th Cir., 755 F.2d 1415, 57 R.R. 1452 (1985).
8. Joe Flint, "FCC Lets TV Networks into Cable Ownership," *Broadcasting* (June 22, 1992): 4.

Cases

Central Telecommunications v. TCI Cablevision, Inc., 800 F.2d 711 (8th Cir., 1986)

Century Communications Corp. v. FCC, 835 F.2d 292 (DC Cir., 1987), cert. denied 108 S.Ct. 2014 (1988)

City of Los Angeles et al. v. Preferred Communications Inc., 476 U.S. 488 (1986)

Cruz v. Ferre, U.S. Ct.App. 11th Cir., 755 F.2d 1415, 57 R.R. 1452 (1985)

Economic Relationship Between TV Broadcasting and CATV, 71 F.C.C.2d 632 (1979)

FCC Redefines Effective Competition for Cable; Seeks Comment on Mandatory Signal Carriage Requirements, MM Docket 90–4, (June 13, 1991)

First Report and Order, Docket Nos. 14895 and 15253, 38 F.C.C. 683 (1965)

Fortnightly Corp. v. United Artists Television Inc., 392 U.S. 390 (1968)

Frontier Broadcasting v. Collier, 24 F.C.C. 251 (1958)

Group W Cable Inc. v. Santa Cruz, 14 Med.L.Rptr. 1769 (1987)

Home Box Office Inc. v. FCC, 567 F.2d 9, 44–45 (DC Cir., 1977), cert. denied, 434 U.S. 829 (1977)

Jones v. Wilkinson, (CA 10, 1986) 13 Med.L.Rptr. 1913

New York City v. FCC, (U.S. Sup.Ct., 1988) 15 Med.L.Rptr. 1542

Notice of Proposed Rule Making and Notice of Inquiry, Docket No. 18397, 15 F.C.C.2d 417, 437–49 (1968)

Quincy Cable TV, Inc. v. FCC, U.S. Ct.App. DC, 768 F.2d 1434 (1985), cert. denied 476 U.S. 1169 (1986)

Second Report and Order; Docket Nos. 14895, 15233, and 15971, 2 F.C.C.2d 725 (1966)

Teleprompter Corp. v. CBS, 415 U.S. 394 (1974)

Turner Broadcasting System, Inc. v. FCC, 730 F.2d 1549 (DC Cir., 1983)

United States v. Southwestern Cable Co., 392 U.S. 157 (1968)

United Video Inc. v. FCC, (CA DC, 1989) 17 Med.L.Rptr. 1129

9

□ □ □
□ □ □
□ □ □

Copyright and Music Licensing

Copyright

The first federal Copyright Act was adopted in 1790. The original act protected books and maps from unauthorized use for a 14-year renewable term. In 1802, protection for prints was added to the act. Musical compositions received protection in 1831. Photographs became copyrightable in 1865 and paintings became copyrightable in 1870. It was not until 1978 that sound and video recordings could be copyrighted.

The copyright statute was revised twice in this century in order to accommodate the emergence of new technologies. As a result, many creative works are still protected under the 1909 Copyright Act, while those works registered after January 1, 1978, are protected under the Copyright Act of 1976. The 1976 act preempted all state copyright laws.

The Scope of Copyright Protection

The Copyright Act is found in title 17 of the U.S. Code. Copyright provides protection from unauthorized use of original works of authorship, including literary, dramatic, musical, artistic, and certain other intellectual works. The 1976 act provides protection for published and unpublished works. Section 106 of the Copyright Act gives the owner of a copyright the exclusive right

(1) To reproduce the work in copies or phonorecords;
(2) To prepare derivative works based on the original;
(3) To distribute copies or phonorecords of the work to the public by sale or other transfer of ownership, or by rental, lease, or lending;
(4) To perform the copyrighted work publicly, in the case of literary, musical, dramatic and choreographic works, pantomimes, and motion pictures and other audiovisual works, and
(5) To display the copyrighted work publicly, in the case of literary, musical, dramatic and choreographic works, pantomimes, and pictorial, graphic or sculptural works, including the individual images of a motion picture or other audiovisual work. [1]

A copyright protects the expression of ideas, not the ideas themselves. The historical fact that someone died is not copyrightable, but a particular version of the death is copyrightable. When a television news program copyrights video of a news event, they do not claim rights to the event itself, only to their particular expression of the event. News departments may not keep competitors from covering a news event by copyrighting it, but the competitors must shoot their own video or obtain their own audio.

In *Hoeling v. Universal Studios* (1980), the U.S. Court of Appeals for the Second Circuit dealt with the concept of separating an idea from the expression of that idea.

In 1937, the German dirigible *Hindenberg* exploded just before landing at Lakehurst, New Jersey, killing 36 people. The airship had just completed a trip across the Atlantic. The official explanation for the tragedy was that static electricity had ignited the highly flammable hydrogen gas used to provide the airship's buoyancy.

A.A. Hoeling, after years of research, came to a different conclusion. In 1962, he wrote a book espousing his thesis that the *Hindenberg* was destroyed by a bomb planted by one of the ship's riggers before it left Germany. The bomb was timed to explode after the ship had landed, but a thunderstorm delayed the landing and the bomb exploded while the ship was still airborne.

In 1972, Michael Mooney wrote a work of fiction entitled *The Hindenberg*. Mooney's book was built around Hoeling's thesis. Universal Studios bought the rights to Mooney's book and a motion picture of the same name was released in 1975. Hoeling sued Universal Studios for copyright infringement, arguing that his thesis was copyrighted in his 1962 book.

The court held that Hoeling's thesis was not subject to copyright protection. The theory of the bombing was viewed as "historical fact." The court ruled that facts are not copyrightable—only the expression of the facts is copyrightable. Therefore, a verbatim copying of Hoeling's book would have resulted in copyright infringement, but not a new expression of the facts as found in the Mooney book and subsequent movie.

Works That Can Be Copyrighted

Copyright protection exists for original works of authorship, as soon as they become fixed in a tangible form of expression. This includes works that are perceived by means of a machine, like video or audio tape. Copyrightable works include the following:

literary works, including compilations and computer programs
musical works, including accompanying words
dramatic works, including accompanying music
pantomimes and choreographic works

pictorial, graphic, and sculptural works, including maps and blueprints
motion pictures and other audiovisual works
sound recordings
computer programs

Materials That May Not Be Copyrighted

Any work that is not in a fixed, tangible form and is not an original expression of an idea cannot be copyrighted. Ideas, procedures, methods, concepts, or processes in themselves may not be copyrighted. If a work consists entirely of information that is common property with no original authorship, it may not be copyrighted. Examples include calendars, rulers, or lists and tables taken from public documents or other common sources.

In *WCVB-TV v. Boston Athletic Association*, the appellate court upheld a lower court ruling that allowed Boston's WCVB Channel 5 to televise the Boston Marathon even though race officials asserted that another local television station was licensed to cover the event. Race promoters argued that the use of the words "Boston Marathon" by Channel 5 constituted a trademark infringement and coverage of the event was a copyright violation.

The appellate court ruled that there was no evidence to suggest that use of the words "Boston Marathon" by Channel 5 suggested official sponsorship of the event. Indeed, the station had broadcast a disclaimer noting that it was not the official sponsor. The court could find no evidence suggesting that Channel 5 might profit from viewers who wrongly believed that the Boston Marathon Association had authorized the broadcasts. No trademark or copyright violations occurred. The words "Boston Marathon" describe the event and are not protected.

The concept of "original authorship" served as the basis of the decision in *Production Contractors v. WGN Continental Broadcasting Co.*, which involved the telecasting of a public event. When WGN-TV announced its intentions to televise the 1985 Chicago Christmas parade, Production Contractors, the parade's organizer, sought to prohibit WGN from doing so. Although the parade was a public event, Production Contractors had granted exclusive rights to WLS-TV and ABC. The U.S. District Court for the Northern District of Illinois ruled that the parade was not a work of authorship and not entitled to copyright protection. WLS could not prevent WGN from televising the parade, provided WGN used its own equipment, camera operators, and directors. In so doing, WGN would create its own "authorship." Both WLS and WGN could create copyrightable versions of the event.

Other noncopyrightable material includes titles, names, short phrases, symbols, or designs. These may be registered as trademarks, which are discussed later in this chapter.

Obtaining a Copyright

It should be emphasized that a work is protected by copyright from the moment it is fixed in a tangible form—either as a written copy or other media, such as audiotape or videotape. Authors are not required to register their work with the Copyright Office in order to obtain protection; however, there are advantages to doing so. A major advantage is that registration allows the copyright owner to collect statutory damages and attorney's fees in cases of infringement. Registration also makes prosecution of infringement easier, because a public record of the copyright has been established and serves as *prima facie* evidence in court.

To register a work, the author must complete the proper application form (see Figure 9.1). If a work has been published, two copies must be included. If the work is unpublished, one copy of the work is required. The author must then submit the application, copies of the work, and a filing fee to the Register of Copyrights, Library of Congress, Washington, D.C. 20559 (see Figure 9.2). It is important to submit all materials in one envelope.

For Original Registration

Form TX: for published and unpublished non-dramatic literary works

Form SE: for serials, works issued or intended to be issued in successive parts bearing numerical or chronological designations and intended to be continued indefinitely (periodicals, newspapers, magazines, newsletters, annuals, journals, etc.)

Form PA: for published and unpublished works of the performing arts (musical and dramatic works, pantomimes and choreographic works, motion pictures and other audiovisual works)

Form VA: for published and unpublished works of the visual arts (pictorial, graphic, and sculptural works)

Form SR: for published and unpublished sound recordings

For Renewal Registration
Form RE: for claims to renewal copyright in works copyrighted under the law in effect through December 31, 1977 (1909 Copyright Act)

For Corrections and Amplifications
Form CA: for supplementary registration to correct or amplify information given in the Copyright Office record of an earlier registration.

For a Group of Contributions to Periodicals
Form GR/CP: an adjunct application to be used for registration of a group of contributions to periodicals in addition to an application Form TX, PA, or VA

Application forms are supplied by the Copyright Office free of charge.

COPYRIGHT OFFICE HOTLINE
NOTE: Requestors may order application forms and circulars at any time by telephoning (202) 287-9100. Orders will be recorded automatically and filed as quickly as possible.

Figure 9.1 Copyright application forms.

The Copyright Fees and Technical Amendments Act of 1990 (Public Law 101-318) amends the Copyright Act of 1976 by increasing fees for Copyright Office services, effective January 3, 1991. Citations below are to sections of the Copyright Act of 1976, as amended by Public Law 101-318.

	Fees through 1/2/91	Fees effective 1/3/91	
REGISTRATION OF COPYRIGHT CLAIMS (Forms TX, VA, PA, SR, CA, SE or GR/CP)	$10.00	$20.00	For each registration and renewal you will receive a certificate bearing the Copyright Office seal.
Form SE/Group (minimum fee $20)	N/A	$10/issue	
Form MW	$20.00	$20.00	
Form RE	$6.00	$12.00	
RECORDATION OF DOCUMENTS Recordation, under section 205, of a document of six pages or less listing no more than one title.	$10.00	$20.00	A document which relates to any disposition of a copyright, such as a transfer, will, or license, may be recorded in the Copyright Office. When processing is completed, the submitted document(s) will be returned to you, along with a certificate of recordation for each document.
Additional pages: each	$.50	N/A	
Additional titles: each	$.50	N/A	
Additional titles: each group of 10 or fewer	N/A	$10.00	
CERTIFICATIONS Additional certificates: each	$4.00	$8.00	Certified copy of the record of registration, including certifications of Copyright Office records. NOTE: fees are cumulative; certification fees are in addition to any other applicable fees, i.e., search, photoduplication, etc.
Any other certification: each	$4.00	$20/hr. or fraction	
SEARCHES Reports from official records: per hour or fraction.	$10.00	$20.00	The Copyright Office will, upon request, estimate the fee required for a search; the fee must be received before the search is undertaken.
Locating Office records: per hour or fraction	$10.00	$20.00	
FILING OF NOTICE OF INTENTION TO MAKE AND DISTRIBUTE PHONORECORDS	$6.00	$12.00	For the filing, under section 115(b), of notice of intention to make and distribute phonorecords.
RECEIPT FOR DEPOSITS each receipt	$2.00	$4.00	For the issuance under section 407, mandatory deposit for the Library of Congress, of a receipt for deposit.
SPECIAL HANDLING FEE Registration (plus registration or renewal fee) (see above)	$200.00	$200.00	Special handling is granted at the discretion of the Register of Copyrights in a limited number of cases as a service to those who have compelling reasons for the expedited service. For further information on special handling, you may call (202) 707-9100 and record your request for ML-319 (registration of claims) or ML-341 (recordation of documents).
Additional Fee For each claim given special handling if a single deposit copy covers multiple claims and special handling is requested only for one. This charge may be avoided by submitting a separate deposit copy.	$50.00	$50.00	
Recordation of a Document (plus recordation fee)(see above)	$200.00	$200.00	
FULL-TERM RETENTION OF COPYRIGHT DEPOSITS For the full-term retention of copyright deposits under section 704(e).	$135.00	$135.00	For information on full-term retention, you may call (202) 707-9100 and record your request for Circular 96, Section 202.23.

Fees remitted to the Copyright Office for registration, including those for supplementary or renewal registrations and for special handling, will not be refunded. Payments made in excess of the statutory fee will be refunded, but refunds of $5 or less will not be refunded unless specifically requested.

Copyright Office · Library of Congress · Washington, D.C. 20559

SL-4 September 1990 — 400 000   U.S. GOVERNMENT PRINTING OFFICE: 1990 262-309/20.007

Figure 9.2 Fees charged for copyright registration.

Duration of a Copyright

Under the 1909 Copyright Act, copyright duration was 28 years, with a provision for one renewal for another 28 years. After that time, works fell into the public domain. This means that they are not protected by copyright and may be freely used. Users of public domain works are free to copyright their own arrangements, adaptations, or translations of those works. The 1976 Copyright Act extends the protection of works created under the 1909 act to 75 years. If the work is in its initial

28-year term, it can be protected for an additional 47 years, provided renewal is sought by the copyright holder.

Works created after January 1, 1978, may be copyrighted for the life of the author plus 50 years. Fifty years after the author's death, the work becomes part of the public domain. Copyrights are assignable and may be willed to the heirs of the author for the remainder of the copyright period.

Work for Hire

Section 101 of the Copyright Act defines a "work made for hire" as

(1) A work prepared by an employee within the scope of his or her employment; or
(2) A specifically ordered or commissioned work in one of nine specified categories, provided there is a written agreement signed by the parties specifying that the work shall be considered one made for hire. These categories are: as a contribution to a collective work, as part of a motion picture or other audiovisual work, as a transition, as supplementary work, as a compilation, as an instructional text, as a test, as answer material for a test, or as an atlas.

Many works produced by the electronic media are works for hire (i.e., the work is prepared as part of an employee's job or as an independent contractor conducting work on behalf of an organization). Either way, the primary author or authors do not retain the sole rights to the work. Instead, ownership is retained by another individual or organization. When an evening television newscast is copyrighted, the rights are retained by the television station owner, not by the anchor or producer. The duration of copyright for works for hire is 75 years after publication or 100 years after creation, whichever occurs first.

In *Baltimore Orioles v. Major League Baseball Players*, the Major League Baseball Players Association argued that the players owned the rights to telecasts of games in which they appeared, not the franchise holder. The U.S. Court of Appeals for the Seventh Circuit held that the telecast of major league games consisted of performance by employees acting within the scope of their employment. Therefore, the telecasts were works for hire and the ball players had no ownership rights to the broadcasts.

Notice of Copyright

Copyright notice is not required to protect a work from infringement. Prior to 1989 and the United States accession to the Berne Convention Implementation Act of 1988, formal notice was required to protect published works. Since 1989, the primary significance of copyright notice is protection against a defense of innocent infringement. Even in this case, the burden of proof remains on the infringer.

Formal copyright notice may still protect published works created before 1989. The copyright protection afforded these works can be lost if notice was omitted and not remedied within 5 years of publication. As noted earlier in this chapter, notice and registration are required to obtain certain statutory damages and attorney's fees.

The Copyright Act, as amended by the Berne Convention Implementation Act of 1988, requires that two copies of a work published in the United States be deposited, with or without copyright notice, in the Copyright Office within 3 months of publication. The work need not be registered. The Copyright Office may request that works be deposited. Failure to comply may result in a fine of not more than $250 per work, payment to the Library of Congress of the total retail price of copies requested, and an additional fine of $2,500 for willful or repeated failure to comply.

Elements of Copyright Notice

The traditional copyright notice contains three elements. The Copyright Office suggests that the elements appear together on the protected copies. Copyright notice consists of

the symbol ©, the word "Copyright," or the abbreviation "Copr."
the year of first publication
the name or owner of the copyright

An example of copyright notice is © 1992 Jane Doe.

The copyright notice for records of a sound recording is somewhat different. Records, tapes, or compact disks contain the symbol ℗ in place of the symbol ©. An example of copyright notice on a record is ℗ 1993 ABC Records Inc.

Fair Use

The concept of fair use places limitations on the exclusive rights of the copyright holder. Fair use is usually applied in matters involving educational materials, literary or social criticism, parody, and First Amendment activities. The rights of the copyright holder are balanced against other interests in determining the level of protection afforded by the Copyright Act. The courts have identified four areas that are considered before copyrighted material may be used without securing the permission of the copyright holder:

(1) The purpose and character of the use, including whether such use is of a commercial nature or is for nonprofit educational purposes;
(2) The nature of the copyrighted work;
(3) The amount and substantiality of the portion used in relation to the copyrighted work as a whole; and

(4) The effect of the use upon the potential market for or value of the copyrighted work.

It should be noted that there is no set percentage of material that may be used before the Fair Use Doctrine has been violated. The use of even a few words may constitute copyright infringement if that use adversely affects the economic value of the original work, as evidenced in *Meerpol v. Nizer*. Even paraphrasing copyrighted material can be considered infringement, as evidenced in *Salinger v. Random House Inc.*

The home videotaping of broadcast television programs was deemed to be fair use by the Supreme Court. In *Sony Corp. v. Universal Studios Inc.* (1984), the Court held that noncommercial in-home use of videotaped programs was not copyright infringement. This case has been referred to as the "Betamax" case, so named because of Sony's tape format at the time. Two critical findings resulted from this ruling—most copyright holders of broadcast programming would not object to "time shifting" (i.e., recording a program for viewing at another time) and time shifting has no direct harm on the market.

The decision in the "Betamax" case opened the door to legal, home videotaping of broadcast programs and spurred the purchase of home videotape recorders in the 1980s.

When a television news clipping service videotaped copyrighted television newscasts and sold them to clients who were featured in the newscasts, the District Court for Northern Georgia found that the practice was not fair use, in *Pacific & Southern Co. v. Duncan.*

When Evangelist Jerry Falwell distributed copies of a parody of him published by *Hustler* magazine in order to raise money to rebut the parody's attack on him, a different decision was reached. In *Hustler v. Moral Majority*, the U.S. Court of Appeals for the Ninth Circuit held that Falwell's copying of the copyrighted parody did not interfere with the magazine's potential sales or the parody's marketability.

In *Tin Pan Apple v. Miller Brewing* (1990), the U.S. District Court for the Southern District of New York ruled that a parody of the rap group "The Fat Boys" by comedian Joe Piscapo as part of a beer commercial violated copyright law. The parody, said the court, did not build on the original and was used solely to promote a commercial product. Therefore, the "Fat Boys" rights of publicity were violated.

When *The Nation* magazine published excerpts from Gerald Ford's unpublished manuscript without permission, the Supreme Court ruled that the publication violated the doctrine of fair use.

Harper & Row Publishers Inc. v. Nation Enterprises (1985)
Justice O'Connor delivered the opinion of the Court.

☐ This case requires us to consider to what extent the "fair use" provision of the Copyright Revision Act of 1976, 17 U.S.C. § 107 (hereinafter the Copyright Act), sanctions from a public figure's unpublished manuscript. In March 1979, an undisclosed source provided *The Nation* magazine with the unpublished manuscript of "A Time to Heal: The Autobiography of Gerald R. Ford." Working directly from the purloined manuscript, an editor of *The Nation* produced a short piece entitled "The Ford Memoirs—Behind the Nixon Pardon." The piece was timed to "scoop" an article scheduled shortly to appear in *Time* magazine. *Time* had agreed to purchase the exclusive right to print prepublication excerpts from the copyright holders, Harper & Row Publishers, Inc. . . . and Reader's Digest . . . As a result of *The Nation* article, *Time* canceled its agreement. Petitioners brought a successful copyright action against *The Nation*. On appeal, the Second Circuit reversed the lower court's finding of infringement, holding that *The Nation's* act was sanctioned as a "fair use" of the copyrighted material. We granted certiorari . . . and we now reverse.

. . . Fair use was traditionally defined as "a privilege in others than the owner of the copyright to use the copyrighted material in a reasonable manner without his consent." . . .

. . . Respondents, however, contend that First Amendment values require a different rule under the circumstances of this case. . . . Respondents advance the substantial public import of the subject matter of the Ford memoirs as grounds for excusing a use that would ordinarily not pass muster as a fair use—the piracy of verbatim quotations for the purpose of "scooping" the authorized first serialization. . . . Respondents argue that the public's interest in learning this news as fast as possible outweighs the right of the author to control its first publication.

The Second Circuit noted, correctly, that copyright's idea/expression dichotomy "strike[s] a definitional balance between the First Amendment and the Copyright Act by permitting free communication of facts while still protecting an author's expression." . . .

. . . As this Court long ago observed: "[T]he news element—the information respecting current events contained in the literary production—is not the creation of the writer, but is a report of matters that ordinarily are *publici juris*; it is the history of the day." *International News Service v. Associated Press*, 248 U.S. 215, 234 (1918). But copyright assures those who write and publish factual narratives such as "A Time to Heal" that they may at least enjoy the right to market the original expression contained therein as just compensation for their investment. Cf. *Zacchini v. Scripps-Howard Broadcasting Co.*, 433 U.S. 562, 575 (1977).

. . . The promise of copyright would be an empty one if it could be avoided merely by dubbing the infringement a fair use "news report" of the book. . . .

. . . Nor do respondents assert any actual necessity for circumventing the copyright scheme with respect to the types of works and users at issue here. . . .

In our haste to disseminate news, it should not be forgotten that the Framers intended copyright itself to be the engine of free expression. By establishing a marketable right to the use of one's expression, copyright supplies the economic incentive to create and disseminate ideas. . . .

The four factors identified by Congress as especially relevant in determining whether the use was fair are: (1) the purpose and character of the use; (2) the nature of the copyrighted work; (3) the substantiality of the portion used in relation to the copyrighted work as a whole; (4) the effect on the potential market for or value of the copyrighted work. We address each one separately.

Purpose of the Use. The Second Circuit correctly identified news reporting as the general purpose of *The Nation's* use. News reporting is one of the examples enumerated in § 107 to "give some idea of the sort of activities the courts might regard as fair use under the circumstances." . . .

The Nation has every right to seek to be the first to publish information. But *The Nation* went beyond simply reporting uncopyrightable information and actively sought to exploit the headline value of its infringement, making a "news event" out of its unauthorized first publication of a noted figure's copyrighted expression.

The fact that a publication was commercial as opposed to non-profit is a separate factor that tends to weigh against a finding of fair use. . . .

Nature of the Copyrighted Work. Second, the Act directs attention to the nature of the copyrighted work. "A Time to Heal" may be characterized as an unpublished historical narrative or autobiography. The law generally recognizes a greater need to disseminate factual works than works of fiction or fantasy. . . .

In the case of Mr. Ford's manuscript, the copyrightholders' interest in confidentiality is irrefutable; the copyrightholders had entered into a contractual undertaking to "keep the manuscript confidential" and required that all those to whom the manuscript was shown also "sign an agreement to keep the manuscript confidential." . . . A use that so clearly infringes on the copyrightholder's interests in confidentiality and creative control is difficult to characterize as "fair."

Amount and Substantiality of the Portion Used. . . . In absolute terms, the words actually quoted were an insubstantial portion of "A Time to Heal." The district court, however, found that "*[T]he Nation* took what was essentially the heart of the book." . . .

As the statutory language indicates, a taking may not be excused merely because it is insubstantial with respect to the *infringing* work. As Judge Learned Hand cogently remarked, "[N]o plagiarist can excuse the wrong by showing how much of his work he did not pirate." . . .

Effect on the Market. . . . The trial court found not merely a potential but an actual effect on the market. *Time's* cancellation of its projected serialization and its refusal to pay the $12,500 were the direct effect of the infringement. . . . Rarely will a case of copyright infringement present such clear-cut evidence of actual damage. . . .

The Nation conceded that its verbatim copying of some 300 words of direct quotation from the Ford manuscript would constitute an infringement unless excused as a fair use. Because we find that *The Nation's* use of these verbatim excerpts from the unpublished manuscript was not a fair use, the judgment of the Court of Appeals is reversed and remanded for further proceedings consistent with this opinion.[2]

News and Copyright

Although the facts of news may not be copyrighted, the expression of those facts are protected. It is copyright infringement to read a newspaper or other print media story over the electronic media, verbatim or rewritten, without permission. Using a competitor, such as a newspaper, as a source of tips is acceptable, provided the user generates an original expression of the events. This means calling or otherwise following up the story and presenting an original interpretation.

In cases of exclusive interviews, both the publisher and the subject of the interview may have remedy. In *Cher v. Forum International Ltd.*, entertainer Cher successfully sued *Forum* magazine for the unauthorized use of an interview with a free-lance writer originally intended for *Us* magazine.

Music Rights

The electronic media are required to pay copyright holders for the music used in programming, continuity, and commercials. As discussed in Chapter 8, cable television pays royalties under a compulsory license to the CRT for the programs it transmits. Broadcasters and cable operators also pay a license fee to the three major music performing rights organizations—American Society of Composers, Authors, and Publishers (ASCAP); Broadcast Music Incorporated (BMI); and Society of European Stage Actors and Composers (SESAC). Electronic media organizations wishing to use music as part of their programming usually enter into an agreement for performance rights with these organizations. The fee paid is based on the market size of the medium and the amount of music used.

Performance, Synchronization, and Mechanical Rights

It is important to realize that any transmission of copyrighted music requires a license from a performing rights organization. If music will be used as part of a commercial, or in conjunction with film or videotape, additional rights must be secured. Synchronization rights must be secured for jingles and commercial uses of music, or when music is integrated with video or film. Mechanical rights must be secured if the product is to be duplicated and distributed as a recording or tape.

Parody or "Soundalike" Recordings

Permission must be obtained for parody recordings that alter the words or other elements of a song. "Weird Al" Jankovich's parodies of Michael Jackson and other pop artists of the 1980s were done with such permission.

Soundalikes are popular as commercial jingles. Advertisers often like to employ musicians to imitate well-known performers in spots, because the public often identifies with a "sound" or recent hit, without the cost of hiring the original artist. This practice has been common for a number of years with few successful suits brought against the imitators. In 1988, however, singer Bette Midler brought a successful suit against Ford Motor Company for their imitation of her hit "Do You Wanna Dance." In *Midler v. Ford Motor Company*, the U.S. Court of Appeals for the Ninth Circuit held that the commercial sounded so much like Midler that the average listener might believe it to be her. Therefore, the court ruled that Ford's commercial violated the singer's right of publicity and artistic persona.

Limits of the License

A performance license from ASCAP, BMI, or SESAC is generally granted with limited conditions. For example, a radio station's performing rights agreement applies only to music broadcast on the air. It does not cover uses such as "music on hold," when callers to the station hear the broadcast signal when their call is placed on hold. A separate license is required for this and other uses, like DJ dance appearances and external promotions.

Another area that has generated attention is that of "storecasting." A radio station does not have the authority to grant permission to a retail establishment (or any other public venue) allowing broadcast of the station's signal, including music played, on the premises. The venue must obtain a license from the performing rights societies. The license issued to the radio station does not cover such "performances." Indeed, most retail and other establishments are not free to play records, cassettes, CDs, or other copyrighted music without first obtaining a performing rights license.

Exceptions include small commercial establishments of 600 square feet or less, without sophisticated sound systems, as held in *Sailor Music v. Gap Stores Inc.* Generally, the sound system should have fewer than four speakers and the music should not be provided for the entertainment of customers. Employees may listen for their personal entertainment.

An inferior sound system, such as one that may be found at a miniature golf course, may also defeat the license requirement, as evidenced in *Springsteen v. Plaza Roller Dome*.

Trademark and Service Mark

A trademark protects identifying symbols, words, or names associated with intellectual property. The legislation governing trademarks is the Federal Trademark Act of 1946, also known as the Lanham Act. Trademarks are registered with the United States Patent and Trademark Office. The notice that an intellectual property is protected by trademark is ® or ™.

To obtain a trademark registration, an application must be filed with the United States Patent and Trademark Office in Washington, DC. There is a filing fee of $175 for each trademark application. The applicant must state that there is a bona fide intention to use the mark in commerce or that the mark is already in use. Commercial trademark search firms may be engaged to assist applicants with determining whether a proposed trademark is already in use. Trademarks must be renewed every 10 years.

Eligibility for Trademark Protection

Letters, groups of letters, graphics, type styles, characters, and names are all eligible for trademark (or service mark) protection. The Trademark Law Revision Act of 1988 made it easier for broadcasters to protect call letters and identifying slogans. Prior to 1983, the FCC mitigated disputes over such matters, but deregulation ended FCC intervention. Service marks include broadcast station call letters and identifying symbols and phrases. For example, "Q-95" and "B-103" may be registered within the geographic area served by the station. The same moniker may be trademarked by another station outside the geographic area. However, under a 1989 amendment to the Trademark Law, the mark may be registered for nationwide protection. Because frequencies are generic, they may not be protected. Phrases like "FM 95" or "AM 1230" could not be registered.

Distinctive names may be registered with the Trademark Office. "Billy Joel," "Chicago" (the pop group), and "Johnny Carson" are all registered trademarks.

A trademark must be distinctive to be registered. This means that generic terms may not be trademarked. "Poison" cannot be registered as a trademark for an insecticide product. However, "Poison" can be registered as a trademark by a manufacturer of perfume. It may also be registered as a service mark for a pop metal band. Because there is no confusion as to the differences between the band and the fragrance, this is permissible.

Protecting the Mark

Trademark and service mark owners may lose their protection if the trademark becomes generic. Terms like *aspirin* and *cellophane* were once trademarks for a painkiller and a plastic material, respectively. Both fell into common usage as descriptive of all products similar to the original product. Companies like Xerox and Coca-Cola go to great lengths to protect their trademarks. Xerox, for example, constantly reminds broadcasters that all copies are not Xerox copies and that "Xerox" is not a verb.

Offensive or immoral symbols may not be trademarked. The Trademark Office judges marks on their "primary meaning." If the primary meaning is judged offensive, a trademark cannot be registered. One can only imagine the extent to which this prohibition has been pushed by would-be trademark holders. One particularly interesting phrase denied by the Trademark Office was submitted by a chicken restaurant. The restaurant wanted to trademark the phrase, "Only a breast in the mouth is better than a leg in the hand."

Commercial Exploitation

Noncommercial uses of trademarks are protected by the First Amendment when trademark uses are for purposes of editorial or artistic expression, as ruled in *L.L. Bean Inc. v. Drake Publishers Inc.*

Moviemaker George Lucas objected to the use of his trademark "Star Wars" when describing the Reagan administration's space-based Strategic Defense Initiative. In *Lucasfilm Ltd. v. High Frontier*, the U.S. District Court for the District of Columbia rejected his claim of trademark infringement because the alleged use was noncommercial.

The pop group "New Kids On The Block" filed a trademark infringement claim against a newspaper and a magazine for their use of the group's identifying logo. The publications used the trademark in articles asking readers to call a "900" number and participate in a survey identifying the most popular member of the "New Kids On The Block." The group alleged that use of the trademark in conjunction with a "900" number constituted commercial exploitation. In *New Kids On The Block v. News America Publications*, the District Court for Central California held that the First Amendment barred an infringement claim by the New Kids, because the use of the trademark by the publications was merely descriptive and was related to news gathering—to determine who was the most popular member of the group. The court ruled that commercial exploitation did not occur.

Summary

The Copyright Act is found in title 17 of the U.S. Code. A copyright provides protection from unauthorized use of original works of authorship, including literary, dramatic, musical, artistic, and certain other intellectual works.

The electronic media are required to pay copyright holders for the music used in programming, continuity, and commercials. Cable television pays royalties, under a compulsory license, to the CRT for the programs it transmits. Broadcasters and cable operators also pay a license fee to the three major music performing rights organizations—ASCAP, BMI, and SESAC.

A trademark protects identifying symbols, words, or names associated with intellectual property. The legislation governing trademarks is the Federal Trademark Act of 1946, also known as the Lanham Act. Trademarks are registered with the United States Patent and Trademark Office.

Notes/References

1. *Copyright Basics*, Circular 1 (Washington, D.C.: Copyright Office, Library of Congress, 1987), 3.
2. Harper & Row Publishers, Inc. v. Nation Enterprises, 471 U.S. 539 (1985).

Cases

Baltimore Orioles v. Major League Baseball Players, (CA 7, 1986) 13 Med.L.Rptr. 1625

Cher v. Forum International, Ltd., 692 F.2d 634 (9th Cir., 1982)

Harper & Row Publishers, Inc. v. Nation Enterprises, 471 U.S. 539 (1985)

Hoeling v. Universal Studios, 618 F.2d 972 (2nd Cir., 1980), Cert. denied 499 U.S. 841 (1980)

Hustler v. Moral Majority, (CA 9, 1986) 13 Med.L.Rptr. 1151

L.L. Bean Inc. v. Drake Publishers Inc., (CA 1, 1987) 13 Med.L.Rptr. 2009

Lucasfilm Ltd. v. High Frontier, 622 F.Supp 931 (DC DC, 1985)

Meerpol v. Nizer, 560 F.2d 1061, (2d Cir., 1977) 2 Med.L.Rptr. 2269, Cert. denied 434 U.S. 1013 (1978)

Midler v. Ford Motor Company, 849 F.2d 460 (9th Cir., 1988)

New Kids On The Block v. News America Publications, (DC C.Cal, 1990) 18 Med.L.Rptr. 1089

Pacific & Southern Co. v. Duncan, (DC N.Ga., 1985) 12 Med.L.Rptr. 1221

Production Contractors v. WGN Continental Broadcasting Co., (ND. Ill., 1985) 12 Med.L.Rptr. 1708

Sailor Music v. Gap Stores Inc., 668 F.2d 84 (2d Cir., 1981), Cert. denied 456 U.S. 945 (1982)

Salinger v. Random House Inc., 811 F.2d 90, (2d Cir., 1987) 13 Med.L.Rptr. 1954

Sony Corp. v. Universal Studios Inc., 464 U.S. 417 (1984)

Springsteen v. Plaza Roller Dome, 602 F.Supp. 113 (M.D. NC, 1985)

Tin Pan Apple v. Miller Brewing, (DC So.NY, 1990) 17 Med.L.Rptr. 2273

WCVB-TV v. Boston Athletic Association, (CA 1, 1991) 18 Med.L.Rptr. 1710

10

Defamation: Libel and the Media

Libel may be generally defined as a publication or broadcast that is injurious to the reputation of another. Libel includes defamatory material that is expressed in print, pictures, signs, or is broadast by radio, television, or cable communications media. Gillmor and Barron define libel as a defamatory, false, malicious, and/or negligent publication that tends to hold a person up to hatred, contempt, or ridicule causing him or her to be shunned or avoided.[1] Essentially, libel changes the way an individual is viewed by others. In the United States, there is no single definition of libel, because each state and the District of Columbia defines libel for its own jurisdiction. Fortunately, the definitions are similar, which allows for general characteristics of libel to be deduced.

Libel and its spoken counterpart, slander, have roots in English common law. Traditionally, libel involved printing a defamatory statement, while slander was a verbal defamation. Records indicate that slander was recognized as a cause of action as far back as the thirteenth century. Libel was criminal in its origin and has remained a common law crime. Slander could only become a criminal offense when the words amounted to another offense, such as blasphemy or sedition. Defamation was part of England's ecclesiastical law of the Middle Ages and was punishable as a sin until the Protestant reformation. The common law of the Middle Ages provided that

> If one calls a man "wolf" or "hare" one must pay him three shillings, while if one calls a woman "harlot" and can not prove the truth of the charge, one must pay forty-five shillings. . . . the man who falsely called another a "thief" or "manslayer" must pay damages, and, holding his nose with his fingers, must publicly confess himself a liar.[2]

Although the punishment was refined over the centuries, libel became a part of England's statutory law in 1792 with the passage of the Fox Libel Act.

Slander is usually heard by fewer individuals and is more ephemeral in impact, while libel usually commands a wider audience and, since it involves printed or broadcast matter, is usually more permanent. Because libel represents a potentially greater harm to a person's reputation, greater damages are awarded. Although it would seem that defamatory material broadcast on radio or television would be prosecuted as slander, the pervasive nature of the broadcast media, coupled with the fact that most broadcasts are scripted, causes most broadcast defamation to be treated as libel.

An exception to this rule occurred in the case of a San Diego woman mistakenly identified as a prostitute in a 1983 news report by KCST-TV. The California Supreme Court refused to review a Fourth District Court of Appeals ruling ordering KCST to pay Naomi O'Hara $300,000 plus $165,000 in interest as a judgment in her slander case against the station. However, this is not always the case, as evidenced in *Brauer v. Globe Newspaper Co.* An actionable libel may involve only three people—the plaintiff, defendant, and a witness.

As in England, common law courts in America were concerned with the protection of reputation. Until 1964, all libel cases in the United States were governed by the common law, as applied by the various states. The landmark Supreme Court decision in *New York Times v. Sullivan* (1964) brought libel law under the constitutional umbrella. Since then, the courts have viewed libel as a First Amendment issue that balances the right of free speech against the protection of an individual's or corporation's reputation.

Elements of Actionable Libel

No libel suit may succeed unless a plaintiff can establish that three elements have been met. The plaintiff must establish that a false defamatory statement was made by the defendant, that the plaintiff is clearly identified as the person defamed, and that the defamatory statement was published in some manner.

Defamation

Direct Libel—*per se*

The words in question must be interpreted as damaging to the plaintiff's reputation. Under the common law, libel *per se* (or direct libel) might have included calling someone a "thief" or a "murderer." Libel *per se* survives today. However, the words need not be specific. The average reader or listener must merely conclude that plaintiffs were engaged in activites that are damaging to their reputations. For example, in *Donaldson v. Washington Post Co.*, the *Washington Post* was guilty of libel when it falsely reported that Michael Donaldson pleaded guilty to a murder charge. When journalist Victor Lasky referred to West Virginia college professor Luella Mundel as a "Communist" in an ABC television broadcast about the McCarthy era of the 1950's, a New York district court ruled in *Lasky v. ABC* that the statement was libelous.

It is defamatory to say that someone is a drunkard, has attempted suicide, is immoral or unchaste, is "queer," is a hypocrite, is a coward, has made improper advances to women, is having "wife trouble," is "unfair" to labor, or has done something dishonorable.

Courts do attempt to separate statements made in the heat of an argument from assertions of fact. Calling someone a "sleaze bag" may not be libel *per se*, because it is difficult to define just what is meant by the term. In *Fleming v. Kane County*, an Illinois court ruled that when a fired employee called his former supervisor a "gutless bastard" and a "black son of a bitch," the terms were not libel *per se*. But when the former employee called him a "liar," the court found the statement actionable as defamation.

The use of the word "alleged" before accusing someone of a crime or other potentially libelous act does not render the statement non-defamatory. As we shall see later in this chapter, it is not libelous to accurately report that someone has been charged with murder. It is libelous to call someone an "alleged murderer."

Indirect Libels—*per quod*

Libel *per quod* (or indirect libel) is libel that is not evident from the words themselves, but is implied. Although libel *per quod* is a common law concept, courts still often distinguish between indirect and direct libel. The working journalist or broadcaster must understand the concept, since the choice of language may invite an unanticipated libel suit. The classic common law example of libel *per quod* would be the newspaper publication that erroneously indicates that a newly married woman has just given birth to a child. Under the common law of libel *per quod*, the woman could sue for damages, provided she could show that her reputation had been harmed by the announcement. These classic cases still occur. When a Charlottesville, Virginia, newspaper identified a married woman (who had filed charges against a man for rape) as "Miss" and then casually mentioned in the same article that she was pregnant, the Virginia Supreme Court agreed, in *Charlottesville Newspapers Inc. v. Debra C. Matthews*, that she had been libeled. The mistake cost *The Daily Progress* $25,000 in damages. In 1961, the *Spokane Chronicle* falsely reported that Phillip Pitts had obtained a divorce in 1961. Pitts married his second wife shortly after actually obtaining the divorce in 1960. In *Pitts v. Spokane Chronicle Co.*, the Washington Supreme Court ruled that Pitts was defamed because the newspaper article made it appear that he was a bigamist.

Indirect libels are seldom easy to identify in reality. They lurk in the interpretation of seemingly innocent words. For example, the word "fix" can have several meanings. When used in the context of "fixing" a court case, the word can take on a defamatory meaning, as evidenced in *McCall v. Courier Journal*. When a defamatory meaning is not apparent, the plaintiff has the burden of proving that a defamatory meaning was intended. A statement that someone has burned down their own house is not defamatory *per se*. If, however, it can be shown the words were understood to mean that he had done so in order to defraud an insurance company, the statement would be defamatory.

In *Tavoulareas v. Washington Post*, the President of Mobil Oil, William Tavoulareas, sued the *Washington Post* for libel as a result of a 1979 article that stated that the oil company president had "set up" his son in a shipping venture. The article was originally found defamatory in 1982 by a trial court because it implied that Tavoulareas had engaged in nepotisim, breached his fiduciary duty, and misused corporate assets. A jury awarded Tavoulareas $2 million. In 1983, the presiding judge declared that the article was not libelous because it represented "unbiased investigative journalism." In 1985, a three-judge panel reinstated the jury verdict once again. An appellate court overturned the decision on grounds that the *Washington Post* story was substantially true and was not published with actual malice. In 1987, 8 years after the publication of the article, the Supreme Court refused to review the case, allowing the court of appeals decision to stand. Although, ultimately, the decision was in favor of the media, the cost of defending against such a case can be time-consuming and costly. For this reason the media will usually try to avoid going to court.

Headlines

Courts have ruled that headlines may be the basis for a libel action, even if the story that follows is not defamatory. A headline must be a "fair index" of an accurate article with which it appears. A headline reading, "Records Reveal Gifts to Police Jury Members," followed by references to "gestures of friendship" in a report about the plaintiff's unethical activities, was judged defamatory in *Buratt v. Capital City Press*.

Headlines are supposed to attract a reader's attention. Some newspapers feel the urge to "spice up" an otherwise bland story with tantalizing banners that are not exactly related to the story that follows. Supermarket tabloids are notorious for this practice. Captions like "Aliens Found in Arizona Desert" are usually followed by stories about a tour bus loaded with German tourists that broke down on the way to Las Vegas. Although sometimes irritating, such mismatched stories do no real harm. There are times, however, when an individual's reputation is at stake. The courts have taken a dim view of misleading headlines because, often, it is only the headlines that are read.

Broadcasters must use similar caution when it comes to "promos," "bumpers," and "teases" used to build an audience for upcoming newscasts. In addition, the use of "B-roll" or "generic" shots can be sources of trouble. Although, in recent years, most cases of this type have been decided in favor of the media, the cost of successfully defending such suits warrants caution.

Innocent Construction Rule

Some states, including Illinois, Ohio, and Indiana, adhere to the innocent construction rule. This means that if the language is capable of nondefamatory meaning, it should be interpreted that way. In most states, the words must be given their natural meaning and courts are not to seek inferences that may be unintended. Some states require that a jury determine the meaning of language that is susceptible to both defamatory and nondefamatory meanings.

Identification

Plaintiffs must show that defamatory statements refer to them. Anyone exposed to the defamatory material must reasonably infer that it is intended to describe the plaintiff. The identification need not refer to the plaintiff by name. In *New York Times v. Sullivan*, the term "Southern violators" was sufficient identification for L.B. Sullivan to establish identification in his libel suit filed against the *New York Times* in Alabama.

Author Gwen Davis Mitchell lost a libel suit resulting from a work of fiction. Even though the physical characteristics of the character in her novel *Touching* did not resemble the plaintiff, a California court ruled that there were enough other similarities to permit identification and, ultimately, libel.

In her novel *Touching*, Gwen Davis Mitchell created a character called Simon Herford. Herford was a psychiatrist who conducted nude therapy sessions. Prior to writing the novel, Mitchell had attended similar sessions under Dr. Bindrim, a psychologist. Mitchell had signed a contract with Bindrim agreeing not to disclose what had taken place in the therapy sessions. Upon publication of the novel, Bindrim asserted that the character of Simon Herford was identifiable as himself. Bindrim also asserted that the book contained several false statements of fact and that several incidents described in the book were libelous. One such incident dipicted an encounter group patient who became so distressed after a weekend of nude therapy that she is killed when she crashes her car. Bindrim also objected to his being depicted as "pressing," "clutching," and "ripping" a patient's cheeks, and calling a female patient a "bitch."

Mitchell claimed that the character Herford was not Bindrim. She also claimed that there can be no statement of false fact, since *Touching* is a novel and is not based on fact. In *Bindrim v. Mitchell*, the court ruled in favor of the plaintiff.

☐ ... In the case at bar the only differences between plaintiff and the Herford character in *Touching* were physical appearance and that Herford was a psychiatrist rather than psychologist. Otherwise, the character Simon Herford was very similar to the actual plaintiff.

... Plaintiff was identified as Herford by several witnesses and plaintiff's own tape recordings of the marathon sessions show that the novel was based substantially on plaintiff's conduct in the nude marathon. ... There is overwhelming evidence that plaintiff and "Herford" were one.

... The test is whether a reasonable person, reading the book, would understand that the fictional character therein pictured was, in actual fact, the plaintiff acting as described.[3]

The court went on to say that if only one reader assumed that Bindrim was Herford, that would be sufficient for identification. The false facts, based on real incidents, gave rise to the libel verdict.

Publication

The real harm in libel comes in publication. It is when others are exposed to the defamation that damage to reputation may occur. Publication may be in the form of a magazine or newspaper story, a radio or television broadcast, a handbill distributed on the street, or a memo to a secretary in the office. The publication must also be intended by the defamer. The victim may not publish a private defamatory communication and then sue for libel. Unlike defamation and identification, publication is usually not a contested issue in a libel case. The printed matter or tape containing the alleged defamation is most often the basis on which a libel suit is originally filed. Any repetition or republication of the original defamation is grounds for additional libel action. Many states adhere to the single publication rule, which treats all copies of a single edition or press run of a defamatory statement as one count of libel.

Under the complicity rule, reporters, editors, and publishers are all liable in a defamation suit. This liability is based on the premise that editors and publishers have the responsibility for approving the work of the reporters. Therefore, any published defamatory material should have been checked by them. Some contributing personnel may not be named in the publication process, including technicians and office workers. In 1986 in *Catalfo v. Jensen*, a U.S. district court held that a free-lance photographer who was responsible only for the photographs accompanying an allegedly defamatory article was not part of the publishing process. The photographer had no hand in writing or editing the article.

Common Law Defenses

Under the common law, once a plaintiff establishes the three elements of an actionable libel (i.e., defamation, identification, and publication), the burden of proof shifts to the defendant. The defamation is assumed to be false unless the defendant can prove otherwise. Therefore, in common law libel cases, the burden of proof is said to be on the defendant. Publishers accused of libel could defend themselves by claiming that the defamatory statement was true, that the defamatory statement was protected by privilege, or that the defamatory statement was a fair comment or criticism of the public performance of an official or entertainer.

Truth

The defendant who pleads truth in a libel case does not have to literally prove every aspect of the charge, but must show that the statement that is charged as defamatory is substantially true. For example, in *Baia v. Jackson Newspapers*, a newspaper article stating that a man had been charged with "pulling off" a bank robbery, when, in fact, he had been charged with conspiracy to commit bank robbery, was judged substantially true by a Connecticut court.

In *Action Repair v. ABC*, when a television station accurately reported, as part of an investigative story on auto repair shops, that the Action Repair Company was unwilling to talk and had cancelled interviews, a California court ruled the report true and thus nondefamatory.

A court may determine that alleged defamatory statements are true if a reasonable jury could come to only one conclusion. In *Redco Corporation v. CBS*, when "60 Minutes" aired a story that contained the statement "multipiece tire rims kill people," the statement was found to be true, even though no one had died from injuries incurred in accidents involving multipiece rims manufactured by the plaintiff.

Proving truth is not always as simple as it first appears. Reporters are sometimes convinced that the charges they have made are true. Circumstantial evidence may be in a defendant's favor. However, convincing a jury is another matter. Sometimes the evidence needed is simply not available. Although truth may be a complete defense, it can be costly and may not be practical.

Privilege

There are two types of privilege—absolute and qualified. Absolute privilege applies to agencies of government, the courts, and government officials when they are conducting official business. One cannot sue for defamatory remarks made as part of an official court proceeding. A similar absolute privilege exists for remarks made as part of political campaigns and broadcast on radio and television stations. Stations may not edit remarks, nor may they be sued for broadcasting defamatory material under Section 315 of the Communications Act.

Qualified privilege protects the media in their coverage of public affairs. The underlying rationale is that in a democracy, the public has a right to be informed about public issues. The qualification is that these reports be fair and accurate.

Under the common law, journalists could publish a fair and accurate report of any public or official meeting at any level of government. Information contained in reports or proceedings of these meetings could also be published. Additional protection was afforded under the "actual malice" ruling of *New York Times v. Sullivan* and the "negligence" standard of *Gertz v. Robert Welch Inc.* (1974).

Information found in public records, such as official arrest reports, court records, and other local or state documents, is protected under the defense of privilege. Although state laws regarding privilege differ, protection is usually afforded for publication of material that has been acted on in an official manner, and contains accurate and current information. The point at which "official action" took place is sometimes questionable. Reporting based only on information gathered from a police scanner would not be privileged information. An arrest that has not formally been entered on the police blotter would not constitute offical action and therefore would not be privileged.

The common law standards of "fair and accurate reporting" must also be observed in order for privilege to be an effective defense. When *Playboy* magazine reported the criminal conviction of Thelma Torres, a federal customs inspector, they relied on out-of-date records. During the 4 months between her initial conviction and the publication of the *Playboy* article, Torres was given a new trial and acquitted. In *Torres v. Playboy*, *Playboy* lost the defenses of privilege as well as truth, since the court ruled that the article did not accurately represent Torres' case.

In some states, privilege includes information gathered at all public meetings where public issues are discussed. This would include public meetings of unions, church boards, political parties, and medical or bar associations.

Fair Comment

The defense of fair comment traditionally involved an honest expression of opinion on a matter of public interest. The common law defense has now been incorporated into the constitutional defense outlined in *New York Times v. Sullivan* and by dicta found in *Gertz v. Welch*. This includes commentary on the conduct of government and public officials, and criticisms of various entertainment media, including restaurant reviews, theater, television, sports, and movies. Provided these commentaries limit themselves to opinion and are not published with actual malice (i.e., knowing falsehood or reckless disregard for the truth), they enjoy absolute immunity from libel. In *Gertz v. Welch* the Supreme Court stated,

☐ Under the First Amendment there is no such thing as a false idea. However pernicious an opinion may seem, we depend for its correction not on . . . judges and juries but on the competition of other ideas.[4]

Other Defenses

Neutral Reportage

Some states recognize the privilege of neutral reportage. This privilege protects all accurate and neutral republications of defamatory statements made by persons involved in public controversies against public figures involved in that controversy. The defense was first articulated in *Edwards v. National Audubon Society* (1977). Essentially, neutral reportage provides immunity from defamation suits when journalists believe that they are reporting an accurate account of defamatory remarks or charges against a public figure.

In *Barry v. Time*, the privilege of neutral reportage protected *Time* magazine's accurate account of a basketball player's charge that he had received illegal payments from his coach, even though the player had pleaded guilty to aggravated assault and had failed to pass a lie detector test regarding that assault. Similarly, in *J.V. Peters v. Knight Ridder*, the *Akron Beacon Journal*'s accurate report of a statement made by a state attorney regarding the dumping of toxic wastes by J.V. Peters & Company, was ruled to be newsworthy and protected as neutral reportage. The report was a statement made by a public person, about a public controversy, and directed at another public person involved in the controversy.

Most states, including New York and Kentucky, do not recognize the privilege of neutral reportage. In *McCall v. Courier Journal*, the Kentucky Supreme Court rejected the privilege defense, noting that the "doctrine has not been approved by the Supreme Court of the United States and has not received approval in other jurisdictions."[5] The U.S. Supreme Court declined to review both *Edwards* and *McCall*, therefore placing the defense of neutral reportage on somewhat uncertain ground.

The Libel Proof Doctrine— A Mitigating Factor

Questions of moral character and fidelity may be direct libel, but courts sometimes consider the previous reputation of a plaintiff when determining if suit may be brought. Courts have ruled that the reputations of some individuals render them libel proof. In *Cardillo v. Doubleday Inc.*, the Libel Proof Doctrine was established. The Second Circuit Court of Appeals ruled that the reputation of a man convicted on several charges, including conspiracy, could not be further damaged by allegations that he had participated in a robbery and attempted to fix a horse race. Subsequent cases in which plaintiffs' reputations were classified as libel proof include *Ray v. Time Inc.*, in which the convicted assassin of Dr. Martin Luther King objected to allegations he had been involved in other criminal activity; *Jackson v. Longcope*, in which a convicted murderer objected to a newspaper report that he raped and strangled his victims, when *all* were not killed in that manner; and *Logan v. District of Columbia*, in which an admitted drug user claimed the media exaggerated the number of times he tested positive for drug use.

In *Schiavone Construction v. Time*, *Time* magazine's publication of a report linking the president of a construction company with organized crime and the disappearance of Jimmy Hoffa was originally found libelous *per se* by a New Jersey district court. Later, the court ruled that because of numerous published reports linking the company to organized crime, and because information had been obtained from FBI files, both the company and its president were libel proof.

In *Guccione v. Hustler*, when *Hustler* published the false statement that *Penthouse* magazine publisher Bob Guccione "is married and has a live-in girlfriend," a U.S. district court found the statement to be libelous *per se*, since it implied that Guccione was engaged in an adulterous relationship. The jury awarded Guccione $1.6 million in punitive damages and $1 in actual damages.

However, the U.S. court of appeals overturned the verdict because of Guccione's long-term relationship with his "girlfriend" prior to and following his divorce. Guccione's reputation rendered him libel proof. Writing for the court, Judge Newman noted that as publisher of *Penthouse*, Guccione often advocated conduct that he now asserted was libelous to him. While statements calling someone an adulterer would generally be libelous *per se*, since the duration of Guccione's adultery had encompassed 13 of the past 17 years, the court concluded that his reputation had not been further damaged by the *Hustler* article.

Like neutral reportage, the Libel Proof Doctrine is by no means universally accepted. It is not a part of federal constitutional law and states are free to accept or reject the doctrine.

Damages

Plaintiffs who successfully sue publishers or broadcasters may recover three kinds of damages—compensatory or general damages, special or actual damages, and punitive damages. State laws and the landmark Supreme Court case *Gertz v. Robert Welch Inc.* greatly affect the kinds of damages that may be awarded. Some states allow only actual damages to be collected and many prohibit punitive damages. The *Gertz* ruling prohibits punitive damages if actual malice has not been demonstrated by the plaintiff.

Compensatory or general damages are awarded for injury to reputation. These damages were assumed in most libel *per se* cases and were based on humiliation, shame, embarrassment, and emotional distress. A jury may set the amount of the award, which may be reviewed by a judge.

Special or actual damages are meant to compensate for proven monetary loss suffered as a result of a defamatory statement. Kentucky and Indiana allow libel plaintiffs to recover only special or actual damages. In the Kentucky Code, "special damages" are defined as pecuniary (monetary) damages that are suffered by a libel plaintiff in respect to his property, business, trade, profession, or occupation. Plaintiffs may also recover money spent as a result of any defamation.[6] In the Indiana Code, "actual damages" is defined in much the same way. Indiana plaintiffs may only recover damages suffered in respect to character, property, business, trade, profession, or occupation, and no other damages whatever.[7]

Punitive damages are meant to punish a publisher or broadcaster for communicating a defamatory statement. Punitive damage awards are high in order to serve as a deterrent to others who may consider publishing similar material. This tactic, however, raises the issue of prior restraint. Punitive damages are controversial in that publishers may shy away from potentially libelous material for fear of incurring fines that might put them out of business. They may also be a death sentence for small publications. For example, in 1981, a small newspaper in Illinois was nearly put out of business after losing a $9.2 million judgment in *Green v. Alton Telegraph*. The case was settled for $1.4 million and the *Alton Telegraph* managed to borrow just enough money to stay in business. Similarly, in *Pring v. Penthouse*, although eventually reversed, *Penthouse* magazine originally lost a $26 million judgment for publishing a work of fiction espousing "Miss Wyoming's Unique Talents."

In 1986 in *Newton v. NBC*, a jury awarded singer Wayne Netwon $19.3 million in punitive damages in his suit against NBC. That figure was reduced to $5.27 million by the court and overturned completely by the Ninth U.S. Circuit Court. The U.S. Supreme Court refused to hear the case in 1991. Newton alleged he was defamed by NBC broadcasts linking him to organized crime.

Retraction Statutes

A number of states have retraction statutes. These laws allow a publisher to mitigate (or lessen) the harm done by a defamatory statement. Most retraction statutes require that a publisher essentially admit that the defamatory statement was false and apologize for that statement. Usually, the retraction must be timely, without comment, and as prominently displayed as the original libelous statement. Burying the retraction with the crossword puzzles will not suffice. It should be remembered that, in most jurisdictions, a retraction merely mitigates damages and may help to demonstrate a lack of malice. A retraction may result in a disallowance of punitive damages, but special or actual damages may still be awarded. For example, Indiana requires that a plaintiff notify a publisher, in writing, 3 days before filing a libel suit, as to which statements in an article are thought to be false and defamatory. The publisher then has 3 days to print a "full and fair retraction" or a suit may be filed. Many publishers are reluctant to retract, for to do so is a direct admission of fault and injures their credibility.

States may not force a publisher to retract defamatory statements. Ohio's retraction statutes once required newspapers to print, within 48 hours, any demanded correction of any false statement, allegation, or rumor. This statute was found to be in violation of the First Amendment. In *Beacon Journal v. Lansdowne*, the Summitt County Common Pleas Court of Ohio noted that the Ohio retraction statutes "clearly result in the coerced publication of particular views and thus violate the First Amendment."[8]

Publishing a retraction in and of itself may not be enough to mitigate a charge of actual malice. When a New York newspaper published a defamatory article based on research that did not comply with accepted standards of the news-gathering profession, the court ruled in *Kerwick v. Orange County Publications* that the paper's retraction was not sufficient to establish a lack of actual malice. Conversely, in *Pelzer v. Minneapolis Tribune*, the failure to retract an allegedly libelous statement did not automatically show that the publisher had acted with actual malice.

Statute of Limitations

Libel suits must be filed within a certain period of time. Most states have statutes of limitations of 2 years, although some require suits to be brought within 1 year or as much as 3 years after a defamatory statement has been published.

In all cases, the statute begins running when a publication goes into general circulation for the first time. For newspapers, this usually means the date on the edition containing the alleged defamatory statement. For broadcasters, it means the date of the first broadcast in question. Since magazines often distribute editions months ahead of the date listed on the cover, statutes of limitations are not triggered by that date. Instead, magazines are governed by the date on which substantial distribution occurred.

National publications whose materials are distributed in states with varying statutes of limitations may find that, although the statute has run out in one state, a plaintiff may file suit in another state. In *Keeton v. Hustler*, the Supreme Court ruled that plaintiffs may search for states having lengthy statutes of limitations and bring suits in those states, provided a substantial number of copies of the offending publication are regularly sold and distributed there.

Consent

A minor defense against a libel suit is that of consent. A written statement giving permission to publish a statement, provided that the statement has not been edited so as to change its meaning, may be a complete defense. Other times, consent may serve to mitigate damages and charges of actual malice.

In *Falwell v. Penthouse* (1981), the Reverend Jerry Falwell sued *Penthouse* magazine for the publication of an accurate account of an interview he had granted to a free-lance journalist. Falwell, a public figure and an outspoken critic of magazines like *Penthouse*, granted the interview under conditions given verbally to the author. Essentially, Falwell stated that the interview should be sold to a magazine that was consistent with the image of his ministry. When the interview was published in the March 1981 issue of *Penthouse*, Falwell appeared on the cover of the magazine. That space was usually reserved for scantily clad women. Falwell contended that the reporter had violated his consent and had acted with actual malice by selling the article to a publication embarrassing to Falwell. The court dismissed the suit noting,

☐   . . . The mere fact that the plaintiff may not approve of publications such as *Penthouse*, or may not desire *Penthouse* to discuss his activities or publish his spoken words, does not give rise to an action cognizable under the law. The First Amendment freedoms of speech and press are too precious to be eroded or undermined by the likes and dislikes of persons who invite attention and publicity by their own voluntary actions.[9]

The Constitutional Defense

Before 1964 and the *New York Times* decision, libel suits were a matter of state law. States, for the most part, recognized the previously discussed common law defenses. However, they sometimes differed in their application of principles. One such principle involves the criticism of public officials. The constitutional defense extends qualified privilege and bases it on the First Amendment guarantee of freedom of the press, coupled with the Warren Court's belief that our elected officials should expect public criticism of their official conduct. The media are now given wide latitude in reporting on public officials, public figures, and public issues. The constitutional defense recognizes that individual reputations must yield to the greater constitutional right to freely report the news, even if it may be false.

The Burden of Proof

The constitutional defense has superseded the common law defense of fair comment and has shifted the burden of proving truth from the defendant to the plaintiff. Case law since 1964 has established that libel plaintiffs must establish the falsity of a defamatory statement. Public figure plaintiffs must also establish that misstatements of fact were made with actual malice. The Supreme Court defined actual malice in *New York Times v. Sullivan* as a false statement made "with knowledge that it was false or with reckless disregard of whether it was false or not."[10]

The constitutional defense grew out of a case that was representative of the turbulent 1960s. The principals involved were the major leaders of the burgeoning civil rights movement. As the movement altered America's social laws over the next decade, so too would *New York Times* alter American libel law.

New York Times v. Sullivan (1964)

On March 29, 1960, the *New York Times* published a full-page editorial advertisement under the headline "Heed Their Rising Voices." The advertisement was placed by civil rights activists in the South. They were soliciting funds to aid in the legal defense of Dr. Martin Luther King, Jr. The activists also sought support for what they called "embattled students" and for the voting rights movement in the South. The advertisement follows:

Heed Their Rising Voices

As the whole world knows by now, thousands of Southern Negro students are engaged in wide-spread non-violent demonstrations in positive affirmation of the right to live in human dignity as guaranteed by the U.S. Constitution and the Bill of Rights. In their efforts to uphold these guarantees, they are being met by an unprecedented wave of terror by those who would deny and negate that document which the whole world looks upon as setting the pattern for modern freedom. . . .

In Orangeburg, South Carolina, when 400 students peacefully sought to buy doughnuts and coffee at lunch counters in the business district they were forcibly ejected, tear gassed, soaked to the skin in freezing weather with fire hoses, arrested en masse and herded into an open barbed-wire stockade to stand for hours in the bitter cold.

In Montgomery, Alabama, after students sang "My Country 'Tis of Thee" on the State Capitol steps their leaders were expelled from school, and truckloads of police armed with shotguns and tear gas ringed the Alabama State College Campus. When the entire student body protested to state authorities by refusing to re-register, their dining hall was padlocked in an attempt to starve them into submission.

In Tallahassee, Atlanta, Nashville, Savannah, Greensboro, Memphis, Richmond, Charlotte, and a host of other cities in the South, young American teenagers, in the face of the entire weight of official state apparatus and police power, have boldly stepped forth as protagonists of democracy. Their courage and amazing restraint have inspired millions and given a new dignity to the cause of freedom.

Small wonder that the Southern violators of the Constitution fear this new, non-violent brand of freedom fighter . . . even as they fear the upswelling right-to-vote movement. Small wonder that they are determined to destroy the one man who, more than any other, symbolizes the new spirit now sweeping the South—the Rev. Dr. Martin Luther King, Jr., world-famous leader of the Montgomery Bus Protest. . . .

Again and again the Southern violators have answered Dr. King's peaceful protests with intimidation and violence. They have bombed his home, almost killing his wife and child. They have assaulted his person. They have arrested him seven times—for "speeding," "loitering" and similar "offenses." And now they have charged him with "perjury"—a felony under which they could imprison him for ten years. Obviously, their real purpose is to remove him physically as the leader to whom the students—and millions of others—look for guidance and support, and thereby to intimidate all leaders who may rise in the South. . . . The defense of Martin Luther King . . . is an integral part of the total struggle for freedom in the South.

Decent-minded Americans cannot help but applaud the creative daring of the students and the quiet heroisim of Dr. King. But this is one of those moments in the story history of Freedom when men and women of good will must do more than applaud the rising-to-glory of others. . . .

We must heed their rising voices—yes—but we must add our own.

We urge you to join hands with our fellow Americans in the South by supporting, with your dollars, this Combined Appeal for all three needs—the defense of Martin Luther King—the support of the embattled students—and the struggle for the right to vote.[11]

The ad was signed by 64 prominent Americans, including former First Lady Eleanor Roosevelt, journalist Nat Hentoff, and major league baseball's first black player, Jackie Robinson. Also among the signatories were show business personalities such as Marlon Brando, Sammy Davis Jr., Harry Belafonte, Sidney Poitier, Nat "King" Cole, Diahann Carroll, Hope Lange, Robert Ryan, and Shelley Winters. In addition, 16 southern clergymen were purported to have signed the ad. They included the Reverends Ralph D. Abernanthy, Fred L. Shuttlesworth, and Martin Luther King, Sr.

A coupon appeared in the lower right-hand corner of the ad urging readers to "mail this coupon TODAY!" along with a contribution to the Committee to Defend Martin Luther King and The Struggle For Freedom In The South.

L.B. Sullivan, the elected police commissioner of Montgomery, Alabama, objected to several passages contained in the third and fifth paragraphs of the ad. The ad contained several factual errors that related to questionable or illegal activities by the Montgomery police. Although Sullivan was not mentioned by name, he contended that he represented the "police" and was therefore being accused of "ringing the campus" and "starving the students into submission." He also claimed that he was characterized as one of the "Southern violators" being accused of "intimidation and violence," bombing Dr. King's home, and falsely charging King with perjury. Sullivan filed suit against four of the clergymen who had signed the ad and who had been critical of the conduct of the police during civil rights demonstrations in Montgomery. In accordance with Alabama law, Sullivan demanded a retraction from the clergymen and the *New York Times*. The clergymen said that their signatures were unauthorized and took no further part in the case. The *New York Times* could not understand how the ad applied to Sullivan.

Under the common law, the burden of proof was on the *New York Times* and a trial court in Alabama found portions of the ad libelous *per se*. The court also ruled that Sullivan could be identified as representing the "police" and "Southern violators." The Alabama Supreme Court upheld the trial court's award of $500,000 to Sullivan and the *New York Times* appealed to the United States Supreme Court. The Supreme Court unanimously reversed the judgment and, in its decision, granted the media greater protection from libel suits filed by public officials. This was done by bringing such suits into the realm of constitutional law. Justice Brennan delivered the opinion of the Court.

☐ We hold that the rule of law applied by the Alabama courts is constitutionally deficient for failure to provide the safeguards for feedom of speech and of the press that are required by the First and Fourteenth Amendments in a libel action brought by a public official against critics of his official conduct. . . .

The general proposition that feedom of expression upon public questions is secured by the First Amendment has long been settled by our decisions. The constititutional safeguard, we have said, "was fashioned to assure [sic] the unfettered interchange of ideas for bringing about political and social changes desired by the people." Roth v. United States, 354 U.S. 476 (1957), . . . "It is a prized American privilege to speak one's mind,

although not always with perfect good taste, on all public institutions."
Bridges v. California 314 U.S. 252 (1941). . . .

Thus we consider this case against the background of a profound national commitment to the principle that debate on public issues should be
uninhibited, robust, and wide-open, and that it may well include vehe-
ment, caustic, and sometimes unpleasantly sharp attacks on government
and public officials.

The present advertisement, as an expression of grievance and protest
on one of the major public issues of our time, would seem clearly to qualify for constitutional protection. . . .

Authoritative interpretations of the First Amendment guarantees have
consistently refused to recognize an exception for any test of truth,
whether administered by judges, juries, or administrative officials—and
especially not one that puts the burden of providing truth on the
speaker. . . .

The constitutional guarantees require, we think, a federal rule that
prohibits a public official from recovering damages for a defamatory falsehood relating to his official conduct unless he proves that the statement
was made with "actual malice"—that is, with knowledge that it was false
or with reckless disregard of whether it was false or not. . . .

We conclude that such a privilege is required by the First and Fourteenth Amendments.

We hold today that the Constitution delimits a state's power to award
damages for libel in actions brought by public officials against critics of
their official conduct.[12]

Extensions of the Public Official Doctrine

Although *New York Times* sought to limit libel suits brought by
public officials against the media, it left uncertainties about who was to be included
in the definition of a "public official." Certainly, elected officials were to be included
in the defintion, but was it to include off-duty police officers, firefighters, and teachers? How were prominent persons who move in and out of government service to be
classified? In *New York Times*, the Court also redefined actual malice from the
traditional meaning of "evil motive," "spite," or "ill will" to that of knowing falsehood or reckless disregard for the truth. The standards for determining actual malice,
however, were unclear. The Supreme Court would rule on these questions in the
decade following *New York Times v. Sullivan.*

In 1967, the Supreme Court combined two libel cases in a decision that extended
the Public Official Doctrine to include public figures. Public figures were defined as
those individuals not holding public office, but who willingly take part in public
affairs. In *Curtis Publishing Co. v. Butts* and *Associated Press v. Walker*, the Court

unanimously extended the constitutional defense against libel to include public figures. A divided Court also extended the "actual malice" and "reckless disregard" tests of *New York Times* to public figures. Four justices would have preferred a standard based on "extreme departure from the standards of investigation and reporting ordinarily adhered to by responsible publishers."[13] This standard would be clarified in *Gertz v. Robert Welch Inc.* and would make it easier for plaintiffs to successfully sue the media.

In *Butts*, University of Georgia Athletic Director Wally Butts originally sued for $5 million, but was awarded $460,000 in damages against the *Saturday Evening Post*, based on an article that charged that Butts and Alabama coach Bear Bryant had conspired to "fix" a football game. The *Post* article, entitled "The Story of a College Football Fix," was based on notes taken by an insurance salesman named George Burnett, who was on probation for writing bad checks. Burnett claimed to have overheard the conspiracy to "fix" the game when he picked up the receiver of a pay telephone and was accidentally cut into the conversation. This somewhat questionable evidence was printed in the article, which compared the Butts/Bryant collusion to the Chicago Black Sox scandal of the 1919 World Series.

In *Walker*, retired army General Edwin Walker had secured a $500,000 judgment against the Associated Press, which falsely reported that Walker had "assumed command" of rioters at Mississipi State University who were protesting the admission of the first black student to the school. The Associated Press report stated that Walker personally led a charge against federal marshals and encouraged rioters to use violence. The article also stated that Walker provided technical advice to the rioters on combating the effects of tear gas.

Technically, Walker was a private citizen at the time, but had enjoyed an illustrious military career before resigning to engage in political activity. Walker had been in command of federal troops during the Little Rock Central High School desegregation confrontation in 1957. He now spoke out strongly against such federal intervention and had become a politcal activist. The Supreme Court found that although he was not a public official, Walker certainly was a public figure. The Supreme Court ruled in favor of Butts and against General Walker. Justice Harlan delivered the opinion of the Court.

☐   In *New York Times Co. v. Sullivan*, this Court held that "the constitutional guarantees (of freedom of speech and press) require a federal rule that prohibits a public official from recovering damages for a defamatory falsehood relating to his official conduct unless he proves that the statement was made with 'actual malice'—that is, with knowledge that it was false or with reckless disregard of whether it was false or not." We brought these two cases here to consider the impact of that decision on libel actions instituted by persons who are not public officials, but who are "public figures" and involved in issues in which the public has a justified and important interest.

. . . We consider and would hold that a "public figure" who is not a public official may also recover damages for a defamatory falsehood whose substance makes substantial danger to reputation apparent, on a showing of highly unreasonable conduct constituting an extreme departure from the standards of investigation and reporting ordinarily adhered to by responsible publishers. . . .

. . . The Butts story was in no sense "hot news" and the editors of the magazine recognized the need for a thorough investigation of the serious charges. Elementary precautions were, nevertheless, ignored. The *Saturday Evening Post* knew that Burnett had been placed on probation in connection with bad check charges, but proceeded to publish the story on the basis of his affidavit without substantial independent support. Burnett's notes were not even viewed by any of the magazine's personnel prior to publication. John Carmichael, who was supposed to have been with Burnett when the phone call was overheard, was not interviewed. . . . In short, the evidence is ample to support a finding of highly unreasonable conduct constituting an extreme departure from the standards of investigation and reporting ordinarily adhered to by responsible publishers.

. . . In contrast to the **Butts** article, the dispatch which concerns us in **Walker** was news which required immediate dissemination. The Associated Press received the information from a correspondent who was present at the scene of the events and gave every indication of being trustworthy and competent. His dispatches in this instance, with one minor exception, were internally consistent and would not have seemed unreasonable to one familiar with General Walker's prior publicized statements on the underlying controversy. **Considering the necessity for rapid dissemination, nothing in this series of events gives the slightest hint of a severe departure from accepted publishing standards.** We therefore conclude that General Walker should not be entitled to damages from the Associated Press.[14]

Expansion of the Public Figure Test

Subsequent cases attempted to define "public officials" and "public figures" for purposes of the constitutional defense against libel. The definitions increasingly became more expansive. The courts included in the definition elected officials, such as mayors and judges, and civil servants. County clerks, police chiefs, and their deputies were defined as public officials. In *Rosenblatt v. Baer*, the Supreme Court defined public officials as those

☐   government employees who have, or appear to the public to have, substantial responsibility for the conduct of government affairs.[15]

Ultimately, the Supreme Court was to expand the doctrine from public officials, to public figures, and finally to private individuals caught up in public issues. A plurality of the Supreme Court held in *Rosenbloom v. Metromedia* (1971), that First Amendment protection should be extended to

☐ all discussion and communication involving matters of public or general concern, without regard to whether the persons involved are famous or anonymous.[16]

The *Rosenbloom* decision stretched the constitutional defense to its limits. For a brief time, the media enjoyed immunity from libel suits involving virtually anyone caught up in a public issue. Three years later, in *Gertz*, the Supreme Court overruled the Public Issues Doctrine as outlined in *Rosenbloom*.

Gertz v. Robert Welch Inc. (1974)

In 1968, a Chicago police officer named Richard Nuccio shot and killed a youth named Nelson. Nuccio was convicted of second-degree murder. The Nelson family retained attorney Elmer Gertz to represent them in civil litigation against Nuccio.

Robert Welch was the founder of the staunchly anticommunist, ultra-conservative John Birch Society and publisher of *American Opinion*, a monthly magazine espousing the views of the organization. In the early 1960s, *American Opinion* warned of a nationwide conspiracy to discredit local law enforcement agencies and of a movement to create a national police force capable of supporting a Communist dictatorship. As part of this continuing effort to warn the public of this conspiracy, *American Opinion* commissioned an article on the murder trial of Richard Nuccio.

In March 1969, *American Opinion* published an article entitled "FRAME-UP: Richard Nuccio And The War On Police." The article asserted that Nuccio's conviction was part of a Communist campaign against the police. Although Gertz took no part in the criminal prosecution of Nuccio, he had been retained by the Nelson family as counsel in the civil proceeding. *American Opinion*, however, portrayed Gertz as an architect of the frame-up. The article stated that Gertz had a criminal record, was an official in several Communist organizations, and had assisted in the planning of the demonstrations during the 1968 Democratic Convention in Chicago. All of these assertions were false and *American Opinion* made no effort to verify the accuracy of the statements.

When Gertz sued *American Opinion* for libel, the magazine claimed constitutional privilege, asserting that Gertz was a public official or a public figure and that the article concerned an issue of public concern. Although the trial court found in favor of Gertz, a federal district court and an appellate court, in citing *Rosenbloom*, ruled in favor of *American Opinion*. The Supreme Court overruled the decision and the Public Issues Doctrine. Justice Powell delivered the opinion of the Court.

☐   ... [T]hose classed as public figures have thrust themselves into the forefront of particular public controversies in order to influence the resolution of the issues involved. In either event, they invite attention and comment. ... [T]he communications media are entitled to act on the assumption that public officials and public figures have voluntarily exposed themselves to increased risk of injury from defamatory falsehood concerning them. No such assumption is justified with respect to a private individual. ... [P]rivate individuals are not only more vulnerable to injury than public officials and public figures, they are also more deserving of recovery. For these reasons we conclude that the states should retain substantial latitude in their efforts to enforce a legal remedy of defamatory falsehood injurious to the reputation of a private individual. The extension of the *New York Times* test proposed by the *Rosenbloom* plurality would abridge this legitimate state interest to a degree that we find unacceptable.

    ... We hold that, so long as they do not impose liability without fault, the states may define for themselves the appropriate standard of liability for a publisher or broadcaster of defamatory falsehood injurious to a private individual.

    ... Our accommodation of the competing values at stake in defamation suits by private individuals allows the States to impose liability on the publisher or broadcaster of defamatory falsehood on a less demanding showing than that required by *New York Times*.

    ... In some instances an individual may achieve such pervasive fame or notoriety that he becomes a public figure for all purposes and in all contexts. More commonly, an individual voluntarily injects himself or is drawn into a particular public controversy and thereby becomes a public figure for a limited range of issues. In either case such persons assume special prominence in the resolution of public questions.

    Petitioner [Gertz] has long been active in community and professional affairs. ... Although ... well known in some circles, he had achieved no general fame or notoriety in the community. None of the prospective jurors called at the trial had ever heard of petitioner prior to this litigation ... Absent clear evidence of general fame or notoriety in the community and pervasive involvement in the affairs of society, an individual should not be deemed a public personality for all aspects of his life.

    ... In this context it is plain that petitioner was not a public figure. ... He plainly did not thrust himself into the vortex of this public issue, nor did he engage the public's attention in an attempt to influence its outcome.[17]

The Court added that private individuals who establish liability under a less demanding standard than *New York Times* may only recover actual damages.

In *Gertz*, the Court redefined the public figure/public issues standard and lessened the libel immunity enjoyed by the media that began with *New York Times* and continually expanded through *Rosenbloom*. The Court also returned to the states the freedom to define the standards of liability for libel when private individuals are involved. The Court suggested that this standard should not require a showing of actual malice, but a less demanding standard. At this writing, 20 states, the District of Columbia, and Puerto Rico have opted for a negligence standard for private individual libel actions. New York has adopted a gross negligence standard. Simply defined, negligence may result when "due care" is not exercised by publishers or broadcasters. Among the jurisdictions adopting the negligence standard are Arkansas, Arizona, California, District of Columbia, Georgia, Hawaii, Illinois, Kansas, Kentucky, Maryland, Massachusetts, Mississippi, Ohio, Oklahoma, Pennsylvania, Puerto Rico, Tennessee, Texas, Utah, Virginia, West Virginia, and Washington. Alaska, Colorado, Indiana, and Michigan still adhere to the actual malice standard. This concept is discussed further, later in this chapter.

The State of Libel Since *Gertz*

Public Figures

The definition of a public figure narrowed considerably following the *Gertz* ruling. In 1976, the Supreme Court ruled that Mary Alice Firestone, a fixture in Palm Beach, Florida, society and former wife of tire and rubber heir Russell Firestone, was not a public figure. *Time* magazine had reported inaccurate information about her recent divorce. When she filed a libel suit, *Time* claimed a constitutional defense. In *Time Inc. v. Firestone*, the Supreme Court rejected the defense, stating that involvement in a public trial does not necessarily make one a public figure. They added that the dissolution of a marriage is not a public controversy as defined in *Gertz*.

The impact of *Gertz* was modified further in the 1990 Supreme Court ruling in *Milkovich v. Lorain Journal*. In this case, the Court held that defamatory opinion that is susceptible to being proved true or false is not protected by the First Amendment.

Milkovich v. Lorain Journal (1990)

A high school wrestling team was involved in an altercation during a match. Several people were injured during the fracas. The state athletic commission held a hearing on the matter and testimony from Coach Milkovich was taken. The day after the hearing, a local newspaper, the *News Herald*, ran an editorial that was critical of Milkovich. The paper stated that Milkovich "had beat the law with a big lie" and that anyone who attended the meet "knows in his heart that [Milkovich] lied at the hearing after giving his solemn oath to tell the truth." Milkovich sued for libel. The paper claimed the statement was protected opinion. Chief Justice Rehnquist wrote,

> ☐ We are not persuaded that . . . an additional separate constitutional privi-
> lege for "opinion" is required to ensure the freedom of expression guaran-
> teed by the First Amendment. The present case then becomes whether or
> not a reasonable fact finder could conclude that the statements in the . . .
> column imply that petitioner Milkovich perjured himself in a judicial pro-
> ceeding. We think this question must be answered in the affirmative. . . .
>
>   . . . [W]e also think the connotation that petitioner committed perjury
> is sufficiently factual to be susceptible of being proved true or false. . . .
>
>   . . . The numerous decisions discussed above establishing First
> Amendment protection for defendants in defamation actions surely dem-
> onstrate the Court's recognition of the amendment's vital guarantee of
> free and uninhibited discussion of public issues. But there is also another
> side to the equation; we have regularly acknowledged the "important so-
> cial values which underlie the law of defamation" and recognize that
> "[S]ociety has a pervasive and strong interest in preventing and redress-
> ing attacks upon reputation" Rosenblatt v. Baer, 383 U.S. 75,86.[18]

Although it was generally more difficult for the media to claim a constitutional defense since *Gertz*, in 1986, the Supreme Court slowed the swing of the pendulum away from the *Rosenbloom* standard when it decided *Philadelphia Newspapers v. Hepps.* In *Philadelphia*, the Court reversed a lower court ruling and required that private figure libel plaintiffs bringing suit against the media for defamatory statements involving matters of public concern, demonstrate the falsity of such statements. Previously, falsity was assumed and the burden of proof fell on the defendant. This decision indicates that *Rosenbloom* still has some residual impact on post-*Gertz* interpretations.

In *Philadelphia Newspapers v. Hepps* (1977), the *Philadelphia Inquirer* published a series of articles stating that Maurice Hepps, the owner of a chain of stores called "Thrifty," had connections to organized crime. The articles also alleged that Hepps had used those connections to influence Pennsylvania's government processes. Hepps was a private figure. However, the allegations that he had influenced the Pennsylvania government made the issue one of public concern. The trial court and the Pennsylvania Supreme Court found in favor of Hepps, following the common law assumption that a defamatory statement is assumed to be false unless the plaintiff proves otherwise. The U.S. Supreme Court reversed the decision. Justice O'Connor delivered the opinion of the Court.

> ☐ Here as in *Gertz*, the plaintiff is a private figure and the newspaper arti-
> cles are of public concern. In *Gertz*, as in *New York Times*, the common-
> law rule was superceded by a constitutional rule. We believe that the
> common law's rule on falsity—that the defendant must bear the burden of
> proving truth—must similarly fall here to a constitutional requirement that
> the plaintiff bear the burden of showing falsity, as well as fault, before
> recovering damages. . . .

To ensure that true speech on matters of public concern is not deterred, we hold that the common-law presumption that defamatory speech is false cannot stand when a plaintiff seeks damages against a media defendant for speech of public concern.[19]

The Negligence Standard of Fault

As previously noted, since *Gertz*, most states have opted for a lesser standard of fault for private figures who are objects of a defamatory falsehood. Negligence usually results from failure to exercise normal care in reporting a story (i.e., departing from accepted journalistic procedures), thereby risking the publication of a defamatory falsehood.

A Little Rock Arkansas television station was guilty of negligence in its reporting of a "robbery/hostage" situation. Interestingly, in *KARK-TV v. Simon*, the Arkansas Supreme Court technically ruled in favor of the TV station, since the trial court had found the station guilty of the more serious charge of actual malice. Although the $12,500 award of compensatory damages was vacated as being excessive, the court did suggest that further proceedings could result in damages against KARK-TV based on a finding of negligence.

At 8:30 P.M. on the evening of August 11, 1982, police were called to the Galleria Shopping Center on Little Rock's west side. They were responding to a report that the Custom Design store was being robbed by two men. At the Galleria, Andre Smith and Barry Simon were handcuffed, searched, and placed in a squad car by police. A reporter for KARK-TV, Carolyn Long, happened to be shopping in the Galleria. She received information from someone who had been listening to a police scanner that there was a potential robbery situation. Long met a camera crew that had been dispatched to the scene from KARK. She questioned police on the scene and interviewed a clerk at Custom Design. The police provided no information and the store clerk gave vague responses to Long's questions. At approximately 9:00 P.M., police released Smith and Simon and decided that no crime had taken place, nor had any crime been attempted.

On the 10 o'clock news, KARK broadcast the following report:

Quick action by Little Rock Police tonight stopped a robbery attempt at Custom Design at the Galleria Shopping Center. Details are sketchy; however, it appears two suspects backed their car up to the store in order to rob it. For a time, the two men allegedly held a store clerk hostage. The clerk was shaken, and wasn't sure about exactly what had happened.[20]

Although Simon and Smith were not named in the report, the newscast included scenes of the police putting the two men in a police car. It was broadcast to approximately 82,000 households.

Judge Hays wrote:

☐   . . . The court instructed the jury here that the defendant [KARK-TV] was held to the standard of care a reasonably careful person would exercise under circumstances similar to those shown by evidence.

. . . The reporter could get no information from police officers at the scene nor could the producer of the news get any information verified by police headquarters. The story was written and shown a little over an hour later. We cannot say that a news report with its sources consisting of information from a police scanner, uncorroborated by police on the scene, in conjunction with an eyewitness account by a news reporter who did not know the surrounding circumstances of what she observed, will be found to be due care as a matter of law. We think the issue of negligence was properly submitted to the jury.[21]

Negligence can also result when reporters and editors fail to check facts or misrepresent information that may be part of the public record.

Actual Malice

Under *New York Times*, for public figures to bring a successful libel suit they must demonstrate that a defamatory falsehood was published with reckless disregard of whether it was false or not. In *Curtis Publishing v. Butts*, the Supreme Court extended the definition of actual malice to include an extreme departure from normal standards of journalism (see discussion earlier in this text). The Supreme Court refined the definition of actual malice in *St. Amant v. Thompson*. In that decision, the Court ruled that there must be "sufficient evidence to permit the conclusion that the defendant entertained serious doubts as to the truth of the publication."[22]

In *Herbert v. Lando*, the Supreme Court ruled that a public figure defendant could be questioned as to his state of mind when writing a defamatory article. This, according to six members of the Court, was essential for a plaintiff to establish actual malice. Since *Herbert*, reporters can be asked to identify their sources of information and to produce transcripts of notes and tapes of interviews. Prior to this ruling, it was generally assumed that a reporter's thoughts and opinions on the editorial process were privileged. Since *Herbert*, any information that would enable a plaintiff to establish that a reporter acted with reckless disregard for the truth—thereby establishing actual malice—can now be asked during trial procedures.

In *Bose Corporation v. Consumers Union* (1985), a trial court found *Consumer Reports* magazine guilty of libeling the Bose Corporation in a 1970 review of the Bose 901 loudspeakers. Because Bose Corporation was found to be a public figure, it had to show that false material in the article was published with actual malice. Based on testimony provided by the author of the article, a trial court found that a false statement was published with reckless disregard of its truth or falsity. The statement in question accused the loudspeakers of producing sound that "wandered about the room." The issue at question was whether the author's word choice accurately described what he heard when listening to the Bose 901 speakers. The court of appeals reversed the trial court's libel verdict on grounds that, based on facts before the court, the statement was not made with actual malice. The Supreme Court affirmed the holding.

This decision is significant in that when media defendants appeal a ruling based on actual malice, the appellate court does not hear testimony. That court does not have the chance to evaluate the demeanor of witnesses. State-of-mind questioning, like that allowed under *Herbert*, is not possible. Justices Rehnquist and O'Connor dissented in *Bose*, noting that the trial court based its original finding of actual malice on the credibility of the defendant's testimony. Rehnquist could not see how the appellate court could rule on actual malice without having the opportunity to hear testimony from the defendant and thereby evaluating his intentions.

Although a newspaper's accurate summary of charges made in a recall petition filed against a Washington state county prosecutor under investigation for racketeering was ruled privileged, the Washington State Supreme Court found that a television report of the same story may have been made with actual malice. In *Herron v. Tribune Publishing Co.*, KING-TV reporter Don McGaffin's statement that he would "get" Pierce County Prosecutor Don Herron, the subsequent broadcast of a story riddled with defamatory falsehoods supported by unreliable sources, and the destruction of the tapes of the broadcast after Herron filed a complaint, were enough to warrant a trial based on actual malice.

Entertainer Wayne Newton brought a suit against NBC as a result of a news report linking him to organized crime. A Nevada district court found that the NBC broadcast concerning Newton's purchase of a Las Vegas hotel was defamatory and could be found by a jury to have been made with actual malice. The jury awarded Newton $7.9 million for loss of past income, $1.1 million for loss of future income, $5 million for damages to his reputation, $225,000 for physical and mental suffering, and $5 million in punitive damages—for a total judgment of $22 million. Although the trial judge found some of the jury's damage awards excessive, the court upheld the jury award of $5 million in punitive damages, and established an award of $225,000 to Newton for physical and mental injury, and $50,000 for presumed damage to his reputation. A motion for a new trial was granted on the question of damages only. In January 1989, in *Newton v. NBC*, Newton filed a remittitur of all damages except $225,000 for physical and mental injury, $50,000 as presumed damages for reputation, and $5 million in punitive damages. The judgment was reduced to $5.2 million and, before being overturned in the summer of 1990, was the highest award ever entered in a libel case against a news organization.

On August 2, 1989, a Clearwater, Florida, court awarded the largest libel judgment in history. GTE Corporation was awarded $100 million in a suit against Home Shopping Network. While the amount of the award was described as "mindboggling," libel experts agree that the award will likely be reduced on appeal.

Summary Judgment

In some libel suits, after the plaintiff has presented his allegations before the court, the defendant may ask for *summary judgment*. Summary judgment is an immediate ruling by the judge based on the facts before the court. If the judge believes that a jury could not reasonably find in favor of the plaintiff, he may grant a summary judgment in favor of the defendant. This means that the case will not go to trial. Since *New York Times*, and the requirement that public figures prove actual malice, many public figure libel suits have been dismissed on a motion for summary judgment. This policy has been encouraged by the Supreme Court. In order to overcome a motion for summary judgment, a plaintiff may present evidence of facts from which a jury could reasonably infer actual malice and is required to show the existence of actual malice with convincing clarity.

Columnist Jack Anderson published three articles in the October 1981 issue of *The Investigator* magazine about a not-for-profit corporation called the Liberty Lobby. The Liberty Lobby complained that 30 statements in the articles were defamatory. Essentially, *The Investigator* articles characterized the Liberty Lobby as being "infiltrated by Nazis," anti-Semitic, and "a nest of Nazis."

Both Anderson and the Liberty Lobby were limited-purpose public figures and the constitutional defense was used. In *Liberty Lobby v. Anderson* (1986), the district court granted the defendant's motion for summary judgment on grounds that the actual malice standard of *New York Times* had not been met. The appellate court reversed, in part, noting that nine of the 30 statements in question were capable of defamatory meaning and that a jury could reasonably conclude that they were made with actual malice. One year later, the U.S. Supreme Court reversed the appellate court's decision. Interestingly, the appellate court judge who authored the opinion was Antonin Scalia. Scalia was appointed to the Supreme Court in June 1986. In July, the Supreme Court overruled Scalia's interpretation of summary judgment.

Writing for the three-judge court, 2 years before his appointment to the U.S. Supreme Court, Appellate Court Judge Antonin Scalia authored this opinion on the application of summary judgment:

☐   . . . To prevail in a libel trial, not only must the public figure plaintiff prove the existence of actual malice; he must prove it with "convincing clarity." . . . The issue we address in this portion of our opinion is whether these requirments of "convincing clarity" . . . apply at the summary judgement stage.

     . . . [T]he issue can be framed as follows: whether, in order to deny the defendant's motion for summary judgement, the court must conclude that a reasonable jury not only could (on the basis of the facts taken in the light most favorable to the plaintiff) find that it had been established with "convincing clarity." We conclude that the answer is no. Imposing the increased proof requirement at this stage would change the threshold summary judgement inquiry from a search for a minimum of facts supporting the plaintiff's case to an evaluation of the weight of those facts and (it would seem) of the weight of at least the defendant's uncontroverted facts as well. It would effectively force the plaintiff to try his entire case in pretrial affidavits and depositions—marshalling for the court all the facts supporting his case, and seeking to contest as many of the defendant's facts as possible. . . . In other words, disposing of a summary judgement motion would rarely be the relatively quick process it is supposed to be.[23]

In July 1986 in *Anderson v. Liberty Lobby*, the Supreme Court struck down this opinion. The Court ruled that in actual malice cases, the plaintiff must establish with convincing clarity that the defendant acted with reckless disregard of the truth or the case will be disposed of with a summary judgment in favor of the defendant. Justice White delieverd the opinion of the Court.

☐   . . . [W]here the factual dispute concerns actual malice, clearly a material issue in a *New York Times* case, the appropriate summary judgement question will be whether the evidence in the record could support a reasonable jury finding either that the plaintiff has shown actual malice by clear and convincing evidence or that the plaintiff has not. . . .

In sum, a court ruling on a motion for summary judgement must be guided by the *New York Times* "clear and convincing" evidentiary standard in determining whether a genuine issue of actual malice exists—that is, whether the evidence presented is such that a reasonable jury might find that actual malice had been shown with convincing clarity. Because the Court of Appeals did not apply the correct standard in reviewing the District Court's grant of summary judgement, we vacate its decision and remand the case for further proceedings consistent with this opinion.[24]

Group Libel

Sometimes the publication of a false, defamatory statement about a group of people may give rise to suits against the media. When a defamatory statement is published about a particular group of people, any one of them may sue for libel, provided they can show that they are readily identified as members of that group and that the defamatory statement applies to them personally. Obviously, the smaller the group, the more likely that individuals can be identified and may sue as a result of a defamatory publication. Generally, groups consisting of more than 25 individuals have some difficulty establishing identity. However, in 1962 in *Fawcett Publications v. Morris*, a member of a football team that consisted of 60 players brought a successful group libel suit.

In the classic group libel case, *Neiman-Marcus Co. v. Lait*, nine models and 15 of 25 salesmen employed by the Dallas department store were allowed to bring suit against *U.S.A. Confidential* for calling them prostitutes and homosexuals, respectively. The publication also referred to the 382 Neiman-Marcus saleswomen as prostitutes, but the 30 women who attempted to sue were not able to bring suit, because the group was too large.

Not surprisingly, in *McCullough v. Cities Service* (1984), the Oklahoma Supreme Court ruled that a doctor of osteopathy could not sue for an allegedly defamatory article on behalf of the 19,686 osteopaths in the United States. The court did, however, attempt to clarify the standards under which group libel suits may be brought. The Oklahoma Supreme Court rejected the notion that a simple numerical limit could determine when a group was too large for a suit to be brought. They noted that although Prosser's *Restatement of Torts* had set an arbitrary limit of 25, a New York Court had determined that a suit by a member of a group of 53 was legally actionable.

Citing *Brady v. Ottaway Newspapers* (1981), the Oklahoma Supreme Court outlined the following principles for determining when a group libel action may be actionable:

☐ From the teaching of **Brady**, we glean the following principles to which we subscribe:
1. The "of and concerning" element in defamation actions requires that the allegedly defamatory comment refer to the plaintiff.
2. Generally an impersonal reproach of an indeterminate class is not actionable. The underlying premise of this principle is that the larger the collectivity named in the libel, the less likely it is that a reader would understand it to refer to a particular individual. The rule was designed to encourage frank discussions of matters of public concern under the First Amendment guarantees. Thus the incidental and occasional injury to the individual resulting from the defamation of large groups is balanced against the public's right to know.
3. In contrast to the treatment of an individual in a large group which has been defamed, an individual belonging to a small group may maintain an action for individual injury resulting from a defamatory comment about the group, by showing that he is a member of the group. Because the group is small and includes few individuals, reference to the individual plaintiff reasonably follows from the statement and the question of reference is left for the jury.
4. *Size alone is too narrow a focus to determine the issue of individual application in group defamation.* [Emphasis added by the author.]
5. The **intensity of suspicion** test recognizes that even a general derogatory reference to a group may affect the reputation of every

member. In order to determine personal application it requires that a factual inquiry be made to determine the degree that the group accusation focuses on each individual member of the group. The numerical size of the group is a consideration, but is not the only factor to be considered. One element to be considered is the prominence of the individual within the group.[25]

In keeping with these standards, in 1987, the Tenth U.S. Court of Appeals ruled in *Weatherland v. Globe International* that a group of 955 was too large to bring a group libel action. The attempted action stemmed from an article in the *Midnight Globe* entitled "America's Dog 'Death Camps'." The report depicted cruel methods employed by some dog breeders in the raising of puppies. The court ruled that although some breeders may practice these methods, the entire group of breeders was too large to permit individual identification of those engaged in such practices.

Criminal Libel

Thus far we have discussed the civil law of libel. Civil law provides monetary awards for successful plaintiffs. On the other hand, jail sentences are part of the punishiment for those who violate criminal law. Many states have criminal libel laws on the books. These laws were designed to punish those who might utter words that provoke riots or otherwise threaten the public order and are rarely enforced today. In fact, *New York Times* has made many of these laws unconstitutional.

In some jurisdictions, group libel is part of criminal law. Illinois enacted a law in 1949 that made it a crime to disseminate or publish racist material. The law was not enforced, however, when American Nazis displaying swastikas marched through the predominately Jewish Chicago suburb of Skokie in 1978. It is unlikely that the law would stand today.

In civil libel, a dead person cannot be defamed. No action can be attempted unless the statement in question reflects on those still living, who are in turn defamed. Criminal libel laws, however, often provide for punishment if one defames the memory of one who is dead, and scandalizes or provokes surviving relatives or friends. These laws were based on the theory that riots and other civil disorders can be started by the defamation of a deceased political or social leader. The laws were designed primarily to protect the public order, not the surviving relatives.

Like many states, Indiana's criminal libel law had its roots in the nineteenth century and provided for a fine of up to $1000 and 6 months in jail for the false publication of material that "imputes official dishonesty and corruption in an officer."[26] A northern Indiana newspaper was prosecuted for criminal libel in 1881 for accusing the town's mayor of "rascally conduct." Indiana's law was modified several times before being repealed in 1976.

As was the case in Indiana, some of these state laws have been modified or declared unconstitutional. However, many remain on the books. In a number of states, including Louisiana, the truth of the utterance was of no concern in criminal libel. The rationale was that even a true defamatory statement is capable of disturbing the public order. In the wake of *New York Times*, the Supreme Court ruled this concept to be unconstitutional where public figures are concerned. In *Garrison v. Louisiana*, the Supreme Court stated that

☐ only those false statements made with the high degree of awareness of their probable falsity demanded by *New York Times* may be the subject of either civil or criminal actions.[27]

The *Garrison* decision forced many states to revise their criminal libel laws.

Humor and Fiction

Generally, defamatory remarks published as humor are protected as the expression of opinion. Many such publications lampoon only public figures and the added protection of *New York Times* allows a wide range of commentary. Editorial cartoons, political satirists, stand-up comics, and other humorists are essentially free to offer their opinions on people and issues facing society. Rhetorical hyperbole is protected as opinion, provided that such language is not a defamatory statement of fact. For example, in *Keller v. Miami Herald*, a federal district court found that an editorial cartoon in the *Miami Herald* that used stereotyped images and caricatures to comment on the character of a person involved with a nursing home was a statement of opinion and not fact. The state of Florida had closed the nursing home for numerous health code violations and the court ruled that the cartoon was pure opinion, based on publicly available information.

When a television and radio talk show host was lampooned by *Heavy Metal* magazine, the New York Supreme Court found the allegedly defamatory statements to be protected opinion.

Joe Franklin hosted a talk show on New York City broadcast stations WOR-TV and WOR-AM. The television show was syndicated throughout the country on various cable telvision systems. *Heavy Metal* was a publication owned by National Lampoon Inc., and was self-described as an "adult fantasy magazine." *Heavy Metal* consisted of science fiction and fantasy stories done in cartoon or comic strip form. The magazine also included some textual material, such as book and music reviews.

The November 1984 issue contained a one-page comic strip headed "HM's Star Dissections," in which the plaintiff was referred to as "The Incredible Shrinking Joe Franklin." In the cartoon that followed, Franklin was caricaturized on the set of his TV show. One of the guests on Franklin's program is drawn as saying "Joe, you look good . . . you lose some weight?" The panels that follow show Franklin in various situations, each of which shows him as getting physically smaller, until his head is barely visible above his desk. The final panel depicts a meeting between Franklin and WOR-TV executives in which he is told that he will be "let go."

Franklin found the cartoon to be defamatory. He noted that he was represented as "shrinking in stature" and was told he will be fired, thereby meeting the standards for actionable libel. The New York Supreme Court did not agree.

☐   ... Where it appears in the context of fiction and deliberate humor which does not purport to relate to actual events, or is obvious satire ... a statement cannot reasonably be susceptible of libelous meaning. . . .

At worst, the cartoon could be read as the obvious pun: Joe Franklin is shrinking in stature and will be fired. However, even if so read it is not a defamatory statement. Any reader interpreting it as a pun would understand it not as fact but as criticism.[29]

The fact that *Heavy Metal* billed itself as a "fantasy magazine" was important in the decision. Readers expect humor and fantasy when reading publications like *Heavy Metal* and are less likely to interpret material in these publications as fact.

Although sometimes difficult to identify, a defamatory statement of fact would still be actionable libel, especially when a private person is involved. The student newspaper published by the Medical College of Georgia crossed that line when responding to a criticism of its editorial policy.

Brooks v. Stone (1984)

Students at the Medical College of Georgia published the *Cadaver*, a newspaper for medical students. The *Cadaver* can be characterized as an irreverent publication, often satirical and risqué. The editors of the paper published under the pen name of "Bones."

A student nurse named Susan Brooks wrote a letter to the editors of the *Cadaver*, criticizing the nature and quality of the paper. The editors responded in their usual irreverent style. However, Ms. Brooks found the editors' reply to be defamatory. The following is how Susan Brooks' letter to the editors was published:

GRADUATE NURSING STUDENT COMPLAINS OR
50 WAYS TO IRRITATE THE EDITORS

Dear Editors:

During orientation I caught myself almost wishing things would be the same here at MCG as they were two years ago. *Almost* everything that is.

This year I hope that the editors of the *Cadaver* have more sense of humor (in a less sick way), have more respect for the students that aren't in the School of Medicine, and that they just have more sense!

If things aren't going to change in the Editor's Office, I hope that the nursing students and allied health students won't put up with it.

Nursing students, I appeal to you—Write! Add articles, announcements, and letters so that the pages will not be filled up with junk this year. Write—so articles by "Ramondo" won't have to be dug out of the garbage heap again.

Editors—I appeal to you. Make the *Cadaver* a paper everyone can read. There is a difference in humor and trash. If you do—maybe the *Cadaver* will be in the hands of students more—and in the bottom of bird cages less.

Sincerely,

S. Brooks, Graduate Student

The editors of the *Cadaver* published this reply:

Dear Ms. Brooks:

You are obviously a sensitive, caring member of society. We appreciate that, we really do, and certainly with your God given sensitivity, you should try to understand how and why those less fortunate members of our society deviate from acceptable forms of behavior. Take us for example, our style of humor is really out of control. Well, let us give you a little family history and you'll understand.

We have backgrounds different from the rest of you. Our mothers were German Shepherds; our fathers were Camels, so naturally we love to hump bitches in heat. Say, Ms. Brooks, when do you come in season?

Bones

Had "Bones" omitted the last sentence, no libel action would have been possible. However, in *Brooks v. Stone*, the Georgia court of appeals found that Ms. Brooks had cause for a libel action. They noted that affidavits indicated that readers of the reply understood the editors to be questioning her chastity. The court also said the reply connoted that Ms. Brooks was sexually promiscuous and was one with whom the editors would like to have sex. The court also distinguished between the normal, humorous content of the newspaper and the "letters to the editor" column:

☐ (1) A letters-to-the-editor feature customarily serves as a forum for reader opinion, including criticism of the newspaper itself; and (2) the plaintiff obviously was criticizing the nature and quality of the newspaper, and did not launch a personal invective upon the editors.[29]

Libel Insurance

As we have seen, libel suits can result from relatively routine situations. Failure to double-check facts, the writing of a "sexy" headline, the zeal of an investigative reporter to "nail" a social offender, or the lack of a budget to hire properly schooled reporters can all be costly. Responsible publishers do not usually begin a day's work with the intention of libeling someone. Although most complaints do not go to trial, daily news gathering often brings the threat of a libel suit. The cost of defending against even a *threat* of a libel suit can be extremely high. If a dispute actually goes to court, it may cost a newspaper or broadcaster more than $150,000 in attorney's fees and court costs alone. Damage awards have averaged in the millions of dollars since the early 1980s. These costs can have a chilling effect on the media's willingness to publish some stories. Small publications and broadcast stations may choose to shy away from controversial stories rather than risk a lawsuit.

Many publishers and broadcasters carry libel insurance to guard against a potentially devastating libel suit. Although prohibited in some states, libel insurance policies are offered both by private underwriters and the major trade organizations such as the American Newspaper Publishers Association and the National Association of Broadcasters.

Premiums are generally based on a percentage of the overall revenue of a broadcast station or publication and, like all insurance, on the risk of a particular medium. For example, some states have a higher percentage of libel suits and some publications tend to be involved in more libel suits than others. Obviously, in these cases, premiums will be higher.

Not all libel insurance policies are alike. There are differences in coverage, exclusions, and conditions. Many do not cover punitive damage awards. Some cover only judgments and not defense costs. But, like automobile or health insurance, various libel policies are available to protect the responsible publisher or broadcaster from financial ruin. Libel insurance may also serve to lessen the chilling effect that rising damage awards and defense costs have had on the media.

Summary

Libel is, essentially, the publication of material that is injurious of the personal reputation of an individual or the business reputation of a corporation. No libel suit can succeed unless the three elements of libel are met—identification, defamation, and publication. In addition, the plaintiff must establish some degree of fault. Private individuals may recover damages by demonstrating a lesser standard of fault than public figures. While public figures must show that a publisher or broadcaster acted with actual malice, most states require that a private individual only establish negligence on the part of the media defendant.

The traditional defenses against a libel suit are truth, privilege, and fair comment. Media defendants usually seek a constitutional defense if the plaintiff is a public figure. Minor defenses include statutes of limitations and consent. The publication of a retraction may mitigate damages, but will not usually serve as a complete defense. If judges believe that a jury cannot reasonably find in favor of a libel plaintiff, they will grant a summary judgment in favor of the defendant. Depending on the jurisidiction, successful libel plaintiffs may recover compensatory damages, special or actual damages, and/or punitive damages.

While opinion is generally protected, if defamatory opinion can be proved true or false, it may not be protected by the First Amendment.

Notes/References

1. Donald M. Gillmor and Jermome A. Barron, *Mass Communication Law*, 4th ed. (St. Paul: West Publishing, 1984), 185.
2. Sir Frederick Pollack and Frederic William Maitland, *The History of English Law*, vol.II (Cambridge: University Press, 1968), 537.
3. Bindrim v. Mitchell, 92 Cal.App.2d 61, 155 Cal.Rptr. 29 (1979).
4. Gertz v. Robert Welch Inc., 418 U.S. 323, 339–40; 94 S.Ct. 2997, 3007 (1974).
5. McCall v. Courier Journal, (KY Sup.Ct., 1981) 7 Med.L.Rptr. 2118 at 2121.
6. 411.061(6) *Kentucky Code* (Sept. 1979 Replacement).
7. *Indiana Code*, 34–4-14–2 Civil Procedure (1982).
8. Beacon Journal v. Lansdowne, (OH Ct.Comm.Pleas, 1984) 11 Med.L.Rptr. at 1096.
9. Falwell v. Penthouse, (DC VA, 1981) 7 Med.L.Rptr. at 1896.
10. New York Times v. Sullivan, 376 U.S. 279–80 (1964).
11. "Heed Their Rising Voices," *The New York Times* (Tuesday, March 29, 1960):L-25.
12. New York Times v. Sullivan, 376 U.S. 279–80 (1964).
13. Curtis Publishing Co. v. Butts and Associated Press v. Walker, 388 U.S. 130 (1967).
14. Ibid.
15. Rosenblatt v. Baer, 383 U.S. 75 (1966).
16. Rosenbloom v. Metromedia, 403 U.S. 29 (1971) at 57.
17. Gertz v. Robert Welch Inc., 418 U.S. 323, 339–40; 94 S.Ct. 2997, 3007 (1974).
18. Milkovich v. Lorain Journal, (U.S. Sup.Ct., 1990) 17 Med.L.Rptr. 2009.
19. Philadelphia Newspapers v. Hepps, (U.S. Sup.Ct., 1986) 12 Med.L.Rptr. 1977.
20. KARK-TV v. Simon, (Ark. Sup.Ct., 1983) 10 Med.L.Rptr 1050.
21. Ibid.
22. St. Amant v. Thompson, 390 U.S. 731 (1968).
23. Liberty Lobby v. Anderson, (U.S. App.Ct. DC, 1984) 11 Med.L.Rptr. at 1010.
24. Anderson v. Liberty Lobby, (U.S. Sup.Ct., 1986) 12 Med.L.Rptr. 2303.
25. McCullough v. Cities Service, (Okla. Sup.Ct., 1984) 10 Med.L.Rptr. 1411.
26. *West's Annotated Indiana Code* (St. Paul: West Publishing, 1985), 398. 35–1-59–1 (1985).

27. Garrison v. State of Louisiana, 379 U.S. 64 (1964).
28. Franklin v. Friedman, (NY Sup.Ct., 1985) 12 Med.L.Rptr. 1146.
29. Brooks v. Stone, (Ga. Ct.App., 1984) 10 Med.L.Rptr. 1517.

Cases

Action Repair v. ABC, (CA 7, 1985) 12 Med.L.Rptr. 1809
Anderson v. Liberty Lobby, (U.S. Sup.Ct.,1986) 12 Med.L.Rptr. 2297
Baia v. Jackson Newspapers, (Conn. Sup.Ct., 1985) 12 Med.L.Rptr. 1780
Barry v. Time, (DC N.Cal., 1984) 10 Med.L.Rptr. 1809
Beacon Journal v. Lansdowne, (OH Ct.Comm.Pleas, 1984) 11 Med.L.Rptr. 1096
Bindrim v. Mitchell, 92 Cal.App.2d 61, 155 Cal.Rptr. 29 (1979)
Bose Corporation v. Consumers Union, (Sup.Ct., 1985) 10 Med.L.Rptr. 1625
Brady v. Ottaway Newspapers, Inc., (NYS 2d, 1981) 8 Med.L.Rptr. 1671
Brauer v. Globe Newspaper Co., 217 N.E.2d 736, 739 (1966)
Brooks v. Stone, (Ga. Ct.App., 1984) 10 Med.L.Rptr. 1517
Buratt v. Capital City Press, (La. Ct.App., 1981) 7 Med.L.Rptr. 1856
Cardillo v. Doubleday & Co. Inc., 518 F.2d 638 (2d Cir., 1975)
Catalfo v. Jensen, (DC NH, 1986) 12 Med.L.Rptr. 1867
Charlottesville Newspapers Inc. v. Debra C. Matthews, (Va. Sup.Ct., 1986) 11
    Med.L.Rptr. 1621
Curtis Publishing Co. v. Butts and Associated Press v. Walker, 388 U.S. 130
    (1967)
Donaldson v. Washington Post Co., (DC Sup.Ct., 1977) 3 Med.L.Rptr. 1436
Edwards v. National Audubon Society, 566 F.2d 113 (2d Cir., 1977)
Falwell v. Penthouse, (DC VA, 1981) 7 Med.L.Rptr. 1891
Fawcett Publications v. Morris, Okla. 1962, 377 P.2d 42, appeal dismissed,
    cert. denied 376 U.S. 513, 84 S.Ct. 964, 11 L.Ed.2d 968, rehearing denied
    377 U.S. 925, 84 S.Ct. 1218, 12 L.Ed. 2d 217
Fleming v. Kane County, (DC N.Ill., 1986) 13 Med.L.Rptr. 1014
Franklin v. Friedman, (NY Sup.Ct., 1985) 12 Med.L.Rptr. 1146
Garrison v. State of Louisiana, 379 U.S. 64 (1964)
Gertz v. Robert Welch Inc., 418 U.S. 323, 339–40; 94 S.Ct. 2997, 3007 (1974)
Green v. Alton Telegraph, 8 Med.L.Rptr. (1982)
Guccione v. Hustler, (DC S.NY, 1986) 12 Med.L.Rptr. 2042
Guccione v. Hustler, (CA 2, 1986) 13 Med.L.Rptr. 1316
Herbert v. Lando, 60 L.Ed.2d 115 (1979)
Herron v. King Broadcasting Co., (Wash Sup.Ct., 1988) 14 Med.L.Rptr. 2017
J.V. Peters v. Knight-Ridder, (Ohio Ct.App., 1984) 10 Med.L.Rptr. 1576
Jackson v. Longcope, 394 Mass. 577, 580; 476 N.E.2d 617 (1985)
KARK-TV v. Simon, (Ark. Sup.Ct., 1983) 10 Med.L.Rptr. 1049
Keeton v. Hustler, (U.S. Sup.Ct., 1984) 10 Med.L.Rptr. 1409–10

Keller v. Miami Herald, (DC SD FL, 1984) 11 Med.L.Rptr. 1032

Kerwick v. Orange County Publications, (NY Ct.App., 1982) 7 Med.L.Rptr. 1152

Lasky v. ABC, (DC So.NY, 1986) 13 Med.L.Rptr. 1379

Liberty Lobby v. Anderson, (U.S. App.Ct. DC, 1984) 11 Med.L.Rptr. 1010

Logan v. District of Columbia, 447 F.Supp. 1328 (DC DC, 1978)

McCall v. Courier Journal, (KY Sup.Ct., 1981) 7 Med.L.Rptr. 2118

McCullough v. Cities Service, (Okla. Sup.Ct., 1984) 10 Med.L.Rptr. 1411

Milkovich v. Lorain Journal, (U.S. Sup.Ct., 1990) 17 Med.L.Rptr. 2009

Neiman-Marcus Co. v. Lait, 13 F.R.D. 311 (D NY, 1952)

New York Times v. Sullivan, 376 U.S. 279–80 (1964)

Newton v. NBC, (DC Nev., 1987) 114 Med.L.Rptr. 1914

Pelzer v. Minneapolis Tribune, (Minn. Dist.Ct., 1982) 7 Med.L.Rptr. 2507

Philadelphia Newspapers v. Hepps, (U.S. Sup.Ct., 1986) 12 Med.L.Rptr. 1977

Pitts v. Spokane Chronicle Co., 388 P.2d 976 (1964)

Pring v. Penthouse, (DC WY, 1981) 7 Med.L.Rptr. 1101

Ray v. Time Inc., 582 F.2d 1280 (6th Cir., 1978)

Redco Corporation v. CBS, (U.S. Ct.App.3d, 1985) 11 Med.L.Rptr. 1861

Rosenblatt v. Baer, 383 U.S. 75 (1966)

Rosenbloom v. Metromedia, 463 U.S. 29 (1971)

Schiavone Construction v. Time, (DC NJ, 1985) 12 Med.L.Rptr. 1153

Schiavone Construction v. Time, (DC NJ, 1986) 13 Med.L.Rptr. 1664

St. Amant v. Thompson, 390 U.S. 731 (1968)

Tavoulareas v. Washington Post, (CA DC, 1985) 11 Med.L.Rptr. 1777

Time Inc. v. Firestone, 424 U.S. 448 (1976)

Torres v. Playboy, (DC So.TX, 1980) 7 Med.L.Rptr. 1185

Weatherland v. Globe International, (CA 10, 1987) 14 Med.L.Rptr. 1949

11

Invasion of Privacy

As we have learned, defamation changes the way society feels about an individual. Invasions of privacy change the way individuals feel about themselves. Today, invasion of privacy suits may be based on personal humiliation, shame, suffering or emotional distress. While defamation involves the communication of a falsehood, invasions of privacy may involve the publication of true, but embarrassing facts. Other invasions of privacy include appropriation of a person's likeness for commercial gain, intrusion by cameras or other devices into the privacy of one's home or office, and the publication of material that places one in a "false light"—that is, appearing to do something that is embarrassing or socially unacceptable. False light is closest to defamation and is sometimes prosecuted as libel.

Most invasion of privacy suits against the media result from individuals caught up in newsworthy situations who object to the way their involvement in the event has been communicated by the press. In a majority of cases, responsible journalists prevail over individuals in court. Most restraints placed on the news media when covering a newsworthy event are in the form of professional ethics, rather than law. While it may be revolting to see close-ups of persons mangled in an auto accident on the local TV news, nothing but good taste prevents a station from broadcasting such a scene. The only recourse is that if enough viewers object to this kind of news coverage, ratings will decline, thereby forcing an editorial policy change by management in the never-ending pursuit of viewers and advertising dollars.

Also of concern over the past two decades has been the protection from surveillance by government and other components of society. Advances in technology have allowed a myriad of users access to information about individuals. Organizations ranging from businesses to law enforcement agencies can easily retrieve information about a person's finances, legal and medical history, arrest records, and recent purchases, to name a few. Needless to say, many people are concerned about who is granted access to such information, how it can be used, and for what purposes. The Federal Privacy Act of 1974 was passed to deal with some of these issues. The Privacy Act defines how individuals are protected from government invasions of privacy and is discussed later in this chapter. Protection from privacy invasions by individuals and the news media developed quite differently than protection from government snooping.

The Development of Privacy Law

While libel has its roots in English common law of the Middle Ages, the law of privacy is a nineteenth century American development. Before 1890, no American court had recognized a right of privacy. One hundred years later, some right of privacy was recognized in almost all jurisdictions. To this day, the extent of our personal rights of privacy are not clearly delineated and remain somewhat controversial.

Although there were a few cases in the early nineteenth century based on the nonexistent right to privacy, it was not until 1888 that Judge Cooley defined privacy as "the right to be let alone."[1] In 1890, an article entitled "The Right of Privacy" by Samuel D. Warren and future Supreme Court Justice Louis Brandeis was published in the *Harvard Law Review*. Although there is little evidence to support the assertion, the two Boston lawyers claim inspiration for the article from gossip in the press about the social affairs of the wealthy Warren family. Warren and Brandeis argued that the growing excesses of the press required the courts to consider granting private individuals protection against the hounding media.[2] In essence, "The Right of Privacy" attempted to establish a common law right of privacy using property rights, defamation, and breach of confidence as its basis. The authors argued that property owners should be allowed to apply the same right to protect their houses and lands from trespass to the protection of their private lives. Warren and Brandeis wrote,

> Instantaneous photographs and newspaper enterprise have invaded the sacred precincts of private and domestic life and numerous mechanical devices threaten to make good the prediction that "what is whispered in the closet shall be proclaimed from the house-tops."
>
> . . . Gossip is no longer the resource of the idle and vicious, but has become a trade, which is pursued with industry as well as effrontery. . . . The intensity and complexity of life attendant upon an advancing civilization have rendered necessary some retreat from the world, and man, under the refining influence of culture, has become more sensitive to publicity, so that solitude and privacy have become more essential to the individual; but modern enterprise and invention have, through invasions of his privacy, subjected him to mental pain and distress, far greater than could be inflicted by mere bodily injury.[3]

Although Brandeis and Warren protested the excesses of the press, they offered no specific evidence to support their claim. Nor did they deal with the problems that would inevitably result when this new privacy right came into conflict with the First Amendment right of a free press. Brandeis' biographer, Lewis Paper, summarizes the impact of the article:

> None of these defects seemed to matter much to readers. The reaction to the article was nothing short of incredible. Lawyers read it, and courts relied on it—all to the seeming end of creating a new right to privacy. Twenty-six years after its publication, Dean Roscoe Pound of the Harvard Law School observed

that the article "did nothing less than to add a chapter to our law." Subsequent scholars were just as impressed. One commentator referred to it as "the outstanding example of the influence of legal periodicals upon the American law." Another writer said that the article was "perhaps the most influential law journal piece ever published." In some sense all of this praise was justified. After all, concerns for privacy in part motivated the American Revolution; and there could be no doubt that protection of privacy was a central concern of the populace.[4]

Despite this critical acclaim, there was no great rush to enact privacy statutes across the country. In fact, the first major test of the theory in 1902 resulted in a New York appellate court ruling that found no common law right of privacy. Ironically, it was this ruling that gave New York the first statutory right of privacy in the United States.

In *Roberson v. Rochester Folding Box Co.* (1902), a flour company lithographed a picture of a girl on boxes of their brand of flour without her consent. She objected to the use of her likeness on flour boxes, noting that it violated her right of privacy. Although the lower courts in that state had earlier relied on the Warren and Brandeis article in upholding a right to privacy, the New York court of appeals rejected her claim.

Although this was what we now would call an "appropriation" case, and unrelated to the kind of privacy Warren and Brandeis outlined, *Roberson* generated enough controversy to prompt the New York legislature to act. *Manola v. Stevens* was the first case to allow recovery on the basis of a privacy claim. It enjoined an individual from publishing a photograph of an actress "scandalously" attired in tights, snapped from a box in the theater. In 1903, New York passed Section 50 of the state Civil Rights Law, making it unlawful to use a person's name or likeness for trade purposes without their consent.

Two years later, a Georgia court became the first to recognize a common law right to privacy. *Pavesich v. New England Life Insurance Co.* (1905) was similar to the *Roberson* case. A newspaper ad for the insurance company contained an unauthorized photograph of the plaintiff. The ad also attributed statements to him that urged the purchase of life insurance from the company. The Georgia Supreme Court ruled in favor of Pavesich and established that a common law right of privacy existed in that state.

It was not until the 1930s that a pattern emerged in the states, that favored the general recognition of a right to privacy.

In 1965, the Supreme Court recognized a "penumbral" right to privacy in the First, Third, Fourth, and Ninth Amendments to the Constitution. In *Griswold v. Connecticut* (1965), the Court struck down a state law making the use of contraceptives—even by married couples—a crime and upheld the right of Planned Parenthood to publish advice on their use. Justice Douglas wrote,

> ☐ [S]pecific guarantees in the Bill of Rights have penumbras, formed by emanations from those guarantees that help give them life and substance. Various guarantees create zones of privacy. The right of association

contained in the First Amendment is one . . . The Third Amendment in its prohibition against the quartering of soldiers . . . is another facet of that privacy. The Fourth Amendment explicitly affirms the "right of people to be secure in their persons, houses, papers, and effects, against unreasonable searches and seizures." The Fifth Amendment in its Self Incrimination Clause enables the citizen to create a zone of privacy which government may not force him to surrender to his detriment. The Ninth Amendment provides: "The enumeration in the Constitution, of certain rights, shall not be construed to deny or disparage others retained by the people."[5]

While Douglas' opinion specifically addressed privacy invasions by the state, subsequent court decisions, including *Roe v. Wade* (1973), which legalized abortions, recognized a right of personal privacy.

Today, all states except Minnesota recognize some common law or statutory right of privacy. Some states recognize very limited privacy rights and there is no universal agreement recognizing the categories of these rights.

Categories of Invasion of Privacy

Most jurisdictions recognize some or all of the four categories of privacy invasion originally developed by Dean William Prosser. Prosser was an expert on tort law and, through his studies, organized the subject of invasions of privacy into the following areas—appropriation, intrusion, embarrassing facts, and false light. You should check your state laws to determine which of these categories are recognized in your state.

Appropriation

Appropriation involves the use of a person's name or likeness for commercial gain. This form of the tort is the earliest to be recognized and has its roots in the *Roberson* case. The first privacy statute in New York was designed to deal with appropriation, as was the first common law decision in Georgia, as previously discussed.

Illegal appropriation occurs when consent is not obtained before using someone's name, picture, or likeness to advertise a product, to accompany an article sold, or to add "luster" to a company name.

Courts have held, however, that the incidental use of a person's name or picture in a book, film , magazine, or other medium is not an invasion of privacy. If a name or likeness is not published for commercial gain, it cannot be appropriation. Therefore, the primary defenses against a claim of misappropriation are newsworthiness and consent. A signed release that shows that persons agreed to allow publication of their likeness for commercial gain will defeat a claim, provided that the publication has not been altered beyond the terms of the agreement.

Examples of the application of the law of appropriation include a television station's use of a photograph taken while the plaintiff was receiving emergency medical treatment, in *Anderson v. Fisher Broadcasting Companies*. The photo was later used in an advertisement for the station's special news report. Although the plaintiff objected to the use of the picture, it was judged newsworthy by an Oregon court of appeals and, hence, no misappropriation occurred. Similarly, in *Lawrence v. A.S. Abell Co.*, republication of a front-page photograph by *The Baltimore Evening Sun* of two children attending a festival in the city as part of the paper's advertising campaign was found not to be illegal appropriation. Finally, the players on the Baltimore Orioles baseball team could not prevent team owners from using portions of videotaped games in which they appeared. In *Baltimore Orioles v. Major League Baseball Players*, the seventh circuit court ruled that the performances were "owned" by the teams—not the players—and, essentially, consent had been given.

Right of Publicity

More recently, concern over what has come to be called the "right of publicity" has emerged. Most cases in this category involve entertainers, sports figures, and other well-known personalities whose actual name or likeness, or that of a character they have created, is used to promote a product or other commercial gain.

When *Forum* magazine, a *Penthouse* magazine affiliate, borrowed portions of an exclusive interview with singer/entertainer Cher that were originally published in *Us* magazine and implied that Cher had also spoken with *Forum* reporters, a California court ruled that the singer's right of publicity had been misappropriated. In *Cher v. Forum International* (1982), the court noted that a celebrity retains the right to control the publicity and establish conditions for the use of his or her name or likeness when he or she chooses voluntarily to give an "exclusive interview" to a particular publication.[6]

Similarly, in *Eastwood v. Superior Court*, actor Clint Eastwood had cause for action when a newspaper used his name and photograph in the paper and in television ads (without his consent) that promoted a nondefamatory false article about the actor.

Author Jackie Collins' right of publicity was violated when *Adelina* magazine published her name on its cover under the heading "In the Nude from the Playmen Archives." Although the nude picture was not really Collins, in *Lerman v. Chuckleberry*, the court ruled that the magazine had used Collins' name solely for the purpose of enhancing the sale of magazines, rather than for the purpose of informing the public about a newsworthy event.

In *Brinkley v. Casablancas*, model Christie Brinkley successfully sued for misappropriation of her right of publicity when an unauthorized pin-up poster of her likeness was distributed in 1980. In *Onassis v. Christian Dior*, Jackie Onassis was successful in her claim against Christian Dior's advertising series that used a model who strongly resembled the former first lady to sell their line of clothing. Citing *Negri v. Schering*, in which silent film star Pola Negri objected to the publication of a scene from one of her movies that was captioned so as to appear that she endorsed use of the antihistamine drug Polaramine, the Supreme Court of New York noted that

☐   if a picture is a clear and identifiable likeness of a living person, he or she is entitled to recover damages suffered by reason of such use.[7]

To date, only one appropriation case has reached the U.S. Supreme Court. It involved Hugo Zacchini, known as the "Human Cannonball," and a Cleveland Ohio television station.

Zacchini v. Scripps-Howard (1977)

Hugo Zacchini made his living by performing an act that consisted of shooting himself from a cannon into a net some 200 feet away. The entire act lasted about 15 seconds. Zacchini was performing the act at a county fair in Ohio. WEWS-TV asked to film Zacchini's act as part of a news story about the county fair. Zacchini refused to grant the station permission to film the act. The next day, acting on instructions from his employer, a reporter from WEWS came to the fair and filmed Zacchini's act in its entirety. The 15-second act was subsequently broadcast on the WEWS evening news.

Zacchini sued WEWS on grounds that his personal property had been appropriated without his consent. He contended that if people could watch his act for free on television, they would not pay to see the act live at the fair. WEWS contended that the filming of the act depicted a newsworthy event of public interest and that commercial exploitation of Zacchini's personal property had not occurred.

The trial court ruled in favor of the television station, an appellate court reversed in favor of Zacchini, and the Ohio Supreme Court reversed again and found in favor of WEWS. The U.S. Supreme Court reversed again and Zacchini ultimately won the case. Justice White delivered the opinion of the Court.

☐   The Ohio Supreme Court held that respondent is constitutionally privi-
     leged to include in its newscasts matters of public interest that would
     otherwise be protected by the right of publicity, absent an intent to injure
     or to appropriate for some nonprivileged purpose. If under this standard
     respondent had merely reported that petitioner was performing at the fair
     and described or commented on his act, with or without showing his pic-
     ture on television, we would have a very different case. But petitioner is
     not contending that his appearance at the fair and his performance could
     not be reported by the press as newsworthy items. His complaint is that
     respondent filmed his entire act and displayed that film on television for
     the public to see and enjoy. This, he claimed, was an appropriation of his
     professional property. . . .

     The broadcast of a film of petitioner's entire act poses a substantial
     threat to the economic value of that performance. As the Ohio court recog-
     nized, this act is the product of petitioner's own talents and energy, the
     end result of much time, effort and expense. Much of its economic value
     lies in the "right of exclusive control over the publicity given to his perfor-
     mance"; if the public can see the act for free on television, they will be

less willing to pay to see it at the fair. The effect of a public broadcast of the performance is similar to preventing petitioner from charging an admission fee. . . . " No social purpose is served by having the defendant get for free some aspect of the plaintiff that would have market value and for which he would normally pay." Kalven, *Privacy in Tort Law—Were Warren and Brandeis Wrong?*, 31 Law and Contemporary Problems 326, 331 (1966). Moreover, the broadcast of petitioner's entire performance, unlike the unauthorized use of another's name for purposes of trade or the incidental use of a name or picture by the press, goes to the heart of petitioner's ability to earn a living as an entertainer. Thus in this case, Ohio has recognized what may be the strongest case for a "right of publicity"—involving not the appropriation of an entertainer's reputation to enhance the attractiveness of a commercial product, but the appropriation of the very activity by which the entertainer acquired his reputation in the first place.[8]

Descendibility

Although the appropriation of the entire act of a performer is unlikely and limits the impact of *Zacchini*, a related issue gained momentum in the 1980s. The issue was the question of descendibility, which means that the right of publicity can be retained even after the death of an individual. Although recent decisions have upheld this right, this was not always the case. In 1979 in *Lugosi v. Universal Pictures*, the California Supreme Court held that the heirs of Bela Lugosi, Hollywood's original Count Dracula, did not have exclusive rights to exploit his name and likeness for those commercial situations not exploited by him during his lifetime.

Much litigation on the question of descendibility followed the death of Elvis Presley and, consequently, forced Tennessee to deal with the issue before other jurisdictions. Questions ranging from the legality of marketing Elvis memorabilia, to the performances of Elvis impersonators eventually found their way into courtrooms. In *Memphis Development Foundation v. Factors Etc. Inc.* (1980), the sixth circuit reversed a trial court decision protecting exclusive exploitation of the Elvis Presley character, noting that the right of publicity terminates at death.

The following year, the state of Tennessee recognized a right of descendibility in *Commerce Union Bank v. Coors*. In this case, deceased bluegrass singer Lester Flatt's likeness was used in a Coors beer advertisement. Tennessee now assigns the right of publicity to the heirs of the deceased. In 1987, the sixth circuit adopted Tennessee's recognition of descendibility when it ruled that celebrities' right of publicity is descendible under the common law of Tennessee.

Several other states now recognize descendibility. Some states automatically assign the right of publicity of a public figure to that person's heirs for a period of 50 years from the date of death. Among them are Kentucky, California, Florida, Virginia, Nebraska, Oklahoma, and Utah. In *Marx Productions v. Day and Night Co.*, it was ruled that a Marx Brothers imitation violates the common law right of publicity to that which they exploited during their lifetimes.

Litigation in this area remains dynamic. It must be remembered that descendibility is by no means a universally recognized concept. Some states still contend that right of publicity terminates at death, others limit the right to those activities exploited by the deceased before death.

Intrusion

This form of privacy invasion involves an unreasonable intrusion by an individual on the seclusion or personal affairs of another. While the Fourth Amendment protects Americans from unreasonable searches and seizures by government, tort law protects us from one another. Civil intrusion occurs most often in the course of news gathering and, while linked to trespass, can take place without physically invading someone else's property. Examples of intrusion consist of unreasonable searches; eavesdropping on conversations; surveillance by cameras, telescopes, or other devices; telephone harassment; peering into windows; and wiretapping. The latter is prohibited by federal law. Clearly, intrusion must pry into matters that are of no public concern and the prying must be judged offensive by a reasonable person.

It is not intrusion to watch, follow, photograph, or attempt to communicate with someone on a public street or other public place. As ruled in *Mark v. Seattle Times*, a television station did not intrude when it broadcast video showing the interior of a pharmacy taken from outside the building as part of a piece on Medicare fraud. Additionally, in *Wehling v. CBS*, a television broadcast showing a private residence—but no more than what could be seen from a public street—was not intrusion.

It is not an invasion of privacy when police or other officials, acting within the scope of their authority, ask for fingerprints, photographs, or other information in the course of their duties. News reports, photographs, or videotapes of individuals caught up in newsworthy events are generally not treated as intrusion. When a newspaper reported information from the private diary of a murdered girl that had been obtained from police, the girl's family sued for intrusion. In *Andren v. Knight-Ridder*, a Michigan district court ruled that no intrusion had taken place because the topic was newsworthy.

It is safe to say that it is very difficult to bring a successful intrusion suit against the news media during the course of normal events. Red flag areas are those situations that take place on private property or involve news personnel in criminal activities such as trespass, breaking and entering, illegal wiretapping, or misrepresentation of facts in order to gain entry to a private locale. For example, CBS News entered an expensive French restaurant in New York City, uninvited, and with cameras rolling. The network was working a story on city health code violations. The restaurant asked CBS to leave. When they didn't, the restaurant ejected the news crew and filed suit. In *Le Mistral, Inc. v. CBS*, CBS lost a judgment amounting to $250,000 in punitive and $1,200 in compensatory damages for intrusion and trespass. The trial judge noted that the right to gather news does not include the right to break and enter or trespass.

In *Huskey v. NBC*, an Illinois court found cause for intrusion when an NBC television camera crew filmed an inmate at Marion Penitentiary without his consent. The inmate was stripped to the waist in gym shorts and engaged in "private activities" in the prison's exercise cage.

Defenses

The primary defenses against a claim of intrusion are newsworthiness and consent; however, unlike the other forms of privacy invasion, actual publication of information gained from intrusion is immaterial. The damage occurs at the information gathering stage.

Sometimes, what would normally be considered trespass is legal when done in the course of following a breaking news story, particularly when reporters are accompanying or working with law enforcement officials. It was not intrusion when journalists accompanied Florida officials onto private property that was the scene of a fatal fire. A 17-year-old girl had been burned to death. In what has come to be known as the "Silhouette of Death" case, the girl's mother first learned of her daughter's death by reading a newspaper account of the tragedy that included a photograph taken by a news photographer in the girl's bedroom. A silhoutte of the girl's body had been formed on the floor where she was burned to death. In *Florida Publishing Co. v. Fletcher*, although ethically questionable, the Florida Supreme Court ruled that no intrusion had occurred because the fire marshall had asked the news photographer to take the picture as part of the offical investigation. The photograph was technically part of the public record. Recognition of this privilege differs from state to state and caution must be exercised.

In 1971, a *Life* magazine reporter gained access to the home of a former plumber named A. A. Dietemann who claimed to have special healing abilities. The reporter pretended to be a friend of a woman who had gone to Dietemann for an examination of feigned breast cancer. The woman had been planted by police and health department officials who were investigating complaints that Dietemann was practicing medicine without a license. The reporter took pictures inside Dietemann's home and relayed tape recordings of the diagnosis and treatment to police waiting outside. Dietemann was arrested for quackery and *Life* published a story on the episode. Dietemann sued for invasion of privacy, contending that the hidden camera constituted intrusion. Dietemann won the case. In *Dietemann v. Time Inc.* (1971), Ninth Circuit Court Judge Shirley Hufstedler noted,

☐ Plaintiff's den was a sphere from which he could reasonably expect to exclude eavesdropping newsmen. He invited two of the defendant's employees to the den. One who invites another into his home or office takes a risk that the visitor may not be what he seems, and that the visitor may repeat all he hears and observes when he leaves. But he does not and should not be required to take the risk that what is heard and seen will be transmitted by photograph or recording, or in our modern world, in full living color and hi-fi to the public at large or to any segment of it that the visitor may select.[9]

The ruling in *Dietemann* is a narrow one. Later rulings suggest that had the police been acting directly in the line of duty and had the photographer not been in a private home, the outcome may have been different. For example, when a TV undercover investigator gained access to an alcoholic treatment center by posing as an alcoholic, in *WCH of Waverly v. Meredith Corp.*, a Missouri court ruled that no intrusion occurred. The reporter was subject to state action for fraud and prosecution under the federal eavesdropping statute.

Convicted murderer David Berkowitz, suspected of being New York City's "Son of Sam" serial killer, objected to reporters entering his apartment after his arrest. In *People v. Berliner*, a New York City court said reporters were not guilty of criminal trespass because only Berkowitz, who would have to have been in the apartment, or the apartment owner could have withheld consent to enter the apartment. However, police could have excluded reporters from the premises while a search was being conducted.

In 1981 in *Anderson v. WROC-TV*, another New York court ruled against a television station reporter who accompanied a Rochester Humane Society official into the home of an individual suspected of mistreating animals. The court said that public officials had no right to invite others, including journalists, to accompany them onto private property during performance of their duties. Reporters are advised to use caution and be familiar with practices accepted in their state regarding accompanying officials onto private property.

Generally speaking, the media must go out of their way and harass newsmakers to lose an intrusion case. Free-lance photographer Ron Galella did just that in his attempts to photograph former first lady Jacqueline Kennedy Onassis. Galella made the bulk of his living photographing Mrs. Onassis, who objected to his continual pursuit of her. He was known to go to all extremes in search of a photo, including shadowing Mrs. Onassis and her children, jumping into their path and taking a picture, using telephoto lenses to snap pictures on private property, and reputedly romancing the Onassis' housekeeper in order to gain access to their home. Having lost a husband and brother-in-law to assassins' bullets, Mrs. Onassis found Galella's erratic behavior and surveillance of her family disturbing. In *Galella v. Onassis*, the former first lady persuaded a New York district court to enjoin Galella's incessant behavior. Although a judge ordered Galella to remain at least 300 feet from the Onassis and Kennedy homes, and 150 feet from Mrs. Onassis and 225 feet from her children, an appellate court reduced the distances to 25 and 30 feet, respectively. Galella continued his pursuit of Mrs. Onassis. In 1982, however, the original New York court found Galella in contempt of its order and fined him $10,000. Galella also promised never to take another picture of Onassis.

Taping Telephone Calls and Third Party Monitoring

Per the Electronic Communications Privacy Act of 1986, federal and state law prohibits the surreptitious recording of telephone and other conversations between individuals. Included are both wire and wireless telephone conversations, electronic mail, satellite transmissions and computer data. Per the Omnibus Crime Control and Safe Streets Act of 1968, bugging, wiretapping, and other third-party monitoring are also prohibited.

One-sided recording of telephone calls is a separate issue. In many states, it is legal for an individual to record his or her personal telephone calls without informing the other party that the conversation is being recorded. Reporters in Indiana, for example, may record all telephone interviews without violating the law. Broadcasting these recordings is another matter. While state law governs single-party recording, the FCC requires broadcasters to inform persons that their call will be broadcast. Similarly, if the phone call is to be broadcast live, the FCC requires broadcasters to inform callers that they are "on the air," thereby allowing them to terminate the call if they object to the broadcast.

Stolen or Illegally Obtained Materials

Sometimes, newsworthy material comes to the attention of journalists as a result of trespass or theft by a third party. If journalists publish stolen information, are they liable for intrusion? Case law would indicate that, for the most part, they are not. Both major cases in this area involved national columnist Drew Pearson and his young assistant, Jack Anderson.

In *Liberty Lobby v. Pearson* (1968), the U.S. Court of Appeals for the District of Columbia ruled that unless the Liberty Lobby could show that Pearson or Anderson had actually stolen the documents in question, they could not successfully sue. Additionally, then Circuit Judge Warren Burger ruled that if the publication of documents is found to be in the public interest, journalists will prevail.

A year later in *Pearson v. Dodd* (1969), Senator Thomas Dodd brought suit against Pearson and Anderson. The senator alleged that the journalists had received copies of private memoranda from disgruntled staff members relating to Dodd's misappropriation of campaign funds. Although Pearson and Anderson had not physically intruded into the senator's files, Dodd claimed that since the journalists knew that the material was stolen, they should be held liable for conversion (i.e., the unauthorized use of someone else's property). The court ruled that no conversion had occurred since the files themselves were not taken. Pearson had received photocopies and the originals remained in place.

Although newsworthiness is a sturdy defense in cases such as these, journalists must be careful not to run afoul of state and local laws that may have consequences that result from the publication of stolen material. When the *Los Angeles Free Press* published a stolen list containing names, addresses, and phone numbers of undercover narcotics agents under the heading "Know Your Local Narc," the paper's publisher was indicted for violation of California's penal code. The code makes it a crime to receive stolen property. In *People v. Kunkin* (1972), the publisher was convicted by a trial court and the conviction was upheld by the California court of appeals. In *People v. Kunkin* (1973), the California Supreme Court reversed the conviction on a technicality. There was reason to doubt that the reporters who had obtained the list knew that it was stolen.

Embarrassing Facts

Sometimes, an invasion of privacy action can be brought against the media for the publication of truthful, nondefamatory facts that are embarrassing to an identified individual. Generally these facts must be communicated to a widespread public, be private in nature (not newsworthy), and be highly offensive and objectionable to a reasonable person.

The major case dealing with public disclosure of embarrassing facts involved a child prodigy named William James Sidis. Sidis graduated from Harvard in 1910 with a degree in mathematics. Because he was 16 years old at the time of graduation, he naturally received a great deal of media attention. Predictions about his future contributions to society appeared in the news media. In reality, however, Sidis was to become a recluse and certainly did not meet the expectations of one so intellectually endowed. In 1937, the *New Yorker* magazine published an article entitled "Where Are They Now?," which exposed personal facts about Sidis' uneventful life. Although the tone of the article was sympathetic, Sidis filed suit noting that detailing his unsuccessful life was an invasion of privacy.

In *Sidis v. F-R Publishing Corporation* (1940), the court ruled in favor of the magazine, noting that Sidis was a public figure—even though 20 years had passed since he had first received media attention. The story, said the court, had legitimate news interest. Finally, the court postulated what has come to be known as "the rule of Sidis." This standard has been used to measure the legitimacy of embarrassing facts claims ever since. Circuit Judge Clark wrote,

☐   ... Everyone will agree that at some point the public interest in obtaining information becomes dominant over the individual's desire for privacy. Warren and Brandeis were willing to lift the veil somewhat in the case of public officers. We would go further, though we are not yet prepared to say how far. At least we would permit limited scrutiny of the "private" life of any person who has achieved or has had thrust upon him, the questionable and indefinable status of a "public figure."

   ... We express no comment on whether or not the newsworthiness of the matter printed will always constitute a complete defense. Revelations may be so intimate and so unwarranted in view of the victim's position as to outrage the community's notions of decency. But when focused upon public characters, truthful comments upon dress, speech, habits and the ordinary aspects of personality will usually not transgress this line. Regrettably or not, the misfortunes and frailties of neighbors and "public figures" are subjects of considerable interest and discussion to the rest of the population. And when such are the mores of the community, it would be unwise for a court to bar their expression in the newspapers, books, and magazines of the day.[10]

Newsworthiness

It should be noted that "newsworthiness" is a strong defense in these kinds of cases and it is difficult to bring a successful embarrrassing facts case against the news media. The rule of Sidis must be exceeded in order to defeat a claim of newsworthiness. It is safe to say that embarrassing facts cases cannot be successfully brought by persons caught up in newsworthy events, including innocent bystanders. Although it may be embarrassing to be arrested, it is not an invasion of privacy for the local news to report the arrest. This is true even if the arrest is based on mistaken identity.

When a temporarily deranged man in Idaho ran out of his house brandishing a shotgun, in the nude, a local television station filmed the event. On regaining his senses, the man filed an embarrassing facts privacy suit against the TV station. He claimed that the station could have edited the film so that he was not pictured in the nude. Although he won the initial judgment, in *Taylor v. KTVB, Inc.*, the Idaho Supreme Court ordered a new trial since the event was newsworthy.

When Oliver Sipple, a veteran confined to a wheel chair, grabbed would-be presidential assassin Sarah Jane Moore's arm as she fired a shot at Gerald Ford, he was hailed a hero. Sipple was also a homosexual, which was disclosed to the news media by members of San Francisco's gay community. The disclosure was not meant to be defamatory, but rather to show that gays could be positive forces in society. In any case, Sipple had not volunteered the information aboout his sexual preference and filed suit. In *Sipple v. Chronicle Publishing Co.*, the court ruled that disclosure of the fact that one is homosexual is not an invasion of privacy, especially when it is part of a newsworthy story such as an attempted assassination of a president.

Consent

Another defense is consent. Provided an individual has granted permission for information to be published, there can be no cause for action. When *Sports Illustrated* published an interview with a rather eccentric body surfer named Mike Virgil, he brought suit against the magazine because he was embarrassed by statements and actions attributed to him. Virgil told *Sports Illustrated* that he sometimes dove head first down flights of stairs to "impress girls," intentionally injured himself working construction in order to collect unemployment compensation, and ate spiders and other insects. The thrust of the article was that body surfing is a particularly rugged sport and requires a special individual to be successful at it. In *Virgil v. Time Inc.*, the Ninth Circuit Court ruled that although these things may now embarrass Virgil, they were relevant to the story and he had given consent to *Sports Illustrated* by granting the interview and making these statements. The rule of Sidis had not been breached.

How far can the press go before the rule of Sidis is breached? In 1964 in *Daily Times Democrat v. Graham*, Flora Bell Graham won a $4000 judgment against the Cullman County Alabama *Daily Times Democrat*. The paper had published a picture of Graham taken as she emerged from a Fun House at a county fair. The 44-year-old housewife's skirt had been blown over her head by air jets, exposing her legs and panties. Although the picture had been taken in a public place, the Alabama Supreme Court found the picture offensive to modesty and decency because it revealed private information in which the public had no legitimate interest.

Certainly *Time* magazine crossed the line when it photographed hospital patient Dorothy Barber against her will. Barber had a rare disease that caused her to lose weight even though she ate a great deal of food. *Time* referred to Barber as the "starving glutton" and "Insatiable Eater Barber" who "eats for ten." In *Barber v. Time Inc.*, the Missouri Supreme Court found the story to be an invasion of privacy and noted that privacy rights include the receipt of medical treatment without "personal publicity."

Similarly, the Dow Chemical company lost an invasion of privacy suit in *Lambert v. Dow Chemical Co.* when it exhibited pictures of an employee injured in an industrial accident as part of the company's on-the-job safety program. The court ruled that pictures taken during the employee's surgery and used without his permission embarrassed and humiliated him.

Stories dealing with matters of public concern are generally not subject to successful invasion of privacy claims. When the *Washington Post* printed an article about heroin addiction and included the photograph of Monica Little, who had been interviewed as part of the story, she sued for privacy invasion. Little contended that although she had agreed to be interviewed, she had used a false name and her family did not know she was an addict. The use of a photograph had damaged her anonymity. She claimed that the *Post* had intentionally caused her emotional distress.

In *Little v. Washington Post*, the U.S. District Court for the District of Columbia ruled against Little, stating that the public interest supports dissemination of accurate information about the risk of drugs and drug addiction, and that she waived her privacy rights when she agreed to the interview. In short, the *Post* did not go beyond the limits of her consent.

The Public Record

The courts have ruled that if the news media exceed the limits outlined in the rule of Sidis, successful invasion of privacy suits may be brought. In the only embarrassing facts case to reach the Supreme Court, however, the media found protection even when publication might "outrage the community's notions of decency." When newsworthy private facts are part of the public record, suit cannot be brought. In 1975 in *Cox Broadcasting Corp. v. Cohn*, some constitutional protection was granted to embarrassing facts found in the open records of court proceedings.

Cox Broadcasting Corp. v. Cohn (1975)

This case resulted from the controversy surrounding the release of the name by police in Atlanta of a 17-year-old rape and murder victim. A Georgia statute protected the identity of rape victims, but the girl's name was obtained by WSB-TV from a court clerk as part of an official record of indictment. On April 2, 1972, WSB-TV broadcast a story that identified the girl. Relying on the Georgia statute, the girl's father brought suit against the television station, claiming that his right of privacy had been invaded by the broadcast.

Although the trial court and the Georgia Supreme Court ruled in favor of the plaintiff, the U.S. Supreme Court reversed the decision. The Georgia statute was an unconstitutional limitation on freedom of the press. Essentially, the Court ruled that an accurate account of material obtained from a public record is not actionable as an embarrassing facts invasion of privacy. Justice White delivered the opinion of the Court:

☐ . . . The version of the privacy tort now before us—termed in Georgia "the tort of public disclosure"—is that in which the plaintiff claims the right to be free from unwanted publicity about his private affairs, which although wholly true, would be offensive to a person of ordinary sensibilities. . . .

The face-off is apparent, and the appellants urge upon us the broad holding that the press may not be made criminally or civilly liable for publishing information that is neither false nor misleading but absolutely accurate, however damaging it may be to reputation or individual sensibilities.

. . . Rather than address the broader question whether truthful publications may ever be subjected to civil or criminal liability consistently with the First and Fourteenth Amendments, or to put it another way, whether the State may ever define and protect an area of privacy free from unwanted publicity in the press, it is appropriate to focus on the narrower interface between press and privacy that this case represents, namely, whether the State may impose sanctions on the accurate publication of the name of a rape victim obtained from public records—more specifically, from judicial records which are maintained in connection with a public prosecution and which themselves are open to public inspection. We are convinced that the State may not do so.

. . . We are reluctant to embark on a course that would make public records generally available to the media but forbid their publication if offensive to the sensibilities of the supposed reasonable man. Such a rule would make it very difficult for the media to inform citizens about the public business and yet stay within the law. The rule would invite timidity and self-censorship and very likely lead to the suppression of many items that would otherwise be published and that should be made available to the public.[11]

It is important for journalists to remember that reports from the public record must be accurate and timely. The *Oakland Tribune* published a story stating that the first female student body president at the College of Alameda, Toni Diaz, had received a sex change operation. The paper used what it thought were public records to establish that Toni was the former Antony Diaz. In *Diaz v. Oakland Tribune Inc.*, the court ruled that the *Tribune* could not rely on identification records such as drivers' licenses and high school transcripts issued before her operation, because Diaz had legally changed those records. The court also could not see how this story was newsworthy.

False Light

The false light tort involves the publication of false information that is highly offensive to an ordinary person. False light invasions of privacy are similar to libel, but the important distinction is that the false light is nondefamatory. Libel actions are instigated in order to protect persons' reputations (i.e., the way they are viewed by society). False light privacy actions stem from a person's right to be let alone and is based on the way people view themselves. Emotional distress is often the basis for false light privacy suits. Unlike libel, false light invasions of privacy may actually embellish one's reputation. When an unauthorized biography of famous baseball pitcher Warren Spahn portrayed him as a war hero, Spahn was able to bring a successful suit in *Messner Inc. v. Warren E. Spahn*. Even though the material was flattering, the "gross misstatement of fact" portrayed the former pitcher in a false light, thereby causing him emotional distress.

False light claims often result from dramatizations and fictional accounts of real-life incidents. In 1931, a former prostitute was awarded damages as a result of her portrayal in a 1924 film entitled *The Red Kimono*. Gabrielle Darley Melvin was acquitted of murder in 1918 and began a new life. She married and became a respectable housewife. Her new family was unaware of her sordid past, until she was identified in the motion picture. Although it is questionable whether a court would reach the same decision today (her past is part of the public record), in *Melvin v. Reid*, Melvin won the case on appropriation grounds and "willful and wanton disregard of that charity which should actuate us in our social intercourse."[12]

The first false light case to reach the U.S. Supreme Court began with a drama review in *Life* magazine and ended some 15 years later, when the case was sent back for retrial.

In 1952, James Hill, his wife, and five children were held hostage in their home by three escaped convicts. The family was not harmed during the ordeal, nor were they abused in any way. This situation naturally attracted a great deal of media attention. A novel entitled *Desperate Hours* was eventually written about the episode. In order to spice up the story, some license was taken by the author. The book included fictionalized violence against the family. So gripping was the story that it was adapted into a Broadway play. Although based on the Hills' story, the play changed the names of the characters, thereby making identification of the actual family difficult. When *Life* magazine reviewed the play, it noted that *Desperate Hours* was based on the Hill family and mirrored their actual experiences. James Hill found this identification offensive, noting that there was little similarity between what had happened to his family and the contents of the drama. The play eventually became a film with Frederick March starring as the hero-like father and Humphrey Bogart as the convict leader.

Because Hill was not directly identified in the play, he could not bring suit against the playwright. Since *Life* magazine did identify him as the father in the drama, he filed a false light suit against the magazine. *Life* contended that the Hill family had been caught up in a public issue and members of the family were, therefore, public figures, even if reluctantly so. Hill argued that by identifying his family as the one in *Desperate Hours*, *Life* had acted with reckless disregard for the truth and therefore had violated the actual malice standard of *New York Times v. Sullivan*.

In *Time Inc. v. Hill*, a jury awarded Hill $30,000 in compensatory damages. The decision was affirmed by the court of appeals, but in 1967 the Supreme Court reversed the decision and sent the case back to trial. Justice Brennan delivered the opinion of the Court.

☐ The question in this case is whether appellant, publisher of Life Magazine, was denied constitutional protections for speech and press by the application by the New York courts of Pts. 50–51 of the New York Civil Rights Law . . . to award appellee damages on allegations that *Life* falsely reported that a new play portrayed an experience suffered by appellee and his family.

. . . [A]lthough the New York statute affords "little protection" to the "privacy" of a newsworthy person, "whether he be such by choice or involuntarily" the statute gives him a right of action when his name, picture, or portrait is the subject of a "fictitious" report or article.

. . . We hold that the constitutional protections for speech and press preclude the application of the New York statute to redress false reports of matters of public interest in the absence of proof that the defendant published the report with knowledge of its falsity or in reckless disregard of the truth.

. . . One need only pick up any newspaper or magazine to comprehend the vast range of published matter which exposes persons to public view, both private citizens and public officials. . . . We create grave risk of serious impairment of the indispensable service of a free press in a free society if we saddle the press with the impossible burden of verifying to a certainty the facts associated in news articles with a person's name, picture or portrait, particularly as related to nondefamatory matter. Even negligence would be a most elusive standard, especially when the content of the speech itself affords no warning of prospective harm to another through falsity. A negligence test would place on the press the intolerable burden of guessing how a jury might assess the reasonableness of steps taken by it to verify the accuracy of every reference to a name, picture or portrait.

. . . But the constitutional guarantees can tolerate sanctions against *calculated* falsehood without significant impairment of their essential function. We held in *New York Times* that calculated falsehood enjoyed no immunity in the case of alleged defamation of a public official's official conduct. Similarly calculated falsehood should enjoy no immunity in the situation here presented us. . . .

The judgement of the Court of Appeals is set aside and the case is remanded for further proceedings not inconsistent with this opinion.[13]

The Court's decision was based on the opinion that although Time Inc. had published a falsehood, it did not exceed the actual malice standard of *New York Times*. The Hills had been in litigation since 1952 and, facing the prospect of beginning the case all over again, decided not to pursue the matter further.

Seven years after *Hill*, the Supreme Court heard another false light case. This time the Court found that *The Cleveland Plain Dealer* had acted with actual malice when it published a story about Margaret Cantrell. Mrs. Cantrell's husband had been one of 44 persons killed 10 days before Christmas in 1967 in the collapse of the Silver Bridge, which spanned the Ohio River at Point Pleasant, West Virginia. She had been left to care for four children with little money. The story was published in August 1968 as part of a follow-up on the lives of the families of the bridge disaster.

In *Cantrell v. Forest City Publishing Co.* (1974), according to testimony taken in court, the story contained a number of inaccuracies. It implied that reporters had spoken with Mrs. Cantrell in her home and that the home was untidy and her children were poorly clothed. Mrs. Cantrell charged that the story made them the objects of pity and ridicule.

In reality, Mrs. Cantrell had not been present when reporter Joseph Eszterhaus came to call. Eszterhaus spoke with one of her children, while a photographer snapped some pictures. Writing for the Supreme Court, Justice Potter Stewart noted,

☐   There was no dispute during the trial that Eszterhaus . . . must have known that a number of the statements in the feature story were untrue. In particular, his article plainly implied that Mrs. Cantrell had been present during his visit to her home and that Eszterhaus had observed her "wear(ing) the same mask of non-expression she wore at the funeral." These were "calculated falsehoods," and the jury was plainly justified in finding that Eszterhaus had portrayed the Cantrells in a false light through knowing or reckless untruth.[14]

Even unintentional distortion of facts can be dangerous to the media. When a Washington, DC, television station broadcast a report on the growing herpes epidemic in America, it opened the story with video of pedestrians standing on a street corner. One of the pedestrians, Linda Duncan, happened to turn and face the camera as it zoomed in on the persons standing on the corner. Ms. Duncan's face was clearly recognizable to those who knew her. She filed a false light claim, charging that reports on the 6:00 P.M. and 11:00 P.M. news implied that she had herpes. The report broadcast at 6:00 P.M. was an on-the-street report, narrated by a reporter on the scene. Even though Ms. Duncan was recognizable, the court ruled that no invasion of privacy had taken place because she was shown on the street with other pedestrians. At 11:00 P.M., however, the report had been edited and the anchorman in the studio read lines over the video shot on the street. With the camera focused on Ms. Duncan, the anchorman said, "[f]or the twenty million Americans who have herpes, its not a cure . . ." The video concluded as Ms. Duncan turned away from the camera and proceeded down the street. In *Duncan v. WJLA-TV*, the court ruled that the 11:00 P.M. broadcast did cast Ms. Duncan in a false light. The video had been edited so that other pedestrians did not appear in the scene.

False light problems may also lurk in "ambush" interviews. Arnold Diaz, a reporter for WCBS-TV in New York conducted such an on-the-street interview with Irving Machleder. Diaz implied that Machleder was involved in the illegal dumping of chemical waste in New Jersey. In *Machleder v. Diaz*, a jury found CBS guilty of false light invasion of privacy and awarded Machleder $1 million in punitive damages and $250,000 in compensatory damages.

Although the Supreme Court refused to set a "negligence" standard for false light claims in *Hill* and *Cantrell*, some states, including Texas, have adopted that standard. Journalists are expected to follow accepted practices to ensure that potentially offensive material is true, newsworthy, or has been obtained with the consent of individuals involved.

When LaJuan and Billy Wood went camping in a state park, they went swimming in the nude. They took several pictures of one another. Upon returning home, the couple had the film developed and stored the nude photos in their dresser drawer. They did not show the photos to anyone else. One day, their neighbor Steve Simpson broke into the Wood's home, stole the photographs, and submitted a nude photo of LaJuan to *Hustler* magazine for publication. Simpson filled out a consent form that provided personal information about LaJuan. Simpson included some true information, such as LaJuan's name and hobbies, but added some false statements including a fantasy attributed to LaJuan of being "tied down and screwed by two bikers." Simpson's wife forged LaJuan's signature on the consent form and mailed the package to *Hustler*.

The magazine has a policy of calling persons who submit photos to verify that they really wish to have them published. The consent form asks that a telephone number be included with all submissions. Simpson did not include a phone number, so the magazine sent a mailgram to the address on the consent form, which was Simpson's. The mailgram asked LaJuan to call the magazine collect. Simpson's wife did just that, pretending to be LaJuan. The *Hustler* representative asked a series of leading "yes" and "no" questions, and terminated the conversation in about 2 minutes.

Assuming incorrectly that a magazine representative had spoken with LaJuan, *Hustler* published the photographs in the February 1980 issue of the magazine.

LaJuan and Billy Wood first learned of the publication of the photos when friends began to tease them. LaJuan was mortified and had to undergo psychological counseling. Ultimately, in *Wood v. Hustler*, LaJuan Wood was able to recover $150,000 in damages for false light invasion of privacy. As a private figure, she needed only to show that *Hustler* was negligent in checking the identity of the person in the photograph.

Protection from Misuse of Personal Data by the Government

The cases and issues discussed thus far have traced the development of the right to privacy concerning individuals—that is, privacy protection from one another and the news media. A separate issue concerns the protection of certain information about individuals by federal and state laws. While there has been a tendency toward the opening of public records, as in *Cox Broadcasting Corp. v. Cohn*, the Federal Privacy Act of 1974 and accompanying state legislation has excluded some data from public scrutiny.

The Privacy Act of 1974 seeks to protect individuals against the misuse of personal information contained about them in government files. Under the act, a government agency must obtain an individual's permission before divulging the contents of certain files containing information about them. Although the Privacy Act regulates what may be divulged about a person, it in no way limits what may be collected about an individual.

There are, of course, exemptions to the Privacy Act. Law enforcement agencies and the CIA have access to all information collected about an individual. There are 11 exemptions or conditions of disclosure built into the act:

1. Officers and employees of the agency maintaining the record may have access to the record in the performance of their duties.
2. Information may be given if disclosure is required by the Freedom of Information Act.
3. Information may be accessed for routine use (i.e., information may be used for the purpose for which it was collected).
4. Information may be divulged for use by the Bureau of the Census.
5. Information may be given to recipients who assure the agency that information will be used for statistical purposes only and that the information will not specifically identify any individuals.
6. If a record has national historical value, it may be given to the National Archives.
7. Information may be provided to law enforcement agencies.

8. Disclosure may be given provided the person requesting information can show that there are "compelling circumstances affecting the health or safety of an individual."
9. Information may be given if requested by Congress.
10. Information may be given to the General Accounting Office.
11. Information may be given pursuant to the order of a court.

Since 1974, several states, including Minnesota, Indiana, California, Arkansas, Kentucky, Ohio, Utah, Connecticut, Virginia, and Massachusetts, have enacted similar privacy protection laws. All allow law enforcement agencies access to information. These state laws are based on the openness of public records.

Privacy and the Electronic Media

While wiretapping and other uninvited forms of electronic snooping are prohibited by law, some invited technologies may generate privacy concerns. While the 1984 Cable Communications Policy Act protects consumers against unauthorized use of personal information gathered by cable operators, interactive computer and video services pose potential privacy problems. So too do personal communications services such as caller identification (caller ID).

On-line Computer Privacy

The use of computer networks for both commercial and personal services has grown dramatically in the past few years. Electronic mail (E-mail), bulletin boards, on-line services such as CompuServe and Prodigy are but a few examples of this growing industry. While wiretap law applies to systems providing some form of E-Mail, the law is vague in other areas. Users of these networks should use caution when transmitting information they do not wish to become available to anyone accessing the system.

Caller ID

Caller ID is a service that provides telephone subscribers with a visual display of the telephone number of all incoming calls. This enables the subscriber to "screen" the incoming call. Theoretically, the subscriber can determine who is calling and decide whether to answer or how to respond when the phone is picked up.

Opponents of caller-ID fear that callers who are unaware that numbers they dial have caller ID may unwittingly sacrifice some privacy. Businesses and others with the feature may automatically log the phone number of callers and thereby access other data bases containing information about the caller without the caller's permission.

Summary

The concept of personal privacy has its roots in an 1890 law journal article by Brandeis and Warren. The right of privacy has been divided into four forms—appropriation, intrusion, embarrassing facts, and false light. Privacy invasions generally change the way persons feel about themselves and defamation is not present. Defenses against invasions of privacy are consent and newsworthiness.

While the common law in most states recognizes some right of personal privacy, all four forms of the tort are not universally recognized. The common law protects against privacy invasions by individuals, while the Federal Privacy Act and various state laws protect against misuse of private information by the government.

The number of telecommunications offerings have grown so quickly that privacy law has not been applied to many of them. As these technologies continue to develop, so will the application of law and regulatory activity.

Notes/References

1. Thomas M. Cooley, *A Treatise on the Law of Torts* (Chicago: Callaghan & Co., 1888) p. 29.
2. Samuel D. Warren and Louis D. Brandeis, "The Right of Privacy," *Harvard Law Review* 4 (December 15, 1890): 193.
3. Ibid., 195–96.
4. Lewis J. Paper, *Brandeis* (New York: Citadel Press, 1983), 34.
5. Griswold v. Connecticut, 381 U.S. 479 (1965).
6. Cher v. Forum International, 213 U.S.P.Q. 96, (DC CA, 1982) 7 Med.L.Rptr 2593.
7. Onassis v. Christian Dior, (NY Sup.Ct., 1984) 10 Med.L.Rptr. at 1861.
8. Zacchini v. Scripps-Howard, 433 U.S. 562 (1977).
9. Dietemann v. Time Inc., 449 F.2d 245 (9th Cir., 1971).
10. Sidis v. F-R Publishing Corporation, 113 F.2d 806 (1940).
11. Cox Broadcasting Corp. v. Cohn, 420 U.S. 469, 95 S.Ct. 1029, 43 L.Ed.2d 328 (1975).
12. Melvin v. Reid, 112 Cal.App. 285, 297, p.91 (1931).
13. Time Inc. v. Hill, 385 U.S. 374 (1967).
14. Cantrell v. Forest City Publishing Co., 419 U.S. 245, 95 S.Ct. 465, 42 L.Ed.2d 419 (1974).

Cases

Anderson v. Fisher Broadcasting Companies, (OR Ct.App., 1985) 11 Med.L.Rptr. 1839

Anderson v. WROC-TV, 441 N.Y.S.2d 220 (Sup.Ct., 1981)

Andren v. Knight-Ridder, (DC E.Mich, 1984) 10 Med.L.Rptr. 2109

Baltimore Orioles v. Major League Baseball Players, (CA 7, 1986) 13 Med.L.Rptr. 1625

Barber v. Time Inc., 348 Mo. 1199, 159 S.W.2d 291 (1942)

Brinkley v. Casablancas (NY Sup.Ct. App.Div., 1981) 7 Med.L.Rptr. 1457

Cantrell v. Forest City Publishing Co., 419 U.S. 245, 95 S.Ct. 465, 42 L.Ed.2d 419 (1974)

Cher v. Forum International, 213 U.S. P.Q. 96, (DC CA, 1982) 7 Med.L.Rptr 2593

Commerce Union Bank v. Coors, (Tenn. Chanc.Ct, 1981) 7 Med.L.Rptr. 2204

Cox Broadcasting Corp. v. Cohn, 420 U.S. 469, 95 S.Ct. 1029, 43 L.Ed.2d 328 (1975)

Daily Times Democrat v. Graham, 162 So.2d 474 (Ala., 1964)

Diaz v. Oakland Tribune Inc., 188 Cal.Rptr. 762 (Cal. App., 1983)

Dietemann v. Time Inc., 449 F.2d 245 (9th Cir., 1971)

Duncan v. WJLA-TV, (DC DC, 1984) 10 Med.L.Rptr. 1395

Eastwood v. Superior Court, (Cal. Ct.App., 1983) 10 Med.L.Rptr. 1073

Florida Publishing Co. v. Fletcher, 340 So.2d 914 (Fla., 1976) cert. denied 431 U.S. 930 (1977)

Galella v. Onassis, 353 F.Supp. 196 (SD NY, 1972), 533 F.Supp. 1076 (DC NY, 1982), 487 F.2d 986 (CA NY, 1973)

Griswold v. Connecticut, 381 U.S. 479 (1965)

Huskey v. NBC, (U.S. DC N.Ill., 1986) 12 Med.L.Rptr. 2105

Lambert v. Dow Chemical Co., 215 So.2d 673 (LA. App., 1968)

Lawrence v. A.S. Abell Co., (MD CA, 1984) 10 Med.L.Rptr. 2001

Le Mistral, Inc. v. CBS, 61 A.D.2d. 491, 402 N.Y.S.2d 815 (NY App.Div., 1978)

Lerman v. Chuckleberry, (US DC S.NY, 1981) 7 Med.L.Rptr. 2282, 2284

Liberty Lobby v. Pearson, 390 F.2d 489 (DC Cir., 1968)

Little v. Washington Post, (DC DC, 1985) 11 Med.L.Rptr. 1428

Lugosi v. Universal Pictures, 25 Cal.3d 813, 603 P.2d 425, 5 Med.L.Rptr. 2185 (1979)

Machleder v. Diaz, (U.S. DC So.NY, 1985) 12 Med.L.Rptr. 1193

Manola v. Stevens, N.Y. Sup.Ct. 1890

Mark v. Seattle Times, (Wash. Sup.Ct., 1982) 7 Med.L.Rptr. 2209

Marx Production v. Day and Night Co., (DC S.NY, 1981) 7 Med.L.Rptr. 2030

Melvin v. Reid, 112 Cal.App. 285, 297, p.91 (1931)

Memphis Development Foundation v. Factors Etc. Inc., (6th Cir., 1980) 5 Med.L.Rptr. 2521, cert. denied 449 U.S. 953 (1980)

Messner Inc. v. Warren E. Spahn, 393 U.S. 1046 (1967)

Negri v. Schering Corp., 333 F.Supp. 101, 105 (1969)

Onassis v. Christian Dior, (NY Sup.Ct., 1984) 10 Med.L.Rptr. 1861

Pavesich v. New England Life Insurance Co., 122 Ga. 190, 50 S.E. 68, 69 L.R.A. 101 (1905)

Pearson v. Dodd, 410 F.2d 701 (DC Cir., 1969), cert. denied, 395 U.S. 947 (1969)

People v. Berliner, (NYC Ct., 1978) 3 Med.L.Rptr. 1942

People v. Kunkin, 100 Cal.Rptr. 845 (1972)

People v. Kunkin, 107 Cal.Rptr. 184 (1973)

Roberson v. Rochester Folding Box Co., 171 NY 538, 64 N.E. 442 (1902)

Roe v. Wade, 410 U.S. 113 (1973)

Sidis v. F-R Publishing Corporation, 113 F.2d 806 (1940)

Sipple v. Chronicle Publishing Co., (CA Ct.App., 1984) 10 Med.L.Rptr. 1690

Taylor v. KTVB, Inc., 96 Idaho 202, 525 P.2d 984 (1974)

Time Inc. v. Hill, 385 U.S. 374 (1967)

Virgil v. Time Inc., 527 F.2d 1122 (9th Cir., 1975)

WCH of Waverly v. Meredith Corp., (DC W.Mo., 1986) 13 Med.L.Rptr. 1648

Wehling v. CBS, (CA 5, 1983) 10 Med.L.Rptr. 1125

Wood v. Hustler, (U.S. CA 5, 1984) 10 Med.L.Rptr. 2113

Zacchini v. Scripps-Howard, 433 U.S. 562 (1977)

12 ⬚⬚⬚
     ⬚⬚⬚
     ⬚⬚⬚

Free Press/Fair Trial: A Conflict of Rights

Selecting an Impartial Jury

Although the First Amendment guarantees the rights of freedom of speech and press, these rights are not absolute. With freedom comes the knowledge that irresponsible actions can lead to the regulation of that freedom by others. As is often the case, the protection against outside regulation of freedoms lies in self-restraint. When one right guaranteed by the Constitution comes in conflict with another, the courts must attempt to balance the two rights. Such is the case regarding press coverage of criminal trials. Irresponsible behavior by press, bench, and bar led to an imbalance between First and Sixth Amendment rights.

The Sixth Amendment to the Constitution guarantees those accused of criminal actions a right to a speedy and public trial by an impartial jury. These rights of a defendant often conflict with rights also guaranteed to the press under the First Amendment. Since a jury is selected after pretrial proceedings, media coverage of the arrest and pleadings of a criminal suspect may prejudice the opinion of prospective jurors. The media have always claimed a First Amendment right to cover trials. However, historically, this coverage has sometimes compromised the conduct of trials. The courts reserve the right to preserve judicial discipline, while citizens and the press maintain a right to comment on and view the judicial process. When these rights collide, conflict and inequities result. Uncontrolled publicity about a criminal trial can result in an innocent person's conviction or a guilty person's acquittal. In either case, justice is not served. For the First and Sixth Amendments to function as intended, the press and the judiciary must respect one another's role in American society.

News coverage of crimes and criminal proceedings may create prejudice in prospective jurors and bias jurors who have already been selected. Reports of crimes, arrests, and evidence that has been admitted at trial usually pose no problem. Two areas that pose the greatest problem are the publication of confessions and prior criminal records of defendants when neither are admissible as evidence.

Criminal defendants are entitled to a speedy and public trial by an impartial jury. Pretrial publicity is assumed to have an effect on the impartiality of that jury. Therefore, it would appear that every effort should be made to insulate prospective jurors from publicity that might influence their decision. Critics argue that our system assumes a truly impartial juror is one who is totally ignorant of the facts surrounding a case. An impartial juror has cynically been described as an uninformed moron who does not read the newspapers, watch television news, or listen to the radio. Of course, this is not the case. Since the early days of our republic, it has been recognized that an impartial juror need not be completely unaware of the defendant or of the crime. In *United States v. Burr* (1807), Chief Justice John Marshall defined an impartial juror as one holding "light impressions which may be supposed to yield to testimony"[1] (i.e., one who is willing to listen to arguments and base any final decision on testimony).

The American Bar Association (ABA) has suggested that the publication of certain types of information may influence potential jurors and may make a fair trial impossible. The ABA recommended that the following material not be published:

opinions about an accused's character, guilt, or innocence

admissions or confessions of guilt by the defendant

references to the results of any examinations or tests, such as lie detectors or laboratory tests

statements about the credibility of witnesses or anticipated testimony

opinions concerning evidence or arguments in a case and the likelihood that such evidence will be used at trial

prior charges and convictions, even though such information may be part of the public record[2]

These recommendations, although by no means universally adhered to, are the result of a long struggle between the press and the judiciary. This struggle began in the early nineteenth century and is by no means over. Now judges regularly attempt to control prejudicial pretrial publicity by granting a change of venue, a continuance, or sequestering the jury. A change of venue moves the location of the trial away from an area in which prospective jurors are likely to hold preconceived opinions about the guilt or innocence of an accused person. A continuance postpones the starting date of a trial so that the strong emotions felt by a community, often accompanying the arrest of a suspect, have had time to subside. "Sequestering the jury" means limiting jurors' contact with the outside world during a trial. This is done in the hope that jurors will not be influenced by media reports of the proceedings or by others desiring to affect the outcome of the trial. A judge may also limit the number of reporters allowed in the courtroom or he may seal the past records of a defendant. In rare instances, he may actually close pretrial proceedings to reporters. However, recent rulings have made this practice even less likely.

The media are somewhat more restrained in their coverage of crimes and trials than in the past, and the relationship between the press and the bar has steadily improved since the 1970s. This lessening of tensions follows a rocky tradition of crime reporting in America, culminating in the infamous murder trials of Leslie Irvin and Dr. Sam Sheppard. The fallout from these two cases set the stage for a difficult period in the history of the free press/fair trial debate.

The Tradition of Crime Reporting

The reporting of crime news in the United States has been a staple of journalism since the 1830s when Benjamin Day's *New York Sun* revolutionized the American newspaper by publishing for the masses instead of the elite. Crime news later contributed to the success of papers like Pulitzer's *World* and Hearst's *Journal*.

The growth of the tabloid press in the early part of this century led to a sensationalistic form of journalism in the 1920s often dubbed "jazz journalism." Publications like the *New York World*, the *Illustrated Daily News*, and Bernard MacFadden's notorious *Graphic* built readership on reports of crime, sex, and gossip. Competition among the tabloids was fierce and each attempted to out-sensationalize the other in order to boost circulation.

One of the more egregious examples of this sensationalism occurred during and after the 1927 trial of a corset salesman named Judd Gray and his sweetheart, Ruth Snyder. The two were on trial for the murder of Snyder's husband. Not only was the trial covered in great detail, but the execution of Ruth Snyder in the electric chair at Sing Sing prison became one of the most outrageous examples of the bad taste exhibited by the tabloid press of that era. The *Graphic* teased its readers with the following:

> Don't fail to read tomorrow's *Graphic*. An installment that thrills and stuns!
> A story that fairly pierces the heart and reveals Ruth Snyder's last thoughts on earth; that pulses the blood as it discloses her final letters. Think of it! A woman's final thoughts just before she is clutched in the deadly snare that sears and burns and FRIES AND KILLS! Her very last words! Exclusively in tomorrow's *Graphic*.[3]

Not to be outdone, the *News* sent photographer Tom Howard inside the execution chamber with a tiny camera strapped to his ankle where he photographed Snyder's execution. The gruesome picture made up page one of the January 14, 1928, *Daily News* and was captioned "When Ruth Paid Her Debt to the State." The *News* sold 250,000 extra copies of that edition.[4]

The 1930s saw the demise of the tabloids and a somewhat more responsible form of reporting emerged. But crime stories continued to be a staple of American journalism. Questionable behavior by journalists in search of a "scoop" still outraged press critics. The trial of Bruno Hauptmann in 1935 for the kidnapping and murder of aviator Charles Lindbergh's baby, drew more than 800 reporters who wrote during a 28-day period. Reporters were joined at the trial by show business personalities, politicians, and an estimated 20,000 members of the general public. The jury was photographed in the jury box, vendors sold souvenir "kidnap ladders," and regular reports about the guilt of Hauptmann appeared in newspapers across the country.

These excesses were not without consequence, however. Although Hauptmann was found guilty, the judge was criticized for permitting a "trial by newspaper." Judges were more careful to control the atmosphere of the trial, and the conduct of reporters and others present in the courtroom. As a result of the conduct of the press during

the Hauptmann trial, the American Bar Association adopted Canon 35 which prohibited the taking of pictures in the courtroom.

The Road to the Supreme Court

After the Second World War, a string of murders and other sensationalistic stories hit the news wires. The stage was set for another conflict between the
press and the judiciary, centering on the public's right to be informed and a defendant's right to a fair trial by an impartial jury.

In 1951, the Supreme Court considered the first of several cases concerning
jury prejudice fostered by the news media. It would be 8 years, however, before the
Court would order a new trial solely on the grounds that pretrial publicity made a fair
trial impossible.

In *Shepherd v. Florida* (1951), four black men were accused of the rape of a white
girl in Lake County, Florida. Two were convicted and sentenced to death. During the
trial, community prejudice was pervasive. The defendants had been threatened with
lynching, one of their parents' homes had been burned, and the National Guard had
been called out to protect other blacks living in the community. Some blacks left the
community after threats on their lives.

The newspapers had quoted the local sheriff as saying that the defendants had
confessed, but no confession was offered at the trial. The papers published several
prejudicial articles during the investigation of the crime, including a cartoon picturing
four electric chairs that were headed "No Compromise—Supreme Penalty." Although
there had been motions for a change of venue and continuance, they had been denied.

A mistrial was declared, however, not on grounds of pretrial publicity, but on
racial prejudice. Justice Jackson did note that if racial discrimination had not been a
factor, the defendants probably would not have received a fair trial anyway.

☐   ... [P]rejudicial influences outside the courtroom, becoming all too typical
    of a highly publicized trial, were brought to bear on this jury with such
    force that the conclusion is inescapable that these defendants were pre-
    judged as guilty and the trial was but a legal gesture to register a verdict
    already dictated by the press and the public opinion which is generated.[5]

The following year, the Supreme Court heard another case in which a confession
was published and newspaper reports were somewhat sensationalistic. This time, the
Court did not order a new trial. In *Stroble v. State of California* (1952), the Court did
require Stroble to demonstrate that pretrial publicity hurt his case—a requirement
that the Court would return to 24 years later in *Nebraska Press*.

The defendant, Stroble, was charged with the first-degree murder of a 6-year-old
girl. The Los Angeles newspapers published excerpts from an alleged confession. The
district attorney had also offered his opinion of the defendant's guilt to the press.
Newspaper articles referred to Stroble as a "werewolf," a "fiend," and a "sex-mad
killer." Stroble pleaded not guilty to the murder charge. The trial itself was covered by

the papers and no objection to press coverage was entered by Stroble, except for the newspapers' occasional reference to him as a "werewolf."

Stroble was convicted by the trial court and the Supreme Court affirmed the conviction. The Court rejected claims that Stroble was deprived of a fair trial because of prejudicial newspaper coverage. The Court noted,

☐ The matter of prejudicial newspaper accounts was first brought to the trial court's attention after petitioner's conviction, as one of the grounds in support of a motion for a new trial. At that time petitioner's present attorney urged that petitioner had been "deprived of the presumption of innocence by premature release by the District Attorney's office of the details of the confession," and offered in support of that allegation certain Los Angeles newspapers published at the time of petitioner's arrest. . . .

. . . [A]t no stage of the proceedings has petitioner offered so much as an affidavit to prove that any juror was in fact prejudiced by the newspaper stories. He asks this Court simply to read those stories and then to declare . . . that [two state courts] deprived him of due process. That we cannot do, at least where, as here, the inflammatory newspaper accounts appeared approximately six weeks before the beginning of petitioner's trial, and there is no affirmative showing that any community prejudice ever existed or in any way affected the deliberation of the jury.[6]

The majority of the Court established that potentially prejudicial, pretrial publicity, in and of itself, does not automatically result in an unfair trial. The Court ruled that in order for a mistrial to be declared, there must be a strong showing by the defendant that community prejudice affected the jury's verdict.

Justices Douglas and Frankfurter wrote dissents, however, that would later serve as foundations for a policy favoring a lesser showing by a defendant. Justice Frankfurter wrote,

☐ . . . I cannot agree to uphold a conviction which affirmatively treats newspaper participation instigated by the prosecutor as part of the "traditional concept of the American way of the conduct of a trial." Such passion as the newspapers stirred in this case can be explained (apart from mere commercial exploitation of revolting crime) only as want of confidence in the orderly course of justice.[7]

Essentially, Justice Frankfurter's position was that if the press cannot act responsibly voluntarily, it is up to the trial judge to ensure that they do. This line of thinking would dominate rulings following the Court's *Sheppard* decision in 1966.

Between 1952 and 1961, the Supreme Court heard several cases in which defendants claimed to have been denied a fair trial as a result of pretrial publicity. None of the cases resulted in a strong call for a reversal based on the conduct of the media. In both *Marshall v. United States* (1959) and *Janko v. United States* (1961), the Supreme Court did call for new trials. But because the Supreme Court acted only in a supervisory capacity and did not attempt to determine whether the defendant had been denied due process, these cases had little impact on the conduct of trials at the state and local levels.

Trial by Newspaper: "Mad Dog Irvin" and "Dr. Sam"

In 1961, the Supreme Court agreed to hear the case of Leslie Irvin, who had been convicted of murder. *Irvin v. Dowd* would be the first *state* case in which a mistrial was declared by the Supreme Court solely on grounds of prejudicial pretrial publicity. *Marshall v. United States* was the first conviction in a *federal* court that was reversed solely on grounds of pretrial publicity.

Irvin v. Dowd (1961)

On December 24, 1954, the news media in the southwestern Indiana city of Evansville began reporting on what was to become one of the most highly publicized murder trials in Indiana. The *Irvin* trial focused attention on the way criminal trials were reported and conducted. Ultimately, it changed the practices of both journalists and judges.

At issue was the way that the news media reported information about Irvin before his arrest and trial. This included the publication of his past criminal record and references to him as a "maniac killer" and a "mad dog." A second problem involved a state law that allowed a change of venue only one county away. Although Irvin's trial was moved from Vanderburgh to Gibson County, most potential jurists had been exposed to the same barrage of pretrial publicity, since the predominate media were the same in both counties. The media and the court failed to safeguard Leslie Irvin's Sixth Amendment right to a fair trial.

The road to the Supreme Court began on Christmas Eve, 1954, when the *Evansville Press* bannered "Police All Out in Hunt for 'Mad Dog' Killer." Two very similar murders had occurred within a 3-week period. On December 2, 1954, Mary Holland, a 33-year-old expectant mother and clerk at the Bellemeade Liquor Store, was forced to kneel over the commode and was shot in the head. On December 23, 1954, Whitney Wesley Kerr, an attendant at a gas station, was found shot in a similar manner. The cash registers at both businesses had been emptied, netting $318.11.

The news reports contributed to a growing siege mentality in the city. The papers warned that a "mad dog killer" was on the prowl. They noted that off-duty policemen had given up their Christmas shopping to join the hunt for what was described as a "maniac killer." A $1000 reward was offered to the public for information leading to the arrest of the killer and one headline advised, "Your Tip May Help Police Trap Killer." Evansville's police chief described the slayings as "acts of cold-blooded murder" and an "act of a homicidal maniac."

No killer was found and it appeared that the Christmastime murders did not signal a reign of terror after all. All was calm until the spring of 1955. Then, within a week, four persons were killed in their homes within the greater Evansville area. As in the December slayings, the motive seemed to be burglary, with money, jewelry, and guns missing from each of the homes.

On March 21, 1955, Mrs. Wilhelmina Sailer was murdered in Posey County and on March 28, three members of the Duncan family were killed in Henderson County, Kentucky. In both incidents, the victims had been shot through the head, with their hands bound. The community was once again gripped by fear. Residents were afraid to walk alone at night and they kept their doors locked tightly during the day.

Finally, on April 9, the *Evansville Press* reported that police had apprehended a suspect. The headline read, "Tight Secrecy Screens Quiz of 'Hottest' Murder Suspect, Evansville Ex-Convict." The chief of detectives issued a statement to the media in which he said that a suspect was being held for questioning. He added that the suspect had admitted some burglaries, but he refused to divulge the suspect's name. The detective expressed concern that to give any more information might "mess up the case." The article continued by stating that the suspect had left his "trademark" in the burglaries. The Henderson County sheriff told reporters that the trademark was the manner in which the suspect entered the houses of the victims. The article also stated that a two-year-old child was found near the body of her mother in the Duncan home. The *Press* ran a photo of the child and indicated that the toddler had picked the suspect out of a police lineup. The photo caption read, "Although the testimony of a two-year-old couldn't be used in court, it may aid the police." The police would neither confirm nor deny the existence of the two-year-old witness.

Leslie Irvin's name was first associated with the killings on April 10th when the *Press* headline read, "Junior Sheriffs Spotted Irvin's Black Sedan." The article continued,

> It was the two young sheriffs' patrol members who first got the license number of the car of Leslie Irvin, 30-year-old parolee, whom police have been questioning since last Friday in connection with the slayings. . . .[8]

Although Irvin had not yet been formally charged with the slayings, the article pointed out that Irvin had "admitted more than two dozen burglaries in Vanderburgh, Posey, Warrick and Gibson counties." The article also noted that Irvin's method of operation matched the way the Duncan home had been broken into either the night before or the morning of the triple slayings.

A subheading in the April 10th article called Irvin "emotionally unstable." An investigating officer is quoted as saying,

> The suspect says he threw the gun away which he stole. . . . The method of operation of the subject has been the same in all cases of burglary and his car fits the description of the car that has been seen in the neighborhoods

where the burglaries have been committed, some of the burglaries being in the murder area. . . . it should be again pointed out that evidence which is being worked cannot be made public until such evidence has been completely worked.[9]

The next day, readers were treated to a triple headline that read, "Murder Suspect Named By Police," "Leslie Irvin Taking Lie Detector Test," "Parole Violator Arrested Near Yankeetown; Car Matches One Seen at Duncan Home." Accompanying this headline was a full-length, police lineup photograph of Irvin, showing the suspect with a police ID tag hanging from his waist.

Statements of Irvin's prior criminal record appear throughout the article. Police are quoted as saying that, "Irvin is a parolee sentenced for first-degree burglary from Indianapolis. He served approximately nine years before being paroled and has approximately nine years to serve on his parole."[10] The article also mentions that Irvin had agreed to submit to a lie detector test, that he admitted numerous burglaries, and that the prosecutor believed enough evidence was available to convict Irvin of first-degree burglary.

On April 12th, an article appeared that again reported Irvin as "emotionally unstable." More circumstantial evidence was reported in the article, noting that Irvin was absent from work on the days the killings took place.

On Wednesday, April 13th, the *Press* headline read, "Irvin Placed At Murder Scene: Reported Seeking To Make Deal." The subheading stated, "Car Seen Turning Into Duncan Lane." A subsequent headline read, "Henderson Sheriff Ready To Ask For Extradition; Local Police Deny Earlier Report of 'Confession.' " Irvin still had not been charged with the murders; however, there was little doubt in the minds of Evansville citizens that the killer had been caught.

Finally, on Thursday, April 14th, Leslie Irvin was officially charged with two counts of murder. He was held without bond. Although he had not yet been convicted, the *Press* was so convinced of his guilt that it ran a headline that boldly asked, "What Made Leslie Irvin A Killer? Known as 'Likeable Fellow' With 'No Problems.' " Once again, a confession was published. The paper reported that Irvin had told Kentucky state police that he had killed three members of the Duncan family and left another for dead. A side bar to this article contained a clipping from the June 2, 1939, *Press*, which was a news report headed, "Boy, 15, Admits Starting Fires at Bosse High." That "boy" was, of course, Leslie Irvin. The *Press* noted that this was his "first brush with the law."

Subsequent news coverage of the trial preparations included references to Irvin's assistance in the recovery of a gun from a ditch, and an admission that he shot three members of the Duncan family and killed Wilhelmina Sailer.

The April 28 *Press* headline read, "2 Innocent Pleas Entered by Irvin." The story goes on to say,

The 31-year-old parolee, who led police to the murder weapons and told them how he killed six persons, will be examined by court-appointed doctors to determine if he is mentally competent to stand trial.[11]

Irvin's trial began in November and was moved from Vanderburgh County, where he was charged, to adjoining Gibson County. His attorneys objected, stating that Irvin could not receive a fair trial so close to the counties of the crimes. Indiana law, however, permitted a change of venue to be merely one county away and the trial proceeded even though eight of the 12 jurors seated thought Irvin was guilty. Irvin was found guilty of murder and sentenced to death by electrocution by the Gibson County jury.

On January 19, 1956, he was to have returned to court to formally request a new trial, but instead he became the first prisoner to escape from the newly constructed Gibson County jail. In February, he was found in San Francisco and brought back to Indiana. Irvin's attorneys appealed his conviction on grounds that he had not received a fair trial by an impartial jury. Eventually the case was reviewed by the Supreme Court. Justice Clark delivered the opinion of the Court.

☐   . . . It is not required that jurors be totally ignorant of the facts and issues involved . . . To hold that the mere existence of any preconceived notions as to the guilt or innocence of an accused, without more, is sufficient to rebut the presumption of a prospective juror's impartiality would be to establish an impossible standard. It is sufficient if the juror can lay aside his impression or opinion and render a verdict based on the evidence presented in court.

. . . Here the build up of prejudice is clear and convincing. An examination of the then current community pattern of thought as indicated by the popular news media is singularly revealing. For example, petitioner's first motion for a change of venue from Gibson County alleged that the trial of petitioner had become the *cause celebre* of this small community—so much so that curbstone opinions, not only as to the petitioner's guilt but even as to what punishment he should receive, were solicited and recorded on the public streets by a roving reporter, and later were broadcast over the local stations. A reading of the 46 exhibits which petitioner attached to his motion indicates that a barrage of newspaper headlines, articles, cartoons and pictures was unleashed against him during the six or seven months preceding his trial. The motion further alleged that the newspapers in which the stories appeared were delivered regularly to approximately 95% of the dwellings in Gibson County and that, in addition, the Evansville radio and TV stations, which likewise blanketed that county, also carried extensive newscasts covering the same incidents.

... It cannot be gainsaid that the force of this continued adverse publicity caused a sustained excitement and fostered a strong prejudice among the people of Gibson County. In fact, on the second day devoted to the selection of the jury, the newspapers reported that "strong feelings," often bitter and angry, rumbled to the surface," and that "the extent to which the multiple murders—three in one family—have aroused feelings throughout the area was emphasized Friday when 27 of the 35 prospective jurors questioned were excused for holding biased pretrial opinions.... Spectator comments, as printed by the newspapers, were "my mind is made up"; "I think he is guilty"; and "he should be hanged."

Finally, and with remarkable understatement, the headlines reported that "impartial jurors are hard to find" ... An examination of the 2,783-page *voir dire* record shows that 370 prospective jurors or almost 90% of those examined ... entertained some opinion as to guilt—ranging in intensity from mere suspicion to absolute certainty.

... Here the "pattern of deep and bitter prejudice" shown to be present throughout the community, was clearly reflected in the sum total of the *voir dire* examination of a majority of the jurors finally placed in the jury box.... Eight of the 12 thought petitioner was guilty.... With his life at stake, it is not requiring too much that petitioner be tried in an atmosphere undisturbed by so huge a wave of public passion and by a jury other than one in which two-thirds of the members admit, before hearing testimony, to possessing a belief in his guilt.[12]

Leslie Irvin was eventually granted a new trial in a less emotional atmosphere. He was found guilty of murder and sentenced to life in prison. He died of cancer in the Indiana State Penitentiary in 1983.

Six months before the first murders attributed to Irvin, a Cleveland, Ohio, osteopath became the chief suspect in the bludgeon slaying of his wife. The classic "trial by newspaper" case of Dr. Sam Sheppard would reach the Supreme Court 5 years after the Irvin decision and have even wider reaching effects.

Sheppard v. Maxwell (1966)

Dr. Sam Sheppard was convicted of second-degree murder in the July 4, 1954, slaying of his pregnant wife, Marilyn. His conviction was upheld by the Ohio Supreme Court and the U.S. Supreme Court refused to hear his appeal. Sheppard served 10 years of a life sentence in the Ohio State Penitentiary. Throughout this time, Sheppard maintained that he was innocent and, ultimately, his attorneys were able to bring a *habeas corpus* proceeding to a federal court. The proceeding argued that Sheppard had been denied a fair trial because of the conduct of the press before and during the trial. In *Sheppard v. Maxwell* (1964), the federal district court agreed, calling Sheppard's first trial a "mockery of justice."

The appellate court disagreed and ordered Sheppard to continue serving his sentence. However, Sheppard once again appealed to the Supreme Court. Sheppard's attorneys argued that the conduct of the press denied Sheppard his constitutional right to be tried by a fair and impartial jury. The Supreme Court agreed to hear this most bizarre case. This time, Sheppard was defended by F. Lee Bailey. Justice Clark delivered the opinion of the Court.

☐   . . . On the day of the tragedy, July 4, 1954, Sheppard pieced together for several local officials the following story: He and his wife had entertained neighborhood friends, the Ahrens, on the previous evening at their home. After dinner they watched television in the living room. Sheppard became drowsy and dozed off to sleep on a couch. Later, Marilyn partially awoke him saying that she was going to bed. The next thing he remembered was hearing his wife cry out in the early morning hours. He hurried upstairs and in the dim light from the hall saw a "form" standing next to his wife's bed. As he struggled with the "form" he was struck on the back of the neck and rendered unconscious. On regaining his senses he found himself on the floor next to his wife's bed. He raised up, looked at her, took her pulse and "felt that she was gone." He then went to his son's room and found him unmolested. Hearing a noise he hurried downstairs. He saw a "form" running out the door and pursued it to the lake shore. He grappled with it on the beach and again lost consciousness. Upon his recovery he was laying face down with the lower portion of his body in the water. He returned to his home, checked the pulse on his wife's neck, and "determined or thought that she was gone." He then went downstairs and called a neighbor, Mayor Houk of Bay Village. The Mayor and his wife came over at once, found Sheppard slumped in an easy chair downstairs and asked, "What happened?" Sheppard replied: "I don't know but somebody ought to try to do something for Marilyn." Mrs. Houk immediately went up to the bedroom. . . . After Mrs. Houk discovered the body, the Mayor called local police, Dr. Richard Sheppard, petitioner's brother, and Ahrens. The local police were the first to arrive. . . . Richard Sheppard then arrived, determined that Marilyn was dead, examined his brother's injuries, and removed him to the nearby clinic operated by the Sheppard family. . . . The Sheppard home and premises were taken into "protective custody" and remained so until after the trial.

From the outset officials focused suspicion on Sheppard. . . . Dr. Gerber, the Coroner, is reported—and it is undenied—to have told his men, "Well, it is evident the doctor did this, so let's go get the confession out of him." . . . The newspapers played up Sheppard's refusal to take a lie detector test and the "protective ring" thrown up by his family. . . . More stories appeared when Sheppard would not allow authorities to inject him with "truth serum."

On the 20th, the "editorial artillery" opened fire with a front page charge that somebody is "getting away with murder." . . . The following day . . . another page-one editorial was headed: "Why No Inquest? Do It Now, Dr. Gerber." The Coroner called an inquest the same day and subpoenaed Sheppard. It was staged the next day in a school gymnasium. . . . In the front of the room was a long table occupied by reporters, television and radio personnel, and broadcasting equipment. The hearing was broadcast with live microphones placed at the Coroner's seat and at the witness stand. . . . Sheppard was brought into the room by police who searched him in view of several hundred spectators. Sheppard's counsel were present during the three-day inquest but were not permitted to participate. When Sheppard's chief counsel attempted to place some documents in the record, he was forcibly ejected from the room by the Coroner, who received cheers, hugs, and kisses from ladies in the audience. Sheppard was questioned for five and one-half hours about his actions on the night of the murder, his married life, and a love affair with Susan Hayes. At the end of the hearing the Coroner announced that he "could" order Sheppard held for the grand jury, but did not do so.

Throughout this period the newspapers emphasized evidence that tended to incriminate Sheppard and pointed out discrepancies in his statements to authorities. At the same time, Sheppard made many public statements to the press and wrote feature articles asserting his innocence . . . On July 28, an editorial entitled "Why Don't Police Quiz Top Suspect" demanded that Sheppard be taken to police headquarters. It described him in the following language:

> Now proved under oath to be a liar, still free to go about his
> business, shielded by his family, protected by a smart lawyer
> who has made monkeys of the police and authorities, carrying
> a gun part of the time, left free to do whatever he pleases . . .

A front-page editorial on July 30 asked: "Why Isn't Sam Sheppard In Jail?" It was later titled "Quit Stalling—Bring Him In." . . .

That night at 10 o'clock Sheppard was arrested at his father's home on a charge of murder. He was taken to the Bay Village City Hall where hundreds of people, newscasters, photographers and reporters were awaiting his arrival.

. . . The publicity then grew in intensity until his indictment [by a grand jury] on August 17. . . . Headlines announced, *inter alia*, that: "Doctor Evidence Is Ready for Jury," "Corrigan Tactics Stall Quizzing," "Sheppard 'Gay Set' Is Revealed by Houk," "Blood Is Found, Police Claim," "Dr. Sam Faces Quiz At Jail On Marilyn's Fear Of Him." . . .

With this background the case came on for trial two weeks before the November general election at which the chief prosecutor was a candidate for municipal judge and the presiding judge, Judge Blythin, was a candidate to succeed himself. Twenty-five days before the case was set, a list of 75 veniremen were called as prospective jurors. This list, including the addresses of each venireman, was published in all three Cleveland newspapers. . . . [A]nonynous letters and telephone calls . . . regarding the impending prosecution were received by all of the prospective jurors.

The courtroom in which the trial was held measured 26 by 48 feet. A long temporary table was set up inside the bar, in back of the single counsel table. . . . Approximately 20 representatives of newspapers and wire services were assigned seats at this table by the court. Behind the bar railing there were four rows of benches. . . . The first row was occupied by representatives of television and radio stations, and the second and third rows by reporters from out-of-town newspapers and magazines. . . . Representatives of the news media also used all the rooms on the courtroom floor, including the room where cases were ordinarily called and assigned for trial. . . . Station WSRS was permitted to set up broadcasting facilities on the third floor of the courthouse next door to the jury room . . .

. . . In the corridors outside the courtroom there was a host of photographers and television personnel with flash cameras, portable lights and motion picture cameras. This group photographed the prospective jurors during selection of the jury.

. . .The jurors themselves were constantly exposed to the news media. Every juror, except one, testified at *voir dire* to reading about the case in the Cleveland papers or to having heard broadcasts about it. . . . During the trial, pictures of the jury appeared over 40 times in the Cleveland papers alone. . . . The day before the verdict was rendered—while the jurors were at lunch and sequestered by two bailiffs—the jury was separated into two groups to pose for photographs which appeared in the newspapers.

We now reach the conduct of the trial. While the intense publicity continued unabated, it is sufficient to relate only the more flagrant episodes: . . .

On the second day of *voir dire* examination a debate was staged and broadcast live over WHK radio. The participants, newspaper reporters, accused Sheppard's counsel of throwing roadblocks in the way of the prosecution and asserted that Sheppard conceded his guilt by hiring a prominent criminal lawyer. Sheppard's counsel objected to this broadcast and requested a continuance, but the judge denied the motion. When counsel asked the court to give some protection from such events the judge replied that "WHK doesn't have much coverage . . ."

On November 24, a story appeared under an eight-column headline: "Sam Called A 'Jekyll-Hyde' by Marilyn, Cousin To Testify." . . . No such testimony was ever produced at the trial. . . . Defense counsel made motions for change of venue, continuance and mistrial, but they were denied.

. . . When the trial was in its seventh week, Walter Winchell broadcast over WXEL television and WJW radio that Carole Beasley, who was under arrest in New York City for robbery, had stated that, as Sheppard's mistress, she had borne him a child. The defense asked that the jury be queried on the broadcast. Two jurors admitted in open court that they had heard it. The judge asked each: "Would that have any effect on your judgement?" Both replied "No." This was accepted by the judge as sufficient; he merely asked the jury to "pay no attention whatever to that type of scavenging . . ."

. . . After the case was submitted to the jury, it was sequestered for its deliberations, which took five days and four nights. After the verdict, defense counsel ascertained that the jurors had been allowed to make telephone calls to their homes every day while they were sequestered in the hotel. . . . The calls were placed by the jurors themselves; no record was kept of the jurors who made calls, the telephone numbers or the parties called. The bailiffs sat in the room where they could hear only the jurors' end of the conversation. The court had not instructed the bailiffs to prevent such calls. . . . [D]efense counsel urged that this ground alone warranted a new trial, but the motion was overruled and no evidence was taken on the question.

The principle that justice cannot survive behind walls of silence has long been reflected in the "Anglo-American distrust for secret trials." *In Re Oliver, 333 U.S. 257, 268 (1947).* A responsible press has always been regarded as the handmaiden of effective judicial administration, especially in the criminal field. . . . The press does not simply publish information about trials but guards against the miscarriage of justice by subjecting the police, prosecutors, and judicial processes to extensive public scrutiny and criticism. . . . But the Court has also pointed out that "[l]egal trials are not like elections, to be won through the use of the meeting hall, the radio, and the newspaper." *Bridges v. State of California, 314 U.S. at 271 (1941).* . . . " [O]ur system of law has always endeavored to prevent even the probability of unfairness."

. . . Sheppard was not granted a change of venue to a locale away from where the publicity originated; nor was his jury sequestered. . . . [J]urors were subjected to newspaper, radio and television coverage of the trial while not taking part in the proceedings. They were allowed to go their separate ways outside the courtroom, without adequate directions not to read or listen to anything concerning the case. . . . Moreover the jurors were thrust into the role of celebrities by the judge's failure to insulate them from reporters and photographers.

. . . [W]e believe that arrangements made by the judge with the news media caused Sheppard to be deprived of that "judicial serenity and calm to which [he] was entitled."

. . . The carnival atmosphere at trial could easily have been avoided since the courthouse premises are subject to the control of the court.[13]

Sam Sheppard was released from prison and was tried a second time for the murder of Marilyn in 1966. This time he was acquitted—a murder weapon had never been found and the case was difficult to prosecute 12 years after the fact. The 10 years in the Ohio State Penitentiary had taken their toll on Sheppard. He found it difficult to readjust to society. He had married a German immigrant with whom he had corresponded while in prison. When he tried to resume his medical practice, several malpractice suits ended his career. His second marriage ended in divorce, with accusations by his German wife that he had threatened her with physical harm. With no hope of resuming his medical practice, and surrounded by the notoriety of his past, Sheppard became a professional wrestler. Billed as "Dr. Sam," he married the 19-year-old daughter of his promoter and adopted the lifestyle of a biker. He died of liver disease in 1970.

The Impact of Sheppard

Justice Clark faulted Judge Blythin for failure to control the conduct of reporters and photographers in the courtroom. Early in the trial, Judge Blythin stated that neither he, nor anyone else could restrict prejudicial news accounts. Clark disagreed and made several suggestions for curbing the excessive behavior of the news media. These suggestions included limiting the number of reporters in the courtroom; insulating the witnesses from the press; controlling the release of leads and gossip to the press by police, witnesses, and counsel for both sides; and proscribing extrajudicial statements by anyone involved in the trial. Clark also suggested that judges should consider continuance, change of venue, and sequestering of the jury as means of safeguarding the trial process from outside influence.

Justice Clark did not blame the press for Sheppard's lack of a fair trial, but blamed Judge Blythin for not ensuring that a fair trial was obtained. Clark did not suggest that courtrooms be closed to the press. In fact, he noted that nothing prevented the press from reporting the events that transpired in the courtroom. However, as we shall see, the fallout from *Sheppard* included the issuance of prior restraints against the media to the closing of the courtroom as a means of preserving "judicial serenity." No judge wanted to risk becoming the next "Judge Blythin" and the backlash against media coverage of trials was swift in coming.

As a result of *Sheppard*, judges now looked for effective ways to control publicity about trials and the conduct of reporters in the courtroom. The suggestions made by Justice Clark in *Sheppard* and recommendations made by the Warren Commission, investigating the assassination of President Kennedy, prompted the American Bar Association to adopt the *Reardon Report* in 1968. The report resulted from a study by the ABA Advisory Committee on Fair Trial, headed by Massachusetts Supreme Court Justice Paul Reardon. Essentially, the report attempted to define acceptable conduct by bench, bar, and press that would ensure that a defendant received a fair trial. It incorporated Justice Clark's *Sheppard* suggestions with others promulgated by the committee. Although not legally binding, enforcement of these recommendations was to be as a standing order against members of the bar under the code of professional responsibility. Law enforcement agencies would regulate the conduct of their personnel and court personnel were to be controlled by rules of the court.

The most controversial aspect involved the means of controlling the news media and other "outside" agencies. The report recommended that judges use their somewhat questionable power to cite for contempt, for actions committed outside of the courtroom. This meant that members of the press could be cited for printing stories designed to influence the outcome of a trial. A press threatened by the use of this power would be less likely to print stories that might be construed as containing prejudicial material. This created a chilling effect on First Amendment rights. Additionally, the report recommended closing pretrial hearings to the press and public if the judge deemed that a fair trial was in jeopardy. The pendulum had begun to swing in a direction favoring Sixth Amendment over First Amendment rights.

Examples of information not to be published about a defendant included prior criminal records, character references, confessions, test results, and out-of-court speculation on guilt, innocence, or the merits of evidence. Obviously, all of these prohibitions were violated in *Irvin* and *Sheppard*.

The *Reardon Report* allowed publication of facts and circumstances of an arrest, identity of the person arrested, name of the arresting officer or agency, descriptions of physical evidence in hand, and the next step in the judicial process.

Needless to say, the *Reardon Report* was not well received by the press. It was also criticized by certain elements of the bench and bar. The out-of-court contempt power was never used. However, in the years following *Sheppard*, prior restraints (or gag orders) became a relatively common practice. Gag orders are restrictive orders against the media designed to limit the impact of publication on the trial process. In other words, the court prohibits the news media from publishing certain information about a trial. If a news medium violates the order, they are held in contempt of court.

The *Reardon Report* did foster dialogue between the press and bar. In the interest of harmony, lawyers, judges, and journalists in many states began formulating voluntary guidelines designed to alleviate the conflict between free press and fair trial. These guidelines were fashioned after the *Reardon Report* and suggestions found in the Katzenbach rules. The Katzenbach rules were a set of guidelines formulated by U.S. Attorney General Nicholas Katzenbach in 1965 that were designed to govern the release of potentially prejudicial information by federal law enforcement officials. Although less controversial than the *Reardon Report*, the rules prohibited Justice Department officials from voluntarily releasing information about a defendant's guilt or innocence, past criminal record, confessions or alibis, and the results of polygraph, ballistic, or other laboratory tests. For a period, the voluntary guidelines seemed to be alleviating much of the tension between press and bar. In 1971, however, tensions resumed with a vengeance.

United States v. Dickinson (1972) was set against the backdrop of racial unrest in the south during the early 1970s. A young VISTA worker was charged with conspiracy to murder the mayor of Baton Rouge, Louisiana. VISTA stands for Volunteers in Service to America, which is a government program begun in 1964 that sends volunteers into poor areas to teach various job skills and improve living conditions. VISTA workers were often viewed as "outside agitators" by white southerners and were sometimes harassed. Hence the possibility in *Dickinson* that the VISTA worker had been framed.

A preliminary hearing was set in U.S. district court to determine whether the state had a legitimate case or whether its action was based on racial prejudice.

Judge E. Gordon West, who would conduct the hearing, knew that the prosecution would offer evidence against the civil rights worker that, although damaging, may not be admissible in court. Although the hearing was to be public, Judge West ordered reporters not to publish any of the testimony heard during the preliminary hearing. Two reporters, Larry Dickinson of the *Baton Rouge State Times* and Gibbs Adams of the *Baton Rouge Morning Advocate*, felt that the order was in violation of the First Amendment and chose to write stories that included testimony offered at the hearing. When the stories were published, Judge West found the two reporters in contempt and fined each $300. They appealed the decision.

Appellate Judge John R. Brown noted that while Judge West's gag order violated the First Amendment, the reporters were not free to simply ignore the order. Chief Judge Brown wrote,

☐ The conclusion that the District Court's order was constitutionally invalid does not necessarily end the matter of the validity of the contempt convictions. There remains the very formidable question of whether a person may with impunity knowingly violate an order which turns out to be invalid. We hold that in the circumstances of this case he may not.

We begin with the well-established principle in proceedings for criminal contempt that an injunction duly issuing out of a court having subject matter and personal jurisdiction must be obeyed, irrespective of the validity of the order. Invalidity is no defense to criminal contempt. . . . Court orders have to be obeyed until they are reversed or set aside in an orderly fashion.

. . . Where the thing enjoined is publication and the communication is "news," this condition presents some thorny problems. Timeliness of publication is the hallmark of "news" and the difference between "news" and "history" is merely a matter of hours. Thus, where the publishing of news is sought to be restrained, the incontestable inviolability of the order may depend on the immediate accessibility of orderly review. . . . But newsmen are citizens too. They too may sometimes have to wait. They are not yet wrapped in immunity or given the absolute right to decide with impunity whether a judge's order is to be obeyed. . . .

Under the circumstances, reporters took a chance. As civil disobedients have done before they ran a risk . . . Having disobeyed the Court's decree, they must, as civil disobeyers, suffer the consequences for having rebelled at what they deem injustice, but in a manner not authorized by law.[14]

The case was returned to the district court, where Dickinson and Adams were once again convicted and fined $300. In *Dickinson v. United States*, the U.S. Supreme Court refused to review the case in 1973.

Dickinson gave rise to an increasing number of prior restraints against the press. Until 1976, judges wishing to control media publicity about a trial often considered some form of restrictive order to be a regular part of the arsenal for maintaining courtroom "sanctity."

Four years after *Dickinson*, the issue of the constitutionality of whether a trial court could issue a gag order against the press to ensure a fair trial came to the Supreme Court. In *Nebraska Press Assn. v. Stuart* (1976), the Court opposed the use of prior restraints against the media.

On the night of October 18, 1975, Erwin Charles Simiants killed six members of the James Kellie family in Sutherland, Nebraska. Simiants then confessed the killings to his family. His father told him to turn himself in to police. Instead, Simiants stopped by a local bar and had a drink before hiding out in some high weeds behind his victims' house. Sutherland is a town of 840 people located in Lincoln County, which has 36,000 residents. The largest city is North Platte, with a population of 24,000. Needless to say, the news of the crime spread quickly that night. Before long, reporters and cameramen were pouring into tiny Sutherland from as far away as Denver. At 8:00 the next morning, Simiants walked into the home of his uncle, where he was immediately arrested by state police and the local sheriff.

By 9:00 A.M. Simiants had been booked and confessed to police. Although that confession had not been witnessed by the media, the chief prosecutor was quoted by the Associated Press as saying "Simiants apparently walked into his father's home after the shooting and told his father he was responsible for the deaths."[15]

News coverage of the crime was pervasive. A report on NBC's *Today* program noted that "Simiants reportedly confessed to his father and fled."[16] Additionally, the *North Platte Telegraph* included a report that quoted Simiant's father as saying "My son killed five or six people here."[17]

Because of the wide news coverage, both the county attorney and the defense counsel asked the county court to close the preliminary hearing to the public and issue a restrictive order against further news coverage so that an impartial jury could be selected. County Judge Ronald Ruff refused to close the hearing, but ordered the news media not to report on any testimony or evidence taken at the hearing.

The news media, represented by the Nebraska Press Association, appealed the order to the U.S. district court in Lincoln. After all, argued the Press Association, the state of Nebraska had already drawn up a set of press-bar guidelines, patterned after the *Sheppard* decision, designed to deal with just this sort of matter. The gag order would have to stand, however, until overturned by a higher court.

Judge Hugh Stuart heard the Press Association's appeal and modified the order. Acknowledging the Nebraska press-bar voluntary guidelines, Judge Stuart made the guidelines mandatory in this case. Stuart noted that because of the nature of the crimes, pretrial publicity could present a clear and present danger to Simiants' right to a fair trial. Judge Stuart's order would only apply until a jury was selected and prohibited the reporting of the existence or contents of a confession, statements made by Simiants to other persons, the contents of a note written by Simiants on the night of the crime, the results of medical testimony taken at the preliminary hearing, and the identity of victims who had been sexually assaulted during the crime.[18] Stuart then ordered the media not to report that they were operating under a gag order. In essence, Judge Stuart had issued a "gag on a gag." Any news medium reporting on the five issues listed above, or informing the public that they were under a restraining order, would be cited for contempt of court.

Again, appeals were filed and, after much legal manuevering, the U.S. Supreme Court agreed to hear the *Nebraska Press* case. In the meantime, *State v. Simiants* continued. Before the Supreme Court decided on the constitutionality of the "gag on a gag," Simiants' trial was over. Simiants was found guilty of six counts of murder and sentenced to death. In 1979, Simiants was awarded a new trial on a technicality (not related to the media coverage of his first trial) and was found innocent by reason of insanity.

In *Nebraska Press*, Chief Justice Burger delivered the opinion of the Court.

☐ . . . Our review of the pretrial record persuades us that the trial judge was justified in concluding that there would be intense and pervasive publicity concerning this case. He could also reasonably conclude, based on common human experience, that publicity might impair the defendant's right to a fair trial. He did not purport to say more, for he found only a "clear and present danger that pretrial publicity could impinge on a fair trial." His conclusion as to the impact of such publicity on prospective jurors was of necessity speculative, dealing as he was with factors unknown and unknowable.

We find little in the record that goes to another aspect of our task, determining whether measures short of an order restraining all publication would have insured the defendant a fair trial. Although the entry of the order might be read as a judicial determination that other measures would not suffice, the trial court made no express findings to that effect . . .

. . . There is no finding that alternative measures would not have protected Simiants' rights . . .

. . . [W]e note that the events disclosed by the record took place in a community of 850 people. It is reasonable to assume that, without any news accounts being printed or broadcast, rumors would travel swiftly by word of mouth. One can only speculate on the accuracy of such reports, given the generative propensities of rumors; they could well be more damaging than reasonably accurate news accounts. But plainly a whole community cannot be restrained from discussing a subject intimately affecting life within it. . . .

. . . Our analysis ends as it began, with a confrontation between prior restraint imposed to protect one vital constitutional guarantee and the explicit command of another that freedom to speak and publish shall not be abridged. We reaffirm that the guarantees of freedom of expression are not an absolute prohibition under all circumstances, but the barriers to prior restraint remain high and the presumption against its use continues intact. We hold that, with respect to the order entered in this case prohibiting reporting or commentary on judicial proceedings held in public, the barriers have not been overcome; to the extent that this order restrained publication of such material, it is clearly invalid. To the extent that it prohibited publication of information gained from other sources we conclude that the heavy burden imposed as a condition to securing a prior restraint was not met . . .[19]

In *Nebraska Press* the Supreme Court said that three elements must be met before a judge can issue a valid restraining order against the press in order to ensure a fair trial. First, there must be a likelihood of widespread prejudicial publicity. Second, all other methods of controlling such publicity must have been exhausted. This includes rigorous *voir dire*, change of venue, and continuance. Finally, there must be a showing that a restraining order will control prejudicial publicity. All three of these guidelines must be met for a restraining order to be constitutional. Obviously, meeting these criteria is difficult—hence the "heavy presumption against prior restraint" by the Supreme Court.

One year later, the Supreme Court once again struck down prior restraints against the media. In *Oklahoma Publishing v. District Court*, the Court noted that although the press could be barred from attending juvenile proceedings, if the press was allowed to attend they could not be prohibited from publishing information obtained at such proceedings.

In the years following *Nebraska Press* and *Oklahoma Publishing*, the number of restraining orders against the press declined. However, some judges still felt compelled to issue prior restraints. In 1983, a federal district court judge issued a restraining order against CBS. The order forbade the broadcast of videotapes of former automobile manufacturer John DeLorean's conversations with federal undercover narcotics agents during his investigation for alleged cocaine dealing. The judge said that broadcast of the tapes would prejudice potential jurors. CBS appealed the order and won the right to broadcast the videotapes. In *CBS v. U.S. District Court*, in a decision based on *Nebraska Press*, the U.S. court of appeals said that the district court had not exhausted all other alternatives available for protecting DeLorean's right to a fair trial.

Closing the Courtroom

While *Nebraska Press* addressed the issue of prior restraint, the closing of pretrial hearings to the press and public continued to be a major issue into the 1980s. Because of the unlikelihood that a prior restraint order would be upheld after *Nebraska Press*, some courts sought to control potentially prejudicial news coverage by limiting access to the courtroom. The Supreme Court first gave apparent support to the concept that there is no First Amendment right on the part of the press to attend pretrial proceedings in *Gannett v. DePasquale* (1979). In a 5–4 decision, the Court upheld a New York judge's order excluding a Gannett newspaper reporter from a pretrial hearing in a second-degree murder case. Writing for the majority, Justice Potter Stewart's opinion was unclear as to whether reporters had no constitutional right to attend pretrial hearings or trials themselves. Not only did the confusion created by *Gannett* lead to an outcry by the press, but it also led to a number of courtroom closings. Between July and September of 1979, more than 50 courtrooms were closed for some or all portions of pretrial or trial proceedings.

The *Gannett* decision was weakened only a year later in *Richmond Newspapers v. Virginia* (1980), when the Court ruled that trials were presumptively open to the public. Chief Justice Burger used language in writing the majority opinion in *Richmond Newspapers* to emphasize that *Gannett* dealt with pretrial hearings and that, in *Richmond Newspapers*, the issue was trial proceedings.

The defendant in *Richmond* was about to be tried for a fourth time for the murder of a hotel manager. The first trial had been reversed on appeal and the two subsequent trials had ended in mistrials. Because of the great deal of publicity surrounding the case and the unusual circumstances of two mistrials, the defense counsel moved that the trial be closed to the public. The prosecution did not object and the judge granted the motion. Two newspaper reporters objected and they filed a motion to vacate the closure order. The motion was denied, the press appealed, and the case eventually found its way to the Supreme Court. The Court used this case to clarify language in *Gannett* and to establish that there is a First Amendment right to attend trials and that there is no right to a private trial. The pendulum had begun to swing back toward the center. Chief Justice Burger delivered the opinion of the Court.

☐   . . . In *Gannett Co. v. DePasquale* . . . the Court was not required to decide whether a right of access to trials, as disinguished from pretrial motions, was guaranteed. The Court held that the Sixth Amendment's guarantee to the accused of a public trial gave neither the public nor the press an enforceable right of access to a pretrial suppression hearing. One concurring opinion specifically emphasized that "a hearing on a motion before trial to suppress evidence is not a trial . . ." Moreover, the Court did not decide whether the First and Fourteenth Amendments guarantee a right of the public to attend trials . . .

. . . We hold that the right to attend criminal trials is implicit in the guarantees of the First Amendment; without the freedom to attend such trials, which people have exercised for centuries, important aspects of freedom of speech and "of the press could be eviscerated." *Branzburg, supra* at 681

. . . [A]lthough the Sixth Amendment guarantees the accused a right to a public trial, it does not give a right to a private trial. . . . Absent an overriding interest articulated in findings, the trial of a criminal case must be open to the public . . .[20]

The Court emphasized that this right of access applies only to *criminal* trials. It did not apply the right to civil proceedings.

Two years later, the Supreme Court reaffirmed the *Richmond Newspapers* holding in *Globe Newspaper Co. v. Superior Court* (1982). At issue was a Massachusetts statute that required closure of all trials dealing with certain sex crimes. The defendant was on trial for forcible rape against two juveniles. When the judge closed the trial, reporters from the *Boston Globe* appealed the order. Eventually, the Supreme Court found that Massachusetts' mandatory closure statute violated the First Amendment right of access to criminal trials recognized in *Richmond Newspapers*.

By the mid 1980s, the Supreme Court had further rejected the *Reardon Report's* suggestion that a trial might be closed on a motion from the defendant if there is reason to believe a fair trial may be in jeopardy. In two cases involving Press-Enterprise, the Supreme Court dealt serious blows to this concept and returned to a more balanced position regarding First and Sixth Amendment rights.

In *Press Enterprise I* (1984), the Supreme Court extended the *Richmond Newspapers* ruling by mandating that jury selection, like trials, should be conducted in public. Chief Justice Burger also provided an interesting history of the jury selection process and its role in the guarantee of a fair trial. Chief Justice Burger delivered the opinion of the Court.

□   . . . Albert Greenwood Brown, Jr. was tried and convicted of the rape and murder of a teenage girl, and sentenced to death in California Superior Court. Before the *voir dire* examination of prospective jurors began, petitioner, Press-Enterprise Co., moved that *voir dire* be open to the public and to the press. Petitioners contend that the public had an absolute right to attend the trial, and asserted that the trial commenced with the *voir dire* proceedings. The State opposed petitioner's motion, arguing that if the press were present juror responses would lack the candor necessary to assure [sic] a fair trial.

The trial judge agreed and permitted petitioner to attend only the "general voir dire." He stated that counsel would conduct the "individual voir dire with regard to death qualifications and any other special areas that counsel may feel some problem with . . . ." The *voir dire* consumed six weeks and all but approximately three days was closed to the public.

After the jury was empaneled, petitioner moved the trial court to release a complete transcript of the *voir dire* proceedings. . . . The court denied petitioner's motion . . .

After Brown had been convicted and sentenced to death, petitioner again applied for release of the transcript. In denying this application, the judge stated:

> The jurors were questioned in private relating to past experiences, and while most of the information is dull and boring, some of the jurors had special experiences in sensitive areas that do not appear to be appropriate for public discussion.

Petitioner then sought in the California Court of Appeal a writ of mandate to compel the Superior Court to release the transcript and vacate the order closing the *voir dire* proceedings. The petition was denied. The California Supreme Court denied petitioner's request for a hearing. We granted certiorari. . . . We reverse.

. . . The roots of open trials reach back to the days before the Norman Conquest when cases in England were brought before "moots," a town meeting kind of body such as the local court of the hundred or the county court.[21] Attendance was virtually compulsory on the part of free men of the community . . . in rendering a judgement. The public aspect thus was "almost a necessary incident of jury trials since the presence of a jury . . . already insured the presence of a large part of the public."[22]

As the jury system evolved in the years after the Norman Conquest, and the jury came to be but a small segment representing the community, the obligation of all free men to attend criminal trials was relaxed; however, the public character of the proceedings, including jury selection, remained unchanged. . . .

The presumptive openness of the jury selection process in England, not surprisingly, carried over into proceedings in Colonial America. . . . Public jury selection thus was the common practice in America when the Constitution was adopted.

. . . No right ranks higher than the right of the accused to a fair trial. But the primacy of the accused's right is difficult to separate from the right of everyone in the community to attend the *voir dire* which promotes fairness.

The open trial thus plays as important a role in the administration of justice today as it did for the centuries before our separation from England.

The value of openness lies in the fact that people not actually attending trials can have confidence that standards of fairness are being observed . . .

"People in an open society do not demand infallibility from their institutions, but it is difficult for them to accept what they are prohibited from observing." *Richmond Newspapers, supra, at 572.* Closed proceedings, although not absolutely precluded, must be rare and only for cause shown that outweighs the value of openness. . . .

The presumption of openness may be overcome only by an overriding interest based on findings that closure is essential to preserve higher values and is narrowly tailored to serve that interest. . . .

To preserve fairness and at the same time protect legitimate privacy . . . those individuals believing public questioning will prove damaging because of embarrassment, may properly request an opportunity to present the problem to the judge *in camera* but with counsel present and on the record.

By requiring the prospective juror to make an affirmative request the trial judge can ensure that there is in fact a valid basis for a belief that disclosure infringes a significant interest in privacy.

The judge at this trial closed an incredible six weeks of *voir dire* without considering alternatives to closure. Later the court declined to release a transcript of the *voir dire* even while stating that "most of the information" in the transcript was "dull and boring." . . . Those parts of the transcript reasonably entitled to privacy could have been sealed without such a sweeping order; a trial judge should explain why the material is entitled to privacy.

Thus not only was there a failure to articulate findings with requisite specificity, but there was also a failure to consider alternatives to closure and to the total suppression of the transcript.[23]

In *Press Enterprise II*, in a 7–2 vote, the Court said that defendants wishing to close a preliminary hearing must demonstrate that an open courtroom would have a "substantial probability" of endangering their right to a fair trial. This case all but overrules the validity of *Gannett* and continues movement toward opening the entire judicial process begun in *Nebraska Press* and developed in *Richmond Newspapers, Globe Newspaper,* and *Press-Enterprise I.* In *Press-Enterprise Co. v. Riverside County Superior Court* (1986), Chief Justice Burger delivered the opinion of the Court.

☐   On December 23, 1981, the State of California filed a complaint . . . charging Robert Diaz with 12 counts of murder and seeking the death penalty. The complaint alleged that Diaz, a nurse, murdered 12 patients by administering massive doses of the heart drug, lidocaine. The preliminary hearing commenced on July 6, 1982. Diaz moved to exclude the public from the proceedings . . .[24] The Magistrate granted the motion, finding that closure was necessary because the case had attracted national publicity and "only one side may get reported in the media."

The preliminary hearing continued for 41 days. Most of the testimony and the evidence presented by the State was medical and scientific; the remainder consisted of testimony by personnel who worked with Diaz on the shifts when the 12 patients died. Diaz did not introduce any evidence, but his counsel subjected most of the witnesses to vigorous cross-examination. Diaz was held to answer on all charges. At the conclusion of the hearing, Press-Enterprise Company asked that the transcript of the proceedings be released. The Magistrate refused and sealed the record.

On January 21, 1983, the State moved in Superior Court to have the transcripts of the hearing released to the public; petitioner later joined in support of the motion. Diaz opposed the motion, contending the release of the transcripts would result in prejudicial pretrial publicity. The Superior Court found that . . . there was . . . "a reasonable likelihood that the release of all or any part of the transcript might prejudice defendant's right to a fair and impartial trial." [Cited from California's statute.]

Petitioner then filed a peremptory writ of mandate with the Court of Appeal. That court originally denied the writ but, after being so ordered by the California Supreme Court, set the matter for a hearing. Meanwhile, Diaz waived his right to a jury trial and the Superior Court released the transcript. After holding that the controversy was not moot, the Court of Appeal denied the writ of mandate.

The California Supreme Court thereafter denied petitioner's peremptory writ of mandate . . .

. . . We granted certiorari. . . . We reverse.

. . . In *Press-Enterprise I*, we summarized the holdings of prior cases, noting that openness in criminal trials, including the selection of jurors "enhances both the fairness of the criminal trial and the appearance of fairness so essential to public confidence in the system." 464 U.S. at 501

. . . The considerations that led the Court to apply the First Amendment right of access to criminal trials in *Richmond Newspapers* and *Globe* and the selection of jurors in *Press-Enterprise I* lead us to conclude that the right of access applies to preliminary hearings as conducted in California.[25]

Once again, the Court did not rule out closing some pretrial hearings, but the standards were clearly defined. In *Press-Enterprise II*, the Court reiterated criteria established in *Press-Enterprise I* and *Richmond Newspapers*—that there must be a substantial probability that the defendant's right to a fair trial will be prejudiced by publicity, which closure will prevent, and that reasonable alternatives to closure cannot adequately protect the defendant's trial rights.

Shortly after the *Press-Enterprise* cases, several state and federal courts were quick to apply the Supreme Court's "presumption of openness" policy. In *Associated*

Press v. Bell, a New York court of appeals reversed a district court ruling that closed a pretrial hearing. The court based the reversal on the fact that the defendant did not specifically note how his trial would be prejudiced if the hearing remained open. On similar grounds, the New York Supreme Court ruled in *Orange County Publications v. Dallow* that a lower court erred in closing a hearing to decide whether a 15-year-old boy accused of the murder of a 9-year-old girl should be held for a grand jury. In *In Re: New York Times* (1987) the Court of Appeals for the Second Circuit found a First Amendment right of access by the press to pretrial motions and procedures filed under seal in criminal proceedings. Finally, in *U.S. v. Raffoul*, a U.S. court of appeals ruled that federal courts must grant a preclosure hearing before ruling on closure motions made at criminal trials. This, said the court, is a "matter of right" to those persons actually present in the courtroom. Personal notice to the news media is not required.

The most significant case to date following *Press-Enterprise I*, however, involved the July 1987 trial of Michael Deaver, a former aide to President Reagan. Michael Deaver was charged with perjury as a result of lobbying activities conducted after leaving President Reagan's staff. Federal Judge Thomas Penfield Jackson odered the *voir dire* closed in order to protect the privacy of potential jurors. The judge gave prospective jurors the option to be questioned in open court, but only five of the 30 to be questioned agreed to do so in open court. In *CNN v. United States (1987)*, the Cable News Network and other news organizations appealed the order, requesting that jury selection be conducted in open court. The appeal was denied, but a Washington, DC, appellate court swiftly granted a summary reversal of Judge Jackson's order. The court cited the three conditions for closing *voir dire* set forth in *Press-Enterprise I*.

1. Specific findings that open *voir dire* would jeopardize the defendant's fair trial interests or the jurors legititmate privacy interests.
2. Jurors suspecting that privacy interests may be damaged by open *voir dire* must make "affirmative requests" for closure.
3. "Alternatives to closure" must be considered.

The appellate court noted that Judge Jackson's closure order met none of the conditions. The Suprmeme Court denied review of the case on October 19, 1987.

These rulings do not affect the secrecy of grand jury deliberations. The Court acknowledged that "the proper functioning of our grand jury system depends upon the secrecy of grand jury proceedings."[26] There are five reasons commonly given for the policy of grand jury secrecy. In essence, they are to

prevent the escape of someone who may be indicted
protect deliberations from outside influence
prevent tampering with witnesses
encourage free disclosures by potential witnesses
protect the innocent accused who is later exonerated

Although *Globe Newspaper Co.* struck down the Massachusetts statute that automatically closed trials dealing with certain sex crimes, the Michigan Supreme

Court upheld a statute that suppresses the names of persons involved and the details relating to criminal sexual conduct cases. In *Midland Publishing v. District Court Judge*, the court held that such information may be withheld until the defendant is arraigned, the case is dismissed, or is otherwise concluded. Unlike the unconstitutional Massachusetts statute, the press is eventually granted access to the information.

Similarly, in *In Re: Pacific & Southern Co.* (1987) the Georgia Supreme Court ruled that the news media did not have a right of access to criminal trial evidence consisting of videotapes of a crime scene and a convicted murder defendant's statement to police. The basis of the holding was that the appeals process had not been completed and broadcast of the material could, if a new trial were granted, deny the defendant a fair trial.

The Camera in the Courtroom

The movement toward greater openness of the judicial process to the press, has resulted in an increasing number of states that permit videotaping and broadcasting trial proceedings. The gradual acceptance of cameras in the courtroom has come about in much the same manner as the "opening" of the courts. The excessive practices of the press with cameras during the Hauptmann trial resulted directly in ABA Canon 35, which banned photographic equipment from the courts. Experiences with the new medium of television in the 1950s and 1960s resulted in that medium's expulsion as well. The primary argument for keeping cameras—both moving and still—out of courts centered around their intrusive nature. The need for bright lights and the bulkiness of early television hardware was cited as depriving defendants of "judicial serenity." Other concerns about the broadcast of trials included the possibility of negative effects on witnesses, "grandstanding" by lawyers and judges up for reelection, and harassment of witnesses who might now be seen on television. Although there was no scientific evidence to support these concerns, the *Hauptmann* and *Sheppard* cases stood as examples of the possible abuse of cameras and broadcasting. Still, cameras found their way into the trial process.

In 1961, Wilbert Rideau was arrested for a bank robbery in Lake Charles, Louisiana, during which a bank employee was killed. Rideau confessed to the local sheriff in his jail cell, without counsel present, while a local TV news crew filmed the confession. This confession was broadcast by KPLC-TV to the Lake Charles area a total of three times in 2 days. An estimated 106,000 of the 150,000 residents of Calcasieu Parish saw the broadcast. Rideau's request for a change of venue was denied. Rideau was found guilty and sentenced to death. Subsequent appeals resulted in the case being heard by the Supreme Court.

In *Rideau v. Louisiana* (1963), the Supreme Court ordered a new trial. Coming on the heels of *Irvin*, the Court held that the broadcast confession had made the selection of an impartial jury impossible. Justice Stewart wrote,

☐ For anyone who has ever watched television, the conclusion cannot be avoided that this spectacle, to the tens of thousands of people who saw and heard it, in a very real sense was Rideau's trial—at which he pleaded guilty of murder. Any subsequent court proceedings in a community so pervasively exposed to such a spectacle could be but a hollow formality.[27]

Rideau was granted a new trial, where he was convicted and sentenced to life in prison. Like Leslie Irvin, prejudicial media coverage had spared him from capital punishment. Irvin had been denied a fair trial because jurors testified that they had been influenced by media coverage. This became known as the "Irvin test."

Rideau extended the Irvin test even further. Now the defense did not have to prove that any jurors were actually influenced by the broadcast, only that they were *probably* influenced by it. Like *Sheppard,* a change of venue was denied in *Rideau* and a continuance was not considered. The courts preferred that the media bear the brunt of ensuring the fairness of a trial.

The thinking during this period with regard to the potential harm that cameras might bring to the judicial process was similar to the attitudes of the time toward the open courtroom. It was better to err on the side of the Sixth Amendment, than on the side of the First Amendment. So, when the Supreme Court heard its first television-cameras-in-court case, a list of potential harm to the fair trial process was generated. Once again, this list was based only on speculation and was not supported by any testimony of fact. *Estes v. State of Texas* (1965) was television journalism's *Sheppard.*

Billie Sol Estes, a Texas financier closely associated with Lyndon Johnson, was tried in 1962 on charges of theft, swindling, and embezzlement. Although Estes objected, the trial judge permitted television coverage of the pretrial hearing and portions of the trial itself. Estes was convicted and appealed on grounds that the television coverage denied him a fair trial. The case reached the Supreme Court, which agreed that the Texas court had not adhered to Canon 35 and that Estes had not received a fair trial. Justice Clark delivered the opinion of the Court.

☐ The question presented here is whether the petitioner . . . was deprived of his right under the Fourteenth Amendment to due process by televising and broadcasting of his trial. Both the trial court and the Texas Court of Criminal Appeals found against the petitioner. We hold to the contrary and reverse his conviction.

While petitioner recites his claim in the framework of Canon 35 of the Judicial Canons of the American Bar Association he does not contend that we should enshrine Canon 35 in the Fourteenth Amendment, but only that the time-honored principles of a fair trial were not followed in his case and that he was thus convicted without due process of law.

. . . Petitioner's case was originally called for trial on September 24, 1962, in Smith County after a change of venue from Reeves County, some 500 miles west. Massive pretrial publicity totaling 11 volumes of press clippings . . . had given it national notoriety. All available seats in the courtroom were taken and some 30 persons stood in the aisles. However, at that time a defense motion to prevent telecasting, broadcasting by radio and news photography and a defense motion for continuance were presented, and after a two-day hearing the former was denied and the latter granted.

These initial hearings were carried live by both radio and television, and news photography was permitted throughout. The videotapes of these hearings clearly illustrate that the picture presented was not one of that judicial serenity and calm to which petitioner was entitled. Indeed, at least 12 cameramen were engaged in the courtroom throughout the hearing taking motion and still pictures and televising the proceedings. Cables and wires were snaked across the courtroom floor, three microphones were on the judge's bench and others were beamed at the jury box and the counsel table. It is conceded that the activities of the television crews and news photographers led to considerable disruption of the hearings.

. . . When the case was called for trial on October 22 the scene had been altered. A booth had been constructed at the back of the courtroom which was painted to blend with the permanent structure of the room. It had an aperture to allow the lens of the cameras an unrestricted view of the courtroom. All television cameras and newsreel photographers were restricted to the area of the booth when shooting film or telecasting.

Because of continual objection, the rules governing live telecasting, as well as radio and still photos, were changed as the exigencies of the situation seemed to require. As a result, live telecasting was prohibited during a great portion of the actual trial. Only the opening and closing arguments of the State, the return of the jury's verdict and its receipt by the trial judge were carried live with sound. . . .

. . . Because of varying restrictions placed on sound and live telecasting, the telecasts of the trial were confined largely to film clips shown on the stations' regularly scheduled news programs. The news commentators would use the film of a particular part of the day's trial activities as a backdrop for their reports. Their commentary included excerpts from testimony and the usual reportorial remarks. On one occasion the videotapes of the September hearings were rebroadcast in place of the "late movie." . . .

We start with the proposition that it is a "public trial" that the Sixth Amendment guarantees to the accused. The purpose of the requirement of a public trial was to guarantee that the accused would be fairly dealt with and not unjustly condemned. . . .

It is said, however, that freedoms granted in the First Amendment extend a right to the news media to televise from the courtroom, and that a refusal to honor this privilege is to discriminate between the newspapers and television. This is a misconception of the rights of the press. . . . The news reporter is not permitted to bring his typewriter or printing press. When the advances in these arts permit reporting by printing press or by television without their present hazards to a fair trial we will have another case. . . .

As has been said, the chief function of our judicial machinery is to ascertain the truth. The use of television, however, cannot be said to contribute materially to this objective. Rather its use amounts to the injection of an irrelevant factor into court proceedings. In addition, experience teaches that there are numerous situations in which it might cause actual unfairness—some so subtle as to defy detection by the accused or controlled by the judge.[28]

The Court then listed four components of the trial that might be adversely affected if trials were telecast:

1. *The jury* might feel pressure from outside forces, knowing that a trial will be televised. Additionally, television might affect the attentiveness of the jury in the jury box. They may pay attention to cameras and not to details of the case. They might also feel self-conscious on television and be "preoccupied with the telecasting rather than the testimony." They may return home and see the broadcasts of the day's proceedings and be influenced by that. Finally, said the Court, new trials would be jeopardized because potential jurors might have seen the original trial on television.

2. *Witnesses* might be influenced by televised trials. Some may be "demoralized and frightened, some cocky and given to overstatement; memories may falter," and accuracy may be undermined. Witnesses may be harassed on the street by those having seen their testimony on television and some witnesses may refuse to testify at all, for fear of being on television. Finally, the Court noted that upcoming witnesses may watch the testimony of others on television and change their testimony accordingly.

3. *Judges* would be saddled with an additional burden while performing the task of controlling the decorum of the courtroom. Judges up for reelection might also be tempted to use television as a means of reaching the electorate.

4. *The defendant* might be subjected to undue pressures, knowing that there will be "inevitable close ups of his gestures and expressions during the ordeal of his trial."[29]

Reading these potential concerns today gives the impression that the Supreme Court was grasping at straws in an effort to keep television out of the courtrooms. Just as *Sheppard* spawned the closing of courtrooms, *Estes* signaled the demise of cameras in court. By 1974, all states except Colorado had banned cameras from the courtroom.

While there is no question that intrusive and irresponsible behavior by television in the coverage of trials would probably affect the outcome of the proceedings, most of the previous arguments can be easily refuted or controlled. Cooperation between bench and broadcasters has alleviated much of the tension, and most of these four arguments are no longer serious impediments to a fair trial today. A key to understanding *Estes*, however, lies in the statement that references the developments in technology that may permit television coverage, without the intrusiveness of the bulky equipment used in 1962. Technological advancements began to reduce "the hazards to a fair trial" referred to by Justice Clark and television slowly made its way back into the courtroom.

In the late 1970s, states like Alabama, Texas, New Hampshire, and Florida experimented with cameras in the courtrooms. The Supreme Court upheld Florida's use of cameras in the courtroom in *Chandler v. Florida* (1981). The court ruled that the mere presence of cameras did not automatically result in an unfair trial.

By the 1990s, a majority of states had experimented with cameras in the courtroom, but federal courts and the Supreme Court remained off-limits. In September 1990, the U.S. Judicial Conference adopted a general policy statement that allowed the use of photography and electronic media in federal courtrooms for a 3-year period. The experiment allows cameras in up to six district courts and two federal appellate courts. At this writing, the Supreme Court does not allow cameras in its proceedings.

The Challenges of the 1990s

The pervasive nature of the electronic media continues to strain the boundaries between the defendant's right to a fair trial and the right to gather news. Can defendants involved in nationally publicized cases be guaranteed a trial by an impartial jury? The question has often been asked, Could Lee Harvey Oswald have been assured of a fair trial? The trial of former Panamanian President Manuel Noriega in the fall of 1991 was another prime example of a public figure who is so well known that no change of venue can guarantee an impartial jury. The notoriety of Jeffrey Dahmer, accused of a series of bizarre murders in Milwaukee in 1991, gained more national attention than Sam Sheppard in his day. Finally, the popularity of "reality" programs like "Top Cops" and "America's Most Wanted" often cast a disparaging shadow on individuals not yet convicted of a crime. Do these programs interfere with the delicate balance between First and Sixth Amendment rights?

The televised trial of William Kennedy Smith, who was accused of raping a woman on the grounds of the Kennedy estate in Florida, seems to indicate that a highly publicized trial can be televised without compromising judical standards. The rape trial of boxer Mike Tyson proceeded in a media-intensive atmosphere without a change of venue. The Tyson jury was sequestered and a fair trial ensued.

The legal system and the electronic and print media will undoubtedly be required to develop additional procedures to ease the tensions that result from increased interaction between the electronic media and judicial professions.

Summary

The Sixth Amendment to the Constitution guarantees those accused of criminal actions a right to a speedy and public trial by an impartial jury. These rights of a defendant often conflict with rights also guaranteed to the press under the First Amendment.

Judges regularly attempt to control prejudicial pretrial publicity by granting a change of venue, a continuance, or sequestering the jury. A change of venue moves the location of the trial away from an area where prospective jurors are likely to hold preconceived opinions about the guilt or innocence of an accused person. A continuance postpones the starting date of a trial so that the strong emotions felt by a community, often accompanying the arrest of a suspect, have had time to subside. Sequestering the jury means limiting jurors' contact with the outside world during a trial. This is done in the hope that jurors will not be influenced by media reports of the proceedings or by others desiring to affect the outcome of the trial.

By the 1990s, a majority of states had experimented with cameras in the courtroom, but federal courts and the Supreme Court remained off-limits. In September 1990, the U.S. Judicial Conference adopted a general policy statement that allowed the use of photography and electronic media in federal courtrooms for a 3-year period.

Notes/References

1. United States v. Burr, 24 Fed. Cas. 49 No. 14692g (1807).
2. Fair Trial/Free Press Voluntary Agreements (Chicago: Legal Advisory Committee on Fair Trial and Free Press, 1974), 7–8.
3. Helen M. Hughes, *News and the Human Interest Story* (Chicago: University of Chicago Press, 1940), 235.
4. Edwin Emery, *The Press and America*, 2nd ed. (Englewood Cliffs, NJ: Prentice-Hall, 1962), 629–30.
5. Shepherd v. Florida, 341 U.S. 50 (1951), 71 S.Ct. 549.
6. Stroble v. State of California, 343 U.S. 181 (1952), 72 S.Ct. 599.
7. Ibid., 609.
8. *The Evansville Press* (April 10, 1955): 1.
9. Ibid.
10. "Murder Suspect Named By Police," *The Evansville Press* (April 11, 1955): 1.
11. "2 Innocent Pleas Entered by Irvin," *The Evansville Press* (April 28, 1955): 1.
12. Irvin v. Dowd, 366 U.S. 717 (1961).
13. Sheppard v. Maxwell, 384 U.S. 333 (1966).
14. United States v. Dickinson, 465 F.2d 496 (5th Cir., 1972).

15. Fred W. Friendly and Martha J.H. Elliot, *The Constitution: That Delicate Balance* (New York: Random House, 1984), 150.
16. Ibid., 151.
17. Ibid.
18. Dale Spencer et al., *Free Press & Fair Trial* (Washington, DC: American Society of Newspaper Editors/ American Newspaper Publishers Association Foundation, 1982), 48.
19. Nebraska Press Assn. v. Stuart, 427 U.S. 539 (1976).
20. Richmond Newspapers, Inc. v. Commonwealth of Virginia, 448 U.S. 555 (1980) at 560.
21. Citing Pollack, *English Law Before the Norman Conquest*, 1 Select Essays in Anglo-American Legal History 88, 89 (1907).
22. Citing Radin, *The Right to a Public Trial*, 6 Temp. L.Q. 381,388 (1932).
23. Press-Enterprise v. Riverside County Superior Court, No. 82–556 (1984) 10 Med.L.Rptr. 1161.
24. California law provided that a trial could be closed if such action would protect the defendant's right to a fair and impartial trial.
25. Press-Enterprise Co. v. Riverside County Superior Court, (S.Ct., 1986) 13 Med.L.Rptr. 1002.
26. "News Notes," (November, 1987) 14 Med.L.Rptr. 21.
27. Rideau v. Louisiana, 373 U.S. 723 at 726, 83 S.Ct. 1417 (1963).
28. Estes v. State of Texas, 381 U.S. 532 (1965).
29. Ibid.

Cases

Associated Press v. Bell, (NY Ct.App., 1987) 14 Med.L.Rptr. 1156
CBS v. U.S. District Court, (CA 9, 1984) 10 Med.L.Rptr. 1529
Chandler v. Florida, 449 U.S. 560 (1981)
CNN v. United States, (DC Ct.App., 1987) 14 Med.L.Rptr. 1334
Dickinson v. United States, cert. denied 414 U.S. 979 (1973)
Estes v. State of Texas, 381 U.S. 532 (1965)
Gannett v. DePasquale, 443 U.S. 368 (1979)
Globe Newspaper Co. v. Superior Court, County of Norfolk, 457 U.S. 596 (1982)
In Re: Pacific & Southern Co., (GA Sup.Ct., 1987) 14 Med.L.Rptr. 1764
Irvin v. Dowd, 366 U.S. 717 (1961)
Janko v. United States, 366 U.S. 716 (1961)
Marshall v. United States, 360 U.S. 310 (1959)
Midland Publishing v. District Court Judge, (Mich Sup.Ct., 1984) 11 Med.L.Rptr. 1337
Nebraska Press Assn. v. Stuart, 427 U.S. 539 (1976)

In Re New York Times, (CA 2, 1987) 14 Med.L.Rptr. 1625

Oklahoma Publishing v. District Court, 430 U.S. 308 (1977)

Orange County Publications v. Dallow, (NY Sup.Ct., 1987) 14 Med.L.Rptr. 1311

Press-Enterprise Co. v. Riverside County Superior Court, No. 82–556 (1984) 10 Med.L.Rptr. 1161

Press-Enterprise Co. v. Riverside County Superior Court, (S.Ct., 1986) 13 Med.L.Rptr. 1002

Richmond Newspapers v. Commonwealth of Virginia, 488 U.S. 555 (1980)

Rideau v. Louisiana, 373 U.S. 723, 83 S.Ct. 1417 (1963)

Shepherd v. Florida, 341 U.S. 50 (1951) 71 S.Ct. 549 (1951)

Sheppard v. Maxwell, 231 F.Supp. 37 (S.D. OH, 1964)

Sheppard v. Maxwell, 384 U.S. 333 (1966)

State v. Simiants, 194 Neb. 783, 236 N.W.2d 794 (1975)

Stroble v. State of California, 343 U.S. 181 (1952), 72 S.Ct. 599 (1952)

United States v. Burr, 24 Fed.Cas. 49 No. 14692g (1807)

United States v. Dickinson, 465 F.2d 496 (5th Cir., 1972)

U.S. v. Raffoul, (CA 3, 1987) 14 Med.L.Rptr. 1534

13 ⬚⬚⬚
⬚⬚⬚
⬚⬚⬚

The Future of Electronic Media Regulation

An Evolving Landscape

The decade of the 1990s promises many changes in the regulatory structure of broadcasting, cable, and developing technologies. Traditional broadcasting is threatened further by the continued growth of cable television. The audiences of the traditional broadcast networks continue to erode, while cable audiences have increased. Both industries face challenges posed by the entry of telephone companies into the business of distributing video programming via fiber optic cable. Direct broadcast satellites (DBS), wireless cable (also known as multichannel multipoint distribution services, or MMDS), home satellite dishes, interactive video systems, and digital audio broadcasting (DAB) may also play a greater role in changing the way we receive information now distributed by traditional broadcast and cable technology.

In this chapter, attention is given to current and potential regulatory activity and the ways that this activity may affect the electronic media in the coming decade.

It is clear that current allocation of the electromagnetic spectrum will not accommodate existing and anticipated broadcast and personal communications services (PCS) such as high definition television (HDTV). Reallocation of spectrum space is likely. This reallocation will require the FCC and NTIA to re-think some of the bases for awarding spectrum space. The FCC allocates spectrum space for the private sector. The National Telecommunications Information Agency (NTIA), part of the Department of Commerce, allocates government uses of the radio spectrum. The Commission will be faced with reconsidering both its rules and policies. Who will be displaced? Who will be awarded space and how will this be determined?

Many policy analysts and telecommunications scholars in the early 1990s proclaimed broadcast television as "obsolete." The FCC's Office of Plans and Policy issued a 180-page report in 1991 that predicts the demise of broadcast TV unless existing regulations are relaxed or eliminated so that the medium can compete more effectively in the expanding marketplace.[1] This report, referred to as the "Pepper Report" after OPP Chief Robert Pepper, contends that over-the-air television has suffered an "irreversible decline" as a result of lost audiences and revenue shares brought on by cable television and home satellite dishes. The report says that small

UHF stations will likely be the big losers and many will go dark. The report recommends that the FCC eliminate the multiple ownership rules and that Congress eliminate broadcast/cable cross-ownership rules. The report is also critical of network affiliate regulations.

In response to the "Pepper Report," the FCC, in the summer of 1991, initiated an inquiry in which it sought comments from the public on the changing video marketplace. The inquiry focused on the increasing competition in and fragmentation of the video marketplace and technological advances, such as digital signal compression techniques. Digital compression would allow wide bandwidth signals, like the 23 MHz required for non-compressed HDTV, to be accommodated in the existing 6 MHz bandwidth presently allocated for broadcast television. The inquiry also focused on the ability of some competitors in the video industry to rely on revenue from direct viewer payment in lieu of or in addition to advertising and the growing increase in the availability of national sources of programming.

Convergence

Convergence is the disintegration of distinctions between different technologies. New combinations of technologies have emerged and promise to challenge the way the electronic media are regulated. In the 1980s, computers and digital technologies blended with traditional broadcast technology. This convergence will accelerate in the 1990s. CD ROM—laser disks that store and retrieve video information—break down the differences between the role of the computer and the television set. The TV becomes a computer and the computer becomes a TV. HDTV may transform the living room into the "media room"—a true home movie theater with "surround-sound." Fiber optic cables will further blur the distinction between the telephone, television, and computer as video is transmitted into the home via telephone lines.

As media converge, old rules and policies will have to be discarded. Regulators will be forced to decide whether the marketplace will really decide which electronic media survive and which go the way of the Betamax recorder, or which are to be artificially protected by regulation.

The FCC's Agenda in the "Age of Knowledge"

FCC Chairman Alfred Sikes articulated a policy in the early 1990s that embraced the convergence of electronic media technologies. Sikes described the electronic media landscape in 1991 as a "seminal point" and a "new generation in the information age." He envisions the "information age" of the 1980s giving way to the "age of knowledge" in the 1990s.[2]

In order to reach the "age of knowledge" Sikes would remove those regulations that are barriers to open competition between various portions of the telecommunications industry. Examples of rules inhibiting broadcasters are the multiple ownership, cross-ownership, duopoly, and one-to-a customer rules. Cable and other non-broadcast delivery systems are not subject to these restrictions. Therefore, broadcasters are placed at an economic disadvantage.

The cable compulsory license has also been cited as a regulation that hampers the economic survival of over-the-air broadcasting. FCC Chairman Alfred Sikes believes that the compulsory license provides a disincentive for over-the-air broadcasters to produce quality programs. Since broadcasters bear the major financial risk in program production, and cable television piggybacks on the effort, Sikes sees an eventual end to broadcast-produced programs unless the rules are repealed.[3]

The ideal result of this revised policy will be a communications environment in which telephone companies offer television programs and video services via fiber optic cable. Cable companies may also offer services now only provided by phone companies. Over-the-air broadcasting will be freed of regulations inhibiting its ability to compete in the marketplace. HDTV will be the standard, with more than 400 channels available to the viewer. The wall-sized, flat-screened TV will serve as a television, CD player, computer, CD ROM reference source, video telephone, and more. The electronic media center will be interactive as well, allowing individuals, in the words of former FCC Commissioner Nicholas Johnson, to "talk back to their television sets."

Anticipated Regulatory Activity

High Definition Television

Testing of six different HDTV systems began in the spring of 1991. The FCC plans to select a single system for implementation by 1993. The Commission plans to grant each existing television station a second channel in its market so that stations may broadcast an HDTV signal on one channel, while continuing NTSC (standard) television broadcasting on its original channel. Eventually, the NTSC channel will be phased out and the spectrum space reallocated for a different use.

It appears that HDTV will be treated as an upgrade of an existing service. This means that current broadcasters will be allocated an HDTV channel in the UHF band (470–890 MHz).

Spectrum Reallocation

HDTV and proposed DAB will require a great deal of spectrum space. When these systems are added to the growing number of other spectrum users, like cellular telephones, radio broadcasters, pocket pagers, MMDS, and even garage door openers, the crowding problem becomes enormous. In the fall of 1991 the FCC began to tackle the spectrum problem by expanding the AM band to reduce interference caused by crowding too many stations into too small an area. The FCC will continue to study ways in which the spectrum can be managed more efficiently.

Alternatives include options from digital compression techniques, which allow more signals to be squeezed into less space, to actually deleting some services. Ideally, voluntary reallocation of existing services seems the best policy. If existing services cannot be reallocated, then compensation for frequency loss would seem in order.

One possible target has been UHF television on the high end. In one study, the FCC found that the effect of taking a UHF station off the air in Los Angeles and replacing it with a cellular telephone service was cost-effective. The implementation of an additional cellular phone service would have resulted in a 25% price cut in cellular service because of increased competition. The social cost through the year 2000 would save the city of Los Angeles $892 million. The social cost of losing the UHF station was calculated to be $139 million. The net gain of reallocating the spectrum in this hypothetical situation was $754 million.[4]

Another possible means of freeing spectrum space might be to use fiber optic telco lines to deliver video services, and telephone and other personal communications services. Of course, a radical move such as this would require a great deal of legislative debate and subsequent regulatory activity, which may lead to a change in the hardware needed to implement these services.

Legislation came before Congress in late 1991 that provided for the transfer of 200 MHz of government-controlled spectrum space to the private sector for use by new technologies such as HDTV, DAB, and PCS.

Deregulation of Broadcasting

Deregulation of broadcasting continues to be a stated policy of the FCC. However, it is conceptually different than the deregulation of the 1980s. Under the Sikes commission, deregulatory activity has been aimed at relaxing multiple ownership and cable/broadcast cross-ownership rules in the hope that these moves will allow broadcasters to compete more effectively in the multichannel environment. Sikes' attic-to-basement review of existing regulations was undertaken with this goal in mind. While deregulation continues, enforcement of existing rules has been stepped up.

The 1991 fin-syn rules gave the networks much less of a break in program syndication than Chairman Sikes would have liked. A reexamination of the rules is likely and relaxation of those rules is a strong possibility.

Telco Entry into the Video Marketplace

The modified final judgment (MFJ) in 1984 set the terms for the breakup of AT&T. The MFJ prohibited the seven regional Bell operating companies (RBOCs) (which are Ameritech, Bell Atlantic, Bell South, NYNEX, Pacific Telesis,

Southwestern Bell, and U.S. West) from engaging in information services. These services included video newspapers, video classified ads, and video program services outside their regional service areas. In 1991, District Court Judge Harold Greene lifted the ban on information services. The decision is under review by the U.S. court of appeals, but it is likely to be upheld.

In July 1992 the FCC relaxed the ban on cable-telco cross-ownership and allowed telephone companies to distribute video programming to households. Telephone companies are permitted to transmit video programming without having to obtain a municipal franchise as required for cable systems.

Under the "video dialtone" plan, telcos may acquire up to 5% equity interest in and provide financing for program services they offer. However, they may not set prices, own, or exercise editorial control over programming.

Under the Cable Act of 1984, telcos may not own co-located cable systems and are limited to a common carrier relationship with program producers. The FCC has recommended that Congress repeal the telco-cable cross-ownership ban.[5]

Interactive Video

In March 1991, the FCC issued a Notice of Proposed Rule Making that modified Part 95 of the FCC Rules establishing Interactive Video Data Service (IVDS) as a personal radio service. The FCC authorized the service in early 1992.

IVDS would allow television viewers to interact with television programming. Viewers could access over-the-air television, cable, pay-per-view, and direct broadcast satellite services. They could also perform electronic banking, home shopping, and video mail activities by using this service. IVDS systems can be provided by cable, fiber optic lines, or over the air.

The system authorized by the FCC is an over-the-air system. Program providers distribute services via satellite, which are downlinked to cell sites around the country and relayed to subscribing households over the air. The two-way service is accomplished by reversing this process. The FCC proposed to assign 500 kHz of spectrum in the 218–218.5 MHz band for IVDS.

The rule making was initiated in response to a petition filed by TV Answer, Inc., purveyor of an IVDS service (see Figure 13.1). TV Answer Inc. planned to make IVDS services available to subscribers for $12.95 per month. Subscribers are given a set-top unit and remote control keypad (see Figure 13.2) which enable interaction with vendors. Viewers would choose services with the help of a menu screen.[6] In the fall of 1991, TV Answer, Inc., signed a contract with Hughes Network Systems for distribution of its interactive service.

In years to come, the FCC will probably create several hundred service areas nationwide for interactive services (similar to that which exists for cellular telephone service). Current plans call for two licenses per service area. TV Answer, Inc., expects service to begin in 1993.[7]

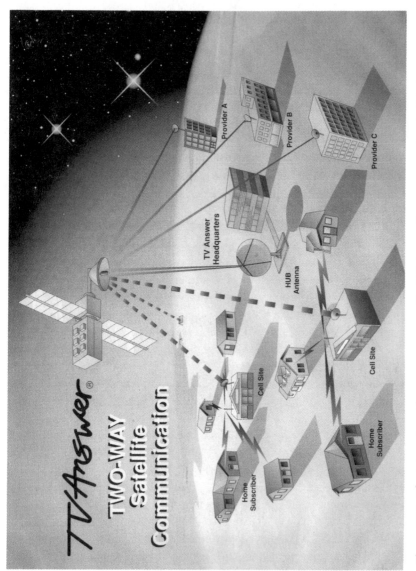

Figure 13.1 The interactive video system proposed by TV Answer Inc. is an over-the-air digital system. Viewer data will be transmitted via satellite to local calls that consist of about 10,000 homes.

Figure 13.2 In a proposed interactive video system data is received and transmitted to and from each home through the use of a wireless set-top unit and hand-held remote cursor control device.

Other Distribution Systems

The changing technological climate promises new challenges for electronic media regulation in both traditional and nontraditional forms of information distribution. Developing technologies like MMDS, wireless cable, and DBS may either be poised for wider acceptance or face extinction, depending on congressional and FCC policy. In the summer of 1991, Congress struggled with the question of whether MMDS was "cable" as defined by the Copyright Act and the Cable Act of 1984. Congress may conclude that the compulsory license does not apply to MMDS. Wireless cable would suffer because it would be unable to clear copyrighted material for transmission to subscribers.

Direct broadcast satellites (DBS) have been a potential means of program distribution in the United States since the early 1980s. But, unlike in Europe and Japan, DBS have remained a stalled technology in the United States. Again, regulatory policy could change that. Perhaps HDTV and DAB will provide the impetus for the realization of DBS. However, it appears that both systems will be terrestrial-based at this time. Presently DBS, while technically feasible, are neither economically nor politically practical. Implementation of the service would require consumers to purchase new hardware to receive the service. Broadcasters and cablecasters would be hurt economically, since DBS would further erode the existing systems' share of the audience.

As audiences of local affiliates continue to fragment, the traditional television networks may expand their role as program producers by distributing their wares on alternate technologies. For example, networks may produce programs for distribution by cable or DBS.

Ultimately, Commission policy toward over-the-air stations will determine their ultimate fate and the pace of new technology integration. If, as appears to be the case, the FCC adopts a protective attitude toward broadcasters, alternative distribution systems will be slow to develop.

Where Is It Going?

It is impossible at this point to predict with certainty which technologies will dominate. However fiber optic cable and high-definition television are likely to be major players. The lines marking the differences between the computer, television set, and telephone will converge. When we emerge on the other side of the 1990s, we will see a landscape quite different from what exists today. It would seem that the development of a regulatory model that promotes diversity of information sources within the framework of the First Amendment would satisfy society's needs.

Henry Geller, a senior fellow with the Annenberg Washington Program in Communications Policy Studies, argues that the present broadcast and cable regulatory models cannot be applied to developing technologies. Geller states,

> The Regulatory model that has best served the diversity of information
> sources in the U.S. is the print model, combined with common carrier delivery (e.g., magazines, newsletters, etc., delivered by mail carriers or facsimile).
> This model can now be adopted for television because of the rapidly increasing
> involvement of local telephone companies in fiber optic transmission.[8]

While fiber optic cable to the home is Geller's choice for video delivery, the common carrier model may be applied to other new technologies as well. DBS, wireless cable (MMDS), and even traditional broadcasting may benefit from this approach to regulation and allow each system to provide diverse communications services to the public. Certainly, as the "Pepper Report" indicates, broadcasters must be able to compete with the new technologies if they are to survive. Additionally, the newer technologies will require a certain amount of freedom from regulation in order to develop their services. It would seem that the print/common carrier model suggested by Geller is best suited to the development of future communications services.

Certainly, all regulation of the electronic media will not disappear. Libel, invasion of privacy, and Sixth Amendment issues will remain. They will, under the common carrier model, be judged against First Amendment values. Protection against fraudulent practices, obscenity, and antitrust by the media will also require regulation. But the content and ownership regulations now faced by broadcasters and cablecasters will probably disappear.

Notes/References

1. See *Broadcast Television in a Multichannel Marketplace*. Washington, D.C.: FCC, Office of Plans and Policy, 1991.
2. Paul Farhi, "Alfred Sikes's Mission at the FCC", *The Washington Post* (June 3, 1991) *National Weekly Edition*, p. 7.
3. "Sikes: Repeal Compulsory License, Take Another Look at PTAR," *Broadcasting* (January 27, 1992): 14.
4. "So Many New Technologies, So Little Space," *Broadcasting* (May 6, 1991): 52.
5. Harry A. Jessell, "FCC Calls For Telco TV," *Broadcasting* (July 20, 1992): 3.
6. Information obtained from *TV Answer Inc.*, 1941 Roland Clarke Place, Reston, VA 22091.
7. "TV Answer Puts Money Down on Infrastructure for Interactive Consumer Service," *Broadcasting* (September 30, 1991): 46.
8. Henry Geller, *Fiber Optics: An Opportunity for a New Policy* (Washington, DC: The Annenberg Washington Program, 1991), 6.

Notice of Inquiry: Increasing Competition in and Fragmentation of the Video Marketplace

6 FCC Rcd No. 17   **Federal Communications Commission Record**   FCC 91-215

Before the
Federal Communications Commission
Washington, D.C. 20554

MM Docket No. 91-221

In the Matter of

Review of the Policy Implications
of the Changing Video Marketplace

NOTICE OF INQUIRY

Adopted: July 11, 1991;   Released: August 7, 1991

Comment Date: October 22, 1991
Reply Comment Date: November 21, 1991

By the Commission: Commissioners Quello, Barrett, and Duggan issuing separate statements.

1. We initiate this proceeding in order to seek wide-ranging comments on changes in the state of the video marketplace and the public policy implications that flow from these changes. This inquiry is prompted by our general concern that some of our television rules and policies may no longer be in step with current industry circumstances and, more particularly, by a number of apparent trends described in a recent Office of Plans and Policy (OPP) staff working paper on the status of the video marketplace.[1]

2. We focus our inquiry on the implications of the findings of the OPP paper, including: 1) the increasing competition in, and fragmentation of, the video marketplace; 2) technological advances such as digital signal compression techniques; 3) the ability of some new competitors to rely on revenue from direct viewer payment instead of, or in addition to, advertising; and 4) the rapid increase in the availability of national sources of programming. We believe that these changes have significant implications for core Commission goals such as localism, diversity, nationwide availability of service, and the public interest standard for broadcasters. We seek general comments concerning the staff's findings and analysis about trends and changes in the video marketplace. If commenters disagree with respect to the conclusions and projections of the staff study, we request that they offer specific evidence to support alternative conclusions. If commenters agree, we request that they provide specific evidence and analysis supporting their position and the relevant policy implications. We also ask commenters to address what steps, if any, we should take to ensure that our policies and rules continue to promote the Commission's goals of localism, diversity, nationwide availability, and broadcasting in the public interest.

**INCREASING COMPETITION IN, AND
FRAGMENTATION OF, THE VIDEO MARKETPLACE**

3. At the outset, we note that television broadcasting now exists in an environment significantly more competitive than in years past and likely to be even more competitive in the years ahead. The statistics in this regard are well known. In 1975, the U.S. had three commercial broadcast networks and no cable networks; cable television was largely a broadcast retransmission medium. By 1990, there were over 100 national and regional cable networks and a major new broadcast network was developing. Cable subscribership rose from 17 percent of television households in 1975 to over 56 percent in 1990; cable now passes over 90 percent of television households. The number of broadcast stations increased by 50 percent over that 15 year period, with independent stations accounting for over three-fourths of that growth. The number of off air stations available to the median household increased from six in 1975 to ten in 1990, and by 1990, 94 percent of television households were located in markets with five or more television stations. In 1975, home videocassette recorders (VCRs) were rare and there were no home satellite dish systems; in 1990, 69 percent of television households owned VCRs and three percent had home satellite dishes.

4. This expansion in the availability of outlets and programming has markedly reduced the audience shares of the broadcast networks and their affiliates. The percentages of prime time viewing of the three major networks dropped from 73 percent in 1982-83 to 58 percent in 1989-90;[2] viewing of cable-originated programming rose from 10 to 20 percent in that period. While each broadcast network still retains a prime time audience share roughly equal to that of all cable networks combined, it appears likely that satellite services such as direct broadcast satellite (DBS), increasingly well-financed cable programming services, and greater cable television channel capacity will perpetuate these trends of the last fifteen years into the 1990s.

5. Although regulation attempts to correct market imperfections, it also serves to further public interest goals not strictly limited to purely economic forces. These dual purposes for regulation must be balanced in any review of changing market conditions. To the extent that certain Commission regulations and policies were adopted to respond to problems created by limitations on entry and concentration of control, such regulation should reflect the amount of diversity and competition that exists and any remaining barriers to entry. Accordingly, we seek comment on the implications of the growth of competition in the video marketplace for our regulatory policies, including:

(1) What is the long-term forecast for these current trends, and any identifiable countervailing trends, in viewing choices and their implications for broadcast television?

---

[1] Office of Plans and Policy Working Paper # 26. *Broadcast Television in a Multichannel Marketplace*, DA 91-817, 6 FCC Rcd 3996 (1991) ("OPP paper").
[2] *See* OPP paper, p. 28, Table 8. We also note that, while the total number of television households increased from 70 million in 1975 to 93 million in 1990, over this period the number of homes reached by the three major networks in prime time declined from 36.9 million to 32.7 million. *Id.* at p. 26, Table 7.

(2) What are the policy implications of a continued decline in the viewing shares of broadcast television networks? Are the effects of declining audience shares mitigated by the continued increase in the total number of television households?

(3) What impact will increased competition have on local broadcast stations, whether network affiliates or independents, and how will this affect their share of advertising revenues? Will increased competition for advertising revenues have an impact on their programming, including local programming?

(4) Which Commission policies and regulations, if any, hamper the ability of the networks, their affiliates, or independents to compete with multichannel delivery systems?

(5) Do our ownership rules, for example, prevent realization of economies of scale and limit program investment which might otherwise promote the vitality of local stations?

(6) To what extent should the number of competing programming choices provided by cable television and satellite services affect our broadcast multiple ownership policies, consistent with diversity and other public interest goals?

(7) If changes are proposed to the broadcast multiple ownership or crossownership rules, what effect will such proposals have on the traditional concerns for diversity embodied in the Commission's public interest mandate?

(8) To what extent, if any, might changes in ownership rules permit broadcasters to increase investments in programming that would increase diversity?

TECHNOLOGY

6. Technology and economics have combined in recent years to change the face of video distribution in the United States. The principal changes that have taken place involve expansion in the availability and channel capacity of multichannel video service providers, in particular increases in cable availability and channel capacity and the development of a market for direct-to-home satellite service. Other important developments include widespread ownership and use of home video recording and playback systems, and use of hand-held television remote control devices.

7. Other technological changes, in particular the development and refinement of digital video compression technologies, could be even more revolutionary in their consequences in the years ahead. Compression systems, which are likely to be used first in conjunction with satellite program delivery and then on cable systems, also hold the potential for increasing the channel capacity of terrestrial broadcasting systems. Dramatic increases in channel capacity will be possible through the implementation of this technology. In addition, increased use of currently available technologies, including addressability and interactivity, which allow viewers to select specific programming or send messages for transactions such as home shopping and banking, could permit enhanced service offerings.

8. With respect to these and other new technological changes, we ask:

(1) At what point will technologies with compression capabilities become a competitive factor in the marketplace? What type of market penetration is projected for such video services?

(2) Are any existing Commission technical, ownership or other regulations likely to have a negative effect on the development and widespread use of these technologies? Are there technical rules that could be modified to increase the competitiveness of broadcast television stations vis-a-vis multichannel providers?

(3) Does the combination of these ongoing technological developments plus existing Commission regulations have any positive or negative implications for the widespread availability of video service? For example, what will be the impact on broadcast television if video compression techniques are introduced first by satellite and cable systems, as expected?

(4) What are the implications, if any, of these technological changes for the diversity of video programming and editorial viewpoints?

(5) What are the implications of these technological changes for provision of locally produced or originated versus nationally produced service to viewers?

(6) To what extent will broadcast licensees, particularly those who own a single or small group of stations, be able to participate in these technological changes and enhance their local service? How do such changes implicate the Commission goal of localism embodied in Section 307(b) of the Communications Act?

(7) More generally, in what ways, if any, will these changes affect the ability of the Commission to carry out its mandate to regulate broadcasting and other ancillary services "in the public interest?"

RELIANCE ON DUAL REVENUE STREAMS

9. One of the most significant trends in the economics of video distribution in recent years is the change from advertising as virtually the sole revenue source for distributors to an environment in which a significant portion of distributors receive both advertising and direct consumer revenues. The primary example of this phenomenon, the cable industry, derives revenues from both subscription fees and advertising sales. Indeed, pay and pay-perview services derive their revenues solely from viewer payment. A satellite DBS provider would also be able to capture these dual revenue sources. The television broadcasting industry, on the other hand, has almost uniformly derived revenue solely from advertising sales, directly or through network compensation.

10. We seek comment on the implications of this development for our regulatory policies:

(1) What are the implications of increased specialization as a competitive programming strategy for the single-channel broadcaster? What practical and legal impediments would affect the ability of a broadcaster to follow a niche programming strategy?

6 FCC Rcd No. 17   **Federal Communications Commission Record**   FCC 91-215

(2) Is multichannel transmission capability or the ability to deliver a specialized program service the only means to attain dual revenue streams?

(3) What are the projections for advertising revenue growth during the next decade? Will local broadcasters experience a net growth or net loss in advertising revenue during this same period? To what extent do underlying economic conditions in the national and local market affect this analysis?

(4) To what extent would the loss of advertising revenues to competitive media services affect a broadcast licensee's ability to provide local service? To the extent local broadcast service is diminished, what are the implications for local services provided by other competitive media outlets? What are the implications for the system of local stations fostered by Commission policies and Section 307(b) of the Communications Act?

(5) Would repeal of the compulsory license for cable television and/or implementation of a scheme of retransmission consent enable local stations to compete more effectively?[3]

(6) Does viewer payment for programming affect the diversity of voices, both broadcast and non-broadcast, available in local video markets? How are broadcast viewers who do not pay directly for programming affected by the growth of pay program services? What are the implications for our current regulatory framework for over-the-air broadcasting?

CHANGES IN DISTRIBUTION AND SUPPLY OF VIDEO PROGRAMMING AT THE NATIONAL LEVEL

11. As the number of local video programming outlets has increased, so have the sources of and distributors of national television programming. As space satellite relay systems have replaced microwave routes as the principal technology for delivery of programming to local broadcast stations, programs increasingly are available nationwide rather than on a local or regional basis. Starting in 1975, programmers to the cable television industry began using satellite relay systems to deliver programming for cable use. Today satellites are used not only to relay numerous channels of video programming to cable systems within the U.S. (and around the world) but to deliver network and syndicated programming to both regular and low power television stations.

12. In terms of audience, each of the three major broadcast networks still attracts larger audiences than any other individual source. Nevertheless, the sources of supply to local video outlets are becoming increasingly competitive; new broadcast and cable networks are developing and new sources of news and syndicated programming have come into being. These developments, in conjunction with other changes in the marketplace, will affect our understanding of how the video marketplace functions

and the rules and policies that should apply to the various participants. We seek to explore and obtain comment on these consequences through this proceeding.

13. In particular, we seek comment on:

(1) What changes can be anticipated in the sources and supply of video programming at the national level?

(2) To what extent will competition to broadcast television, particularly by cable networks and their cable system affiliates. change the relationships between suppliers of broadcast programming and local television broadcast stations? Will new sources of supply and competition loosen the relationship between networks and their affiliates or will it create pressure for a closer partnership between them?

OTHER ISSUES

14. In addition to comments on the changing video marketplace structure and the Commission policies and rules specifically raised in this notice, we welcome comment on any other events, policies, or rules that may be implicated by our general inquiry into the future of the video marketplace. In this regard, commenters may also wish to address whether changing the multiple ownership rules impacts any prior Commission decisions that deleted or modified rules or policies which were based upon the principles of diversity, localism, or the number of broadcast television outlets in the market.

PROCEDURAL MATTERS

A. Ex Parte Rules - Exempt Proceeding

15. This proceeding is exempt from the *ex parte* requirements pursuant to 47 C.F.R. § 1.1204(a)(4).

B. Comment Dates

16. Pursuant to applicable procedures set forth in Sections 1.415 and 1.419 of the Commission's Rules, 47 C.F.R. §§ 1.415 and 1.419, interested parties may file comments on or before October 22, 1991, and reply comments on or before November 21, 1991. To file formally in this proceeding, you must file an original and five copies of all comments, reply comments, and supporting comments. If you want each Commissioner to receive a personal copy of your comments, you must file an original plus nine copies. You should send comments and reply comments to the Office of the Secretary, Federal Communications Commission, Washington, D.C. 20554. Comments and reply comments will be available for public inspection during regular business hours in the Dockets Reference Room of the Federal Communications Commission, 1919 M Street, N.W., Washington, D.C. 20554.

C. Additional Information

---

[3] The related issue of must carry is the subject of the *Report and Order and Second Further Notice of Proposed Rule Making* in MM Docket Nos. 90-4 and 84-1296, FCC 91-184, 56 FR 33387, 33414 (July 22, 1991).

FCC 91-215   **Federal Communications Commission Record**   6 FCC Rcd No. 17

For additional information on this proceeding, contact
Beverly McKittrick, Mass Media Bureau, (202) 632-5414.

FEDERAL COMMUNICATIONS COMMISSION

Donna R. Searcy
Secretary

6 FCC Rcd No. 17   Federal Communications Commission Record   FCC 91-215

STATEMENT OF COMMISSIONER JAMES H. QUELLO ON
REVIEW OF THE POLICY IMPLICATIONS OF THE CHANGING VIDEO MARKETPLACE

They say that in life timing is everything, and I think it is a particularly appropriate time right now to take a comprehensive look at our policies relating to television. The video marketplace is going through changes as significant as any in its history, and it is incumbent upon the Commission, as the expert agency, to monitor these changes and adjust its policies accordingly.

First, I want to congratulate the staff of the Office of Plans and Policy for their most impressive effort in producing a thought-provoking study on which many of the NOI questions are based. This study is an excellent starting point for our inquiry.

I want to emphasize, however, that the study is just that — a starting point. It has not yet been adopted by the Commission or tested by the adversarial give and take that we expect from the commenters in this proceeding. Consequently, any interpretations in the popular press about the FCC predicting the demise of broadcasting are more than a little premature. We are just beginning the inquiry.

But you don't have to predict the end of broadcasting as we know it to understand that some of our rules no longer relate to the reality of the video marketplace. I believe I made my feelings on this point clear in my dissenting statement in the financial interest and syndication rules proceeding. *Evaluation of the Syndication and Financial Interest Rules*, FCC 91-114 (released May 29, 1991) (dissenting statement). The finsyn rules were adopted during a time of near-absolute network dominance — a fact that has changed drastically during the intervening two decades. In my mind, there can be no justification for retaining rules long after their policy purposes have vanished, especially if the rules hamper the viability of a competitor in the video marketplace. In particular, I think it is time to review the effect of cross-ownership rules on free over-the-air television.

In this regard, the present inquiry presents a much needed opportunity to look at a broad range of policies to determine which ones are still needed, which ones are not, and which ones are counterproductive in terms of the public interest. I am looking forward to reading the comments in this most important proceeding.

SEPARATE STATEMENT
OF
COMMISSIONER ANDREW C. BARRETT

RE: REVIEW OF THE POLICY IMPLICATIONS OF
THE CHANGING VIDEO MARKETPLACE

I look forward to reviewing the comments which will be filed in response to issues raised in this Notice of Inquiry. As I have stated before with respect to our radio "attic to basement" review, periodically the Commission should examine its rules to ensure that they comport with marketplace realities. However, I wish to emphasize, that such reviews must be taken in a balanced manner. In the media area, I believe our regulations exist not only to address market imbalances, but also to address public interest concerns that may or may not be in the best economic self-interest of broadcast licensees. These dual purposes for regulation in the media area should be addressed when analyzing changing market conditions. To the extent that certain Commission regulations and policies were adopted to respond to problems of limitation on entry or concentration of control, I believe such regulations should continue to bear some relationship to: (1) the amount of competition that exists; (2) the remaining barriers to entry; and, (3) the relative diversification of control within segments of the marketplace. To the extent certain Commission regulations were adopted to respond to overarching public interest concerns, I believe that a review of changing market conditions or technologies must also address the implications for these concerns.

In this Notice of Inquiry, I encourage industry members, trade associations, and public interest groups to address the implications of changing technologies on the future of local broadcast stations. I particularly look forward to reviewing comments with respect to the implications of any proposed multiple ownership rule changes on our traditional concerns for diversity and localism. In this regard, I hope that commenters not only address the implications of such changes on traditional First Amendment or diversity concerns, but also comment on the extent to which such changes impact upon the rationale for prior Commission decisions to abolish the Fairness Doctrine or community ascertainment requirements. Finally, I look forward to comments from those who own a single station or a small group of stations as to their ability to participate in future technological and economic changes projected in the OPP working paper.[1]

FOOTNOTE TO THE STATEMENT

[1] F. Setzer & J. Levy, OPP Working Paper 26, *Broadcast Television in a Multichannel Marketplace* (FCC June 1991). I also desire additional input on the economic projections provided in the OPP paper. As I have stated before, the OPP paper is one of several inputs I will look at in making any decisions in this docket.

Separate Statement
of
Commissioner Ervin S. Duggan

In Re: Notice of Inquiry -- Review of the Policy Implications of the Changing Video Marketplace

As I have said in the past, I fully support reviewing the Commission's television rules and policies in light of new realities. Such a review seems to me well-founded, in view of the Staff Working Paper produced by the Office of Plans and Policy: the most thorough recent analysis of the video marketplace.

I fervently hope that the gloomy predictions offered by this paper turn out to be wrong. If we hope to prove them wrong, however, and to shape a happier future for broadcast television, we need to remember one important fact: the fate of the broadcast industry will not be shaped at 20th and M Streets. Regulation is important, but the greatest power to shape the destiny of broadcasting is in the hands of broadcasters themselves: in their courage, their imagination, their agility, their shrewdness. It is far more important, in my judgment, that broadcasters respond vigorously to the change in the marketplace than for the FCC merely to put more stations in the hands of a few owners.

Broadcasters need to invent a whole new future. They need, as never before, to innovate: to launch a new era of research, technical innovation, and imaginative programming. Broadcasters should be creating new services and forging new alliances that will expand their channel capacity and energize their programming. Where, for example, are broadcasters when it comes to exploiting the tantalizing possibilities of interactive television?

It has become a truism that the future belongs to those who know how to produce great programming. Surely the worst thing that could happen now is for broadcasters to respond to new challenges by cutting back drastically on high quality entertainment and local programming, the very thing that has distinguished the broadcast medium in the past.

I was struck by two themes that emerged, again and again, in the recent obituaries of actor-producer Michael Landon. One was that every show he was involved with turned out to be a hit. The other was that every show he was involved with was one that parents and children could sit down and enjoy together. Perhaps this connection is no accident. What does it profit broadcasters to seek "breakthrough" concepts in programming--- if the breakthroughs are to the lowest common denominator of taste and values?

Ever since joining the Commission, I have been troubled by the asymmetry between our regulation of broadcasting and multichannel video industries. We expect broadcasters to continue serving the public interest while competing for ever more scarce advertising revenues. Broadcasters' competitors, on the other hand, are not so constrained when it comes to regulation, to revenue streams, or to channel capacity.

In light of broadcasters' long history of public service, I want to do all that I can to help broadcasters compete in the future video world. I am eager to remove old regulatory barriers, if they prove to be unnecessary. But broadcasters' ultimate fate, I am convinced, lies in their own hands and minds. So I will be interested, as we examine what we must do for broadcasting, to see what broadcasting is doing for itself.

FCC Forms

Federal Communications Commission
Washington, D.C. 20554

APPLICATION FOR RENEWAL OF LICENSE FOR
COMMERCIAL AND NONCOMMERCIAL AM, FM OR TV BROADCAST STATION

Approved by OMB
3060-0110
Expires 5/31/91

For Commission Fee Use Only	
	FEE NO:
	FEE TYPE:
	FEE AMT:
	ID SEQ:

For Commission Use Only: File No.

For Applicant Fee Use Only

Is a fee submitted with this application?   ☐ Yes ☐ No

If No, indicate reason therefor (check one box):
☐ Nonfeeable application

Fee Exempt (See 47 C.F.R. Section 1.1112)

☐ Noncommercial educational licensee
☐ Governmental entity

---

1. Name of Applicant

Mailing Address

City	State	ZIP Code

2. This application is for: ☐ AM ☐ FM ☐ TV

(a) Call Letters:	(b) Principal Community:
	City State

3. Attach as Exhibit No. _____ an identification of any FM booster or TV booster station for which renewal of license is also requested.

4. Have the following reports been filed with the Commission:

(a) The Broadcast Station Annual Employment Reports (FCC Form 395-B) as required by 47 C.F.R. Section 73.3612?   ☐ Yes ☐ No

If No, attach as Exhibit No. _____ an explanation.

(b) The applicant's Ownership Report (FCC Form 323 or 323-E) as required by 47 C.F.R. Section 73.3615?   ☐ Yes ☐ No

If No, give the following information:
Date last ownership report was filed   _____
Call letters of station for which it was filed   _____

FCC 303-S
May 1988

5. Is the applicant in compliance with the provisions of Section 310 of the Communications Act of 1934, as amended, relating to interests of aliens and foreign governments?   ☐ Yes ☐ No

   If No, attach as Exhibit No. _____ an explanation.

6. Since the filing of the applicant's last renewal application for this station or other major application, has an adverse finding been made or final action been taken by any court or administrative body with respect to the applicant or parties to the application in a civil or criminal proceeding, brought under the provisions of any law relating to the following: any felony; broadcast related antitrust or unfair competition; criminal fraud or fraud before another governmental unit; or discrimination?   ☐ Yes ☐ No

   If Yes, attach as Exhibit No. _____ a full description of the persons and matters involved, including an identification of the court or administrative body and the proceeding (by dates and file numbers) and the disposition of the litigation.

7. Would a Commission grant of this application come within 47 C.F.R. Section 1.1307, such that it may have a significant environmental impact?   ☐ Yes ☐ No

   If Yes, attach as Exhibit No. _____ an Environmental Assessment required by 47 C.F.R. Section 1.1311.

   If No, explain briefly why not.

8. Has the applicant placed in its station's public inspection file at the appropriate times the documentation required by 47 C.F.R. Sections 73.3526 or 73.3527?   ☐ Yes ☐ No

   If No, attach as Exhibit No. _____ a complete statement of explanation.

The APPLICANT hereby waives any claim to the use of any particular frequency or of the electromagnetic spectrum as against the regulatory power of the United States because of the previous use of the same, whether by license or otherwise, and requests an authorization in accordance with this application. (See Section 304 of the Communications Act of 1934, as amended.)

The APPLICANT acknowledges that all the statements made in this application and attached exhibits are considered material representations and that all the exhibits are a material part hereof and are incorporated herein as set out in full in the application.

CERTIFICATION: I certify that the statements in this application are true, complete, and correct to the best of my knowledge and belief, and are made in good faith.

Name	Signature
Title	Date

WILLFUL FALSE STATEMENTS MADE ON THIS FORM ARE PUNISHABLE BY FINE AND IMPRISONMENT.   U.S. CODE, TITLE 18, SECTION 1001.

Federal Communications Commission
Washington, D.C. 20554

Instructions for FCC 301
Application for Construction Permit for Commercial Broadcast Station
(FCC Form 301 attached)

GENERAL INSTRUCTIONS

A. This FCC form is to be used to apply for authority to construct a new commercial AM, FM or TV broadcast station, or to make changes in the existing facilities of such a station. It consists of the following sections:

    I.   GENERAL INFORMATION
    II.   LEGAL QUALIFICATIONS
    III.   FINANCIAL QUALIFICATIONS
    IV-A.   PROGRAM SERVICE STATEMENT
    IV-B.   INTEGRATION STATEMENT
    V.   ENGINEERING DATA AND ANTENNA AND SITE INFORMATION
    VI.   EQUAL EMPLOYMENT OPPORTUNITY PROGRAM
    VII.   CERTIFICATIONS

    An applicant for change in facilities need file only Sections I, V and VII. Do not file Sections II, III, IV-A, IV-B and VI.

B. Many references to FCC Rules are made in this application form. Before filling it out, the applicant should have on hand and be familiar with current broadcast rules in 47 Code of Federal Regulations (C.F.R.):

    (1) Part 0   "Commission Organization"
    (2) Part 1   "Practice and Procedure"
    (3) Part 17   "Construction, Marking and Lighting of Antenna Structure"
    (4) Part 73   "Radio Broadcast Services"

    FCC Rules may be purchased from the Government Printing Office, Washington, D.C. 20402. You may telephone the GPO Order desk at (202) 783-3238 for current prices.

C. Prepare an original and two copies of this form and all exhibits. This application with all required exhibits should be filed with the FCC's Washington, D.C. office in accordance with 47 C.F.R. Section 0.401.

D. By law, the Commission is required to collect charges for certain of the regulatory services it provides to the public. Generally, applicants seeking to construct a new commercial AM, FM or TV broadcast station or to make changes in the authorized facilities of such a station are required to pay and submit a fee with the filing of the application. See 47 C.F.R. Section 1.1112. A listing of the required charges is set forth in 47 C.F.R. Section 1.1104. Full payment of the required fee may be made by check, bank draft or money order payable to the Federal Communications Commission. An application submitted with an insufficient payment or with an inappropriate form of payment will be returned, along with the tendered payment, to the applicant without processing. Except for the limited circumstances enumerated in 47 C.F.R. Section 1.1111, an accepted fee payment will be retained by the government irrespective of the subsequent substantive disposition of the underlying application. For further information regarding fees, see 47 C.F.R. Part 1, Subpart G.

E. Public Notice Requirements:

    (1) 47 C.F.R. Section 73.3580 requires that applicants for construction permits for new broadcast stations and major changes in existing facilities (as defined in 47 C.F.R. Sections 73.3571(a)(1) (AM), 73.3572(a)(1) (television), or 73.3573(a)(1) (FM)) give local notice in a newspaper of general circulation in the community to which the station is licensed. This publication requirement also applies with respect to major amendments thereto as defined in 47 C.F.R. Sections 73.3571(b) (AM), 73.3572(b) (television), and 73.3573(b) (FM).

    (2) Completion of publication may occur within 30 days before or after tendering of the application. Compliance or intent to comply with the public notice requirements must be **certified** in Section VII of this application. The information that must be contained in the notice of filing is described in Paragraph (f) of 47 C.F.R. Section 73.3580. Proof of publication need not be filed with this application.

F. A copy of this completed application and all related documents shall be made available for inspection by the public, pursuant to 47 C.F.R. Section 73.3526.

G. Replies to questions in this form and the applicant's statements constitute representations on which the FCC will rely in considering the application. Thus, time and care should be devoted to all replies, which should reflect accurately the applicant's responsible consideration of the questions asked. Include all information called for by this application. If any portions of the application are not applicable, so state. **Defective or incomplete applications will be returned without consideration.** Furthermore, inadvertently accepted applications are also subject to dismissal.

H. In accordance with 47 C.F.R. Section 1.65, the applicant has a **continuing obligation** to advise the Commission, through amendments, of any substantial and significant changes in the information furnished.

I. Amendments to previously filed applications should be prepared and submitted in triplicate (an original and two duplicate copies), signed in the same manner as the original application, and should contain the following information to identify the application being amended:

(1) Applicant's name.

(2) Service (AM, FM or TV).

(3) Call letters or specify new station.

(4) Channel number (FM or TV) or frequency (AM).

(5) Community of license.

(6) File number (if known) of application being amended.

(7) Date of filing of application (if file number not known).

INSTRUCTIONS FOR SECTION I – GENERAL INFORMATION

A. The name of the applicant stated in Section I shall be:

(1) If a corporation, the EXACT corporate name;

(2) If a partnership, the names of all general partners, and the name under which the partnership does business;

(3) If an association, the name of the individual(s) authorized to act on behalf of the association, and the name of the association;

(4) If an individual applicant, the full legal name.

In all other sections of this form, the organization name alone will be sufficient for identification of the applicant.

B. In Section I use the following State abbreviations:

Alabama	AL	Kentucky	KY	Ohio	OH		
Alaska	AK	Louisiana	LA	Oklahoma	OK		
American Samoa	AS	Maine	ME	Oregon	OR		
Arizona	AZ	Marshall Islands	MH	Palau	PW		
Arkansas	AR	Maryland	MD	Pennsylvania	PA		
California	CA	Massachusetts	MA	Puerto Rico	PR		
Colorado	CO	Michigan	MI	Rhode Island	RI		
Connecticut	CT	Minnesota	MN	South Carolina	SC		
Delaware	DE	Mississippi	MS	South Dakota	SD		
District of Columbia	DC	Missouri	MO	Tennessee	TN		
Federal States of		Montana	MT	Texas	TX		
Micronesia	FM	Nebraska	NE	U.S. Minor Outlying			
Florida	FL	Nevada	NV	Islands (etc.)	UM		
Georgia	GA	New Hampshire	NH	Utah	UT		
Guam	GU	New Jersey	NJ	Vermont	VT		
Hawaii	HI	New Mexico	NM	Virginia	VA		
Idaho	ID	New York	NY	Virgin Islands	VI		
Illinois	IL	North Carolina	NC	Washington	WA		
Indiana	IN	North Dakota	ND	West Virginia	WV		
Iowa	IA	Northern Mariana		Wisconsin	WI		
Kansas	KS	Islands	MP	Wyoming	WY		

INSTRUCTIONS FOR SECTION II — LEGAL QUALIFICATIONS

A. As used in Section II, the words "party to this application" have the following meanings:

APPLICANT: The individual or entity seeking the proposed facilities.

INDIVIDUAL APPLICANT: The natural person applying for the facilities in his or her own right.

PARTNERSHIP APPLICANT: All partners, including limited partners. However, limited partners in a limited partnership are not considered parties to the application **IF** the limited partners are not materially involved, directly or indirectly, in the management or operation of the media-related activities of the partnership and the applicant so certifies in response to Question 5(a), Section II. Sufficient insulation of a limited partner for purposes of this certification would be assured if the limited partnership agreement:

(1) specifies that any exempt limited partner (if not a natural person, its directors, officers, partners, etc.) cannot act as an employee of the limited partnership if his or her functions, directly or indirectly, relate to the media enterprises of the company;

(2) bars any exempt limited partner from serving, in any material capacity, as an independent contractor or agent with respect to the partnership's media enterprises;

(3) restricts any exempt limited partner from communicating with the licensee or the general partner on matters pertaining to the day-to-day operations of its business;

(4) empowers the general partner to veto any admissions of additional general partners admitted by vote of the exempt limited partners;

(5) prohibits any exempt limited partner from voting on the removal of a general partner or limits this right to situations where the general partner is subject to bankruptcy proceedings, as described in Sections 402 (4)-(5) of the Revised Uniform Limited Partnership Act, is adjudicated incompetent by a court of competent jurisdiction, or is removed for cause, as determined by an independent party;

(6) bars any exempt limited partner from performing any services to the limited partnership materially relating to its media activities, with the exception of making loans to, or acting as a surety for, the business; and

(7) states, in express terms, that any exempt limited partner is prohibited from becoming actively involved in the management or operation of the media businesses of the partnership.

Notwithstanding conformance of the partnership agreement to these criteria, however, the requisite certification cannot be made if the applicant has actual knowledge of a material involvement of the limited partner in the management or operation of the media-related business of the partnership. In the event that the applicant cannot certify as to the noninvolvement of the limited partners, the limited partners will be considered as parties to this application.

CORPORATE APPLICANT: All officers and directors and each owner of or subscriber to stock accounting for 5% or more of the outstanding votes in the corporation. However, where an individual or a single entity holds more than 50% of the applicant's voting stock, and a simple majority is all that is required to control corporate affairs, other stockholders are not considered parties to this application.

Where a corporation is a party to this application by virtue of its ownership or subscription to 5% or more of the voting stock of the applicant, each of the corporate stockholder's directors and "executive officers (president, vice-president, secretary, treasurer or their equivalents) is considered a party to this application **UNLESS** the applicant submits a statement establishing that an individual director or officer will not exercise authority or influence in areas that will affect the applicant or the proposed station. The applicant should identify the individual by name and title, describe the individual's duties and responsibilities, and explain why that person should not be attributed an interest in the corporate applicant or considered a party to this application. In addition, a person or entity holding an ownership interest in the corporate stockholder of the applicant is considered a party to this application **ONLY IF** that interest, when multiplied by the corporate stockholder's interest in the applicant, would account for 5% or more of the votes of the applicant. For example, where X owns or subscribes to stock accounting for 25% of the applicant's votes, only those stockholders of corporation X which hold stock accounting for 20% or more have a 5% indirect interest in the applicant (.25 x .20 - .05) and, therefore, are considered parties to this application. In applying the multiplier, any entity holding more than 50% of its subsidiary will be considered a 100% owner.

If any stockholder agreement exists pertaining to cooperative voting accounting for 5% or more of the votes, that block of stock is regarded as if held by a single entity and any stockholder holding 5% or more of the stock in that block is considered a party to this application.

An investment company, insurance company or trust department of a bank is not considered a party to this application **IF** its aggregated holding accounts for less than 10% of the outstanding votes in the applicant **AND IF** the applicant certifies that:

(1) such entity exercises no influence or control over the corporation, directly or indirectly; and

(2) such entity has no representatives among the officers and directors of the corporation.

ANY OTHER APPLICANT: All executive officers, members of the governing board and owners or subscribers who hold 5% or more of the votes in the applicant.

B. As used in Section II, the words "non-party equity owners in the applicant" have the following meanings:

PARTNERSHIP APPLICANT: All holders of equity interests in the applicant that are not considered parties to the application, including all limited partners. In the event there are more than fifty (50) owners of equity interests in the applicant, only those who own 5% or more of the total equity in the applicant are considered non-party equity owners for purposes of Section II.

CORPORATE APPLICANT: All holders of equity interests in the applicant that are not considered parties to the application, including all nonvoting stockholders, stockholders with less than 5% voting stock interest and stockholders with less than a majority interest in voting stock where a single entity owns more than 50% of the voting stock. In the event that there are more than fifty (50) stockholders or owners of equity interests in the applicant, only those who own 5% or more of the total equity in the applicant are considered non-party equity owners for purposes of Section II.

ANY OTHER APPLICANT: All holders of equity interests in the applicant that are not considered parties to the application.

C. An attributable interest is an ownership interest in or relation to an applicant or licensee which will confer on its holder that degree of influence or control over the applicant or licensee as should subject it to limitation by the Commission's multiple ownership rules. Parties to the application are holders of attributable interests. Non-party holders of equity interests in the applicant are holders of nonattributable interests. While these holders of nonattributable interests are not considered parties to the application, Section II information must be provided for them. Moreover, they may have attributable interests in other media that are considered under the Commission's cross-interest policy which seeks to ensure the promotion and maintenance of arms' length competition between stations in the same area. For example, a limited partner in an applicant, which has made the above partnership certification, may have an attributable interest in a newspaper or broadcast station in the same area, or in a station with contours that overlap the applicant's proposed station, or in a cable television (CATV) system that is located within the Grade B contour of a proposed television station. See, generally, 47 C.F.R. Sections 73.3555 and 76.501 as to the relevant contours. If so, the applicant is required:

(1) to identify the individuals or entities that have an attributable interest in another medium of mass communications in the area;
(2) to state the nature and extent of the interest in the applicant; and
(3) to identify the other medium and the nature and extent of the interest held.

In situations in which a marital relationship is involved, the interests held by one spouse are presumptively attributed to the other and both spouses may, unless this presumption is rebutted by an appropriate showing, be considered to be holders of attributable interests and parties to this application.

D. All applications must comply with Section 310 of the Communications Act, as amended. Specifically, Section 310 proscribes issuance of a construction permit to an alien, the representative of an alien, a foreign government or the representative thereof, or a corporation organized under the laws of a foreign government. This proscription also applies with respect to any corporation of which any officer or director is an alien or of which more than 20% of the capital stock is owned or voted by aliens, their representatives, a foreign government or its representative, or by a corporation organized under the laws of a foreign country. This proscription could likewise apply to any corporation directly or indirectly controlled by another corporation of which (a) any officer is, (b) more than 25% of the directors are, or (c) more than 25% of the capital stock is owned or voted by aliens, their representatives, a foreign government or its representative. The Commission may also deny a construction permit to a corporation controlled by another corporation organized under the laws of a foreign country.

Section 310 of the Communications Act has been interpreted with respect to limited partnerships to prohibit equity contributions or voting interests of alien limited partners, which in the aggregate exceed 20% in a broadcast licensee or which in the aggregate exceed 25% in a partnership which holds a controlling interest in a broadcast licensee. The interests held by aliens in a licensee through intervening domestically organized limited partnerships can be determined by multiplication of any intervening insulated interests in the manner set forth above with respect to corporate applicants, except that insulated limited partnership interests exceeding 50% may be multiplied rather than considered as a 100% interest. However, the multiplier is not used in calculating the limited partnership link in the ownership chain **UNLESS** the applicant is able to certify that the alien partner is effectively insulated from active involvement in the partnership affairs. For example, see Instruction A, above.

The applicant must determine the citizenship of each officer and director. It must also determine the citizenship of each shareholder or else explain how it determined the relevant percentages. For large corporations, a sample survey using a recognized statistical method is acceptable for this purpose.

E. Commission policies and litigation reporting requirements for broadcast applicants have been revised with a view to focusing on misconduct which violates the Communications Act or a Commission rule or policy and on certain specified non-FCC misconduct which demonstrates the proclivity of an applicant to deal truthfully with the Commission and to comply with its rules and policies. The categories of relevant non-FCC misconduct include: (1) misrepresentations to any other governmental unit resulting in criminal or civil violations; (2) criminal convictions involving false statements or dishonesty; (3) certain felony convictions; and (4) adjudicated violations of anticompetitive or antitrust laws that are broadcast related. The parameters of the revised policies and requirements are fully set forth in Character Qualifications, 102 FCC 2d 1179 (1986), reconsideration denied, 1 FCC Rcd 421 (1986).

INSTRUCTIONS FOR SECTION III — FINANCIAL QUALIFICATIONS

A. All applicants filing Form 301 must be financially qualified to effectuate their proposals. Certain applicants (i.e., for a new station, to reactivate a silent station, or if specifically requested by the Commission) must demonstrate their financial qualifications by filing Section III. DO NOT SUBMIT Section III if the application is for changes in operating or authorized facilities.

B. An applicant for a new station must attest it has sufficient net liquid assets on hand or committed sources of funds to construct the proposed facility and operate for three months without additional funds. In so certifying, the applicant is also attesting that it can and will meet all contractual requirements, if any, as to collateral, guarantees, donations, and capital investments. As used in Section III, "net liquid assets" means the lesser amount of the net current assets or of the liquid assets shown on a party's balance sheet, with net current assets being the excess of current assets over current liabilities.

C. Documentation supporting the certification of financial qualifications need not be submitted with this application but must be available to the Commission upon request. The Commission encourages that all financial statements used in the preparation of this application be prepared in accordance with generally accepted accounting principles.

D. (1)(a) The applicant must estimate the initial costs of constructing and operating the facility proposed in the application. The estimate for constructing the facility should include, but is not limited to, costs incurred for items listed below. In calculating costs for the items below, determine the costs for the items in place and ready for service, including amounts for labor, supervision, materials, supplies, and freight:

Antenna System (including antenna, antenna tower, transmission line, phasing equipment, ground system, coupling equipment and tower lighting);

RF Generating Equipment (including transmitter, tubes, filters, diplexer, remote control equipment, and automatic logger);

Monitoring and Test Equipment (including frequency monitor, modulation monitor, oscilloscope, dummy load, vectorscope, and video monitors);

Program Origination Equipment (including control consoles, film chains, cameras, audio tape equipment, video tape equipment, program and distribution amplifiers, limiters, and transcription equipment);

Acquiring Land;

Acquiring, Remodeling or Constructing Buildings;

Services (including legal, engineering, and installation costs); and

Other Miscellaneous Items (including mobile and STL equipment, non-technical studio furnishings, etc.)

(b) The estimate must also include the costs of operating the proposed facility for the first three months, including the costs of proposed programming, without relying on advertising or other revenues to meet operating costs. To arrive at an estimate of the total costs to be met by the applicant, the total construction costs should be added to the estimated cost of operation for three months.

(2) The applicant must also identify, in the application, its sources of funding for the construction and operation of the proposed facility for the first three months. For each source of funding, the applicant must identify the source's name, address, telephone number, a contact person if the source is an entity, the relationship (if any) of the source to the applicant, and the amount of funds to be supplied by the source. The total amount of funds to be supplied by all the sources listed should equal or exceed the estimated cost of construction and operation computed in accordance with paragraph (1) and stated in the application in response to Question 2, Section III.

The funding sources listed on the application should include, if applicable: existing capital, new capital, loans from banks (identified separately), loans from others (identified separately), profits for existing operations, donations, and net deferred credit from equipment suppliers (identified separately and determined by deducting from the deferred credit the down payment, payments to principal, and interest payments). (Note: If the first equipment payment is due upon shipment, the applicant must include five monthly payments; if due in 30 days, four monthly payments; if due in 60 days, three monthly payments, etc.)

(3) The applicant must also have on hand, at the time it files its application, **BUT NEED NOT SUBMIT WITH THE APPLICATION**, the following documentation:

(a) For the applicant:

A detailed balance sheet at the close of a month within 90 days of the date of the application showing the applicant's financial position.

A statement showing the yearly net income, after Federal income tax, for each of the past two years, received by the applicant from any source.

(b) For each person identified in response to Question 3, Section III, who has **already** furnished funds, purchased stock, extended credit, or guaranteed loans:

A copy of the agreement obligating the party to furnish funds, showing the amount furnished, the rate of interest, the terms of repayment, and security, if any.

(c) For each person identified in response to Question 3, Section III, who has **agreed to** furnish funds, purchase stock, extend credit, or guarantee loans, a balance sheet or a financial statement showing:

All liabilities and current and liquid assets sufficient to meet current liabilities;

Financial ability to comply with the terms of the agreement to furnish funds, purchase stock, extend credit, or guarantee loans; and

Net income after Federal income tax, received for the past two years.

Note: If the statement does not indicate current and liquid assets sufficient to meet the proposed commitments, the financial statement must be supplemented by a statement showing how non-liquid assets will be used to provide the funds, and the extent to which such assets have liens or prior obligations against them.

(d) For financial institutions or equipment manufacturers, identified in response to Question 3, Section III, who have agreed to make a loan or extend credit:

The document by which the institution or manufacturer has agreed to provide the loan or credit, showing the amount of loan or credit, terms of payment or repayment of the loan, collateral or security required, rate of interest to be charged, and special requirements (e.g., moratorium on principal or interest, waiver of collateral, etc.); and

A statement from any parties required to provide special endorsements showing their willingness to provide such endorsements.

E. It is Commission policy not to approve extensions of time for construction on the basis of financial inability or unwillingness to construct.

INSTRUCTIONS FOR SECTION IV–A – PROGRAM SERVICE STATEMENT

Applicants need only file a program service statement called for in Section IV-A of this application. See Deregulation of Radio, 84 FCC 2d 968 (1981), reconsideration denied, 87 FCC 2d 797; and Commercial TV Stations, 98 FCC 2d 1076 (1984), reconsideration denied, 60 RR 2d 526 (1986).

INSTRUCTIONS FOR SECTION IV–B – INTEGRATION STATEMENT

The applicant's integration statement must identify each principal who will participate in the management of the station, his or her position, duties and hours, and for each principal whether a qualitative credit will be claimed for minority status, past local residence, female status, broadcast experience or civic activity. Any claim for "daytimer" preference must also be stated. An applicant may include its integration statement in this application, but it must file its integration statement with the Commission by the amendment as-of-right date in FM proceedings, or the "B" cut-off date in AM and television proceedings. If an applicant fails to disclose its integration statement by the amendment as-of-right or "B" cut-off date, whichever is applicable, it will receive no credit for integration in the comparative hearing.

INSTRUCTIONS FOR SECTION V – ENGINEERING DATA AND ANTENNA AND SITE INFORMATION

A. An indication as to the specific transmitter make and model is not required on the application. Rather, any subsequent permit authorizing construction will require installation of a type accepted transmitter or one complying with the provisions of 47 C.F.R. Section 73.1660. Applicants for AM facilities are reminded of the maximum rated power limitations for transmitters imposed by 47 C.F.R. Section 73.1665.

B. Prior to January 4, 1982, parties submitting AM directional antenna patterns pursuant to 47 C.F.R. Sections 73.150 and 73.152 (standard patterns and modified standard patterns) had to submit patterns which were tabulated and plotted using units of millivolts per meter at one mile. Beginning on January 4, 1982, such patterns must be tabulated and plotted using units of millivolts per meter at one kilometer. Applications which are amended should use the units in effect as of the day of submission of the amendment. Applications which were on file prior to January 4, 1982, need not be amended solely for the purpose of conversion to metric units. Applications which are submitted using the wrong units will be returned unless they are promptly amended to use the correct units. See 47 C.F.R. Section 73.181(f) concerning uses of the metric system with AM stations.

C. When applying for FM station construction permit, one of the submissions required by FCC Form 301, Section V-B, is a 7.5 minute series U.S. Geological Survey topographic quadrangle map upon which is marked the transmitter site. The Commission recommends that applicants submit at least one original copy of each appropriate full-scale USGS quadrangle map, if available, with the transmitter site properly marked and labeled.

In order to allow the Commission's processing staff to verify the correctness of the geographic coordinates provided in an FM application, it is necessary for this site map to show along the printed margin of both axes at least two coordinate markings, specifically labeled by the USGS, one on either side of the marked site. Additionally, a scale of kilometers (if available) or miles and all of the identifying map information must be included. The site should be plotted on a full scale map, and all of the contour lines must be clearly visible. Faded, smudged or otherwise illegible maps are unacceptable. Photocopies are acceptable in lieu of actual USGS maps, provided they are clear, dark and legible. It is not necessary to submit an entire map (although this is perfectly acceptable), but only as much as is necessary to fully comply with the requirements described above.

In certain cases it may be inconvenient to provide a full scale photocopy which includes both the site and the margins. This can occur when the site lies toward the center of the map. In this case the following alternative is acceptable. Provide a full scale copy of the section of the map containing the site. This copy must include either four of the standard printed cross-marks or one margin and two cross-marks. Fine lines should be drawn between the marks in such a fashion as to enclose the site. Each of these lines should be labeled with the appropriate latitude or longitude. This full scale map section must include all of the information specified in the previous paragraph. In addition, a reduced copy of the entire map must be included to allow the Commission's staff to verify that the lines have been correctly labeled.

D. The latitude and longitude coordinates for all points in the United States are based upon the 1927 North American Datum (NAD 27). The National Geodetic Survey is in the process of replacing NAD 27 with the more accurate 1983 North American Datum (NAD 83) and updating current topographic maps with NAD 83 datum. In addition, coordinates determined by use of the satellite-based Global Positioning System already reflect the NAD 83 datum. To prevent intermixing of data using two different datums, however, the Commission announced that until further notice, applicants are to furnish coordinates based on NAD 27 datum on all submissions and the Commission will continue to specify NAD 27 coordinates in its data bases and authorizations. In addition, applicants who have already filed applications with coordinates that reflect NAD 83 datum must provide NAD 27 coordinates to the appropriate Commission licensing bureau. See Public Notice, entitled "FCC Interim Procedures for the Specification of Geographic Coordinates," 3 FCC Rcd 1478 (1988). Accordingly, in furnishing the information called for in Section V (e.g., V-A (AM) #4, V-B (FM) #2, V-C (TV) #2), NAD 27 datum should be used.

E. The following guidance is provided for the questions regarding environmental impact (V-A (AM) #14, V-B (FM) #20, V-C (TV) #20):

(1) Place an (X) in the appropriate box to indicate whether a Commission grant of the proposed communication facility(ies) may have a significant environment impact as defined by 47 C.F.R. Section 1.1307. Briefly, Commission grant of an application may have a significant environmental impact if any of the following are proposed:

    (a) A facility is to be located in sensitive areas (e.g., an officially designated wilderness area, a wildlife preserve area, a flood plain) or will physically or visually affect sites significant in American history.

    (b) A facility whose construction will involve significant change in surface features.

    (c) The antenna tower and/or supporting structure(s) will be equipped with high intensity white lights and are to be located in residential neighborhoods.

    (d) The facilities or the operation of which will cause exposure of workers or the general public to levels of radio frequency radiation in excess of the "Radio Frequency Protection Guides" recommended in "American National Standard Safety Levels with respect to Human Exposure to Radio Frequency Electromagnetic Fields, 300 kHz to 100 GHz," (ANSI C95. 1-1982), by the Institute of Electrical and Electronics Engineers, Inc., 345 East 47th Street, New York, New York 10017.

(2) If you answer Yes, submit the required Environmental Assessment (EA). The EA includes for antenna towers and satellite earth stations:

    (a) A description of the facilities as well as supporting structures and appurtenances, and a description of the site as well as the surrounding area and uses. If high intensity lighting is proposed or utilized within a residential area, the EA must also address the impact of this lighting upon the residents.

    (b) A statement as to the zoning classification of the site, and communications with, or proceedings before and determinations (if any) made by zoning, planning, environmental or other local, state or federal authorities on matters relating to environmental effect.

    (c) A statement as to whether construction of the facilities has been a source of controversy on environmental grounds in the local community.

    (d) A discussion of environmental and other considerations which led to the selection of the particular site and, if relevant, the particular facility; the nature and extent of any unavoidable adverse environmental effects, and any alternative sites or facilities which have been or might reasonably be considered.

(3) The information submitted in the EA shall be factual (not argumentative or conclusory) and concise with sufficient detail to explain the environmental consequences and to enable the Commission, after an independent review of the EA, to reach a determination concerning the proposal's environmental impact, if any. The EA shall deal specifically with any feature of the site which has special environmental significance (e.g., wilderness area, wildlife preserves, natural migration paths for birds and other wildlife, and sites of historic, architectural, or archeological value). In the case of historically significant sites, it shall specify the effect of the facilities on any district, site, building, structure or object listed in the National Register of Historic Places, 39 Fed. Reg. 6402 (February 19, 1974). It shall also detail any substantial change in the character of the land utilized (e.g., deforestation, water diversion, wetland fill, or other extensive change of surface features). In the case of wilderness areas, wildlife preserves, or other like areas, the statement shall discuss the effect of any continuing pattern of human intrusion into the area (e.g., necessitated by the operation and maintenance of the facilities).

(4) The EA shall also be accompanied with evidence of site approval which has been obtained from local or federal land use authorities.

(5) To the extent that such information is submitted in another part of the application, it need not be duplicated in the EA, but adequate cross-reference to such information shall be supplied.

(6) An EA need not submitted to the Commission if another agency of the Federal Government has assumed responsibility (a) for determining whether the facilities in question will have a significant effect on the quality of the human environment and, (b) if it will affect the environment, for invoking the environmental impact statement process.

INSTRUCTIONS FOR SECTION VI – EQUAL EMPLOYMENT OPPORTUNITY PROGRAM

A. Applicants seeking authority to construct a new commercial, noncommercial or international broadcast station, applicants seeking authority to obtain assignment of the construction permit or license of such a station, and applicants seeking authority to acquire control of an entity holding such construction permit or license are required to afford equal employment opportunity to all qualified persons and to refrain from discriminating in employment and related benefits on the basis of race, color, religion, national origin or sex. See 47 C.F.R. Section 73.2080. Pursuant to these requirements, an applicant who proposes to employ five or more full-time station employees must establish a program designed to assure equal employment opportunity for women and minority groups (that is, Blacks not of Hispanic origin, Asian or Pacific Islanders, American Indians or Alaskan Natives, and Hispanics). This is submitted to the Commission as the Model EEO Program on FCC Form 396-A, which should be filed as part of the application. If minority group representation in the available labor force is less than five percent (in the aggregate), a program for minority group members is not required. However, a program must be filed for women since they comprise a significant percentage of virtually all area labor forces. If an applicant proposes to employ less than five full-time employees, no EEO program for women or minorities need be filed.

B. Guidelines for developing an Equal Employment Opportunity program are set forth in FCC Form 396-A.

NOTE: This five-point Broadcast Equal Employment Opportunity Model Program Report (FCC 396-A) is to be utilized only by applicants for new construction permits, assignees and transferees.

INSTRUCTIONS FOR SECTION VII – CERTIFICATIONS

A. Applicants for a new AM, FM or TV broadcast station or for a major modification of the authorized facilities of such stations (as defined in 47 C.F.R. Sections 73.3571(a), 73.3573(a), or 73.3572(a), respectively) are required to give public notice of the filing of their applications by publication in a local newspaper and/or by broadcast announcements in accordance with 47 C.F.R. Section 73.3580.

B. An applicant need not have a binding agreement or absolute assurance of the availability of the transmitter site it proposes to utilize. However, the applicant must be able to show that it has obtained reasonable assurance that the proposed site is available to it. The Commission's requirements will be satisfied where an applicant has contacted the property owner or the owner's representative and has obtained reasonable assurance, in good faith, that the proposed site will be available for the intended purpose.

C. The original of this application form must be signed by the applicant. The required copies can be conformed. See 47 C.F.R. Section 73.3513.

NOTE: Certification of site availability is required only in applications for authority to construct a new station or to change the site of an existing facility.

Federal Communications Commission
Washington, D. C. 20554

FCC 301

Approved by OMB
3060-0027
Expires 2/28/92
See Page 25 for information
regarding public burden estimate

APPLICATION FOR CONSTRUCTION PERMIT FOR COMMERCIAL BROADCAST STATION

For COMMISSION Fee Use Only		
FEE NO:		
FEE TYPE:		
FEE AMT:		
ID SEQ:		

For APPLICANT Fee Use Only

Is a fee submitted with this application? ☐ Yes ☐ No

If fee exempt (see 47 C.F.R. Section 1.1112), indicate reason therefor (check one box):

☐ Noncommercial educational licensee
☐ Governmental entity

FOR COMMISSION USE ONLY

FILE NO.

Section I - GENERAL INFORMATION

1. Name of Applicant

Street Address or P.O. Box

City	State	ZIP Code

Telephone No. *(Include Area Code)*

Send notices and communications to the following person at the address below:

Name

Street Address or P.O. Box

City	State	ZIP Code

Telephone No. *(Include Area Code)*

2. This application is for: ☐ AM ☐ FM ☐ TV

(a) Channel No. or Frequency	(b) Principal Community	City	State

(c) Check one of the following boxes:

☐ Application for **NEW** station

☐ **MAJOR** change in licensed facilities; call sign: _____

☐ **MINOR** change in licensed facilities; call sign: _____

☐ **MAJOR** modification of construction permit; call sign: _____

File No. of construction permit: _____

☐ **MINOR** modification of construction permit; call sign: _____

File No. of construction permit: _____

☐ **AMENDMENT** to pending application; Application file number: _____

NOTE: It is not necessary to use this form to amend a previously filed application. Should you do so, however, please submit only Section I and those other portions of the form that contain the amended information.

3. Is this application mutually exclusive with a renewal application? ☐ Yes ☐ No

If Yes, state:	Call letters	Community of License	
		City	State

FCC 301
June 1989

Section II - LEGAL QUALIFICATIONS

Name of Applicant

1. Applicant is: *(check one box below)*

   ☐ Individual   ☐ General partnership   ☐ For-profit corporation

   ☐ Other   ☐ Limited partnership   ☐ Not-for-profit corporation

2. If the applicant is an unincorporated association or a legal entity other than an individual, partnership, or corporation, describe in an Exhibit the nature of the application.

Exhibit No.

   NOTE: The terms "applicant," "parties to this application," and "non-party equity owners in the applicant" are defined in the instructions for Section II of this form. Complete information as to each "party to this application" and each "non-party equity owner in the applicant" is required. If the applicant considers that to furnish complete information would pose an unreasonable burden, it may request that the Commission waive the strict terms of this requirement with appropriate justification.

3. If the applicant is not an individual, provide the date and place of filing of the applicant's enabling charter (e.g., a limited partnership must identify its certificate of limited partnership and a corporation must identify its articles of incorporation by date and place of filing):

   Date _____ Place _____

   In the event there is no requirement that the enabling charter be filed with the state, the applicant shall include the enabling charter in the applicant's public inspection file. If, in the case of a partnership, the enabling charter does not include the partnership agreement itself, the applicant shall include a copy of the agreement in the applicant's public inspection file.

4. Are there any documents, instruments, contracts or understandings (written or oral), other than instruments identified in response to Question 3 above, relating to future ownership interests in the applicant, including but not limited to, insulated limited partnership shares, nonvoting stock interests, beneficial stock ownership interests, options, rights of first refusal, or debentures?

   ☐ Yes ☐ No

   If Yes, submit as an Exhibit all such written documents, instruments, contracts, or understandings, and provide the particulars of any oral agreement.

Exhibit No.

5. Complete, if applicable, the following certifications:

   (a) Applicant certifies that no limited partner will be involved in any material respect in the management or operation of the proposed station.

   ☐ Yes ☐ No

   If No, applicant must complete Question 6 below with respect to all limited partners actively involved in the media activities of the partnership.

   (b) Does any investment company *(as defined in 15 U.S.C. Section 80 a-3)*, insurance company, or trust department of any bank have an aggregated holding of greater than 5% but less than 10% of the outstanding votes of the applicant?

   ☐ Yes ☐ No

   If Yes, applicant certifies that the entity holding such interest exercises no influence or control over the applicant, directly or indirectly, and has no representatives among the officers and directors of the applicant.

   ☐ Yes ☐ No

Section II – LEGAL QUALIFICATIONS (Page 2)

6. List the applicant, parties to the application and non-party equity owners in the applicant. Use one column for each individual or entity. Attach additional pages if necessary.

(Read carefully – The numbered items below refer to line numbers in the following table.)

1. Name and residence of the applicant and, if applicable, its officers, directors, stockholders, or partners (if other than individual also show name, address and citizenship of natural person authorized to vote the stock). List the applicant first, officers next, then directors and, thereafter, remaining stockholders and partners.

2. Citizenship.

3. Office or directorship held.

4. Number of shares or nature of partnership interests.

5. Number of votes.

6. Percentage of votes.

7. Other existing attributable interests in any broadcast station, including the nature and size of such interests.

8. All other ownership interests of 5% or more (whether or not attributable), as well as any corporate officership or directorship, in broadcast, cable, or newspaper entities in the same market or with overlapping signals in the same broadcast service, as described in 47 C.F.R. Section 73.3555 and 76.501, including the nature and size of such interests and the positions held.

1.			
2.			
3.			
4.			
5.			
6.			
7.			
8.			

FCC 301 (Page 3)
June 1989

Section II - LEGAL QUALIFICATIONS (Page 3)

7. Does the applicant, any party to the application or any non-party equity owner in the applicant have, or have they had, any interest in:

   (a) a broadcast station, or pending broadcast station application before the Commission? ☐ Yes ☐ No

   (b) a broadcast application which has been dismissed with prejudice by the Commission? ☐ Yes ☐ No

   (c) a broadcast application which has been denied by the Commission? ☐ Yes ☐ No

   (d) a broadcast station, the license of which has been revoked? ☐ Yes ☐ No

   (e) a broadcast application in any pending or concluded Commission proceeding which left unresolved character issues against the applicant? ☐ Yes ☐ No

   If the answer to any of the questions in (a)-(e) above is Yes, state in an Exhibit the following information: [Exhibit No.]

   (1) Name of party having interest;
   (2) Nature of interest or connection, giving dates;
   (3) Call letters of stations or file number of application or docket; and
   (4) Location.

8. (a) Are any of the parties to the application or non-party equity owners in the applicant related (as husband, wife, father, mother, brother, sister, son or daughter) to each other? ☐ Yes ☐ No

   (b) Does any member of the immediate family (i.e., husband, wife, father, mother, brother, sister, son or daughter) of any party to the application or non-party equity owner in the applicant have any interest in or connection with any other broadcast station, pending broadcast application or newspaper in the same area *(see Section 73.3555(c))* or, in the case of a television station applicant only, a cable television system in the same area *(see Section 76.501(a))*? ☐ Yes ☐ No

   If the answer to (a) or (b) above is Yes, attach an Exhibit giving full disclosure concerning the persons involved, their relationship, the nature and extent of such interest or connection, the file number of such application, and the location of such station or proposed station. [Exhibit No.]

9. State in an Exhibit any interest the applicant or any party to this application proposes to divest in the event of a grant of this application. [Exhibit No.]

OTHER MASS MEDIA INTERESTS

10. (a) Do individuals or entities holding nonattributable interests of 5% or more in the applicant have an attributable ownership interest or corporate officership or directorship in a broadcast station, newspaper or CATV system in the same area? *(See Instruction 8 to Section II.)* ☐ Yes ☐ No

    (b) Does any member of the immediate family (i.e., husband, wife, father, mother, brother, sister, son or daugther) of an individual holding a nonattributable interest of 5% or more in the applicant have any interest in or connection with any other broadcast station, pending broadcast application, newspaper in the same area *(see Section 73.3555(c))*, or, in the case of a television station applicant only, a cable television system in the same area *(see Section 76.501(a))*? ☐ Yes ☐ No

    If the answer to (a) and/or (b) above is Yes, attach an Exhibit giving a full disclosure concerning the persons involved, their relationship, the nature and extent of such interest or connection, the file number of such application, and the location of such station or proposed station. [Exhibit No.]

Section II — LEGAL QUALIFICATIONS (Page 4)

CITIZENSHIP AND OTHER STATUTORY REQUIREMENTS

11. (a) Is the applicant in violation of the provisions of Section 310 of the Communications Act of 1934, as amended, relating to interests of aliens and foreign governments? *(See Instruction C to Section II.)*   ☐ Yes ☐ No

(b) Will any funds, credits or other financial assistance for the construction, purchase or operation of the station(s) be provided by aliens, foreign entities, domestic entities controlled by aliens, or their agents?   ☐ Yes ☐ No

If the answer to (b) above is Yes, attach an Exhibit giving full disclosure concerning this assistance.   Exhibit No.

12. (a) Has an adverse finding been made or an adverse final action been taken by any court or administrative body as to the applicant, any party to this application, or any non-party equity owner in the applicant in a civil or criminal proceeding brought under the provisions of any law related to the following:

Any felony; broadcast related antitrust or unfair competition; criminal fraud or fraud before another governmental unit; or discrimination?   ☐ Yes ☐ No

(b) Is there now pending in any court or administrative body any proceeding involving any of the matters referred to in (a) above?   ☐ Yes ☐ No

If the answer to (a) and/or (b) above is Yes, attach an Exhibit giving full disclosure concerning persons and matters involved, including an identification of the court or administrative body and the proceeding (by dates and file numbers), a statement of the facts upon which the proceeding is or was based or the nature of the offense alleged or committed, and a description of the current status or disposition of the matter.   Exhibit No.

SECTION III - FINANCIAL QUALIFICATIONS

NOTE: If this application is for a change in an operating facility do not fill out this section.

1. The applicant certifies that sufficient net liquid assets are on hand or that sufficient funds are available from committed sources to construct and operate the requested facilities for three months without revenue.   ☐ Yes ☐ No

2. State the total funds you estimate are necessary to construct and operate the requested facility for three months without revenue. $ _____

3. Identify each source of funds, including the name, address, and telephone number of the source (and a contact person if the source is an entity), the relationship (if any) of the source to the applicant, and the amount of funds to be supplied by each source.

Source of Funds (Name and Address)	Telephone Number	Relationship	Amount

Section IV-A — PROGRAM SERVICE STATEMENT

Attach as an Exhibit, a brief description, in narrative form, of the planned programming service relating to the issues of public concern facing the proposed service area.

> Exhibit No.

Section IV-B — INTEGRATION STATEMENT

Attach as an Exhibit the information required in 1. and 2. below.

> Exhibit No.

1. List each principal of the applicant who, in the event of a grant of the application on a comparative basis proposes to participate in the management of the proposed facility and, with respect to each such principal, state whether he or she will work full-time (minimum 40 hours per week) or part-time (minimum 20 hours per week) and briefly describe the proposed position and duties.

2. State with respect to each principal identified in response to Item 1. above, whether the applicant will claim qualitative credit for any of the following enhancement factors:

    (a) Minority Status
    (b) Past Local Residence
        If Yes, specify whether in the community of license or service area and the corresponding dates.
    (c) Female Status
    (d) Broadcast Experience
        If Yes, list each employer and position and corresponding dates.
    (e) Daytime Preference

Section V-A - AM BROADCAST ENGINEERING DATA	FOR COMMISSION USE ONLY
	File No. _____
	ASB Referral Date _____
	Referred by _____

Name of Applicant

---

1. Purpose of Application: *(check all appropriate boxes)*

☐ Construct new station

☐ Make changes in authorized/existing station   Call Sign _____

    ☐ Principal authorized/licensed community

    ☐ Frequency   ☐ Hours of operation

    ☐ Power   ☐ Transmitter location

    ☐ Main studio location

    ☐ Antenna system*(including increase in height by addition of FM or TV antenna)*

       ☐ New antenna construction

       ☐ Alteration of existing structure

          ☐ Increase height   ☐ Decrease height

          ☐ Non-DA to DA   ☐ DA to Non-DA

   ☐ Other *(Summarize briefly the nature of the changes proposed)*

2. Principal community to be served:

State	County	City or Town

3. Facilities requested:

   Frequency: _____ kHz   Hours of Operations:

   Power: Night: _____ kW   Day: _____ kW   Critical hours: _____ kW

4. Transmitter location:

State	County	City or Town

Exact antenna location *(street address)*. If outside city limits, give name of nearest town and distance *(in kilometers)*, and direction of antenna from town.

Geographical coordinates *(to nearest second)*. For directional antenna give coordinates of center of array. For single vertical radiator give tower location. Specify South Latitude or East Longitude where applicable; otherwise, North Latitude or West Longitude will be presumed.

Latitude ° ' "	Longitude ° ' "

SECTION V–A — AM BROADCAST ENGINEERING DATA (Page 2)

5. Is the proposed site the same transmitter-antenna site of other stations authorized by the Commission or specified in another application pending before the Commission? ☐ Yes ☐ No

   If Yes, indicate call sign or application file number: _____

6. Antenna system *(including ground or counterpoise system)*

   Non–Directional ☐ Day ☐ Night ☐ Critical Hours

   Estimated efficiency _____ mV/m per kW at one kilometer

   If antenna is either top loaded or sectionalized, describe fully in an Exhibit. *(Include apparent electrical height.)* | Exhibit No. |

   Directional ☐ Day only (DA-D) ☐ Night only (DA-N)

   ☐ Same constants and power day and night (DA-1)

   ☐ Different constants and/or power day and night (DA-2)

   ☐ Different constants and/or power day, critical hours and night (DA-8)

   Submit complete engineering data in accordance with 47 C.F.R. Section 73.150 for each Directional antenna pattern proposed.

   Type of feed circuits (excitation) ☐ Series Feed ☐ Shunt Feed ☐ Other (explain)

TOWERS *(In meters, rounded to nearest meter)*	1	2	3	4	5	6
Overall height of radiator above base insulator, or above base, if grounded						
Overall height above ground *(include obstruction lighting)*						
Overall height above mean sea level *(include obstruction lighting)*						

If additional towers, attach information exactly as it appears above.

7. Has the FAA been notified of the proposed construction? ☐ Yes ☐ No

   If Yes, give date and office where notice was filed and attach as an Exhibit a copy of FAA determination, if available. | Exhibit No. |

   Date _____ Office where filed _____

SECTION V-A - AM BROADCAST ENGINEERING DATA (Page 3)

8. List all landing areas within 8 kilometers of antenna site. Give distances and direction to the nearest boundary of each landing area from the antenna site.

	Landing Area	Distance (km)	Direction
(a)	_____	_____	_____
(b)	_____	_____	_____
(c)	_____	_____	_____

9. Attach as an Exhibit a description and vertical plan sketch *(including supporting buildings, if any)* of the proposed structure, giving heights above ground, in meters, for all significant features. Clearly indicate existing portions, noting lighting, and distinguishing between the skeletal or other main supporting structure and the antenna elements. If a directional antenna, give spacing and orientation of towers.

> Exhibit No.

If not fully described above, attach as an Exhibit further details and dimensions, including any other antennas mounted on tower and associated isolation circuits.

> Exhibit No.

Attach as an Exhibit, a plat of the transmitter site clearly showing boundary lines, roads, railroads, other obstructions, and the ground system or counterpoise. Show number and dimensions of ground radials or, if a counterpoise is used, show heights and dimensions.

> Exhibit No.

10. Will the main studio be located within the station's principal community contour as defined by 47 C.F.R. Section 73.24(J)?   ☐ Yes ☐ No

If No, attach as an Exhibit a justification pursuant to 47 C.F.R. Section 73.1125.

> Exhibit No.

11. Is there a remote control location or is one to be established in accordance with 47 C.F.R. Section 73.1400?   ☐ Yes ☐ No

If yes, submit the following:

State	County	City or Town
Street address *(or other identification)*		

12. Attach as an Exhibit a sufficient number of aerial photographs taken in clear weather at appropriate altitudes and angles to permit identification of all structures in the vicinity. The photographs must be marked so as to show compass directions, exact boundary lines of the proposed site, and locations of the proposed 1000 mV/m contour for both day and night operation. Photographs taken in eight different directions from an elevated position on the ground will be acceptable in lieu of the aerial photographs if the data referred to can be clearly shown.

> Exhibit No.

13. Is the population within the 1 V/m (1000 mV/m) contour less than 300 persons or less than 1.0 percent of the population within the 25 mV/m contour?   ☐ Yes ☐ No

If No, attach as an Exhibit a justification pursuant to 47 C.F.R. Section 73.24(g).

> Exhibit No.

14. Environmental Statement. *(See 47 C.F.R. Section 1.1301 et seq.)*

Would a Commission grant of this application come within 47 C.F.R. Section 1.1307, such that it may have a significant environmental impact?   ☐ Yes ☐ No

If you answer Yes, submit as an Exhibit an Environmental Assessment required by 47 C.F.R. Section 1.1311.

> Exhibit No.

If No, explain briefly why not.

SECTION V–A – AM BROADCAST ENGINEERING DATA (Page 4)

15. Allocation Studies

A. Daytime *(For assistance, see 47 C.F.R. Section 73.37)*

(1) For daytime operation, attach as an exhibit map(s) having appropriate scales, showing the 1000, 5, 2 and 0.5 (0.1, if Class I station) daytime contours in mV/m for both existing and proposed operations. On the map(s) showing the 5 mV/m contours **CLEARLY INDICATE THE LEGAL BOUNDARIES OF THE PRINCIPAL COMMUNITY TO BE SERVED.**

| Exhibit No. |

(2) Does the daytime 5 mv/m contour encompass the legal boundaries of the principal community to be served?

□ Yes   □ No

If No, attach as an Exhibit a justification for waiver of 47 C.F.R. Section 73.24(j).

| Exhibit No. |

(3) For daytime operation, attach as an Exhibit an allocation study utilizing Figure M-8 *(Figure R-3 47 C.F.R. Section 73.190)* or an accurate full scale reproduction thereof and using pertinent field strength measurement data where available, a full scale exhibit of the entire pertinent area to show the following:

| Exhibit No. |

(a) Normally protected and the interfering contours for the proposed operation along all azimuths.

(b) Normally protected and interfering contours of existing stations and other proposed stations in pertinent areas with which prohibited overlap would result as well as those existing stations and other proposals which require study to clearly show absence of prohibited overlap. If prohibited overlap were to occur as a result of the proposal, appropriate justification for waiver of 47 C.F.R. Section 73.37 is to be included.

(c) Plot of the transmitter location of each station or proposal requiring investigation, with identifying call letters, file numbers, and operating or proposed facilities.

(d) Properly labeled longitude and latitude degree lines, shown across entire Exhibit.

(4) For daytime operation, attach as an Exhibit a tabulation of the following:

| Exhibit No. |

(a) Azimuths along which the groundwave contours were calculated for all stations or proposals shown on allocation study exhibits required by (3Xa).

(b) Inverse distance field strength used along each azimuth.

(c) Basis for ground conductivity utilized along each azimuth specified in (4Xa). If field strength measurements are used, the measurements must be either submitted or be properly identified as to location in Commission's files.

(d) Calculated distances.

B. Critical Hours *(If applicable, see 47 C.F.R. Section 73.187)*

(1) For critical hour operation, attach as an Exhibit map(s) having appropriate scales, showing the 1000, 5 and 0.5 critical hours contours in mV/m for both existing and proposed operations. On the map(s) showing the 5 mV/m contours **CLEARLY INDICATE THE LEGAL BOUNDARIES OF THE PRINCIPAL COMMUNITY TO BE SERVED.**

| Exhibit No. |

(2) Does the critical hours 5 mV/m contour encompass the legal boundaries of the principal community be served?

□ Yes   □ No

If No, attach as an Exhibit justification for waiver of 47 C.F.R. Section 73.24(j).

| Exhibit No. |

(3) For critical hours operation, attach as an Exhibit an allocation study utilizing Figure M-3 *(Figure R-3 47 C.F.R. Section 73.190)* or an accurate full scale reproduction thereof and using pertinent field strength measurement data where available, a full scale exhibit of the entire pertinent area to show the following: The 0.1 mV/m groundwave contour pertinent arcs of Class I stations and appropriate studies to establish compliance with 47 C.F.R. Section 73.187 when operation is proposed on a U.S. Class I channel.

| Exhibit No. |

SECTION V–A – AM BROADCAST ENGINEERING DATA (Page 5)

C. Nighttime. *(For assistance, see 47 C.F.R. Section 73.182)*

    (1) For nighttime operation, attach as an Exhibit map(s) having appropriate scales, showing the 1000 mV/m and coverage contours (appropriate minimum protected value for proposed class of station, or RSS nighttime interference-free contour, whichever is the greater value) for both existing and proposed operations. On the map(s) showing the interference-free contours. CLEARLY INDICATE THE LEGAL BOUNDARIES OF THE PRINCIPAL COMMUNITY TO BE SERVED.

> Exhibit No.

    (2) Does the nighttime coverage contour encompass the legal boundaries of the principal community to be served?

> ☐ Yes ☐ No

    If No, attach as an Exhibit justification for waiver of, or exemption pursuant to 47 C.F.R. Section 73.24(J).

> Exhibit No.

    (3) For nighttime operation, attach as an Exhibit allocation data including the following:

> Exhibit No.

        (a) Proposed nighttime limitation to other existing or proposed stations with which objectionable interference could result, as well as those other proposals and existing stations which require study to show clearly absence of objectionable interference.

        (b) All existing or proposed nighttime limitations which enter into the nighttime RSS limitation of each of the existing or proposed facilities investigated under (3)(a) above.

        (c) All existing and proposed limitations which contribute to the RSS nighttime limitation of the proposed operation, together with those limitations which must be studied before being excluded.

        (d) A detailed interference study plotted upon an appropriate scale map if a question exists with respect to nighttime interference to other existing or proposed facilities along bearing other than on a direct line toward the facility considered. (Clipping study)

        (e) The detailed basis for each nighttime limitation calculated under (3)(a), (b), (c) and (d) above.

16. Attach as an Exhibit a map *(7.5 minute U.S. Geological Survey topographic quadrangles, if available)* of the proposed antenna location showing the following information:

> Exhibit No.

    A. Proposed transmitter location accurately plotted with the latitude and longitude lines clearly marked and showing a scale in kilometers.

    B. Heights of buildings or other structures and terrain elevations in the vicinity of the antenna, indicating the location thereof.

    C. Transmitter location and call signs of non-broadcast radio stations *(except amateur and citizens band)*, established commercial and government receiving stations in the general vicinity which may be adversely affected by the proposed operation.

    D. Transmitter location and call letters of all AM, FM and TV broadcast stations within three (3) kilometers of the proposed antenna location.

SECTION V—A — AM BROADCAST ENGINEERING DATA (Page 6)

CERTIFICATION

I certify that I have prepared this Section of this application on behalf of the applicant, and that after such preparation, I have examined and found it to be accurate and true to the best of my knowledge and belief.

Name *(Typed or Printed)*	Relationship to Applicant *(e.g., Consulting Engineer)*
Signature	Address *(Include ZIP Code)*
Date	Telephone No. *(Include Area Code)* ( )

Section V-B — FM BROADCAST ENGINEERING DATA	FOR COMMISSION USE ONLY
	File No. _____
	ASB Referral Date _____
	Referred by _____

Name of Applicant

Call letters *(if issued)*

Is this application being filed in response to a window? ☐ Yes ☐ No

If Yes, specify closing date: _____

Purpose of Application: *(check appropriate box(es))*

☐ Construct a new (main) facility

☐ Modify existing construction permit for main facility

☐ Modify licensed main facility

☐ Construct a new auxiliary facility

☐ Modify existing construction permit for auxiliary facility

☐ Modify licensed auxiliary facility

If purpose is to modify, indicate below the nature of change(s) and specify the file number(s) of the authorizations affected.

☐ Antenna supporting-structure height

☐ Antenna height above average terrain

☐ Antenna location

☐ Main Studio location

☐ Effective radiated power

☐ Frequency

☐ Class

☐ Other *(Summarize briefly)*

File Number(s) _____

1. Allocation:

Channel No.	Principal community to be served:			Class *(check only one box below)*
	City	County	State	☐ A ☐ B1 ☐ B ☐ C3
				☐ C2 ☐ C1 ☐ C

2. Exact location of antenna.

(a) Specify address, city, county and state. If no address, specify distance and bearing relative to the nearest town or landmark.

(b) Geographical coordinates (to nearest second). If mounted on element of an AM array, specify coordinates of center of array. Otherwise, specify tower location. Specify South Latitude or East Longitude where applicable; otherwise, North Latitude or West Longitude will be presumed.

Latitude	°	'	"	Longitude	°	'	"

3. Is the supporting structure the same as that of another station(s) or proposed in another pending application(s)? ☐ Yes ☐ No

If Yes, give call letter(s) or file number(s) or both. _____

If proposal involves a change in height of an existing structure, specify existing height above ground level including antenna, all other appurtenances, and lighting, if any. _____

FCC 301 (Page 14)
June 1989

SECTION V-B – FM BROADCAST ENGINEERING DATA (Page 2)

4. Does the application propose to correct previous site coordinates?   ☐ Yes ☐ No
   If Yes, list old coordinates.

Latitude o ' "	Longitude o ' "

5. Has the FAA been notified of the proposed construction?   ☐ Yes ☐ No
   If Yes, give date and office where notice was filed and attach as an Exhibit a copy of FAA
   determination, if available.   Exhibit No. ☐

   Date _____ Office where filed _____

6. List all landing areas within 8 km of antenna site. Specify distance and bearing from structure to nearest point of the
   nearest runway.

Landing Area	Distance (km)	Bearing (degrees True)
(a) _____	_____	_____
(b) _____	_____	_____

7. (a) Elevation: *(to the nearest meter)*

   (1) of site above mean sea level;   _____ meters

   (2) of the top of supporting structure above ground (including antenna, all other   _____ meters
   appurtenances, and lighting, if any); and

   (3) of the top of supporting structure above mean sea level $[(a)(1) + (a)(2)]$ _____ meters

   (b) Height of radiation center: *(to the nearest meter)*   H = Horizontal; V = Vertical

   (1) above ground   _____ meters (H)

      _____ meters (V)

   (2) above mean sea level $[(a)(1) + (b)(1)]$ _____ meters (H)

      _____ meters (V)

   (3) above average terrain   _____ meters (H)

      _____ meters (V)

8. Attach as an Exhibit sketch(es) of the supporting structure, labelling all elevations required   Exhibit No. ☐
   in Question 7 above, except item 7(b)(3). If mounted on an AM directional-array element,
   specify heights and orientations of all array towers, as well as location of FM radiator.

9. Effective Radiated Power:
   (a) ERP in the horizontal plane
      _____ kw (H*) _____ kw (V*)

   (b) Is beam tilt proposed?   ☐ Yes ☐ No

   If Yes, specify maximum ERP in the plane of the tilted beam, and attach as an Exhibit a   Exhibit No. ☐
   vertical elevational plot of radiated field.
      _____ kw (H*) _____ kw (V*)

   *Polarization

SECTION V–B – FM BROADCAST ENGINEERING DATA (Page 3)

10. Is a directional antenna proposed? ☐ Yes ☐ No

If Yes, attach as an Exhibit a statement with all data specified in 47 C.F.R. Section 73.316, including plot(s) and tabulations of the relative field. | Exhibit No. |

11. Will the proposed facility satisfy the requirements of 47 C.F.R. Sections 73.315(a) and (b)? ☐ Yes ☐ No

If No, attach as an Exhibit a request for waiver and justification therefor, including amounts and percentages of population and area that will not receive 3.16 mV/m service. | Exhibit No. |

12. Will the main studio be within the protected 3.16 mV/m field strength contour of this proposal? ☐ Yes ☐ No

If No, attach as an Exhibit justification pursuant to 47 C.F.R. Section 73.1125. | Exhibit No. |

13. (a) Does the proposed facility satisfy the requirements of 47 C.F.R. Section 73.207? ☐ Yes ☐ No

(b) If the answer to (a) is No, does 47 C.F.R. Section 73.213 apply? ☐ Yes ☐ No

(c) If the answer to (b) is Yes, attach as an Exhibit a justification, including a summary of previous waivers. | Exhibit No. |

(d) If the answer to (a) is No and the answer to (b) is No, attach as an Exhibit a statement describing the short spacing(s) and how it or they arose. | Exhibit No. |

(e) If authorization pursuant to 47 C.F.R. Section 73.215 is requested, attach as an Exhibit a complete engineering study to establish the lack of prohibited overlap of contours involving affected stations. The engineering study must include the following: | Exhibit No. |

(1) Protected and interfering contours, in all directions (360°), for the proposed operation.
(2) Protected and interfering contours, over pertinent arcs, of all short-spaced applications and allotments, including a plot showing each transmitter location, with identifying call letters or file numbers, and indication of whether facility is operating or proposed. For vacant allotments, use the reference coordinates as the transmitter location.
(3) When necessary to show more detail, an additional allocation study utilizing a map with a larger scale to clearly show prohibited overlap will not occur.
(4) A scale of kilometers and properly labeled longitude and latitude lines, shown across the entire exhibit(s). Sufficient lines should be shown so that the location of the sites may be verified.
(5) The official title(s) of the map(s) used in the exhibits(s).

14. Are there: (a) within 60 meters of the proposed antenna, any proposed or authorized FM or TV transmitters, or any nonbroadcast *(except citizens band or amateur)* radio stations; or (b) within the blanketing contour, any established commercial or government receiving stations, cable head-end facilities, or populated areas; or (c) within ten (10) kilometers of the proposed antenna, any proposed or authorized FM or TV transmitters which may produce receiver-induced intermodulation interference? ☐ Yes ☐ No

If Yes, attach as an Exhibit a description of any expected, undesired effects of operations and remedial steps to be pursued if necessary, and a statement accepting full responsibility for the elimination of any objectionable interference (including that caused by receiver-induced or other types of modulation) to facilities in existence or authorized or to radio receivers in use prior to grant of this application. *(See 47 C.F.R. Sections 73.315(b), 73.316(e) and 73.318.)* | Exhibit No. |

SECTION V–B – FM BROADCAST ENGINEERING DATA (Page 4)

15. Attach as an Exhibit a 7.5 minute series U.S. Geological Survey topographic quadrangle map that shows clearly, legibly, and accurately, the location of the proposed transmitting antenna. This map must comply with the requirements set forth in Instruction V. The map must further clearly and legibly display the original printed contour lines and data as well as latitude and longitude markings, and must bear a scale of distance in kilometers.

> Exhibit No.

16. Attach as an Exhibit *(name the source)* a map which shows clearly, legibly, and accurately, and with the original printed latitude and longitude markings and a scale of distance in kilometers:

> Exhibit No.

  (a) the proposed transmitter location, and the radials along which profile graphs have been prepared;

  (b) the 3.16 mV/m and 1 mV/m predicted contours; and

  (c) the legal boundaries of the principal community to be served.

17. Specify area in square kilometers (1 sq. mi. = 2.59 sq. km.) and population (latest census) within the predicted 1 mV/m contour.

  Area_____ sq. km.   Population_____

18. For an application involving an auxiliary facility only, attach as an Exhibit a map *(Sectional Aeronautical Chart or equivalent)* that shows clearly, legibly, and accurately, and with latitude and longitude markings and a scale of distance in kilometers:

> Exhibit No.

  (a) the proposed auxiliary 1 mV/m contour; and

  (b) the 1 mV/m contour of the licensed main facility for which the applied-for facility will be auxiliary. Also specify the file number of the license.

19. Terrain and coverage data *(to be calculated in accordance with 47 C.F.R. Section 73.313)*

  Source of terrain data: *(check only one box below)*

  ☐ Linearly interpolated 30-second database   ☐ 7.5 minute topographic map

    (Source: _____)

  ☐ Other *(briefly summarize)*

SECTION V-B - FM BROADCAST ENGINEERING DATA (Page 5)

Radial bearing (degrees True)	Height of radiation center above average elevation of radial from 3 to 16 km (meters)	Predicted Distances	
		To the 3.16 mV/m contour (kilometers)	To the 1 mV/m contour (kilometers)
*			
0			
45			
90			
135			
180			
225			
270			
315			

*Radial through principal community, if not one of the major radials. This radial should NOT be included in the calculation of HAAT.

20. Environmental Statement*(See 47 C.F.R. Section 1.1301 et seq.)*

Would a Commission grant of this application come within Section 1.1307 of the FCC Rules, such that it may have a significant environmental impact? ☐ Yes ☐ No

If you answer Yes, submit as an Exhibit an Environmental Assessment required by Section 1.1311. ☐ Exhibit No.

If No, explain briefly why not.

CERTIFICATION

I certify that I have prepared this Section of this application on behalf of the applicant, and that after such preparation, I have examined the foregoing and found it to be accurate and true to the best of my knowledge and belief.

Name *(Typed or Printed)*	Relationship to Applicant *(e.g., Consulting Engineer)*
Signature	Address *(Include ZIP Code)*
Date	Telephone No. *(Include Area Code)* ( )

	FOR COMMISSION USE ONLY
Section V-C – TV BROADCAST ENGINEERING DATA	File No. _____
	ASB Referral Date _____
	Referred by _____

Name of Applicant	Call letters *(if issued)*

Purpose of Application *(check appropriate box)*:

☐ Construct a new (main) facility

☐ Construct a new auxiliary facility

☐ Modify existing construction permit for main facility

☐ Modify existing construction permit for auxiliary facility

☐ Modify licensed main facility

☐ Modify licensed auxiliary facility

If purpose is to modify, indicate nature of change(s) by checking appropriate box(es), and specify the file number(s) of the authorization(s) affected:

☐ Antenna supporting-structure height

☐ Effective radiated power

☐ Antenna height above average terrain

☐ Frequency

☐ Antenna location

☐ Antenna system

☐ Main Studio location

☐ Other *(Summarize briefly)*

File Number(s) _____

---

1. Allocation:

Channel No.	Offset *(check one)*	Principal community to be served:			Zone *(check one)*
	☐ Plus	City	County	State	☐ I
	☐ Minus				☐ II
_____	☐ Zero				☐ III

2. Exact location of antenna:

(a) Specify address, town or city, county and state. If no address, specify distance and bearing to the nearest landmark.

(b) Geographical coordinates (to nearest second). If mounted on element of an AM array, specify coordinates of center of array. Otherwise, specify tower location. Specify South Latitude or East Longitude where applicable; otherwise, North Latitude and West Longitude will be presumed.

Latitude	°	'	"	Longitude	°	'	"

3. Is the supporting structure the same as that of another station(s) or proposed in another pending application(s)?   ☐ Yes ☐ No

If Yes, give call letter(s) or file number(s) or both. _____

If proposal involves a change in height of an existing structure, specify existing height above ground level, including antenna, all other appurtenances, and lighting, if any. _____

SECTION V-C - TV BROADCAST ENGINEERING DATA (Page 2)

4. Does the application propose to correct previous site coordinates? ☐ Yes ☐ No
   If Yes, list old coordinates.

Latitude	°	'	"	Longitude	°	'	"

5. Has the FAA been notified of the proposed construction? ☐ Yes ☐ No
   If Yes, give date and office where notice was filed and attach as an Exhibit a copy of FAA
   determination, if available.

Exhibit No.

   Date _____ Office where filed_____

6. List all landing areas within 8 km of antenna site. Specify distance and bearing from structure to nearest point of
   the nearest runway.

	Landing Area	Distance (km)	Bearing (degrees True)
(a)			
(b)			

7. (a) Elevation: *(to the nearest meter)*

   (1) of site above mean sea level; _____ meters

   (2) of the top of supporting structure above ground (including antenna, all other _____ meters
       appurtenances, and lighting, if any); and

   (3) of the top of supporting structure above mean sea level [(a)(1) + (a)(2)] _____ meters

   (b) Height of antenna radiation center: *(to the nearest meter)*

   (1) above ground; _____ meters

   (2) above mean sea level [(a)(1) + (b)(1)]; and _____ meters

   (3) above average terrain. _____ meters

8. Attach as an Exhibit sketch(es) of the supporting structure, labelling all elevations required
   in Question 7 above, except item 7(b)(3). If mounted on an AM directional-array element,
   specify heights and orientations of all array towers, as well as location of TV radiator.

Exhibit No.

9. Maximum visual effective radiated power _____ kW

SECTION V–C – TV BROADCAST ENGINEERING DATA (Page 3)

10. Antenna:

(a) Manufacturer_____ (b) Model No._____

(c) Is a directional antenna proposed?   ☐ Yes ☐ No

If Yes, specify major lobe azimuth(s)_____ degrees True and attach   ☐ Exhibit No.
as an Exhibit all data specified in 47 C.F.R. Section 73.685.

(d) Is electrical beam tilt proposed?   ☐ Yes ☐ No

If Yes, specify _____ degrees electrical beam tilt and attach as an Exhibit all data   ☐ Exhibit No.
specified in 47 C.F.R. Section 73.685.

(e) Is mechanical beam tilt proposed?   ☐ Yes ☐ No

If Yes, specify _____ degrees mechanical beam tilt toward azimuth _____ degrees   ☐ Exhibit No.
True and attach as an Exhibit all data specified in 47 C.F.R. Section 73.685.

(f) The proposed antenna is: (check only one box)

☐ horizontally polarized   ☐ circularly polarized   ☐ elliptically polarized

11. Will the proposed facility satisfy the requirements of 47 C.F.R. Sections 73.685(a) and (b)?   ☐ Yes ☐ No

If No, attach as an Exhibit justification therefor, including amounts and percentages of   ☐ Exhibit No.
population and area that will not receive City Grade service.

12. Will the main studio be located within the station's predicted principal community contour   ☐ Yes ☐ No
as defined by 47 C.F.R. Section 73.685(a)?

If No, attach as an Exhibit justification pursuant to 47 C.F.R. Section 73.1125.   ☐ Exhibit No.

13. Does the proposed facility satisfy the requirement of 47 C.F.R. Section 73.610?   ☐ Yes ☐ No

If No, attach as an Exhibit justification therefor, including a summary of any previously   ☐ Exhibit No.
granted waiver(s).

14. Are there: (a) within 60 meters of the proposed antenna, any proposed or authorized FM or   ☐ Yes ☐ No
TV transmitters; or (b) in the general vicinity, any nonbroadcast (except citizens band or
amateur) radio stations or any established commercial or government receiving stations?

If Yes, attach as an Exhibit a description of the expected, undesired effects of operations   ☐ Exhibit No.
and remedial steps to be pursued, if necessary, and a statement accepting full responsibility
for the elimination of any objectionable interference (including that caused by intermodulation)
to facilities in existence or authorized prior to grant of this application. (See 47 C.F.R. Sections
73.685(d) and (g).)

15. Attach as an Exhibit a topographic map that shows clearly, legibly, and accurately, the   ☐ Exhibit No.
location of the proposed transmitting antenna. This map must comply with the provisions of
47 C.F.R. Section 73.684(g). The map must further display clearly and legibly the original
printed contour lines and data as well as latitude and longitude markings, and must bear a
scale of distance in kilometers.

SECTION V-C - TV BROADCAST ENGINEERING DATA (Page 4)

16. Attach as an Exhibit a map *(Sectional Aeronautical Chart or equivalent)* which shows clearly, legibly and accurately, and with the original printed latitude and longitude markings and a scale of distance in kilometers:

Exhibit No.

    (a) The proposed transmitter location, and the radials along which profile graphs have been prepared;
    (b) The City Grade, Grade A and Grade B predicted contours; and
    (c) The legal boundaries of the principal community to be served.

17. Specify area in square kilometers (1 sq. mi. = 2.59 sq. km.) and population *(latest census)* within the predicted Grade B contour.

    Area _____ sq. km.   Population _____

18. For an application involving an auxiliary facility only, attach as an Exhibit a map *(Sectional Aeronautical Chart or equivalent)* that shows clearly, legibly, and accurately, and with latitude and longitude markings and a scale of distance in kilometers:

Exhibit No.

    (a) The proposed auxiliary Grade B contour; and
    (b) The Grade B contour of the licensed main facility for which the applied-for facility will be the auxiliary.
    (Main facility license file number _____)

19. Terrain and Coverage Data *(To be calculated in accordance with 47 C.F.R. Section 73.684.)*
    Source of terrain data: *(check only one box below)*

    ☐ Linearly interpolated 30-second database (Source: _____)

    ☐ 7.5 minute topographic map

    ☐ Other *(briefly summarize)*

Radial bearing (degrees True)	Height of radiation center above average elevation of radial from 3 to 16 km (meters)	Predicted Distances		
		To the City Grade Contour (kilometers)	To the Grade A Contour (kilometers)	To the Grade B Contour (kilometers)
*				
0				
45				
90				
135				
180				
225				
270				
315				

*Radial through principal community, if not one of the major radials. This radial should NOT be included in calculation of HAAT.

FCC 301 (Page 22)
June 1989

SECTION V–C – TV BROADCAST ENGINEERING DATA (Page 5)

20. Environmental Statement*(See 47 C.F.R. Section 1.1301 et seq.)*

Would a Commission grant of this application come within 47 C.F.R. Section 1.1307, such that it may have a significant environmental impact? ☐ Yes ☐ No

If you answer Yes, submit as an Exhibit an Environmental Assessment required by 47 C.F.R. Section 1.1311.

| Exhibit No. |

If No, explain briefly why not.

CERTIFICATION

I certify that I have prepared this Section of this application on behalf of the applicant, and that after such preparation, I have examined the foregoing and found it to be accurate and true to the best of my knowledge and belief.

Name *(Typed or Printed)*	Relationship to Applicant *(e.g., Consulting Engineer)*
Signature	Address *(Include ZIP Code)*
Date	Telephone No. *(Include Area Code)* ( )

SECTION VI – EQUAL EMPLOYMENT OPPORTUNITY PROGRAM

1. Does the applicant propose to employ five or more full-time employees? ☐ Yes ☐ No

If Yes, the applicant must include an EEO program called for in the separate Broadcast Equal Employment Opportunity Program Report (FCC 396-A).

SECTION VII – CERTIFICATIONS

1. Has or will the applicant comply with the public notice requirement of 47 C.F.R. Section 73.3580? ☐ Yes ☐ No

2. Has the applicant reasonable assurance, in good faith, that the site or structure proposed in Section V of this form, as the location of its transmitting antenna, will be available to the applicant for the applicant's intended purpose? ☐ Yes ☐ No

If No, attach as an Exhibit, a full explantion.

☐ Exhibit No.

3. If reasonable assurance is not based on applicant's ownership of the proposed site or structure, applicant certifies that it has obtained such reasonable assurance by contacting the owner or person possessing control of the site or structure.

Name of Person Contacted _____

Telephone No. *(include area code)* _____

Person contacted: *(check one box below)*

☐ Owner   ☐ Owner's Agent   ☐ Other *(specify)*

The APPLICANT hereby waives any claim to the use of any particular frequency as against the regulatory power of the United States because of the previous use of the same, whether by license or otherwise, and requests an authorization in accordance with this application. *(See Section 304 of the Communications Act of 1934, as amended.)*

The APPLICANT acknowledges that all the statements made in this application and attached exhibits are considered material representations, and that all exhibits are a material part hereof and incorporated herein.

The APPLICANT represents that this application is not filed for the purpose of impeding, obstructing, or delaying determination on any other application with which it may be in conflict.

In accordance with 47 C.F.R. Section 1.65, the APPLICANT has a continuing obligation to advise the Commission, through amendments, of any substantial and significant changes in information furnished.

SECTION VII – CERTIFICATION (Page 5)

**WILLFUL FALSE STATEMENTS MADE ON THIS FORM ARE PUNISHABLE BY FINE AND IMPRISONMENT.
U.S. CODE, TITLE 18, SECTION 1001.**

I certify that the statements in this application are true and correct to the best of my knowledge and belief, and are made in good faith.

Name of Applicant	Signature
Date	Title

**FCC NOTICE TO INDIVIDUALS REQUIRED BY THE PRIVACY ACT
AND THE PAPERWORK REDUCTION ACT**

The solicitation of personal information requested in this application is authorized by the Communications Act of 1934, as amended. The principal purpose for which the information will be used is to determine if the benefit requested is consistent with the public interest. The staff, consisting variously of attorneys, analysts, engineers and applications examiners, will use the information to determine whether the application should be granted, denied, dismissed, or designated for hearing. If all the information is not provided, the application may be returned without action having been taken upon it or its processing may be delayed while a request is made to provide the missing information. Accordingly, every effort should be made to provide all necessary information. Your response is required to obtain the requested authority.

Public reporting burden for this collection of information is estimated to vary from 71 hours 45 minutes to 301 hours 30 minutes with an average of 118 hours 28 minutes per response, including the time for reviewing instructions, searching existing data sources, gathering and maintaining the data needed, and completing and reviewing the collection of information. Comments regarding this burden estimate or any other aspect of this collection of information, including suggestions for reducing the burden, can be sent to the Federal Communications Commission, Office of Managing Director, Washington, D.C. 20554, and to the Office of Management and Budget, Paperwork Reduction Project (3060-0027), Washington, D.C. 20503.

THE FOREGOING NOTICE IS REQUIRED BY THE PRIVACY ACT OF 1974, P.L. 93–579, DECEMBER 31, 1974, 5 U.S.C. 552a(e)(3), AND THE PAPERWORK REDUCTION ACT OF 1980, P.L. 96–511, DECEMBER 11, 1980, 44 U.S.C. 3507.

Federal Communications Commission
Washington, D.C. 20554

INSTRUCTIONS

Approved by OMB
3060-0010
Expires 6/30/92

Ownership Report, FCC Form 323

Public reporting burden for this collection of information is estimated to average 7 hours per response, including the time for reviewing instructions, searching existing data sources, gathering and maintaining the data needed, and completing and reviewing the collection of information. Send comments regarding this burden estimate or any other aspect of this collection of information, including suggestions for reducing this burden to Federal Communications Commission, Office of Managing Director, Washington, DC 20554, and to the Office of Information and Regulatory Affairs, Office of Management and Budget, Paperwork Reduction Project (3060-0010), Washington, DC 20503.

1. This report is to be filed by AM, FM, International or Television broadcast stations as indicated below *(see 47 C.F.R. Section 73.3615)*. If there has been no change since the last filing of this form, a letter may be filed in lieu of a new report, stating that the previously filed report has been examined and is currently accurate.

   (a) By licensee once a year on the anniversary of the station's renewal application filing date. Where the licensee, however, is a partnership that is composed entirely of natural persons, the annual reporting requirement does not apply. Similarly, sole proprietorships *(i.e., where the station is licensed to an individual(s))* are not required to file annually.

   (b) By permittee or licensee within 30 days after the grant of an original construction permit or the consummation, pursuant to Commission consent, of a transfer of control or an assignment. A permittee is also required to update its initial report or to certify the continuing accuracy and completeness of that report when the permittee applies for a station license.

   (c) File one copy with the Federal Communications Commission, in accordance with 47 C.F.R. Section 0.401. If information submitted is equally applicable to each listed station, one annual report may be filed for all such stations; otherwise, a separate report shall be filed for each station on the appropriate filing date.

   (d) The person certifying the accuracy of the information in this report must be the individual licensee or permittee, a general partner in the licensee or permittee partnership, or an appropriate officer in the licensee or permittee corporation or association. If this report is filed for a respondent and not for a licensee or permittee, the person certifying the accuracy of the information must be a general partner in the respondent partnership or an appropriate officer in the respondent corporation or association.

2. Any contract or modification of contract relating to the ownership, control, or management of the licensee or permittee or to its stock must be filed with the Commission, as required by 47 C.F.R. Section 73.3613. Attention is directed to the fact that Section 73.3613 requires the filing of *all* contracts of the types specified and is not limited to executed contracts but includes options, pledges, and other executory agreements and contracts relating to ownership, control, or management.

3. If the licensee or permittee is directly or indirectly controlled by another entity or if another entity has an attributable interest in such licensee or permittee, a separate Form 323 should be submitted for such entity. For successive entities, interests are multiplied. See Instruction 6.

4. Limited partners in a limited partnership need not be reported IF the limited partners are not materially involved, directly or indirectly, in the management or operation of the media-related activities of the licensee, permittee or respondent so certifies. A statement assuring this non-involvement must be attached to this report. Sufficient insulation of a limited partner for purposes of this certification would be assured if the limited partnership agreement: (a) specifies that any exempt limited partner *(if not a natural person, its directors, officers, partners, etc.)* cannot act as an employee of the limited partnership if his or her functions, directly or indirectly relate to the media enterprises of the company; (b) bars any exempt limited partner from serving, in any material capacity, as an independent contractor or agent with respect to the partnership's media enterprises; (c) restricts any exempt limited partner from communicating with the licensee or the general partner on matters pertaining to the day-to-day operations of its business; (d) empowers the general partner to veto any admissions of additional general partners admitted by vote of the exempt limited partners; (e) prohibits any exempt limited partner from voting on the removal of a general partner or limits this right to situations where the general partner is subject to bankruptcy proceedings, as described in Sections 402 (4)-(5) of the Revised Uniform Limited Partnership Act or is adjudicated incompetent by a court of competent jurisdiction; (f) bars any exempt limited partner from performing any services to the limited partnership materially relating to its media activities, with the exception of making loans to, or acting as a surety for, the business; and (g) states, in express terms, that any exempt limited partner is prohibited from becoming actively involved in the management or operation of the media businesses of the partnership. Notwithstanding conformance of the partnership agreement to this criteria, however, the requisite certification cannot be made if the licensee, permittee or respondent has actual knowledge of a material involvement of the limited partner in the management or operation of the media-related business of the partnership. In the event that the licensee, permittee or respondent cannot certify as to the noninvolvement of the limited partners, the limited partners will be considered to be holders of attributable interests regarding whom full information is required.

FCC 323 Instructions
February 1990

5. Under "Remarks," Paragraph 7, Page 2, give full information as to any family relationship *(parent-child, husband-wife, brothers, sisters)*, between one or more officers, directors, stockholders, or partners of the licensee or permittee and any other officer, director, stockholder, or partner. In situations in which a marital relationship is involved, the interests held by one spouse are presumptively attributed to the other and both spouses may, unless this presumption is rebutted by an appropriate showing, be considered to be holders of attributable interests regarding whom full information is required. In addition, a permittee or licensee seeking attribution exemption for eligible officers or directors should identify that individual by name and title, fully describe that person's duties and responsibilities, and explain why that individual should not be attributed an interest.

6. The following interests are attributable *(and the holder of the interest is cognizable)* and should be reported in response to Question 8:

If a corporation, all officers and directors and each owner of stock accounting for 5% or more of the outstanding votes in the corporation. (Investment companies, insurance companies or trust departments of banks need be listed only if the aggregated holding accounts for 10% or more of the outstanding votes, provided the licensee certifies that such entities exercise no influence over the corporation, directly or indirectly, and have no representatives among the officers and directors of the corporation).

If a single entity holds more than 50% of the voting stock, and a simple majority is all that is required to control corporate affairs, no other stockholder need be reported.

If any stockholder agreement exists pertaining to cooperative voting accounting for 5% or more of the votes *(listed in response to Question 7)*, list the block of stock as if held by a single entity, and also list *(immediately following)* any stockholder holding 5% or more of the stock in that block.

If a partnership, list all partners. (If a limited partnership and Question 5 is answered "Yes," list only general partners and only those limited partners that hold interests considered attributable under Instruction 4, explaining that involvement.)

If the entity for which this report is filed is not the subject licensee, but a minority, non-controlling stockholder or a partner in the licensee, list only those stockholders whose interest, when multiplied by the reporting entity's interest, would account for 5% or more of the votes of the subject licensee; list all partners. Any entity holding over 50% of its subsidiary will be considered as a 100% owner for reporting purposes. E.g., if this report is filed for corporation X which owns stock accounting for 25% of the subject licensee votes, then only those stockholders of X which hold stock

accounting for 20% or more need be listed (.25 X .20 = .05). Also, such an entity need report the directors "executive" officers *(president, vice-president, secretary, treasurer or their equivalents)* and any other officers with a relationship or responsibility to the licensee including a responsibility in determining how the entity's stock in the licensee is voted. Also, for such an entity, Questions 6 and 7 need not be answered. See Instruction 5 above with respect to the attribution exemption showing necessary for officers and directors with duties unrelated to the licensee.

If the stock is held in trust, if the trustee has the sole power to vote the stock and sole power to dispose of the assets of the trust, and if the trustee is an independent person with no familial or business relationship with the beneficiary or grantor, then only the trustee shall be reported as "owner" of the stock. If the grantor or beneficiary shares the power to vote, has the sole power to dispose of the stock, or has the power to replace the trustee at will, that party shall also be listed as an "owner" of the stock.

7. THIS FORM IS NOT TO BE USED TO REPORT OR REQUEST A TRANSFER OF CONTROL OR ASSIGNMENT OF LICENSE OR CONSTRUCTION PERMIT *(except to report a transfer of control or assignment of license made pursuant to prior Commission consent)*. The appropriate forms for use in connection with such transfers or assignments are FCC Forms 314, 315 and 316. It is the responsibility of the licensee or permittee to determine whether a given transaction constitutes a transfer of control or an assignment. However, for purposes of example only, and for the convenience of interested persons, there are listed below some of the more common types of transfers.

A transfer of control takes place when:

(a) An individual stockholder gains or loses affirmative or negative (50%) control. (Affirmative control consists of control of more than 50% of voting stock; negative control consists of control of exactly 50% of voting stock.)

(b) Any family group or any individual in a family group gains or loses affirmative or negative (50%) control. *(See also Instruction 6.)*

(c) Any group in privity gains or loses affirmative or negative (50%) control.

The following are examples of transfers of control or assignments of licenses requiring *prior* Commission consent:

(a) A, who owns 51% of the licensee's or permittee's stock, sells 1% or more thereof. A transfer has been effected.

(b) X corporation, wholly owned by Y family, retires outstanding stock which results in family member A's individual holdings being increased to 50% or more. A transfer has been effected.

(c) A and B, husband and wife, each owns 50% of the licensee's or permittee's stock. A sells any of his stock to B. A transfer has been effected.

(d) A is the partner in the licensee. A sells any part of his interest to newcomer B or existing partner C. An assignment has been effected.

(e) X partnership incorporates. An assignment has been effected.

(f) Minority stockholders form a voting trust to vote their 50% or more combined stockholdings. A transfer has been effected.

(g) A, B, C, D and E each own 20% of the stock of X corporation, A, B and C sell their stock to F, G and H at different times. A transfer is effected at such time as 50% or more of the stock passes out of the hands of the stockholders who held stock at the time the original authorization for the licensee or permittee corporation was issued.

8. For further information regarding the above, see *Report and Order in MM Docket No. 83-46*, 49 Fed. Reg. 19482 (May 8, 1984), 97 FCC 2d 997, *reconsideration granted in part*, 50 Fed. Reg. 27438 (July 3, 1984), 58 RR 2d 604, *further modified on reconsideration*, 52 Fed. Reg. (January 15, 1987), 61 RR 2d 739 (1986). See also 47 C.F.R. Sections 73.3540 and 73.3541.

Approved by OMB
3080-0010
Expires 6/30/92

CERTIFICATION

I certify that I am _____
(Official title, see Instruction 1)

of _____
(Exact legal title or name of respondent)

United States of America
Federal Communications Commission
Washington, D. C. 20554

that I have examined this Report, that to the best of my knowledge and belief, all statements in the Report are true, correct and complete.

Ownership Report

NOTE: Before filling out this form, read attached instructions

(Date of certification must be within 60 days of the date shown in Item 1 and in no event prior to Item 1 date):

Section 310(d) of the Communications Act of 1934 requires that consent of the Commission must be obtained prior to the assignment or transfer of control of a station license or construction permit. This form may not be used to report or request an assignment of license/permit or transfer of control (except to report an assignment of license/permit or transfer of control made pursuant to prior Commission consent).

_____ _____ , 19 _____
(Signature)   (Date)

1. All of the information furnished in this Report is accurate as of

_____ , 19 _____
(Date must comply with Section 73.3615(a), i.e., information must be current within 60 days of the filing of this report, when 1(a) below is checked.)

Telephone No. of respondent (include area code):

Any person who willfully makes false statements on this report can be punished by fine or imprisonment. U.S. Code, Title 18, Section 1001.

This report is filed pursuant to Instruction (check one)

Name and Post Office Address of respondent:

1(a) ☐ Annual   1(b) ☐ Transfer of Control or Assignment of License   1(c) ☐ Other

for the following stations:

Call Letters	Location	Class of service

4. Name of entity, if other than licensee or permittee, for which report is filed (see Instruction 3):

2. Give the name of any corporation or other entity for whom a separate Report is filed due to its interest in the subject licensee (See Instruction 3):

5. Respondent is:

☐ Sole Proprietorship

☐ For-profit corporation

3. Show the attributable interests in any other broadcast station of the respondent. Also, show any interest of the respondent, whether or not attributable, which is 5% or more of the ownership of any other broadcast station or any newspaper or CATV entity in the same market or with overlapping signals in the same broadcast service, as described in Sections 73.3555 and 76.501 of the Commission's Rules.

☐ Not-for-profit corporation

☐ General Partnership

☐ Limited Partnership

☐ Other: _____

If a limited partnership, is certification statement included as in Instruction 4?

☐ Yes   ☐ No

FCC 323
February 1990

6. List all contracts and other instructions required to be filed by Section 73.3613 of the Commission's Rules and Regulations. (Only licensees, permittees, or a reporting entity with a majority interest in or that otherwise exercises de facto control over the subject licensee or permittee shall respond.)

Description of contract or instrument	Name of person or organization with whom contract is made	Date of Execution	Date of Expiration

7. Capitalization (Only licensees, permittees, or a reporting entity with a majority interest in or that otherwise exercises de facto control over the subject licensee or permittee, shall respond.)

Class of Stock (preferred, common or other)	Voting or Non-voting	Number of Shares		
		Authorized	Issued and Outstanding	Treasury	Unissued

Remarks concerning family relationships, attribution exemptions and certifications: (*See Instructions 4, 5 and 6*)

8. List officers, directors, cognizable stockholders and partners. Use one column for each individual or entity. Attach additional pages, if necessary. See Instructions 4, 5, and 6.

Line (Read carefully - The numbered items below refer to line numbers in the following table.)

1. Name and residence of officer, director, cognizable stockholder or partner (if other than individual also show name, address and citizenship of natural person authorized to vote the stock). List officers first, then directors and, thereafter, remaining stockholders and partners.

2. Citizenship.

3. Office or directorship held.

4. Number of shares or nature of partnership interest.

5. Number of votes.

6. Percentage of votes.

7. Other existing attributable interests in any other broadcast station, including nature and size of such interest.

8. All other ownership interests of 5% or more (whether or not attributable), as well as any corporate officership or directorship, in broadcast, cable, or newspaper entities in the same market or with overlapping signals in the same broadcast service, as described in Sections 73.3555 and 76.501 of the Commission's Rules, including the nature and size of such interests and the position held.

1	(a)	(b)	(c)
2			
3			
4			
5			
6			
7			
8			

**FCC NOTICE TO INDIVIDUALS REQUIRED BY THE PRIVACY ACT
AND THE PAPERWORK REDUCTION ACT**

The solicitation of personal information requested in this Report is authorized by the Communications Act of 1934, as amended. The principal purpose for which the information will be used is to assess compliance with the Commission's multiple ownership restrictions. The staff, consisting variously of attorneys and examiners, will use the information to determine such compliance. If all the information requested is not provided, processing may be delayed while a request is made to provide the missing information. Accordingly, every effort should be made to provide all necessary information. Your response is required to retain your authorization.

**THE FOREGOING NOTICE IS REQUIRED BY THE PRIVACY ACT OF 1974, P.L. 95-579, DECEMBER 31, 1974,
5 U.S.C. 552(d)(3) AND THE PAPERWORK REDUCTION ACT P.L. 96-511, DECEMBER 11, 1980, 44 U.S.C. 3507.**

Approved by OMB
3060-0390
Expires 9/30/93
Estimated Individual Burden:
10 minutes to 1 hour

INSTRUCTIONS FOR COMPLETION OF FCC FORM 395-B

BROADCAST STATION ANNUAL EMPLOYMENT REPORT

1. Who Must File

All licensees and permittees of commercial and noncommercial AM, FM, LPTV, TV and International BROADCAST stations.

2. What Information Must Be Filed

a. If the filing concerns a particular reporting unit (see item 5 below) which had fewer than 5 full-time employees during the selected payroll period (see item 4 below), (a) so indicate in Section III of the form; (b) provide the pertinent identifying information asked for in Sections I and II; (c) complete and sign the certification statement in Section IV of the form. Do not provide the substantive information (statistical data) asked for in Sections V-A and V-B.

b. If the filing concerns a particular reporting unit which had 5 or more full-time employees during the selected payroll period, (a) provide the pertinent identifying information asked for in Sections I and II, and all information asked for in Sections V-A and V-B; and (b) complete and sign the certification statement in Section IV.

3. When and Where to File

Send TWO copies of each Annual Employment Report required under these instructions to the Federal Communications Commission, 1919 M Street, N.W., Washington, D.C. 20554, no later than MAY 31 of each year.

4. Reporting Period

The employment data filed on FCC Form 395-B must reflect the employment figures from any one payroll period in January, February or March. The same payroll period should be used in each year's report.

5. Reporting Units

The employment data filed on FCC Form 395-B must be filed in duplicate:

a. For each AM, FM, LPTV, TV and International Broadcast Station, whether commercial or noncommercial; except that a combined report must be filed for an AM and an FM station, both of which are: (1) under common ownership; and (2) assigned to the same principal city or to different cities within the same metropolitan statistical area.

b. For each Headquarters Office of a multiple station owner report those employees whose primary duties lie in the operation of the individual stations. (A separate Form 395-B need not be filed to cover headquarters employees whose duties relate to the operation of an AM and an FM station covered in a combined AM-FM report under (a) above, if all such employees are included in such combined AM-FM Report).

6. Race/Ethnic Categories

a. White, not of Hispanic Origin – A person having origins in any of the original peoples of Europe, North Africa, or the Middle East.

b. Black, not of Hispanic Origin – A person having origins in any of the black racial groups of Africa.

c. Hispanic – A person of Mexican, Puerto Rican, Cuban, Central or South America or other Spanish Culture or origin, regardless of race.

d. Asian or Pacific Islander – A person having origins in any of the original peoples of the Far East, Southeast Asia, the Indian Subcontinent, or the Pacific Islands. This area includes, for examples, China, Japan, Korea, the Philippine Islands, and Samoa.

e. American Indian or Alaskan Native – A person having origins in any of the original peoples of North America, and who maintain cultural identification through tribal affiliation or community recognition.

7. Job Categories

The following "job category definitions" are provided for your guidance and may be used in completing FCC Form 395-B. A "Comboperson" is to be listed in the job category which represents the work primarily done by that person; a "Comboperson" is to be listed only once. Specific job titles below are not all inclusive or rigid. The proper categorization of any employee depends on the kind and level of the employees' responsibilities.

a. **Officials and Managers** – Occupations requiring administrative personnel who set broad policies, exercise overall responsibility for execution of these policies, and direct individual departments or special phases of a firm's operations. Includes: Presidents and other corporate officers, general managers, station managers, controllers, chief accountants, general counsels, chief engineers, facilities managers, sales managers, business managers, promotion directors, research directors, personnel managers, news directors, operations managers, and production managers.

b. **Professionals** – Occupations requiring either college graduation or experience of such a kind and amount as to provide a comparable background. Includes: On-air personnel, correspondents, producers, writers, editors, researchers, designers, artists, musicians, dancers, accountants, attorneys, nurses, publicists, film buyers, rating and research analysts, systems analysts and programmers, financial analysts, state managers, cinema photographers, senior staff assistants, personnel interviewers, and continuity directors.

c. **Technicians** – Occupations requiring a combination of basic scientific knowledge and manual skill which can be obtained through about 2 years of post high school education, such as is offered in many technical institutes

◄ **DO NOT RETURN THESE INSTRUCTIONS TO THE COMMISSION** ►

and junior colleges, or through equivalent on-the-job training. Includes: Engineers, technicians and engineering aides, including: transmitter, studio maintenance and master control engineers, and news camera, news sound, film lab and drafting technicians. Also film editors, projectionists, and software specialists.

d. **Sales** — Occupations engaging wholly or primarily in direct selling. Includes: Sales account executives, sales analysts, account representatives and sales trainees.

e. **Office and Clerical** — Includes all clerical-type work regardless of level of difficulty, where the activities are predominantly non-manual though some manual work not directly involved with altering or transporting the products is included. Includes: Secretaries, production assistants, traffic managers, traffic department employees, telephone operators, junior rating and research analysts, assistant camera technicians, news and feature assistants, billing clerks, mail clerks, messengers, cashiers, typists, key punch operators, bookkeepers, photo lab assistants, librarians, (music, film or other) readers, administrative assistants, tab operators, TWX operators, PBX operators, printing and duplicating operators, production coordinators, ledger clerks, operations assistants, pages and guides, stock clerks, office machine operators, including computer console operators. (The positions of traffic managers and administrative assistants have been included in the office and clerical category because in most instances they are not truly managerial positions. However, those stations that require managerial functions of either position (director of a full department or special phase of the firm's operation) may include it in the officials and managers category.)

f. **Craftsperson (skilled)** — Manual workers of relatively high skill level having a thorough and comprehensive knowledge of the process involved in their work. Exercise considerable independent judgment and usually receive an extensive period of training. Includes: Electricians, machinists, building construction workers, hair stylists, carpenters, painters, make-up artists, wardrobe person, heating and air conditioning mechanics.

g. **Operatives (semiskilled)** — Workers who operate machine or processing equipment or perform other factory-type duties of intermediate skill level which can be mastered in a few weeks and require only limited training. Includes: Chauffeurs, mobile messengers, drivers, apprentice carpenters and painters, scenic artists, film department assistants, material handlers. (Apprentices — persons employed in a program including work training and related instruction to learn a trade or craft which is traditionally considered an apprenticeship, regardless of whether the program is registered with a Federal or State agency.)

h. **Laborers (unskilled)** — Workers in manual occupations which generally require no special training. Perform elementary duties that may be learned in a few days and require the application of little or no independent judgment. Includes: Studio grips, property persons, laborers performing lifting, pulling, piling, loading, etc., carwashers, set up helpers.

i. **Service Workers** — Workers in both protective and nonprotective service occupations. Includes: Cooks, counter and fountain workers, elevator operators, guards and watchpersons, doorkeepers, stewards, janitors, waiters and waitresses.

8. Total

Include in this column all employees in the Reporting Unit covered in the individual FCC Form 395-B. Consider as "full-time" employees all those working 30 or more hours a week.

9. Minority Group Identification

a. Minority group information necessary for this section may be obtained either by visual surveys of the work force, or from post-employment records as to the identity of employees. An employee may be included in the minority group to which she or he appears to belong, or is regarded in the community as belonging.

b. Since visual surveys are permitted, the fact that minority group identifications are not present on the company records is not an excuse for failure to provide the data called for.

c. Conducting a visual survey and keeping post-employment records of the race or ethnic origin of employees is legal in all jurisdictions and under all Federal and State laws. State laws prohibiting inquiries and record-keeping as to race, etc., relate only to applicants for jobs, not to employees.

d. FCC Form 395-B provides for reporting American Indians or Alaskan Natives; Asians or Pacific Islanders; Blacks, not of Hispanic origin; Hispanics; Whites, not of Hispanic origin; whenever such persons are employed. The category which most closely reflects the individual's recognition in his community should be used to report persons of mixed racial and/or ethnic origins.

10. Networks & Group Owners

Broadcast networks will file employment data in their role as group owners and report employees whose primary duties lie in the operation and/or management of the individual broadcast stations.

Federal Communications Commission
Washington, D.C. 20554

BROADCAST STATION

ANNUAL EMPLOYMENT REPORT 1991

Approved by OMB
3060-0390
Expires 9/30/93

(For FCC Use Only)

Code No.

SECTION I

A. Name of Licensee or Permittee

B. Address

SECTION II

A. TYPE OF RESPONDENT (check ONLY one)

COMMERCIAL BROADCAST STATION

NONCOMMERCIAL BROADCAST STATION

HEADQUARTERS

AM ☐ AM

TV ☐ TV

ER ☐ Educational AM or FM Radio

HQ ☐

FM ☐ FM

LP ☐ Low Power TV

ET ☐ Educational TV

AF ☐ Combined AM & FM in same area (must file a combined report)

IN ☐ International

B. List call letters and location(s) of included stations. AM station is to be listed first in a combined report. Provide former call letters for each station if changed since last 395-B report.

CURRENT CALL LETTERS	LOCATION(S)	FORMER CALL LETTERS

SECTION III

A. PAY PERIOD COVERED BY THIS REPORT (DATE)

B. CHECK APPLICABLE BOX

☐ Fewer than five full-time employees during the selected payroll period (Complete page one only and certification statement and return to FCC)

☐ Five or more full-time employees during selected payroll period (Complete all sections of form and certification statement and return to FCC)

SECTION IV CERTIFICATION

This report must be certified, as follows: (a) By licensee, if an individual; (b) By a partner, if a partnership (general partner, if a limited partnership); (c) By an officer, if a corporation or an association; or (d) By an attorney of the licensee, in case of physical disability or absence from the United States of the licensee.

WILLFUL FALSE STATEMENTS MADE ON THIS FORM ARE PUNISHABLE BY FINE AND IMPRISONMENT.
U.S. CODE, TITLE 18, SECTION 1001.

I certify to the best of my knowledge, information and belief, all statements contained in this report are true and correct.

Signed _____

Title _____

Print Name _____

Date _____ Telephone No. ( ) _____

FCC 395-B
February 1991

SECTION V - EMPLOYEE DATA

A. FULL-TIME PAID EMPLOYEE DATA

JOB CATEGORIES	TOTAL (a-j)	MALE					FEMALE				
		WHITE (NOT HISPANIC) (a)	BLACK (NOT HISPANIC) (b)	HISPANIC (c)	ASIAN OR PACIFIC ISLANDER (d)	AMERICAN INDIAN, ALASKAN NATIVE (e)	WHITE (NOT HISPANIC) (f)	BLACK (NOT HISPANIC) (g)	HISPANIC (h)	ASIAN OR PACIFIC ISLANDER (i)	AMERICAN INDIAN, ALASKAN NATIVE (j)
OFFICIALS & MANAGERS											
PROFESSIONALS											
TECHNICIANS											
SALES WORKERS											
OFFICE & CLERICAL											
CRAFT WORKERS (SKILLED)											
OPERATIVES (SEMI-SKILLED)											
LABORERS (UNSKILLED)											
SERVICE WORKERS											
TOTAL											

B. PART-TIME PAID EMPLOYEE DATA

JOB CATEGORIES	TOTAL (a-j)	MALE					FEMALE				
		WHITE (NOT HISPANIC) (a)	BLACK (NOT HISPANIC) (b)	HISPANIC (c)	ASIAN OR PACIFIC ISLANDER (d)	AMERICAN INDIAN, ALASKAN NATIVE (e)	WHITE (NOT HISPANIC) (f)	BLACK (NOT HISPANIC) (g)	HISPANIC (h)	ASIAN OR PACIFIC ISLANDER (i)	AMERICAN INDIAN, ALASKAN NATIVE (j)
OFFICIALS & MANAGERS											
PROFESSIONALS											
TECHNICIANS											
SALES WORKERS											
OFFICE & CLERICAL											
CRAFT WORKERS (SKILLED)											
OPERATIVES (SEMI-SKILLED)											
LABORERS (UNSKILLED)											
SERVICE WORKERS											
TOTAL											

Federal Communications Commission
Washington, D.C. 20554

Approved by OMB
3060-0120
Expires 9/30/90

BROADCAST EQUAL EMPLOYMENT OPPORTUNITY

MODEL PROGRAM REPORT

1. APPLICANT

Name of Applicant	Address
Telephone Number (include area code)	

2. This form is being submitted in conjunction with:

☐ Application for Construction Permit for New Station   ☐ Application for Assignment of License

☐ Application for Transfer of Control
(a) Call letters (or channel number of frequency) .... _____
(b) Community of License (city and state) .... _____
(C) Service:
☐ AM   ☐ FM   ☐ TV   ☐ Other (Specify) _____

INSTRUCTIONS

Applicants seeking authority to construct a new commercial, noncommercial or international broadcast station, applicants seeking authority to obtain assignment of the construction permit or license of such a station, and applicants seeking authority to acquire control of an entity holding such construction permit or license are required to afford equal employment opportunity to all qualified persons and to refrain from discrimination in employment and related benefits on the basis of race, color, religion, national origin or sex. See Section 73.2080 of the Commission's Rules. Pursuant to these requirements, an applicant who proposes to employ five or more full-time employees must establish a program designed to assure equal employment opportunity for women and minority groups (that is, Blacks not of Hispanic origin, Asians or Pacific Islanders, American Indians or Alaskan Natives and Hispanics). This is submitted to the Commission as the Model EEO Program. If minority group representation in the available labor force is less than five percent (in the aggregate), a program for minority group members is not required. In such cases, a statement so indicating must be set forth in the EEO model program. However, a program must be filed for women since they comprise a significant percentage of virtually all area labor forces. If an applicant proposes to employ fewer than five full-time employees, no EEO program for women or minorities need be filed.

Guidelines for a Model EEO Program and a Model EEO Program are attached.

NOTE: Check appropriate box, sign the certification below and return to FCC:

☐ Station will employ fewer than 5 full-time employees; therefore no written program is being submitted.

☐ Station will employ 5 or more full-time employees. Our Model EEO Program is attached. (You must complete **all** sections of this form.)

I certify that the statements made herein are true, complete, and correct to the best of my knowledge and belief, and are made in good faith.

Signed and dated this _____ day of _____ , 19 ___

Signed _____

Title _____

**WILLFUL FALSE STATEMENTS MADE ON THIS FORM ARE PUNISHABLE BY FINE AND IMPRISONMENT.
U.S. CODE, TITLE 18, SECTION 1001.**

FCC Form 396-A
January 1988

GUIDELINES TO THE MODEL EEO PROGRAM

The model EEO program adopted by the Commission for construction permit applicants, assignees and transferees contains five sections designed to assist the applicant in establishing an effective EEO program for its station. The specific elements which should be addressed are as follows:

I. GENERAL POLICY

The first section of the program should contain a statement by the applicant that it will afford equal employment opportunity in all personnel actions without regard to race, color, religion, national origin or sex, and that it has adopted an EEO program which is designed to fully utilize the skills of qualified minorities and women in the relevant available labor force.

II. RESPONSIBILITY FOR IMPLEMENTATION

This section calls for the name (if known) and title of the official who will be designated by the applicant to have responsibility for implementing the station's program.

III. POLICY DISSEMINATION

The purpose of this section is to disclose the manner in which the station's EEO policy will be communicated to employees and prospective employees. The applicant's program should indicate whether it: (a) intends to utilize an employment application form which contains a notice informing job applicants that discrimination is prohibited and that persons who believe that they have been discriminated against may notify appropriate governmental agencies; (b) will post a notice which informs job applicants and employees that the applicant is an equal opportunity employer and that they may notify appropriate governmental authorities if they believe that they have been discriminated against; and (c) will seek the cooperation of labor unions, if represented at the station, in the implementation of its EEO program and in the inclusion of nondiscrimination provisions in union contracts. The applicant should also set forth any other methods it proposes to utilize in conveying its EEO policy (e.g., orientation materials, on-air announcements, station newsletter) to employees and prospective employees.

IV. RECRUITMENT

The applicant should specify the recruitment sources and other techniques it proposes to use to attract qualified minority and female job applicants. Not all of the categories of recruitment sources need be utilized. The purpose of the listing is to assist the applicant in developing specialized referral sources to establish a pool of qualified minorities and women who can be contacted as job opportunities occur. Sources which subsequently prove to be nonproductive should not be relied on and new sources should be sought.

V. TRAINING

Training programs are not mandatory. Each applicant is expected to decide, depending upon its own individual situation, whether a training program is feasible and would assist in its effort to increase the available pool of qualified minority and female applicants. Additionally, the applicant may set forth any other assistance it proposes to give to students, schools or colleges which is designed to be of benefit to minorities and women interested in entering the broadcasting field. The beneficiary of such assistance should be listed, as well as the form of assistance, such as contributions to scholarships, participation in work study programs, and the like.

MODEL EQUAL EMPLOYMENT OPPORTUNITY PROGRAM

I. GENERAL POLICY

It will be our policy to provide employment opportunity to all qualified individuals without regard to their race, color, religion, national origin or sex in all personnel actions including recruitment, evaluation, selection, promotion, compensation, training and termination.

It will also be our policy to promote the realization of equal employment opportunity through a positive, continuing program of specific practices designed to ensure the full realization of equal employment opportunity without regard to race, color, religion, national origin or sex.

To make this policy effective, and to ensure conformance with the Rules and Regulations of the Federal Communications Commission, we have adopted an Equal Employment Opportunity Program which includes the following elements:

II. RESPONSIBILITY FOR IMPLEMENTATION

(Name/Title) _____ will be responsible for the administration and implementation of our Equal Employment Opportunity Program. It will also be the responsibility of all persons making employment decisions with respect to the recruitment, evaluation, selection, promotion, compensation, training and termination of employees to ensure that our policy and program is adhered to and that no person is discriminated against in employment because of race, color, religion, national origin or sex.

III. POLICY DISSEMINATION

To assure that all members of the staff are cognizant of our equal employment opportunity policy and their individual responsibilities in carrying out this policy, the following communication efforts will be made:

☐ The station's employment application form will contain a notice informing prospective employees that discrimination because of race, color, religion, national origin or sex is prohibited and that they may notify the appropriate local, State or Federal agency if they believe they have been the victims of discrimination.

☐ Appropriate notices will be posted informing applicants and employees that the station is an Equal Opportunity Employer and of their right to notify an appropriate local, State or Federal agency if they believe they have been the victims of discrimination.

☐ We will seek the cooperation of unions, if represented at the station, to help implement our EEO program and all union contracts will contain a nondiscrimination clause.

☐ Other (specify)

IV. RECRUITMENT

To ensure nondiscrimination in relation to minorities and women, and to foster their full consideration whenever job vacancies occur, we propose to utilize the following recruitment procedures:

☐ We will contact a variety of minority and women's organizations to encourage the referral of qualified minority and women applicants whenever job vacancies occur. Examples of organizations we intend to contact are:

☐ In addition to the organizations noted above, which specialize in minority and women candidates, we will deal only with employment services, including State employment agencies, which refer job candidates without regard to their race, color, religion, national origin or sex. Examples of these employment referral services are:

☐ When we recruit prospective employees from educational institutions such recruitment efforts will include area schools and colleges with minority and women enrollments. Educational institutions to be contacted for recruitment purposes are:

☐ When we place employment advertisements with media some of such advertisements will be placed in media which have significant circulation or viewership or are of particular interest to minorities and women. Examples of media to be utilized are:

☐ We will encourage employees to refer qualified minority and women candidates for existing and future job openings.

V. TRAINING

☐ Station resources and/or needs will be such that we will be unable or do not choose to institute programs for upgrading the skills of employees.

☐ We will provide on-the-job training to upgrade the skills of employees.

☐ We will provide assistance to students, schools, or colleges in programs designed to enable qualified minorities and women to compete in the broadcast employment market on an equitable basis:

School or Other Beneficiary   Proposed Form of Assistance

_____   _____

_____   _____

_____   _____

☐ Other (specify)

Federal Communications Commission
Washington, D.C. 20554

Approved by OMB
3060-0113
Expires 9/30/93

BROADCAST EQUAL EMPLOYMENT
OPPORTUNITY PROGRAM REPORT

(To be filed with broadcast license renewal application)

	(For FCC Use Only)
Call Letters _____ _____	Code No.

Name of Licensee _____ _____
City and State which station
is licensed to serve _____ _____

TYPE OF BROADCAST STATION (Check one)

Commercial Broadcast Station   Noncommercial Broadcast Station

☐ AM   ☐ TV   ☐ Educational Radio

☐ FM   ☐ Low Power TV   ☐ Educational TV

☐ Combined AM & FM   ☐ International
   in same area

SEND NOTICES AND COMMUNICATIONS TO THE FOLLOWING NAMED PERSON AT THE ADDRESS INDICATED BELOW:

Name	Street Address		
City	State	ZIP Code	Telephone No. ( )

FILING INSTRUCTIONS

Broadcast station licensees are required to afford equal opportunity to all qualified persons and to refrain from discriminating in employment and related benefits on the basis of race, color, national origin, and sex. See Section 73.2080 of the Commission's Rules. Pursuant to these requirements, a license renewal applicant who employs five or more full-time station employees must file a report of its activities to ensure equal employment opportunity for women and minority groups (that is, Blacks not of Hispanic origin, Asians or Pacific Islanders, American Indians or Alaskan Natives, and Hispanics). If minority group representation in the available labor force is less than five percent (in the aggregate), equal employment opportunity (EEO) program information for minority group members need not be filed. However, EEO program information must be filed for women since they comprise a significant percentage of virtually all area labor forces. If an applicant employs fewer than five full-time employees, no equal employment opportunity activity information need be filed.

A copy of this report must be kept in the station's public file. These actions are required to obtain license renewal. Failure to meet these requirements may result in license renewal being delayed or denied. These requirements are contained in Section 73.2080 of the FCC Rules (47 CFR 73.2080), and are authorized by the Communications Act of 1934, as amended.

☐   If your station employs fewer than five full-time employees, check the box at left, complete the certification below, return the form to the FCC, and place a copy in your station's public file. You do not have to complete the rest of the form.

If your station employs five or more full-time employees, you must complete all of this form and follow all instructions.

☐   If minority group representation in the available labor force is less than 5 percent (in the aggregate) and you choose not to file EEO program information for minority groups, check the box at left and complete the rest of this form with only the information for your program directed towards women.

FCC 396
November 1990

CERTIFICATION

This report must be certified, as follows:

A. By licensee, if an individual;

B. By a partner, if a partnership (general partner, if a limited partnership);

C. By an officer, if a corporation or an association; or

D. By an attorney of the licensee, in case of physical disability or absence from the United States of the licensee.

WILLFUL FALSE STATEMENTS MADE ON THIS FORM ARE PUNISHABLE BY FINE AND IMPRISONMENT (U.S. CODE, TITLE 18, SECTION 1001), AND/OR REVOCATION OF ANY STATION LICENSE OR CONSTRUCTION PERMIT (U.S. CODE, TITLE 47, SECTION 312(a)(11), AND/OR FORFEITURE (U.S. CODE, TITLE 47, SECTION 503).

I certify to the best of my knowledge, information   and belief, all statements contained in this report are true and correct.

Signed
Title
Date
Name of Respondent
Telephone No. (include area code)

FCC NOTICE TO INDIVIDUALS REQUIRED BY THE PRIVACY ACT AND THE PAPERWORK REDUCTION ACT

The solicitation of personal information requested in this application is authorized by the Communications Act of 1934, as amended. The principal purpose for which the information will be used is to determine if the license renewal requested is consistent with the public interest. The staff, consisting variously of attorneys, accountants, engineers, and applications examiners, will use the information to determine whether the license renewal application should be granted, denied, dismissed or designated for hearing. If all the information requested is not provided, the application may be returned without action having been taken upon it or its processing may be delayed while a request is made to provide the missing information. Accordingly, every effort should be made to provide all necessary information. Your response is required to obtain the requested authority.

Public reporting burden for this collection of information is estimated to average 3 hours per response, including the time for reviewing instructions, searching existing data sources, gathering and maintaining the data needed, and completing and reviewing the collection of information. Send comments regarding this burden estimate or any other aspect of this collection of information, including suggestions for reducing this burden to Federal Communications Commission, Office of Managing Director, Washington, DC 20554, and to the Office of Information and Regulatory Affairs, Office of Management and Budget, Paperwork Reduction Project (3060-0113), Washington, DC 20503.

THE FOREGOING NOTICE IS REQUIRED BY THE PRIVACY ACT OF 1974, P.L. 93-579, DECEMBER 31, 1974, 5 U.S.C. 552a(e)(3) AND THE PAPERWORK REDUCTION ACT OF 1980, P.L. 96-511, DECEMBER 11, 1980, 44 U.S.C. 3507.

The purpose of this document is to remind broadcast station licensees of their equal employment opportunity responsibilities and to provide the licensee, the FCC and the public with information about whether the station is meeting these requirements.

GENERAL POLICY

A broadcast station must provide equal employment opportunity to all qualified individuals without regard to their race, color, religion, national origin or sex in all personnel actions including recruitment, evaluation, selection, promotion, compensation, training and termination.

A broadcast station must also encourage applications from qualified minorities and women for hiring and promotion to all types of jobs at the station.

I. RESPONSIBILITY FOR IMPLEMENTATION

A broadcast station must asign a particular official overall responsibility for equal employment opportunity at the station. That official's name and title are:

NAME _____ TITLE _____

It is also the responsibility of all persons at a broadcast station making employment decisions with respect to recruitment, evaluation, selection, promotion, compensation, training and termination of employees to ensure that no person is discriminated against in employment because of race, color, religion, national origin or sex.

II. POLICY DISSEMINATION

A broadcast station must make effective efforts to make management, staff, and prospective employees aware that it offers equal employment opportunity. The Commission considers the efforts listed below to be generally effective. Indicate each practice that your station follows. You also may list any other efforts that you have undertaken.

☐ Notices are posted informing applicants and employees that the station is an Equal Opportunity Employer and that they have the right to notify an appropriate local, State, or Federal agency if they believe they have been the victims of discrimination.

☐ Our station's employment application form contains a notice informing prospective employees that discrimination because of race, color, religion, national origin or sex is prohibited and that they may notify the appropriate local, State, or Federal agency if they believe they have been the victims of discrimination.

☐ We seek the cooperation of the unions represented at the station to help implement our EEO program and all union contracts contain a nondiscrimination clause.

☐ Other (specify)

III. RECRUITMENT

A broadcast station must make efforts to attract qualified minority and women applicants for all types of jobs at the station whenever vacancies occur.

Indicate each practice that your station follows and, where appropriate, list sources and numbers of referrals.

☐ When we place employment advertisements with media some of such advertisements are placed with media which have significant circulation or viewership, or are of particular interest to minorities and women in the recruitment area. Examples of media utilized during the past 12 months and the number of minority and/or women referrals are:

| | Number of Referrals | |
	Minority	Women
_____	_____	_____
_____	_____	_____

☐   Recruit prospective employees from educational institutions, including area schools and colleges with minority and women enrollments. Educational institutions contacted for recruitment purposes during the past 12 months and the number of minority and/or women referrals are:

Educational Institution	Number of Referrals Minority	Women
_____	_____	_____
_____	_____	_____

☐   Contact a variety of minority and women's organizations to encourage the referral of qualified minority and women applicants whenever job vacancies occur. Examples of such organizations contacted during the past 12 months are:

Organization	Number of Referrals Minority	Women
_____	_____	_____
_____	_____	_____
_____	_____	_____

☐   We encourage present employees to refer qualified minority and women candidates for job openings. The number of minority and/or women referrals are:

Minority	Women
_____	_____

☐   Other (specify) and the number of minority and/or women referrals are:

Minority	Women
_____	_____

IV. JOB HIRES

A broadcast station must consider applicants for job openings on a nondiscriminatory basis. Further, to assure that qualified minorities and women are given due consideration for available positions, it must make efforts to encourage them to apply for job openings.

During the twelve-month period prior to filing this application beginning (Month-Day-Year) _____ and ending (Month-Day-Year), _____ we hired:

Total hires _____   Minorities _____   Women _____

During this period, for positions in the upper four job categories, we hired:

Total hires, upper _____   Minorities _____   Women _____
four categories

V. PROMOTIONS

A broadcast station must promote individuals on a nondiscriminatory basis. Further, to assure that qualified minorities and women are given due consideration for promotional opportunities, it must make efforts to encourage them to qualify and apply for advancement.

During the twelve-month period prior to filing this application beginning (Month-Day-Year) _____ and ending (Month-Day-Year) _____, we promoted:

Total promotions _____   Minorities _____   Women _____

During this period, in the upper four job categories, we promoted:

Total promotions, upper _____   Minorities _____   Women _____
four categories

VI. AVAILABLE LABOR FORCE

A broadcast station must evaluate its employment profile and job turnover against the availability of minorities and women in the relevant labor market. The FCC will use labor force data for the MSA in which your station is located, or county data if the station is not located in an MSA, to evaluate your station's equal employment efforts. If you use these data in your evaluation, you need not submit them to the FCC.

This section is optional:

As an alternative to MSA or county labor force data, you may use other data that more accurately reflect the percentages of women and minorities in the labor force available to your station. If such alternative data are used, that data must be submitted on the table below and an explanation attached as to why they are more appropriate.

Percentage in the Labor Force	Women	Blacks not of Hispanic Origin	Asian or Pacific Islanders	American Indians or Alaskan Natives	Hispanics

The above information is for: ☐ M.S.A. ☐ City ☐ County

☐ Other (specify)

VII. COMPLAINTS

You must provide here a brief description of any complaint which has been filed before any body having competent jurisdiction under Federal, State, territorial or local law, alleging unlawful discrimination in the employment practices of the station including the persons involved, the date of filing, the court or agency, the file number (if any), and the disposition or current status of the matter. Examples of such jurisdiction may include the Equal Employment Opportunity Commission, state and local equal opportunity commissions, or other appropriate agencies.

VIII. OTHER INFORMATION

You may also describe other information that you believe would allow the FCC to evaluate more completely your efforts in providing equal opportunity in employment at your station. Submission of such information is optional. Among the additional information you may choose to provide are:

Any training programs the station has undertaken that are designed to enable minorities and women to compete in the broadcast employment market including, but not necessarily limited to, on-the-job training and assistance to students, schools or colleges.

Any problems the station has experienced in assuring equal employment opportunity, or attracting qualified minority and women candidates for employment or promotion.

Any efforts the station has undertaken or will undertake to promote equal opportunity in its employment and to encourage applications from minorities and women.

Copyright Forms

Filling Out Application Form SR

Detach and read these instructions before completing this form. Make sure all applicable spaces have been filled in before you return this form.

BASIC INFORMATION

When to Use This Form: Use Form SR for copyright registration of published or unpublished sound recordings. It should be used where the copyright claim is limited to the sound recording itself, and it may also be used where the same copyright claimant is seeking simultaneous registration of the underlying musical, dramatic, or literary work embodied in the phonorecord.

With one exception, "sound recordings" are works that result from the fixation of a series of musical, spoken, or other sounds. The exception is for the audio portions of audiovisual works, such as a motion picture soundtrack or an audio cassette accompanying a filmstrip; these are considered a part of the audiovisual work as a whole.

Deposit to Accompany Application: An application for copyright registration of a sound recording must be accompanied by a deposit consisting of phonorecords representing the entire work for which registration is to be made.

Unpublished Work: Deposit one complete phonorecord.

Published Work: Deposit two complete phonorecords of the best edition, together with "any printed or other visually perceptible material" published with the phonorecords.

Work First Published Outside the United States: Deposit one complete phonorecord of the first foreign edition.

Contribution to a Collective Work: Deposit one complete phonorecord of the best edition of the collective work.

The Copyright Notice: For published sound recordings, the law provides that a copyright notice in a specified form "shall be placed on all publicly distributed phonorecords of the sound recording." Use of the copyright notice is the responsibility of the copyright owner and does not require advance permission from the Copyright Office. The required form of the notice for phonorecords of sound recordings consists of three elements: (1) the symbol "℗" (the letter "P" in a circle); (2) the year of first publication of the sound recording; and (3) the name of the owner of copyright. For example: "℗ 1981 Rittenhouse Record Co." The notice is to be "placed on the surface of the phonorecord, or on the label or container, in such manner and location as to give reasonable notice of the claim of copyright." For further information about copyright, write: Information and Publications Section, LM-455
Copyright Office, Library of Congress, Washington, D.C. 20559

PRIVACY ACT ADVISORY STATEMENT Required by the Privacy Act of 1974 (P.L. 93-579)
The authority for requesting this information is title 17, U.S.C., secs. 409 and 410. Furnishing the requested information is voluntary. But if the information is not furnished, it may be necessary to delay or refuse registration and you may not be entitled to certain relief, remedies, and benefits provided in chapters 4 and 5 of title 17, U.S.C.
The principal uses of the requested information are the establishment and maintenance of a public record and the examination of the application for compliance with legal requirements.
Other routine uses include public inspection and copying, preparation of public indexes, preparation of public catalogs of copyright registrations, and preparation of search reports upon request.
NOTE: No other advisory statement will be given in connection with this application. Please keep this statement and refer to it if we communicate with you regarding this application.

LINE-BY-LINE INSTRUCTIONS

1 SPACE 1: Title

Title of This Work: Every work submitted for copyright registration must be given a title to identify that particular work. If the phonorecords or any accompanying printed material bear a title (or an identifying phrase that could serve as a title), transcribe that wording completely and exactly on the application. Indexing of the registration and future identification of the work may depend on the information you give here.

Nature of Material Recorded: Indicate the general type or character of the works or other material embodied in the recording. The box marked "Literary" should be checked for nondramatic spoken material of all sorts, including narration, interviews, panel discussions, and training material. If the material recorded is not musical, dramatic, or literary in nature, check "Other" and briefly describe the type of sounds fixed in the recording. For example: "Sound Effects"; "Bird Calls"; "Crowd Noises."

Previous or Alternative Titles: Complete this space if there are any additional titles for the work under which someone searching for the registration might be likely to look, or under which a document pertaining to the work might be recorded.

2 SPACE 2: Author(s)

General Instructions: After reading these instructions, decide who are the "authors" of this work for copyright purposes. Then, unless the work is a "collective work," give the requested information about every "author" who contributed any appreciable amount of copyrightable matter to this version of the work. If you need further space, request additional Continuation Sheets. In the case of a collective work, such as a collection of previously published or registered sound recordings, give information about the author of the collective work as a whole. If you are submitting this Form SR to cover the recorded musical, dramatic, or literary work as well as the sound recording itself, it is important for space 2 to include full information about the various authors of all of the material covered by the copyright claim, making clear the nature of each author's contribution.

Name of Author: The fullest form of the author's name should be given. Unless the work was "made for hire," the individual who actually created the work is its "author." In the case of a work made for hire, the statute provides that "the employer or other person for whom the work was prepared is considered the author."

What is a "Work Made for Hire"? A "work made for hire" is defined as: (1) "a work prepared by an employee within the scope of his or her employment"; or (2) "a work specially ordered or commissioned for use as a contribution to a collective work, as a part of a motion picture or other audiovisual work, as a translation, as a supplementary work, as a compilation, as an instructional text, as a test, as answer material for a test, or as an atlas, if the parties expressly agree in a written instrument signed by them that the work shall be considered a work made for hire." If you have checked "Yes" to indicate that the work was "made for hire," you must give the full legal name of the employer (or other person for whom the work was prepared). You may also include the name of the employee along with the name of the employer (for example: "Elster Record Co., employer for hire of John Ferguson").

"Anonymous" or "Pseudonymous" Work: An author's contribution to a work is "anonymous" if that author is not identified on the copies or phonorecords of the work. An author's contribution to a work is "pseudonymous" if that author is identified on the copies or phonorecords under a fictitious name. If the work is "anonymous" you may: (1) leave the line blank; or (2) state "anonymous" on the line; or (3) reveal the author's identity. If the work is "pseudonymous" you may: (1) leave the line blank; or (2) give the pseudonym and identify it as such (for example: "Huntley Haverstock, pseudonym"); or (3) reveal the author's name, making clear which is the real name and which is the pseudonym (for example: "Judith Barton, whose pseudonym is Madeline Elster"). However, the citizenship or domicile of the author **must** be given in all cases.

Dates of Birth and Death: If the author is dead, the statute requires that the year of death be included in the application unless the work is anonymous or pseudonymous. The author's birth date is optional, but is useful as a form of identification. Leave this space blank if the author's contribution was a "work made for hire."

Author's Nationality or Domicile: Give the country of which the author is a citizen, or the country in which the author is domiciled. Nationality or domicile **must** be given in all cases.

Nature of Authorship: Give a brief general statement of the nature of this particular author's contribution to the work. If you are submitting this Form SR to cover both the sound recording and the underlying musical, dramatic, or literary work, make sure that the precise nature of each author's contribution is reflected here. Examples where the authorship pertains to the recording: "Sound Recording"; "Performance and Recording"; "Compilation and Remixing of Sounds." Examples where the authorship pertains to both the recording and the underlying work: "Words, Music, Performance, Recording"; "Arrangement of Music and Recording"; "Compilation of Poems and Reading."

3 SPACE 3: Creation and Publication

General Instructions: Do not confuse "creation" with "publication." Every application for copyright registration must state "the year in which creation of the work was completed." Give the date and nation of first publication only if the work has been published.

Creation: Under the statute, a work is "created" when it is fixed in a copy or phonorecord for the first time. Where a work has been prepared over a period of time, the part of the work existing in fixed form on a particular date constitutes the created work on that date. The date you give here should be the year in which the author completed the particular version for which registration is now being sought, even if other versions exist or if further changes or additions are planned.

Publication: The statute defines "publication" as "the distribution of copies or phonorecords of a work to the public by sale or other transfer of ownership, or by rental, lease, or lending"; a work is also "published" if there has been an "offering to distribute copies or phonorecords to a group of persons for purposes of further distribution, public performance, or public display." Give the full date (month, day, year) when, and the country where, publication first occurred. If first publication took place simultaneously in the United States and other countries, it is sufficient to state "U.S.A."

4 SPACE 4: Claimant(s)

Name(s) and Address(es) of Copyright Claimant(s): Give the name(s) and address(es) of the copyright claimant(s) in this work even if the claimant is the same as the author. Copyright in a work belongs initially to the author of the work (including, in the case of a work made for hire, the employer or other person for whom the work was prepared). The copyright claimant is either the author of the work or a person or organization to whom the copyright initially belonging to the author has been transferred.

Transfer: The statute provides that, if the copyright claimant is not the author, the application for registration must contain "a brief statement of how the claimant obtained ownership of the copyright." If any copyright claimant named in space 4 is not an author named in space 2, give a brief, general statement summarizing the means by which that claimant obtained ownership of the copyright. Examples: "By written contract"; "Transfer of all rights by author"; "Assignment"; "By will." Do not attach transfer documents or other attachments or riders.

5 SPACE 5: Previous Registration

General Instructions: The questions in space 5 are intended to find out whether an earlier registration has been made for this work and, if so, whether there is any basis for a new registration. As a rule, only one basic copyright registration can be made for the same version of a particular work.

Same Version: If this version is substantially the same as the work covered by a previous registration, a second registration is not generally possible unless: (1) the work has been registered in unpublished form and a second registration is now being sought to cover its first published edition; or (2) someone other than the author is identified as copyright claimant in the earlier registration, and the author is now seeking registration in his or her own name. If either of these two exceptions apply, check the appropriate box and give the earlier registration number and date. Otherwise, do not submit Form SR; instead, write the Copyright Office for information about supplementary registration or recordation of transfers of copyright ownership.

Changed Version: If the work has been changed, and you are now seeking registration to cover the additions or revisions, check the last box in space 5, give the earlier registration number and date, and complete both parts of space 6 in accordance with the instructions below.

Previous Registration Number and Date: If more than one previous registration has been made for the work, give the number and date of the latest registration.

6 SPACE 6: Derivative Work or Compilation

General Instructions: Complete space 6 if this work is a "changed version," "compilation," or "derivative work," and if it incorporates one or more earlier works that have already been published or registered for copyright, or that have fallen into the public domain, or sound recordings that were fixed before February 15, 1972. A "compilation" is defined as "a work formed by the collection and assembling of preexisting materials or of data that are selected, coordinated, or arranged in such a way that the resulting work as a whole constitutes an original work of authorship." A "derivative work" is "a work based on one or more preexisting works." Examples of derivative works include recordings reissued with substantial editorial revisions or abridgments of the recorded sounds, and recordings republished with new recorded material, or "any other form in which a work may be recast, transformed, or adapted." Derivative works also include works "consisting of editorial revisions, annotations, or other modifications" if these changes, as a whole, represent an original work of authorship.

Preexisting Material (space 6a): Complete this space **and** space 6b for derivative works. In this space identify the preexisting work that has been recast, transformed, or adapted. For example, the preexisting material might be: "1970 recording by Sperryville Symphony of Bach Double Concerto." Do not complete this space for compilations.

Material Added to This Work (space 6b): Give a brief, general statement of the **additional** new material covered by the copyright claim for which registration is sought. In the case of a derivative work, identify this new material. Examples: "Recorded performances on bands 1 and 3"; "Remixed sounds from original multitrack sound sources"; "New words, arrangement, and additional sounds." If the work is a compilation, give a brief, general statement describing both the material that has been compiled **and** the compilation itself. Example: "Compilation of 1938 Recordings by various swing bands."

7,8,9 SPACE 7, 8, 9: Fee, Correspondence, Certification, Return Address

Deposit Account: If you maintain a Deposit Account in the Copyright Office, identify it in space 7. Otherwise leave the space blank and send the fee of $10 with your application and deposit.

Correspondence (space 7): This space should contain the name, address, area code, and telephone number of the person to be consulted if correspondence about this application becomes necessary.

Certification (space 8): The application cannot be accepted unless it bears the date and the **handwritten signature** of the author or other copyright claimant, or of the owner of exclusive right(s), or of the duly authorized agent of the author, claimant, or owner of exclusive right(s).

Address for Return of Certificate (space 9): The address box must be completed legibly since the certificate will be returned in a window envelope.

MORE INFORMATION

"Works": "Works" are the basic subject matter of copyright; they are what authors create and copyright protects. The statute draws a sharp distinction between the "work" and "any material object in which the work is embodied."

"Copies" and "Phonorecords": These are the two types of material objects in which "works" are embodied. In general, **"copies"** are objects from which a work can be read or visually perceived, directly or with the aid of a machine or device, such as manuscripts, books, sheet music, film, and videotape. **"Phonorecords"** are objects embodying fixations of sounds, such as audio tapes and phonograph disks. For example, a song (the "work") can be reproduced in sheet music ("copies") or phonograph disks ("phonorecords"), or both.

"Sound Recordings": These are "works," not "copies" or "phonorecords." "Sound recordings" are "works that result from the fixation of a series of musical, spoken, or other sounds, but not including the sounds accompanying a motion picture or other audiovisual work." Example: When a record company issues a new release, the release will typically involve two distinct "works": the "musical work" that has been recorded, and the "sound recording" as a separate work in itself. The material objects that the record company sends out are "phonorecords": physical reproductions of both the "musical work" and the "sound recording."

Should You File More Than One Application? If your work consists of a recorded musical, dramatic, or literary work, and both that "work," and the sound recording as a separate "work," are eligible for registration, the application form you should file depends on the following:

File Only Form SR if: The copyright claimant is the same for both the musical, dramatic, or literary work and for the sound recording, and you are seeking a single registration to cover both of these "works."

File Only Form PA (or Form TX) if: You are seeking to register only the musical, dramatic, or literary work, not the sound recording. Form PA is appropriate for works of the performing arts; Form TX is for nondramatic literary works.

Separate Applications Should Be Filed on Form PA (or Form TX) and on Form SR if: (1) The copyright claimant for the musical, dramatic, or literary work is different from the copyright claimant for the sound recording; or (2) You prefer to have separate registrations for the musical, dramatic, or literary work and for the sound recording.

FORM SR
UNITED STATES COPYRIGHT OFFICE

REGISTRATION NUMBER

_____

SR   SRU

EFFECTIVE DATE OF REGISTRATION

_____

Month   Day   Year

DO NOT WRITE ABOVE THIS LINE. IF YOU NEED MORE SPACE, USE A SEPARATE CONTINUATION SHEET.

1

TITLE OF THIS WORK ▼

PREVIOUS OR ALTERNATIVE TITLES ▼

NATURE OF MATERIAL RECORDED ▼ See instructions.
☐ Musical   ☐ Musical-Dramatic
☐ Dramatic   ☐ Literary
☐ Other _____

2

a

NAME OF AUTHOR ▼

DATES OF BIRTH AND DEATH
Year Born ▼   Year Died ▼

Was this contribution to the work a
"work made for hire"?
☐ Yes
☐ No

AUTHOR'S NATIONALITY OR DOMICILE
Name of Country
OR { Citizen of ▶_____
{ Domiciled in ▶_____

WAS THIS AUTHOR'S CONTRIBUTION TO THE WORK
Anonymous?   ☐ Yes ☐ No   If the answer to either
Pseudonymous? ☐ Yes ☐ No   of these questions is "Yes," see detailed instructions.

NATURE OF AUTHORSHIP Briefly describe nature of the material created by this author in which copyright is claimed. ▼

NOTE

Under the law, the "author" of a "work made for hire" is generally the employer, not the employee (see instructions). For any part of this work that was "made for hire" check "Yes" in the space provided, give the employer (or other person for whom the work was prepared) as "Author" of that part, and leave the space for dates of birth and death blank.

b

NAME OF AUTHOR ▼

DATES OF BIRTH AND DEATH
Year Born ▼   Year Died ▼

Was this contribution to the work a
"work made for hire"?
☐ Yes
☐ No

AUTHOR'S NATIONALITY OR DOMICILE
Name of Country
OR { Citizen of ▶_____
{ Domiciled in ▶_____

WAS THIS AUTHOR'S CONTRIBUTION TO THE WORK
Anonymous?   ☐ Yes ☐ No   If the answer to either
Pseudonymous? ☐ Yes ☐ No   of these questions is "Yes," see detailed instructions.

NATURE OF AUTHORSHIP Briefly describe nature of the material created by this author in which copyright is claimed. ▼

c

NAME OF AUTHOR ▼

DATES OF BIRTH AND DEATH
Year Born ▼   Year Died ▼

Was this contribution to the work a
"work made for hire"?
☐ Yes
☐ No

AUTHOR'S NATIONALITY OR DOMICILE
Name of Country
OR { Citizen of ▶_____
{ Domiciled in ▶_____

WAS THIS AUTHOR'S CONTRIBUTION TO THE WORK
Anonymous?   ☐ Yes ☐ No   If the answer to either
Pseudonymous? ☐ Yes ☐ No   of these questions is "Yes," see detailed instructions.

NATURE OF AUTHORSHIP Briefly describe nature of the material created by this author in which copyright is claimed. ▼

3

YEAR IN WHICH CREATION OF THIS WORK WAS COMPLETED This information must be given in all cases. ◀ Year

DATE AND NATION OF FIRST PUBLICATION OF THIS PARTICULAR WORK
Complete this information ONLY if this work has been published. Month ▶_____ Day ▶_____ Year ▶_____ ◀ Nation

4

COPYRIGHT CLAIMANT(S) Name and address must be given even if the claimant is the same as the author given in space 2.▼

See instructions before completing this space

TRANSFER If the claimant(s) named here in space 4 are different from the author(s) named in space 2, give a brief statement of how the claimant(s) obtained ownership of the copyright.▼

APPLICATION RECEIVED

ONE DEPOSIT RECEIVED

TWO DEPOSITS RECEIVED

REMITTANCE NUMBER AND DATE

DO NOT WRITE HERE OFFICE USE ONLY

MORE ON BACK ▶ • Complete all applicable spaces (numbers 5-9) on the reverse side of this page
• See detailed instructions.   • Sign the form at line 8.

DO NOT WRITE HERE
Page 1 of_____pages

EXAMINED BY	**FORM SR**
CHECKED BY	

☐ CORRESPONDENCE Yes	FOR COPYRIGHT OFFICE
☐ DEPOSIT ACCOUNT FUNDS USED	USE ONLY

DO NOT WRITE ABOVE THIS LINE. IF YOU NEED MORE SPACE, USE A SEPARATE CONTINUATION SHEET.

PREVIOUS REGISTRATION Has registration for this work, or for an earlier version of this work, already been made in the Copyright Office?
☐ **Yes** ☐ **No** If your answer is "Yes," why is another registration being sought? (Check appropriate box) ▼

☐ This is the first published edition of a work previously registered in unpublished form.

☐ This is the first application submitted by this author as copyright claimant.

☐ This is a changed version of the work, as shown by space 6 on this application.

If your answer is "Yes," give: **Previous Registration Number** ▼　　　　**Year of Registration** ▼

5

DERIVATIVE WORK OR COMPILATION Complete both space 6a & 6b for a derivative work; complete only 6b for a compilation.
a. Preexisting Material Identify any preexisting work or works that this work is based on or incorporates. ▼

b. Material Added to This Work Give a brief, general statement of the material that has been added to this work and in which copyright is claimed. ▼

6

See instructions
before completing
this space

DEPOSIT ACCOUNT If the registration fee is to be charged to a Deposit Account established in the Copyright Office, give name and number of Account.
Name ▼　　　　**Account Number** ▼

7

CORRESPONDENCE Give name and address to which correspondence about this application should be sent. Name/Address/Apt/City/State/Zip ▼

Area Code & Telephone Number ▶

Be sure to
give your
daytime phone
◀ number

CERTIFICATION* I, the undersigned, hereby certify that I am the
Check one ▼

☐ author

☐ other copyright claimant

☐ owner of exclusive right(s)

☐ authorized agent of _____
　　　　　Name of author or other copyright claimant, or owner of exclusive right(s) ▲

of the work identified in this application and that the statements made
by me in this application are correct to the best of my knowledge.

8

Typed or printed name and date ▼ If this is a published work, this date must be the same as or later than the date of publication given in space 3.

　　　　　　　　　　　　　　　　　　　　　　　date ▶

☞　**Handwritten signature (X)** ▼

MAIL CERTIFI-CATE TO	Name ▼	**Have you:** ● Completed all necessary spaces? ● Signed your application in space 8?
Certificate will be mailed in window envelope	Number/Street/Apartment Number ▼	● Enclosed check or money order for $10 payable to *Register of Copyrights?* ● Enclosed your deposit material with the application and fee?
	City/State/ZIP ▼	**MAIL TO:** Register of Copyrights, Library of Congress, Washington, D.C. 20559.

9

✩ U.S. GOVERNMENT PRINTING OFFICE: 1984—461-584/10,011　　　　　　　November 1984 — 100,000

FORM PA
UNITED STATES COPYRIGHT OFFICE

REGISTRATION NUMBER

_____

PA   PAU

EFFECTIVE DATE OF REGISTRATION

Month   Day   Year

DO NOT WRITE ABOVE THIS LINE. IF YOU NEED MORE SPACE, USE A SEPARATE CONTINUATION SHEET.

1

TITLE OF THIS WORK ▼

PREVIOUS OR ALTERNATIVE TITLES ▼

NATURE OF THIS WORK ▼ See instructions

2

a

NAME OF AUTHOR▼

DATES OF BIRTH AND DEATH
Year Born ▼   Year Died ▼

Was this contribution to the work a "work made for hire"?
☐ Yes
☐ No

AUTHOR'S NATIONALITY OR DOMICILE
Name of Country
OR { Citizen of ▶ _____
     Domiciled in ▶ _____

WAS THIS AUTHOR'S CONTRIBUTION TO THE WORK
Anonymous?   ☐ Yes ☐ No
Pseudonymous?   ☐ Yes ☐ No
If the answer to either of these questions is "Yes," see detailed instructions

NATURE OF AUTHORSHIP Briefly describe nature of the material created by this author in which copyright is claimed. ▼

NOTE

Under the law, the "author" of a "work made for hire" is generally the employer, not the employee (see instructions). For any part of this work that was "made for hire" check "Yes" in the space provided, give the employer (or other person for whom the work was prepared) as "Author" of that part, and leave the space for dates of birth and death blank.

b

NAME OF AUTHOR ▼

DATES OF BIRTH AND DEATH
Year Born ▼   Year Died ▼

Was this contribution to the work a "work made for hire"?
☐ Yes
☐ No

AUTHOR'S NATIONALITY OR DOMICILE
Name of country
OR { Citizen of ▶ _____
     Domiciled in ▶ _____

WAS THIS AUTHOR'S CONTRIBUTION TO THE WORK
Anonymous?   ☐ Yes ☐ No
Pseudonymous?   ☐ Yes ☐ No
If the answer to either of these questions is "Yes," see detailed instructions.

NATURE OF AUTHORSHIP Briefly describe nature of the material created by this author in which copyright is claimed. ▼

c

NAME OF AUTHOR ▼

DATES OF BIRTH AND DEATH
Year Born ▼   Year Died ▼

Was this contribution to the work a "work made for hire"?
☐ Yes
☐ No

AUTHOR'S NATIONALITY OR DOMICILE
Name of Country
OR { Citizen of ▶ _____
     Domiciled in ▶ _____

WAS THIS AUTHOR'S CONTRIBUTION TO THE WORK
Anonymous?   ☐ Yes ☐ No
Pseudonymous?   ☐ Yes ☐ No
If the answer to either of these questions is "Yes," see detailed instructions.

NATURE OF AUTHORSHIP Briefly describe nature of the material created by this author in which copyright is claimed. ▼

3

YEAR IN WHICH CREATION OF THIS WORK WAS COMPLETED This information must be given in all cases.
◀ Year

DATE AND NATION OF FIRST PUBLICATION OF THIS PARTICULAR WORK
Complete this information ONLY if this work has been published.
Month ▶ _____ Day ▶ _____ Year ▶ _____ ◀ Nation

4

COPYRIGHT CLAIMANT(S) Name and address must be given even if the claimant is the same as the author given in space 2.▼

APPLICATION RECEIVED

ONE DEPOSIT RECEIVED

TWO DEPOSITS RECEIVED

REMITTANCE NUMBER AND DATE

DO NOT WRITE HERE
OFFICE USE ONLY

See instructions before completing this space

TRANSFER If the claimant(s) named here in space 4 are different from the author(s) named in space 2, give a brief statement of how the claimant(s) obtained ownership of the copyright.▼

MORE ON BACK ▶ • Complete all applicable spaces (numbers 5-9) on the reverse side of this page
• See detailed instructions.   • Sign the form at line 8.

DO NOT WRITE HERE
Page 1 of _____ pages

| EXAMINED BY | **FORM PA** |
| CHECKED BY | |

☐ CORRESPONDENCE
Yes

☐ DEPOSIT ACCOUNT
☐ FUNDS USED

FOR
COPYRIGHT
OFFICE
USE
ONLY

DO NOT WRITE ABOVE THIS LINE. IF YOU NEED MORE SPACE, USE A SEPARATE CONTINUATION SHEET.

PREVIOUS REGISTRATION Has registration for this work, or for an earlier version of this work, already been made in the Copyright Office?
☐ **Yes** ☐ **No** If your answer is "Yes," why is another registration being sought? (Check appropriate box) ▼

☐ This is the first published edition of a work previously registered in unpublished form.

☐ This is the first application submitted by this author as copyright claimant.

☐ This is a changed version of the work, as shown by space 6 on this application.

If your answer is "Yes," give: **Previous Registration Number ▼**   **Year of Registration ▼**

5

DERIVATIVE WORK OR COMPILATION Complete both space 6a & 6b for a derivative work; complete only 6b for a compilation.
a. **Preexisting Material** Identify any preexisting work or works that this work is based on or incorporates. ▼

b. **Material Added to This Work** Give a brief, general statement of the material that has been added to this work and in which copyright is claimed.▼

6

See instructions
before completing
this space.

DEPOSIT ACCOUNT If the registration fee is to be charged to a Deposit Account established in the Copyright Office, give name and number of Account.
Name ▼   **Account Number ▼**

CORRESPONDENCE Give name and address to which correspondence about this application should be sent.   Name/Address/Apt/City/State/Zip ▼

Area Code & Telephone Number ▶

7

Be sure to
give your
daytime phone
◀ number

CERTIFICATION* I, the undersigned, hereby certify that I am the
Check only one ▼

☐ author

☐ other copyright claimant

☐ owner of exclusive right(s)

☐ authorized agent of _____
Name of author or other copyright claimant, or owner of exclusive right(s) ▲

of the work identified in this application and that the statements made
by me in this application are correct to the best of my knowledge.

Typed or printed name and date ▼ If this is a published work, this date must be the same as or later than the date of publication given in space 3.

_____ **date ▶** _____

☞ **Handwritten signature (X) ▼**

8

**MAIL
CERTIFI-
CATE TO**

**Certificate
will be
mailed in
window
envelope**

Name ▼

Number/Street/Apartment Number ▼

City/State/ZIP ▼

Have you:
• Completed all necessary
  spaces?
• Signed your application in space
  8?
• Enclosed check or money order
  for $10 payable to *Register of
  Copyrights?*
• Enclosed your deposit material
  with the application and fee?
MAIL TO: Register of Copyrights,
Library of Congress, Washington,
D.C. 20559

9

* 17 U.S.C. § 506(e): Any person who knowingly makes a false representation of a material fact in the application for copyright registration provided for by section 409, or in any written statement filed in
connection with the application, shall be fined not more than $2,500.

U.S. GOVERNMENT PRINTING OFFICE: 1987—181—531 60,002

August 1987—200,000

4 □ □ □
□ □ □
□ □ □

ASCAP Radio
Agreement Form

ANNUAL STATEMENT OF ACCOUNT **FORM AB-86**

ascap
American Society of Composers, Authors & Publishers
ASCAP Building—One Lincoln Plaza, New York, N.Y. 10023

Submitted by:

Signature Title Date

FOR RADIO STATION:

Call Letters

Licensee

Address

PART 1 Account Information

Reporting Period*

*Report must be on Calendar Year Basis

19 ☐

If less than full year Reporting Period

☐ to ☐

Month Day Year   Month Day Year

Type of Station

AM ☐
FM ☐
AM-FM Simulcast ☐

If AM-FM Simulcast
Enter call letters of
second station
☐☐☐☐☐ ☐

Accounting Method

Billing Basis ☐

Cash Basis* ☐
*See Lic. ¶6E

Reporting Method

Standard Deduction ☐

Itemized Deductions ☐

PART 2 Fee Computation

1	Gross Revenue (excluding non-cash payments in goods and or services) (Lic. ¶2F)	1
2	Network Revenue for Programs of Licensed Networks (Lic. ¶2G(1))	2
3	Advertising Agency Commissions (Lic. ¶2G(2))	3
4	Net Revenue for Political Broadcasts (Lic. ¶2G(3))	4
5	Bad Debts (Lic. ¶2G(4))	5
6	Rate Card Discounts (Lic. ¶2G(5))	6
7	Net Revenue Cleared at the Source (Lic. ¶2G(6))	7
8	Total Adjustments to Gross (Add lines 2 thru 7)	8
9	Adjusted Gross Revenue/Revenue Subject to Fee (Subtract line 8 from line 1)	9

Skip lines 10-13 unless you itemize deductions.

10	Total Itemized Deductions (from line 22)	10
11	Enter 15% of Line 9 (Adjusted Gross Revenue)	11
12	Subtract Line 11 from line 10	12
13	Revenue Subject to Fee (Subtract line 12 from line 9)	13
14	License Fee (1.56% of line 9 or line 13 but not less than $360)	14

PART 3 COMPLETE ONLY IF YOU ITEMIZE DEDUCTIONS

15 Schedule: Compensation Under Lic. ¶2H (1) NAMES OF PERSONNEL ANNUAL COMPENSATION

Adjusted Gross Revenue	Amount Not Deductible
Under $ 50,000	$ 5,200
$ 50,000 · $ 149,999	$15,800
$ 150,000 · $ 299,999	$23,400
$ 300,000 · $ 499,999	$35,100
$ 500,000 · $ 749,999	$39,000
$ 750,000 · $ 999,999	$45,500
$1,000,000 and over	$52,000

Total 15

16	Amount Non-Deductible (See Table at right)	16
17	Deductible Compensation (Lic. ¶2H(1)) (Subtract 16 from line 15)	17
18	News Ticker and Audio (Lic. ¶2H(2))	18
19	Remote Pickups (Lic. ¶2H(3)(a))	19
20	Broadcast Rights (Lic. ¶2H(3)(b))	20
21	Other, Specify License Paragraph	21

LOCAL STATION BLANKET RADIO LICENSE

AGREEMENT made between AMERICAN SOCIETY OF COMPOSERS, AUTHORS AND PUB-
LISHERS ("Society") and

("Licensee") as follows:

1.   **Scope of License.** Society grants to Licensee and Licensee accepts for a period commencing as of
        19   and ending December 31, 1990, a license to perform publicly by radio broadcasting on
Licensee's local radio programs from Radio Station

located at

("the Station") non-dramatic performances of the separate musical compositions in the Society's repertory. This
license does not extend to or include the public performance by radio broadcasting or otherwise of any rendition
or performance of any opera, operetta, musical comedy, play or like production, as such, in whole or in part.
Nothing in this agreement shall be construed as authorizing Licensee to grant to others any right to perform
publicly or reproduce in any manner any of the musical compositions licensed under this agreement, or as
authorizing any receiver of any radio broadcast to perform publicly or reproduce the same in any manner. The
radio broadcast performances licensed under this agreement may originate at the Station or at any other place but
nothing in this agreement shall be deemed to grant a license to anyone authorizing any public performance in such
other place of any such composition.

2.   **Definitions.** As used in this agreement:

A.   "Society's repertory" means all musical compositions which the Society has the right to license for public
performance now or hereafter during the term of this agreement. Included for the full term of this agreement are
all compositions written and copyrighted by members of Society and in the repertory on the date this agreement is
executed. Compositions later written or copyrighted by members during the license term shall be included for the
full balance of the term.

B.   "Local radio program" means any program broadcast from the Station other than a network radio
program. For the purposes of this agreement, sports, special events and other programs furnished by networks
not licensed by Society shall be deemed to be "local radio programs".

C.   "Network radio program" means a program broadcast simultaneously or by so-called "delayed" or
"repeat" broadcasts (sometimes known as "rebroadcasts") over two or more affiliated stations.

D.   "Affiliated station" means any radio broadcasting station in the United States which regularly
broadcasts network radio programs of a radio network or which appears on the radio rate card of such network
and which is interconnected with such network by wire or any other means whatsoever. Such station shall only be
deemed to be an affiliated station so long as it regularly broadcasts such programs or appears on such rate cards.
All radio broadcasting stations in the United States which are owned and operated by a network and which
broadcast such network's radio programs shall be deemed to be affiliated stations for the purpose of this
agreement, whether or not they appear on such network's radio rate card.

E.   "Co-operative programs" are programs which are furnished by a network to its affiliated stations under
an arrangement permitting an affiliate to broadcast such programs on a sustaining basis or on a commercial basis
under the sponsorship of a local, regional or national advertiser contracting directly with such affiliated station or
its representative for the incorporation of the commercial credits of such advertiser into the program as broadcast
by such affiliated station. For the purposes of this agreement only, and without prejudice to the position of Society
or Licensee or any network of which Licensee is an affiliated station as to the status of co-operative programs under
Society's television broadcasting licenses, such co-operative radio programs shall be deemed to be "local radio
programs" as defined herein.

F.   "Gross Revenue" means all payments (excluding non-cash payments in goods and/or services) made

(1)   by or on behalf of sponsors or donors for the use of radio broadcasting facilities of the Station,
whether made directly to Licensee or to any other person, including any network not
licensed by Society and under the same or substantially the same ownership, management or control as the
Station.

(2)   by wholly independent "time brokers" or recognized wholly independent companies engaged in
"barter" arrangements with radio or television stations generally for the resale of the radio broadcasting
facilities of the station, and

(3)   by wholly independent networks not licensed by the Society for the broadcasting of such
networks' programs by the station.

G.   "Adjusted Gross Revenue" means gross revenue less:

(1)   any sums received from networks licensed by Society with respect to network radio programs: this deduction shall not apply to that portion of the sums received from a network licensed by Society attributable to announcements in a network program not broadcast by the station, or to announcements furnished by such network not related to network programs;

(2)   advertising agency commission not to exceed 15% actually allowed to an advertising agency that has no direct or indirect ownership or managerial connection with Licensee or the Station;

(3)   any sums received from political local radio programs of Licensee;

(4)   bad debts actually written off and discounts allowed or rebates paid;

(5)   rate card discounts, cash, quantity and/or frequency actually allowed; and

(6)   any sums received with respect to a local radio program of Licensee presented by transcription if a license has been granted by Society (as distinguished from its members) at the source to perform on such local radio program by means of such transcription the musical compositions embodied therein.

H.   "Revenue Subject to Fee" means adjusted gross revenue or, at Station's option, adjusted gross revenue less the total of the following itemized deductions which exceeds 15% of adjusted gross revenue:

(1)   All compensation over and above the total annual amount indicated below, actually paid by the Station to personnel whose duties primarily are acting as (a) master of ceremonies or disc jockey on musical programs, or (b) vocalist or instrumentalist engaged for a specific program; or (c) featured newscaster and news commentator; or (d) featured sportscaster, or (e) master of ceremonies on an entertainment program, or (f) announcer:

Station's Annual "Adjusted Gross Revenue"	Total Annual Amount
Under — $ 50,000	$ 5,200
$ 50,000 — $ 149,999	$15,600
$150,000 — $ 299,999	$23,400
$300,000 — $ 499,999	$35,100
$500,000 — $ 749,999	$39,000
$750,000 — $ 999,999	$45,000
$1,000,000 and Over	$52,000

License may not deduct any compensation paid to any person who has a stock or other ownership interest in Licensee or in the Station of 40% or more.

(2)   The actual payment by the Station to an independent supplier of news ticker or news audio service (i.e., AP or UPI or other similar agencies) for news ticker or news audio service.

(3)   The following actual costs incurred by the Station for a specific local commercial program: (a) payments to the telephone company or like transmission utility for remote pick-up necessary to broadcast such program from a point outside a studio of the Station; and (b) rights for broadcasting a sports or other special event.

(4)   The following actual payments made by the Station to a wholly independent network not licensed by Society for a specific local program: (a) If such network is owned and operated by a college or university, the actual payment made by the station to such college or university; (b) If such network is not owned and operated by a college or university, the actual payments made for talent and for broadcast rights (which may not exceed the amount actually paid to or for the original holder of the broadcast rights for the particular program), and the actual payments made to or for the telephone company or like transmission utility for interconnecting lines and remote lines necessary to broadcast the program from a point outside the studio of the station, which may not exceed the amount actually paid to or for the telephone company or like transmission utility.

(5)   The following actual costs incurred by a network not licensed by Society and under the same or substantially the same ownership, management or control as the Station for network programs: (a) the payments to its affiliated stations in connection with such programs; (b) the actual payments made for talent and broadcast rights (which may not exceed the amount actually paid to or for the original holder of such broadcast rights); and (c) the actual payments made to or for the telephone company or like transmission utility for interconnecting lines and remote lines necessary to broadcast that program from a point outside the studio of the Station, which may not exceed the amount actually paid to or for the telephone company or like transmission utility.

3.   **Music Reports.** Licensee agrees to furnish to Society upon request a list of all musical compositions on Licensee's local radio programs, showing the title, composer and author of each composition. Licensee shall not be obligated to furnish such list for a period or periods which, in the aggregate, exceed one month of any one calendar year during the term of this agreement.

4.   **Right to Restrict.**

A.   The members of Society shall have the right to restrict the radio broadcasting of compositions from musical comedies, operas, operettas and motion pictures, or any other composition being excessively broadcast, only for the purpose of preventing harmful effect upon other interests under the copyrights of such works; provided, however, that (1) the maximum number of compositions which may be restricted at any time shall not exceed 500; (2) limited licenses will be granted upon application to Society entirely free of additional charge as to restricted compositions, if and when the copyright owners thereof are unable to show reasonable hazards to their major interests likely to result from such radio broadcasting; (3) such right to restrict any such composition shall not be exercised for the purpose of permitting the fixing or regulating of fees for the recording or transcribing of such composition; (4) in no case shall any charges, "free plugs", or other consideration be required in respect of any permission granted to perform a restricted composition; and (5) in no event shall any composition, after the initial radio broadcast thereof, be restricted for the purpose of confining further radio broadcasts thereof to a particular artist, station, network or program.

B.   Society reserves the further right in good faith to restrict the radio broadcasting of any composition, over and above the number specified in the previous paragraph, only as to which any suit has been brought or threatened on a claim that such composition infringes a composition not contained in the Society's repertory or on a claim that Society does not have the right to license the public performance of such composition by radio broadcasting.

5.   **License Fee.**

A.   In consideration of the license herein granted, Licensee agrees to pay to Society for each year during the term of this agreement a fee of $360 or 1.56% of "Revenue Subject to Fee", whichever is greater.

B.   In the event that Licensee's payment of fees under this agreement causes Society to incur a liability to pay a gross receipts, sales, use, business use, or other tax which is based on the amount of Society's receipts from Licensee, and (1) Society has taken reasonable steps to be exempted or excused from paying such tax; and (2) Society is permitted by law to pass through such tax to its licensees, Licensee shall pay to Society the full amount of such tax.

6.   **Reports and Payments.**

A.   On or before the first day of April in each year commencing 1987, Licensee shall send to Society a report of the license fee due for the preceding calendar year. Each such report shall be made by completing fully the Statement of Account form supplied free of charge by Society. A copy of the Statement of Account form is annexed and made a part of this agreement.

B.   For each month during the term of this Agreement, Licensee shall pay to Society on or before the first day of the following month, a sum equal to 1/12th of the license fee for the preceding calendar year, plus 8%. If the report required by Paragraph 6.A. for any calendar year is not received by Society when due, the monthly payments shall be in the amount of the monthly payments due for the preceding year, plus 24%, and payments at that rate shall continue until the late report is received by Society. If the station commenced broadcasting after January 1, 1987, Licensee shall furnish Society with a good faith estimate of its revenue for the first year of operation and the monthly payments during the first calendar year of broadcasting shall be 1/12th of the fee provided in Paragraph 5.A. for a station having such Revenue Subject to Fee.

C.   Each report required by Paragraph 6.A. of this agreement for the preceding calendar shall be accompanied by payment to Society of the license fee due over and above all amounts paid to Society for the preceding calendar year pursuant to Paragraph 6.B. If the amount paid by Licensee for the preceding calendar year exceeds the license fee due for the year, Licensee shall apply the excess payment against future monthly payments. If the excess payment is greater than three monthly payments required by Paragraph 6.B., Society shall, upon written request of Licensee, refund the excess payment.

D.   If any payment required under Paragraph 6.B. or 6.C. is not received by Society before the first day of the month following the date when the payment was due, Licensee agrees to pay Society a finance charge of 1% per month from the date the payment was due.

E.   License fee reports shall be made on a billing basis by all stations, except that any station may report on a cash basis if (1) its books have been kept on a cash basis and (2) it reported to Society only on a cash basis and at no time on a billing basis during the entire term of its agreement with Society ending February 28, 1977, and continuously thereafter. All billings made subsequent to the termination of this agreement with respect to radio broadcasts made during the term hereof shall be accounted for by Licensee as and when such billings are made by Licensee.

F.   If a report required by Paragraph 6.A. of the agreement is not received by the Society within 30 days of the date that the report was due, Society may give notice to Licensee that Licensee has an additional 30 days within which to submit the report on either the "Adjusted Gross Revenue" or "Adjusted Gross Revenue less itemized deductions" basis. If Licensee fails to submit the report within the additional 30-day period, the report must be on the "Adjusted Gross Revenue" basis.

G.   AM and FM stations owned by Licensee in the same city shall report and pay separately, and be treated for all purposes as separate stations, provided however that if in any year:

(1)   the combined "gross revenue" for both such stations is less than $75,000, or

(2)   programs which are simultaneously broadcast by both stations account for 80% or more of the total broadcast time both stations are on the air concurrently,

the stations shall report and pay license fees as if they were one station.

7.   **Audits.**

A.   Society shall have the right by its duly authorized representatives, at any time during customary business hours, to examine the books and records of account of Licensee only to such extent as may be necessary to verify any report required by this agreement. Society shall consider all data and information coming to its attention as a result of any such examination of books and records as completely and entirely confidential.

B.   The period for which the Society may audit shall be limited to the four calendar years reported preceding the year in which the audit is made; provided however, that if an audit is postponed at the request of the Station the Society shall have the right to audit for the period commencing with the fourth calendar year reported preceding the year in which notification of intention to audit was first given by the Society to the Station. This limitation shall not apply if the Station fails or refuses after written notice from the Society to produce the books and records necessary to verify any report or statement of accounting pursuant to the agreement.

C.   The period for which Licensee may correct computational errors, or errors relating to deductions permitted under the agreement on its license fee reports shall be limited to four calendar years preceding the year in which such corrected reports were submitted. This provision shall not be construed to permit a station to submit a report on the "Adjusted Gross Revenue less itemized deductions" basis for a period previously reported on the "Adjusted Gross Revenue" basis.

8.   **Breach or Default.** Upon any breach or default by Licensee of any terms herein contained relating to the reports, accountings or payments required to be made by Licensee, Society may give Licensee thirty (30) days' notice in writing to cure such breach or default, and in the event that such breach or default has not been cured within said thirty (30) days, Society may then promptly terminate this license.

9.   **Indemnity Clause.** Society agrees to indemnify, save and hold harmless and to defend Licensee, its advertisers and their advertising agencies, and its and their officers, employees and artists, from and against all claims, demands and suits that may be made or brought against them or any of them with respect to the performance under this agreement of any compositions in the Society's repertory which are written or copyrighted by members of Society. Licensee agrees to give Society immediate notice of any such claim, demand or suit and agrees immediately to deliver to Society all papers pertaining thereto. Society shall have full charge of the defense of any such claim, demand or suit and Licensee shall cooperate fully with Society in such defense. Licensee however shall have the right to engage counsel of its own at its own expense who may participate in the defense of any such action. Society agrees at the request of Licensee to cooperate with and assist Licensee, its advertisers and their advertising agencies and its and their officers, employees and artists in the defense of any action or proceeding brought against them or any of them with respect to the performance of any musical compositions contained in the Society's repertory, but not copyrighted or written by members of Society. This Paragraph 9 shall not apply to performances of any works that may be restricted under Paragraph 4 of this agreement.

10.   **Rights of Termination.**

A.   In the event of the termination or suspension of the governmental licenses covering the Station or any substantial alteration or variation of the terms and conditions thereof, or any major interference with the operations of the Station due to governmental measures or restrictions, Licensee shall have the right to terminate this agreement upon seven (7) days' written notice.

B.   In the event of:

(1)   any major interference with the operation of Society in the state, territory, dependency, possession or political subdivision in which the Station is located, by reason of any law of such state, territory, dependency, possession or political subdivision; or

(2)   any substantial increase in the cost to the Society of operating in such state, territory, dependency, possession or political subdivision, by reason of any law of such state, territory, dependency, possession or political subdivision which is applicable to the licensing of performing rights,

Society shall have the right to terminate this agreement on thirty (30) days' written notice to Licensee.

11. **Notices.** All notices required or permitted to be given by either of the parties to the other under this agreement shall be duly and properly given if mailed to the other party by registered or certified United States mail addressed to the party at its main office.

12. **Successors and Assignees.** This agreement shall enure to the benefit of and shall be binding upon parties and their respective successors and assignees, but no assignment shall relieve the parties of their respective obligations under this agreement.

13. **Per Program License.** The "local station per program license" for the term ending December 31, 1990 is being offered to Licensee simultaneously with this agreement. In accepting this agreement, Licensee acknowledges that it has a choice of entering into either this agreement or the per program license with Society; that Licensee has the opportunity to negotiate for separate licenses with the individual members of Society; and that Licensee is voluntarily entering into this agreement with Society. Licensee may substitute the per program agreement in place of this agreement by giving Society written notice at least 60 days prior to the commencement of any month during the term of this agreement. In such event, effective with the commencement of that month, the per program agreement shall be in full force and effect between Licensee and Society for the balance of the license term.

14. **Applicable Law.** The fees set forth in this agreement have been approved by the United States District Court for the Southern District of New York as reasonable and non-discriminatory in accordance with the amended Final Judgment in *United States v. ASCAP*. The meaning of the provisions of this agreement shall be construed in accordance with the laws of the State of New York.

IN WITNESS WHEREOF, this agreement has been duly executed by Society and Licensee this   day of   , 19   .

AMERICAN SOCIETY OF COMPOSERS,
AUTHORS AND PUBLISHERS

By _____

LICENSEE

_____
(Full corporate or other name of station owner)

By _____

_____
(Fill in capacity in which signed)

(a) If corporation, state corporate office held;
(b) If partnership, write word "partner" under signature of signing partner;
(c) If individual owner, write "individual owner" under signature.

Bibliography

"ABC Relaxes Advertising Guidelines." *Broadcasting* (September 9, 1991): 25.

"ACT Challenges Children's TV Rules." *Broadcasting* (May 20, 1991): 62.

Bessie, Simon Michael. *Jazz Journalism*. New York: E.P. Dutton & Co., 1938.

Blackstone, William. *Commentaries on the Laws of England*. Edited by Charles M. Haar. Boston: Beacon Press, 1962.

Bosmajian, Haig A., ed. *The Principles and Practices of Freedom of Speech*. Boston: Houghton Mifflin, 1971.

Buranelli, Vincent. *The Trial of Peter Zenger*. Washington Square: New York University Press, 1957.

"Cable Rereg Bill Bogs Down." *Broadcasting* (July 15, 1991): 15.

Carter, T. Barton, et al. *The First Amendment and the Fifth Estate: Regulation of Electronic Mass Media*. 2nd ed., Westbury, NY: Foundation Press, 1989.

"Case Dismissed." *Broadcasting* (October 14, 1991): 52.

Chafee, Jr., Zechariah. *Free Speech in the United States*. Cambridge, MA: Harvard University Press, 1964.

Chafee, Jr., Zechariah. *Thirty-Five Years with Freedom of Speech*. New York: Roger N. Baldwin, Civil Liberties Foundation, 1952.

Cole, Barry G., and Mal Gettinger. *Reluctant Regulators: The FCC and the Broadcast Audience*. Reading, MA: Addison-Wesley, 1978.

"Congress All Shook Up Over Rock Lyrics." *Broadcasting* (September 23, 1985): 28.

Copyright Basics, Circular 1. Washington, D.C.: Copyright Office, Library of Congress, 1987.

"Costly Mistake." *Broadcasting* (October 14, 1991): 52.

"Court Throws Out FCC's 24-Hour Indecency Ban." *Broadcasting* (May 20, 1991): 33.

Creech, Kenneth C. "An Historical and Descriptive Analysis of Low-Power Educational Radio Broadcasting in the United States." Ph.D. diss., Wayne State University, 1978.

"Disney Facing Hurdle in Effort to Relax PTAR." *Broadcasting* (December 10, 1990): 102.

"Divided Commission Eases Fin-Syn Restrictions." *TV Today* (April 15, 1991): 2.

Downs, Donald Alexander. *Nazis in Skokie: Freedom, Community and the First Amendment.* Notre Dame, IN: University of Notre Dame Press, 1985.

"EEO Forfeitures and Short-Term License Renewals Continue." *Haley, Bader & Potts Information Memorandum* 16(February 14, 1991): 6.

Emery, Edwin. *The Press and America.* 2nd ed. Englewood Cliffs, NJ: Prentice-Hall, 1962.

Eshelman, David. "The Emergence of Educational FM Broadcasting." *NAEB Journal* 26 (March/April 1967): 57.

"Fairness Doctrine Legislation Re-Emerges." *Broadcasting* (January 12, 1991): 43.

Fair Trial/Free Press Voluntary Agreements. Chicago: Legal Advisory Committee on Fair Trial and Free Press, 1974.

"False Radio Broadcast Evokes FCC Investigation." *Broadcasting* (February 4, 1991): 29.

"FCC Allocates Interactive Video Spectrum." *Broadcasting* (January 20, 1992): 11.

"FCC Broadens Area Considered for License Character." *Broadcasting* (May 14, 1990): 32.

"FCC Considers Restoring Must-Carry Rules." *Broadcasting* (July 22, 1991): 32.

"FCC Creates Adult Country: Midnight–6 A.M." *Broadcasting* (November 30, 1987): 51.

"FCC to Delay Children's Ad Time Limits Until '92." *Broadcasting* (July 29, 1991): 68.

"FCC Gets Tough on Political and EEO Violations, Sets Record Fines." *TV Today* (May 21, 1990): 3.

"FCC Hears Little Support for 24-Hour Broadcasting Indecency Ban." *Broadcasting* (February 26, 1990): 48.

"FCC to Investigate Murder Hoax." *Broadcasting* (April 22, 1991): 48.

"FCC Launches Attack on Indecency." *Broadcasting* (April 30, 1987): 35.

"FCC Report Concedes TV's Future to Cable." *Broadcasting* (July 1, 1991): 19.

"FCC Revamping Comparative Hearings Process." *Broadcasting* (May 14, 1990): 31.

"FCC Takes Action on Process Abuse, Station Licensing Character Policy." *TV Today* (May 14, 1990): 4.

"FCC Takes Tentative Step Toward TV Dereg." *Broadcasting* (July 15, 1991): 13.

"FCC Tells TV Station It May Have Violated Indecency Law." *Broadcasting* (January 18, 1988): 46.

"FCC Turns Up the Heat on Indecency" *Broadcasting* (August 28, 1989): 27.

Federal Communications Commission. *Annual Report, 1945.* Washington, DC: U.S. Government Printing Office, 1946.

"A Foot in the Door for Telcos." *Broadcasting* (July 29, 1991): 23.

"Fox Wins 18½ Hour, One Year Fin-Syn Waiver." *Broadcasting* (May 7, 1990): 28.

Francois, William E. *Mass Media Law and Regulation.* 3rd ed. Columbus, OH: Grid Publishing Co., 1982.

Friedrich, C.J., and J. Sayer Smith. "Radiobroadcasting and Higher Education." In *Studies in the Control of Radio, Numbers 1–6, History of Broadcasting: Radio to Television Series.* Edited by Christopher Sterling. New York: Arno Press and The New York Times, 1971.

Friendly, Fred W., and Martha J.H. Eliot. *The Constitution: That Delicate Balance.* New York: Random House, 1984.

Frost, S.E. *Education's Own Stations.* Chicago: University of Chicago Press, 1937.

"FTC Takes Action on 'Infomercials.' " *Electronic Media* (May 21, 1990): 32. Educational Radio: The Hidden Medium. *Washington, DC: National Association of Educational Broadcasters, 1967.*

Geller, Henry. *Fiber Optics: An Opportunity for a New Policy.* Washington, DC: The Annenberg Washington Program, 1991.

Gillmor, Donald M., and Jerome A. Barron, et al. *Mass Communication Law: Cases and Comment.* 5th ed. St. Paul: West Publishing Co., 1990.

"Gleam in Fowler's Regulatory Eye." *Broadcasting* (September 14, 1981): 27.

Goodale, James, ed. *Communications Law 1982.* New York: Practising Law Institute, 1982.

"Group Ownership on the Rise." *Broadcasting* (February 11, 1991): 69.

Hamlin, David. *The Nazi/Skokie Conflict: A Civil Liberties Struggle.* Boston: Beacon Press, 1980.

Harless, James D. *Mass Communication: An Introductory Survey.* Dubuque, IA: William C. Brown, 1985.

Head, Sydney, and Christopher Sterling. *Broadcasting in America.* 6th ed. Boston: Houghton-Mifflin Company, 1990.

Hernandez, Ruel Torres. "ECPA and Online Computer Privacy." *Federal Communications Law Journal* 41:1 (1990): 17.

"High Court Strikes Blow for Investigative Journalism." *Broadcasting* (October 12, 1987): 79.

"Hill, FCC Face Full Agenda After August Vacation." *Broadcasting* (September 12, 1991): 14.

Hilliard, Robert L. *The Federal Communications Commission: A Primer.* Boston: Focal Press, 1991.

"Hoax Fallout." *Broadcasting* (April 29, 1991): 7.

Holmes, Oliver W. *The Common Law.* Boston: Little, Brown, 1881.

Holonen, Doug. "Big 3, Hollywood Rips Fin-Syn." *Electronic Media* (April 15, 1991): 1, 52.

Hudon, Edward G. *Freedom of Speech and Press in America.* Washington, DC: Public Affairs Press, 1963.

Hughes, Helen M. *News and the Human Interest Story.* Chicago: University of Chicago Press, 1940.

"Imaging: The Merger of Computer and TV." *Broadcasting* (January 27, 1992): 41.

"In Brief." *Broadcasting* (April 29, 1991): 72.

"Indecency Ban Comes Under Fire, Appeals Court Judge Criticizes FCC's 24-Hour Indecency Prohibition Challenging Commission's Contention That It Is 'Narrowly Tailored.' " *Broadcasting* (February 4, 1991): 40–41.

"Indecency Ban Nixed." *Electronic Media* (May 20, 1991): 1.

"Indecency Effort Set." *Electronic Media* (April 22, 1991): 1.

"Infinity Fights Indecency Ban." *Broadcasting* (February 18, 1991): 60.

"Is Wireless Cable 'Cable'?" *Broadcasting* (July 15, 1991): 31.

"Janet Steiger: The FTC's Vigilant Enforcer." *Broadcasting* (February 5, 1990): 76.

Johnson, Nicholas, and John Jay Dystel. "A Day in the Life: The Federal Communications Commission." *The Yale Law Journal* 82:8 (July 1973): 1574.

Keeton, W. Page, et al. *Prosser and Keeton on Torts.* 5th ed. St. Paul: West Publishing Co., 1984.

"Kellner Presses Fox's Case For Fin-Syn Exemption." *Broadcasting* (November 19, 1990): 50.

Kovner, Victor. "Recent Developments in Intrusion, Private Facts, False Light and Commercialization Claims." In *Communications Law 1982.* Edited by James C. Goodale. New York: Practising Law Institute, 1982.

Krasnow, Erwin G., and Lawrence D. Longley. *The Politics of Broadcast Regulation.* 2nd ed. New York: St. Martin's Press, 1978.

"The Laissez Faire Legacy of Charles Ferris." *Broadcasting* (January 19, 1981): 37.

Le Duc, Don R. *Beyond Broadcasting: Patterns in Policy and Law.* New York: Longman, 1987.

"License Pulled for Drug Conviction." *Broadcasting* (January 28, 1991): 49.

Lowery, Shearon A., and Melvin L. DeFleur. "The Invasion from Mars: Radio Panics America." In *Milestones in Mass Communication Research.* 2nd ed. New York: Longman, 1988.

"Making Life a Bit Easier; Reregulation Gets Under Way." *Broadcasting* (November 6, 1972): 19.

Mason, Alpheus Thomas, and William M. Beaney. *American Constitutional Law: Introductory Essays and Selected Cases.* 4th ed. Englewood Cliffs, NJ: Prentice-Hall, 1968.

McCrory, James. "Developments in Libel Law." In *Communications Law 1982.* Edited by James Goodale. New York: Practising Law Institute, 1982.

Mermigas, Diane. "Networks Study Prime-Time Cuts." *Electronic Media* (April 29, 1991): 31.

Mill, J.S. *On Liberty Etc.* London: Oxford University Press, 1969.

Miller, Arthur R., and Michael H. Davis. *Intellectual Property: Patents, Trademarks and Copyright.* St. Paul: West Publishing Co., 1991.

Milton, John. *Areopagitica and Of Education.* Edited by George H. Sabine. New York: Appleton-Century-Crofts, 1951.

Mott, Frank Luther. *American Journalism.* 3rd ed. New York: Macmillan, 1962.

National Association of Broadcasters. "FCC Streamlines Comparative Hearings." *TV Today* (December 17, 1990): 1.

Nelson, Harold L., Dwight L. Teeter, Jr., and Don R. Le Duc. *Law of Mass Communications: Freedom and Control of Print and Broadcast Media.* 6th ed. Westbury, NY: The Foundation Press, 1990.

Paper, Lewis J. *Brandeis.* New York: Citadel Press, 1983.

Pollock, Sir Frederick, and Frederic William Maitland. *The History of English Law.* Vol. II. Cambridge: Cambridge University Press, 1968.

"Record Labeling Could Have Radio Fallout?" *Broadcasting* (April 30, 1990): 58.

Saettler, Paul. *A History of Instructional Technology.* New York: McGraw-Hill, 1968.

Sayre, Jeanette. "An Analysis of the Radiobroadcasting Activities of Federal Agencies." In *Studies in the Control of Radio, Numbers 1–6, History of Broadcasting: Radio to Television Series.* Edited by Christopher Sterling. New York: Arno Press and The New York Times, 1971.

Scofield, Cora L. *A Study of the Court of Star Chamber.* New York: Burt Franklin, 1969.

Shientag, Bernard L. *Moulders of Legal Thought.* Port Washington, NY: Kennikat Press Inc., 1968.

"Sikes the Enforcer." *Broadcasting* (February 12, 1990): 24.

"Sikes Looks to Strengthen Broadcasters' Hand." *Broadcasting* (July 8, 1991): 23.

"Sikes: Repeal Compulsory License, Take Another Look at PTAR." *Broadcasting* (January 27, 1992): 14.

"So Many Technologies, So Little Space." *Broadcasting* (May 6, 1991): 52.

Spencer, Dale, et al. *Free Press & Fair Trial.* Washington, DC: American Society of Newspaper Editors/American Newspaper Publishers Association Foundation, 1982.

Sponseller, Diane. "Who's Got Your Number? Regulators Confront the New Caller ID Services." *Public Utilities Fortnightly* (February 15, 1990): 55

"Station Stunts Tread Fine Line of Humor and Hoax." *Broadcasting* (April 8, 1991): 55.

Sterling, Christopher H., and John M. Kittross. *Stay Tuned: A Concise History of American Broadcasting.* 2nd ed. Belmont, CA: Wadsworth, 1990.

Stevens, George E. "Mass Media and the 'Libel Proof' Doctrine." *Journalism Quarterly* 66:1 (Spring 1989): 177.

Stover, Dawn. "Look Who's Calling." *Popular Science* (July 1990): 76.

"Supreme Court Upholds Noriega Tape Ban." *Broadcasting* (November 26, 1990): 52.

Tresolini, Rocco J., and Martin Shapiro. *American Constitutional Law.* 3rd ed. New York: Macmillan, 1970.

"TV Answer Puts Money Down on Infrastructure for Interactive Consumer Service." *Broadcasting* (September 30, 1991): 46.

"Two More Stations Fined for Indecency Violations." *Radio and Records* (April 26, 1991): 12, 22.

"Under Way." *Broadcasting* (October 22, 1990): 6.

Warren, Samuel D., and Lewis D. Brandeis. "The Right of Privacy." *Harvard Law Review* 4 (December 15, 1890): 193.

West's Indiana Law Encyclopedia. Vol. 18. St. Paul: West Publishing Co., 1959.

White, Llewellyn. *The American Radio.* Chicago: University of Chicago Press, 1947.

Youm, Kyu Ho. "The Impact of *People v. Croswell* on Libel Law." *Journalism Monographs* 113 (June 1989): 6.

Glossary

Administrative Law Judge   individuals who preside over hearings for administrative agencies like the Federal Communications Commission

Amici curiae   literally, "friends of the court." Individuals or organizations not part of a legal action permitted to submit briefs to a court to help the court reach a decision. The American Civil Liberties Union often submits friends of the court briefs in First Amendment cases.

Appellant   the party who appeals a decision of a lower court

Appellee   the party against whom an appeal is filed

Brief   the written legal argument submitted to the court by attorneys as part of a lawsuit

Civil Suit   legal action seeking monetary damages as a result of a private wrong or injury. Criminal actions are brought by a public prosecutor to redress a crime against society at large.

Common Law   law that has evolved over the years as accepted practice. Originating in England, common law is the application of the decisions of judges over time. Common law is often called "discovered law," because judges look to the past to discover a solution to a problem.

Construction Permit (CP)   authorization to build or make changes to a broadcast facility issued by the FCC after receipt of Form 301 (for commercial stations) or Form 340 (for noncommercial educational stations)

Conversion   the unauthorized assumption of ownership over goods or personal property belonging to another. Using someone else's goods or property to the exclusion of the owner's rights.

Defendant   the party against whom a criminal or civil action is brought

Deposition   a sworn statement made by a party out of court in answer to questions posed by an attorney

Discovery   the exchange of information between two parties to a lawsuit prior to the beginning of a trial

Docket 80–90 Stations   three new classes of stations created in May 1983 as part of Docket 80–90 when the FCC opened the FM spectrum. Docket 80–90 stations are afforded a reduced mileage separation between stations and operate with somewhat less power than other classes of FM stations. Docket 80–90 is expected to create about 1000 FM stations.

Grand Jury   a group of citizens appointed to decide whether enough evidence exists to indict an individual or individuals for the commission of a crime. An indictment by the grand jury will result in charges being filed and a trial may follow.

In Camera   in a judge's chambers without the public present

Indictment   a written accusation by a grand jury charging an individual or individuals with a serious crime

Injunction   an order by the court that commands a party to refrain from doing something, or an order to perform a specific act

Memorandum Decision   a court ruling issued without opinions or reasons given

Mistrial   a trial that is stopped because of a major procedural defect. For example, extensive, prejudicial pretrial publicity may result in the declaration of a mistrial based on the grounds that the defendant may not receive a fair trial.

Notice of Inquiry (NOI)   a statement by the FCC that describes a problem or issue and asks for public comments on how the problem should be solved. An NOI is published in the *Federal Register*. (See *Report and Order*.)

Notice of Proposed Rule Making (NOPR)   a statement by the FCC that describes how it plans to change its rules. An NOPR is published in the *Federal Register* and public comments are accepted. (See *Report and Order*.)

Per Curiam   a court ruling that is an unsigned opinion that represents the collective thinking of all justices on the court

Petitioner   the party seeking review of a lower court ruling or other judicial relief by seeking a hearing by a higher court

Plaintiff   the party who initiates a lawsuit

Preliminary Hearing   a hearing held before a judge to determine whether there is enough evidence to proceed to trial

Prima Facie   literally, "on the face of it." A *prima facie* fact is presumably true, unless it is disproved by evidence to the contrary.

Remand   an order of a higher court that instructs a lower court to conform to the decision of the higher court

Report and Order (R & O)   a statement by the FCC that explains how its rules and regulations have been changed. The Commission may use an R & O to adopt a new rule, modify an existing rule, or explain why a proposed rule has not been changed. It may also be issued to terminate a proceeding. An R & O is published in the *Federal Register*. (See *Notice of Inquiry* and *Notice of Proposed Rule Making*.)

Renewal Expectancy   the assumption that existing broadcast licenses will be favored by the FCC at license renewal time over competitive applications, all other things being equal

Respondent   the party opposed to judicial relief requested by the petitioner

Restraining Order   synonymous with *injunction*

Sequester   to quarantine a jury from influences of the outside world during the course of a trial to ensure that the jury remains impartial

Slip Opinion   a copy of a court opinion circulated immediately after the opinion is decided

Stare Decisis   to abide by or hold to. When a court establishes a series of principles over time, they will be applied *stare decisis* in future cases where the facts are substantially the same.

Summary Judgment   a pretrial motion that, if successful, will result in a judgment for a party without the necessity of going to trial

Tort   a private civil wrong or injury

Venireman   a member of a jury

Venue   the location of a trial. It is common practice for a judge to issue a change of venue when there has been substantial media coverage of a case in order to ensure that an impartial jury can be selected from the population

Voir Dire   the process of questioning prospective jurors for the purpose of eliminating those who are unlikely to render an unbiased verdict

Writ of Certiorari   a discretionary order issued by the Supreme Court asking to hear a case from a lower court

Index